A Volume in the Series

Culture, Politics, and the Cold War

Edited by Christian G. Appy and Edwin A. Martini

OTHER TITLES IN THE SERIES

REDEFINING SCIENCE

REDEFINING
SCIENCE

SCIENTISTS, THE NATIONAL SECURITY STATE, AND
NUCLEAR WEAPONS IN COLD WAR AMERICA

PAUL RUBINSON

UNIVERSITY OF MASSACHUSETTS PRESS
Amherst and Boston

Copyright © 2016 by University of Massachusetts Press
All rights reserved
Printed in the United States of America

ISBN 978-1-62534-244-7 (pbk), 243-0 (hardcover)

Designed by Sally Nichols
Set in Minion Pro
Printed and bound by Maple Press, Inc.

Cover design by Jack Harrison

Library of Congress Cataloging-in-Publication Data

Names: Rubinson, Paul, 1977– author.
Title: Redefining science : scientists, the national security state,
    and nuclear weapons in Cold War America / Paul Rubinson.
Description: Amherst : University of Massachusetts Press, [2016] | Series:
    Culture, politics, and the Cold War | Includes bibliographical
    references and index.
Identifiers: LCCN 2016033965| ISBN 9781625342447 (pbk. : alk. paper) | ISBN
    9781625342430 (hardcover : alk. paper)
Subjects: LCSH: Nuclear weapons—Government policy—United
    States—History—20th century. | Science—Social aspects. |
    Scientists—United States—Biography. | Science and state—United
    States—History—20th century. | Nuclear warfare—Government
    policy—United States—History—20th century. | Antinuclear
    movement—United States—History—20th century. | Nuclear
    disarmament—United States—History. | National security—United
    States—History—20th century. | Cold War.
Classification: LCC U264 .R83 2016 | DDC 355.02/17097309045—dc23
LC record available at https://lccn.loc.gov/2016033965

British Library Cataloguing-in-Publication Data
A catalog record for this book is available from the British Library.

To Kristin, Harper, and Camille

Contents

Preface

GREW UP IN BALTIMORE DURING THE 1980s, and I have a distinct memory of Charles Street where it crosses the county line heading south into the city, marked by a street sign that declared Baltimore a nuclear-free zone. While I noticed the sign, it never seemed particularly special—after all, nuclear weapons were everywhere. My friends and I "nuked" each other playing in the backyard; my family and I "nuked" food in the microwave. Nuclear weapons were plot devices in movies and lead stories on the news. Only later did I come to see this aspect of my childhood as bizarre for seeming so normal at the time.

I started college after the end of the Cold War, eager to understand why it had culminated not in the devastation of thermonuclear war but, as I understood it then, the victory of peace movements. In a sociology class on social movements, I studied the antinuclear activism of the 1980s and read oddities like *You Could Be the Hundredth Monkey*. While my generation was constantly accused of apathy, these antinuclear protesters from the '80s seemed incomparably superior, having challenged the superpowers and prevented World War III. Schooled in the sociological literature, I came to believe that social movement success was just a matter of properly "mobilizing resources" or "aligning frames." Years later, having become a historian, I still took it for granted that social movements could influence U.S. foreign policy: obviously, it had to happen—elites simply refused to admit it. When I began to write a book about the antinuclear movement, I decided to look at scientists because they were an unlikely source of activism but also powerful elites who would certainly have influenced policy.

But during a research trip to the University of Chicago over a Halloween weekend, I remember not finding evidence of that influence despite days of combing through documents. Discouraged, I wandered the cold grounds after the archive closed early on Saturday and ended up watching a particularly hapless football game between UC and Carnegie Mellon at Stagg Field. After all, it was beneath this structure some sixty years earlier where Enrico Fermi and his peers had successfully created the world's first controlled fission reaction as part of the Manhattan Project. Perhaps I hoped some sort of insight might trickle up from the radioactive residue of that historic moment, but, like the UC football team that day, luck wasn't on my side.

The feeling recurred as I visited scientists' archives across the country, from the Massachusetts Institute of Technology (MIT) and Harvard to Stanford and Oregon State, at the Johnson and Eisenhower Presidential Libraries, and in countless pages of the *Bulletin of the Atomic Scientists*. I saw the tremendous efforts exerted by scientists to stem the tide of nuclear weapons rewarded only with the incessant growth of nuclear arsenals worldwide. Elite American scientists apparently offered overwhelming logic against nuclear weapons with hardly any effect on policy—much like debates over climate change going on at the time I was researching. Finally, it occurred to me that, instead of asking how scientists influenced nuclear policy, a better question might be why scientists were largely unable to influence policy. Why would the government ignore the expert advice of its brilliant scientists?

Reframing the question in this way allowed me to identify powerful elements of coercion at work. With the rise of the Cold War and thermonuclear weapons in the 1950s, the government asserted its control over scientists, redefining how they could advise the government on nuclear matters. This dictum established new parameters within which questions about and criticisms of nuclear policy would be tolerated. For most of the Cold War, scientists who hoped to retain influence in government circles learned to avoid discussion of personal and moral views when advising the government, especially when they advocated for nuclear arms control and disarmament. These scientists began to couch their advice in strictly technical terms and accepted nuclear deterrence as the fundamental premise of U.S. national security. Those scientists who refused to accept this redefinition found themselves excluded from policymaking and frequently ostracized by large segments of their peers, who had come to internalize the government's distinction between acceptable science that enhanced national security and unacceptable science that challenged the Cold War consensus.

I owe a great deal of thanks to the institutions and people that aided and supported me in the writing of this book. International Security Studies at Yale University awarded me a Smith-Richardson Predoctoral Fellowship that allowed me an entire year of researching and writing that resulted in chapters 7 and 8, for which I am extremely grateful. The History Department of the University of Texas at Austin provided me with numerous travel grants, enabling me to visit several archives, and at the 2013 SHAFR Summer Institute I received valuable feedback on chapter 6. A Small Grant from the Center for the Advancement of Research and Scholarship at Bridgewater State University (BSU) came at a crucial moment, reminding me how appreciative I am that our small institution provides such large support for scholarship.

This book would not have happened without Fran Ramos. Her encouragement, humor, and warmth enabled me to persevere more than once when I would have preferred not to. I utterly treasure our friendship.

Mark Lawrence and Bruce Hunt have been wonderful mentors who have always given generously of their time, feedback, and insight in the past, and they remain role models in the present. D'Arcy Randall mentored me as a writer and a teacher and several times taught me life lessons with empathy and kindness. Michael Bess was inspirational at an early stage of my career, while much more recently Priscilla McMillan graciously read a draft of the entire manuscript. Her willingness to share her vast knowledge as well as her enthusiasm for the project are much appreciated. I would also like to thank Francis Gavin, David Oshinsky, and Michael Stoff for their input, while Peter Kuznick's feedback improved the manuscript tremendously. At the University of Massachusetts Press, I thank Brian Halley, Carol Betsch, Sally Nichols, Karen Fisk, and Yvonne Crevier, as well as Annette Wenda for skillfully copyediting the manuscript.

Generous colleagues have helped me every step of the way. Sarah Snyder, whose advice made the book better in numerous ways, is an ideal friend and colleague. Joy Rohde leant her intellect and humor at an early stage, while Bryant Etheridge never hesitated to perform true yeoman's work, from a place to stay during Cambridge research trips to help moving across the country (and back again). Matt Tribbe read a very early draft of the manuscript, which could not have been much fun. Conversations with Benjamin Greene, David Hecht, and William Knoblauch frequently improved my thinking on this topic.

I thank wonderful friends who have been crucial to this work and my well-being over the years, including Susan Ferber, Benjamin Hinerfeld, Laresh Jayasanker, Jessica Luther, and Kerry Webb. Nathan Keay provided housing for that critical Chicago research trip and Halloween celebration, the memories of which I will always cherish. Dan and Jessica Whelan kindly housed me for a productive visit to the Ava Helen and Linus Pauling Papers at Oregon State University. At BSU I thank my colleagues in the History Department, as well as Elizabeth Veisz for always listening and always laughing—always over lunch.

I have heavily relied on the support and love of my parents, Karen, Deborah, and Rick, as well as my siblings, Claude, Emily, and Max. Never once did they offer anything but unwavering support for me and my work. I thank them for always celebrating my victories and downplaying my defeats. Finally, I dedicate this book to Kristin, Harper, and Camille, who are my world.

A version of chapter 4 appeared as "'Crucified on a Cross of Atoms': Scientists, Politics, and the Test Ban Treaty," *Diplomatic History* 35, no. 2 (2011): 283–319. Portions of chapter 7 appeared in "The Global Effects of Nuclear Winter: Science and Antinuclear Protest in the United States and the Soviet Union during the 1980s," *Cold War History* 14, no. 1 (2014): 47–69. Material from chapter 7 appeared in "Imagining the Apocalypse: Nuclear Winter in Science and the World," in *Understanding the Imaginary War: Culture, Thought, and Nuclear Conflict, 1945–90,* edited by Matthew Grant and Benjamin Ziemann (Manchester: Manchester University Press, 2016). I thank the publishers for permission to include that material here.

REDEFINING SCIENCE

Introduction

A Tale of Two Hearings

A
T NINE ON THE MORNING OF October 25, 1956, a reporter for the *Tonopah Times* of Nevada placed a call to Linus Pauling to inform the Nobel Prize–winning chemist of the death of seven-year-old Martin Bordoli. Although Pauling had no connection to the boy, the reporter felt that the circumstances surrounding his death were "interesting" and sought Pauling's opinion. According to the reporter, residents of Twin Springs, Nevada, lived under clouds of radioactive fallout downwind from the U.S. nuclear testing site. When residents of the tiny town developed "sore eyes," the reporter told Pauling, "they were examined by [Atomic Energy Commission (AEC)] doctors, who said there was nothing for them to worry about." The Bordoli family had also been "troubled by these sore eyes," and in the spring of 1956 Martin developed leukemia; he passed away on October 24. Pauling agreed that "the circumstances were suspicious" and told the reporter that there was a chance that the leukemia had been caused by nuclear fallout. Almost as troubling to Pauling was the reporter's admission that her newspaper had been asked, "as a patriotic duty, not to publish anything about it."[1]

The reporter who chose to ask Pauling about young Martin Bordoli did not make her decision randomly. During the 1950s Pauling had become a public authority on the dangers of nuclear testing. His iconoclastic pacifism distanced him from the U.S. government and boosted his reputation as a source for information that challenged official policies and statements on nuclear weapons. By the time of Martin Bordoli's death, Pauling had already begun a global campaign for a nuclear test ban to prevent the spread of fallout. But while journalists and other members of the public turned to Pauling for information, the U.S. government worked to ensure that the antinuclear messages of Pauling and other influential scientists were never heard, or at least diluted.

Anticommunist witch-hunters within the government adopted many tactics to silence Pauling, but their goal was to fundamentally undermine his credibility. After he distributed an antinuclear petition to scientists around the world, the Senate Internal Security Subcommittee brought Pauling in front of Congress. There, the assembled senators asked him not about Martin Bordoli or the dangers of fallout but rather who had helped him distribute his petition. "Will you tell us who did that work, the mimeographing?" they asked. "Do you know, sir, who supplied the addresses of the scientists to whom letters were sent on that evening of May 15?" "Dr. Pauling, can you tell us what was the cost of printing the copies of your appeal?" "Did you have arrangements with any individual in any foreign country to centralize the circulation of the petition in that country?" More pointed questions, posed by the subcommittee vice chairman, Thomas Dodd (D-CT), lay at the heart of the interrogation: "Was this petition, in any sense, Communist propaganda? . . . Was there substantial Communist participation in the organization of the petition? . . . In the preparation and submission of the petition, were Communist techniques used?"[2] Pauling refused to answer not because he had any communist sympathies but because as a fierce defender of civil liberties, he considered such questions unconstitutional.

Congress, however, did not universally despise scientists during the Cold War. In fact, the government often willingly, and sometimes eagerly, engaged with scientists who opposed nuclear weapons. During Senate hearings on antiballistic missiles (ABMs) in 1969, of the twenty witnesses brought in to testify, thirteen were scientists, in addition to one engineer and one mathematician. And the reception they received could not have been more different from the hostile interrogation that Pauling endured almost a decade earlier. In this case, the senators apparently could not wait to be enlightened by science, represented by James Killian, George Kistiakowsky, and

Herbert York, who had each served as scientific advisers in various presidential administrations. Senator Albert Gore Sr. (D-TN) described the trio as "great" and "uniquely qualified" to advise the upper chamber on ABMs, and after the witnesses finished their statements, Gore gushed, "Your logic, your intellectual eloquence . . . makes me feel proud to be an American." As the lunchtime recess approached, Clifford Case (R-NJ) told the scientists he found it "difficult for us to let you go because this is an extraordinary panel."[3]

The warm reception was not entirely unprecedented; members of Congress had not suddenly transformed into peaceniks. Although they steadfastly opposed ABMs specifically and were uneasy with nuclear weapons in general, Killian, Kistiakowsky, and York were not accusing the government of killing children with leukemia, obscuring the truth about victims of the U.S. testing program, or any other immoral action. Instead, the science advisers assured the subcommittee that they opposed ABMs because these missiles would result in a "loss of secure deterrent" and a loss "for our national security" overall. Reinforcing the Cold War status quo, Killian remarked that "the credibility of our deterrent . . . is vital," while Kistiakowsky declared that the "development of new weapons really does not improve our national security." To support this view, the scientists discussed subjects including sea-based deterrents, functional orbital bombardment, hard-point defense, and the problem of hair triggers versus stiff triggers. This advice was just what the senators wanted to hear: technical and unemotional (although heartfelt) opposition to the arms race that still upheld the fundamental aspects of U.S. nuclear policy. Gore closed the session by praising it as one for the ages, stating, "If I could select one hearing from my 30 years [of] service that I would like my son to listen to for information and inspiration, I would select this one."[4]

These two hearings capture the essence of the most drastic change in the relationship between scientists and the national security state during the Cold War. In 1954 the Atomic Energy Commission redefined how scientists were allowed to advise policymakers on nuclear matters. This dictum, expressed in the verdict that removed the physicist Robert Oppenheimer from his government position, established new parameters within which questions about and criticisms of nuclear policy would be tolerated. In the years after 1954, scientists who hoped to retain influence in government circles learned to avoid discussion of personal and moral views when advising the government, especially when they advocated for nuclear arms control and disarmament. These scientists began to couch their advice in strictly technical terms and accepted nuclear deterrence as the fundamental premise of U.S. national security. Those scientists who refused to accept this redefinition found themselves excluded from policymaking and frequently ostracized by large segments of their peers, who had come to internalize the government's distinction between "objective" science in favor of national security and "emotional" science that challenged the Cold War consensus.

Redefining Science

The Cold War rivalry between the United States and the Soviet Union dominated geopolitics for a half century. Ubiquitous throughout the conflict, nuclear weapons served as the objects of negotiation and intimidation; global tensions rose and fell with their growth and limitation. Ideology lay at the heart of the Cold War, as the West pitted a democratic capitalism against the one-party communism practiced by the East. But vested interests within each superpower propelled the Cold War forward as well, causing the conflict to last much longer than necessary.[5] With the Soviet Union branded as inherently untrustworthy, many Americans put their faith in nuclear deterrence as a simple, reliable method of maintaining their way of life in a hostile world, and the nuclear weapons industry, including labs, scientists, contractors, think tanks, and politicians, obliged by perpetuating an arms race with no apparent end.

The totalizing nature of the Cold War transformed the lives and disciplines of scientists, even those uninvolved with the creation of nuclear weapons. Natural and social scientists alike could rarely distance themselves from the growing demands of national security or at least the controversy surrounding the government's influence over science policy. Funding, basic research goals, and even fundamental concepts such as objectivity came to be defined or justified in Cold War terms as the nation struggled to defend its image, interests, and ideology in the face of hostile nuclear states.[6]

But living with the possibility of mushroom clouds rising over every minor crisis around the world provoked people to rise up against nuclear weapons and Cold War bipolarity. Antinuclear protest occurred in almost every country, and almost every segment of society engaged in activism across a spectrum that spanned moderate protest, mainstream dissent, and radical civil disobedience. These efforts, the historian Lawrence Wittner has shown, "played a central role in curbing the nuclear arms race and preventing nuclear war." Scientists made up a small but influential constituency of this movement and frequently sparked campaigns to abolish or at least regulate the very weapons they or their peers had helped create. During the early

Cold War, U.S. officials came to identify arms control as an alternative to an offensive nuclear policy.[7] Since arms control agreements were often complex and technical in nature, scientists believed their expertise could make a difference in the nuclear age.

Scientists took a variety of approaches toward changing nuclear policy during the Cold War, but policymakers in the government had to respond to these efforts if they were to make a difference. Since the dawn of the atomic age in 1945, the American public heard scientists give conflicting advice about nuclear weapons, ranging from total nuclear disarmament to overwhelming nuclear superiority. How were members of the national security state who sought guidance from experts on nuclear weapons supposed to reconcile these positions? A logical view might have been to make a decision based on scientific prestige—simply to listen to only the "best" scientists. Credentials are, after all, the lifeblood of science, with degrees, prizes, grants, and publications indicating the discipline's most worthy practitioners.

But other factors mattered more to the government than prestige. Most important to policymakers was not finding out what America's best scientists thought of the arms race but instead learning ways of maintaining deterrence and nuclear superiority as the pillars of Cold War policy. Confronted with conflicting views, policymakers came to distinguish between two types of science. One type was like Pauling's: moral, emotional, utopian, and vaguely suspicious. A second type, like York, Killian, and Kistiakowsky's, was technical, unemotional, pragmatic, and patriotic. Although scientific evidence supported a multitude of views on nuclear weapons, the state decided only one view would actually count as objective science, and that was the science that explicitly or implicitly supported the state's idea of proper nuclear policy. Thus, a confrontational relationship evolved, but not simply one that posed the state and pronuclear scientists against antinuclear scientists. Instead, an alliance formed between the state and scientists who adhered to the Cold War redefinition of objective science against those who used science to advocate for nuclear disarmament in explicitly political and moral terms.

By the beginning of the Cold War, scientists had an established, if inconsistent, inclination to act politically and to use science to better humanity. During the Great Depression, as the historian Peter Kuznick has shown, scientists dedicated significant effort to publicizing the ways in which their work improved human lives.[8] This sentiment continued in somewhat altered form during World War II, when scientists worked to build technology, including the atomic bomb and radar, that would help rid the world of the scourge of Nazism. But scientists also wanted a say in how this technology would be used. During the Manhattan Project, some scientists attempted to influence U.S. atomic policy, though this struggle was, not surprisingly, won by President Truman, who ignored pleas that he reconsider military use of the A-bomb against Japan.

The adoption of nuclear weapons as the ultimate guarantor of security during the Cold War further threatened to turn scientists into mere weaponeers of the state, at best, and the authors of genocide, at worst. Asked to enlist on the side of what became known as mutually assured destruction, many scientists struggled against this militarism and worked to reconcile the dangers of the Cold War with an optimistic faith in the scientific life. This sentiment sometimes took the form of wholehearted opposition to nuclear weapons and U.S. Cold War policy. The state, for its part, needed scientists' expertise, but it became clear very early on that scientists would not blindly follow the dictates of national security. Scientists thus found themselves caught between wanting to influence policy, on the one hand, and freedom of expression, on the other. Ultimately, Cold War policymakers decided that if scientists wanted to influence nuclear policy, they could do so only within certain limits.

The AEC set these boundaries at the 1954 security clearance hearing of Robert Oppenheimer, who had served as head of the Los Alamos laboratory during World War II and came to be hailed as "the acknowledged father of the A-bomb." The AEC removed Oppenheimer from his position as the nation's premier science adviser and mandated that government science advisers must, above all else, uphold "the protection of the strongest offensive military interests of the country."[9] This command reset the terms in which scientific advice about nuclear weapons would be judged, limiting advisers to technical advice rather than moral and political considerations. This shift from moral concerns to strictly technical input was part of the contested but successful establishment of the deterrence consensus that evolved into mutually assured destruction and lasted until the end of the Cold War.

Cold Warriors in the U.S. government felt they had to control science because the combination of antinuclear activism and scientific authority offered a major challenge to nuclear weapons and, therefore, U.S. Cold War ideology. This power dynamic has often been described as the state's demand that scientists be "on tap," not "on top." For the most part, the national security state successfully neutralized the substantial threat that scientists' dissent posed to the U.S. nuclear establishment and managed this containment by first redefining what constituted proper scientific advice and then excluding some scientists while granting access to those who internalized this definition.

The antinuclear scientists who rejected the redefinition of science found the state questioning their loyalties, confronting them with scientific opponents, marginalizing them as uninformed, challenging their credibility, co-opting their concerns as its own, or employing several of these tactics simultaneously. Underlying these different methods was the simple question of whether scientists upheld or disputed the concept of nuclear deterrence. Scientists who opposed the continual evolution of nuclear energy into newer and bigger weapons generally failed to influence policy. When outsider scientists gained—or threatened to gain—a degree of influence based on their expertise, the state most often responded by questioning their objectivity, even though to Cold Warriors in the U.S. government, to be objective meant not standing in the way of the nuclear arms race.

The government could not achieve this conformity without the adherence of scientists who accepted the AEC's redefinition of science and the primacy of nuclear deterrence. Maintaining a nuclear arsenal meant that the state needed scientists and not just for the physical upkeep of the nation's weapons. Scientists could also provide legitimacy, expertise, and authority for various branches of government that both supported and questioned nuclear weapons. So while the government frequently excluded scientists from policymaking, it just as often engaged with them, welcoming many who opposed nuclear weapons as long as they played by the new rules of science advice and gave technical recommendations to help the nation achieve the most credible nuclear deterrent. Edward Teller, a tireless advocate of nuclear weapons development, fitted this mold, of course, but so did scientists less obsessed with bigger and deadlier nuclear weapons, including men like Killian, Kistiakowsky, York, and Hans Bethe, who consistently challenged Teller. By accepting deterrence, these scientists had more in common with Teller than they did with Pauling.

But playing by the rules negated the strongest arguments against nuclear weapons. Forbidden from arguing that nuclear weapons were just plain wrong or morally repulsive (views that resonated with large segments of the public), scientists who worked for arms control and disarmament within the government made strictly technical arguments, for these assertions appeared to be more objective and therefore in line with the redefinition of science. From this technical perspective, scientists argued that more powerful nuclear weapons made the country less safe and deterrence less credible—a reasonable argument but one that offended the common sense of many policymakers during the Cold War. The state's new definition of science, then, bolstered rather than challenged the centrality of nuclear weapons in U.S. Cold War strategy. Scientists' professional identities, conservative in nature, further restricted the actions of antinuclear scientists by implicitly assimilating the government's conception of the proper role of scientists and seeing *objectivity* as synonymous with *apolitical.*

Case Studies

Part of the nuclear issue in post–World War II America included a debate over the role of science in the Cold War. Scholars' views on scientists have evolved over time, from labeling them as mere cogs in the military-industrial complex and sinister "wizards of Armageddon" to emphasizing different levels of trust in the U.S. government held by World War II–era and Vietnam-era scientists. One common way of understanding this tension between scientists and politics has been to examine Robert Oppenheimer's career, which— through his rise to fame and subsequent downfall after his 1954 security clearance hearing—arguably altered the course of U.S. science, as scientific internationalism was overtaken by rigid Cold War nationalism. The historian Jessica Wang, however, has shown that Oppenheimer's shaming was but the finale of a long purge of leftist scientists from government institutions after World War II.[10] Yet while the Oppenheimer case was indeed the culmination of the Red Scare campaign against scientists, it was not at all the final word on the issue of scientists and nuclear weapons. *Redefining Science* in many ways picks up where Wang's work ends. The nearly forty years between the Oppenheimer hearing and the end of the Cold War saw continuous conflict between scientists and the national security state, as scientists' attempts to influence nuclear weapons policy continuously reshaped power relations between science and the government.

Scholars across an array of disciplines have investigated the relationship between scientists, nuclear weapons, and politics in many ways. Historians of the early atomic age found instances where scientists nudged public opinion away from nuclearism, while political scientists have explained that antinuclear activists and scientists used various pathways to encourage arms control in the U.S. and Soviet governments. One sociological approach has argued that as scientists became more politically active in the 1960s, they weakened their own social authority. Science and technology scholars, meanwhile, have shown that members of different technical disciplines argued against ABMs in different ways, as well as how debates over nuclear technology shaped the culture and national identity of modern France. Each of these works illuminates our understanding of the role of science in society, yet none of them covers the entire Cold War or the full extent of the internal wrestling within science over the changes taking place. Furthermore, an emphasis on specific achievements (a single treaty, for example) obscures the overall fact that nuclear weapons endured despite tremendous opposition to them.[11]

A clear understanding of the persistence of nuclear weapons in U.S. policy demands an analysis of the array of scientists who fought over this issue for the duration of the Cold War. *Redefining Science* takes as its subjects individuals at or near the top of the U.S. scientific hierarchy, concentrating on those who spoke most effectively for and against nuclear weapons from both within the government and without. The reason for this approach is that these most famous scientists directly engaged the state and had the capacity to shape perceptions of science and nuclear weapons. Influential with both the public and other scientists, these men took it upon themselves to act and speak for science; they were also the focus of government actions and helped shape conceptions about the proper role of scientists in the U.S. government as well as society at large. This book does not, therefore, take up the study of a broad social movement, nor does it provide a social history of the rank and file of U.S. scientists. To include an array of different scientific activists, not every important antinuclear scientist (Barry Commoner, for example) is covered in detail. Instead, *Redefining Science* examines a variety of notable scientists whose actions and beliefs directly shaped the relationship between scientists and the state by speaking to each other, the government, and the public about the role and responsibility of scientists in a geopolitical system ruled by nuclear weapons.

Of the scientists who grappled with the nuclear issue during the Cold War, many are discussed, but several stand out, some for their renown but all for representing a unique approach in their attempts to shape nuclear policy. Although his reputation is currently in some disrepair, Linus Pauling tirelessly opposed nuclear weapons in the 1950s and early 1960s. As a Nobel Prize winner, Pauling brought unimpeachable credentials to the antinuclear crusade, and his "morality of science" offered a powerful antinuclear message that inspired activists in the United States and overseas while also exasperating critics. Years of controversial activism, however, including widespread petitions, contentious lawsuits, prolific writings, and public demonstrations, eventually brought professional and political retribution for Pauling, showing both how far scientific activism from outside the halls of government could reach and how short it could fall.

Pauling's nemesis, Edward Teller, is known to anyone familiar with the history of nuclear weapons. His career spanned the Cold War and beyond, and for his entire life he steadfastly promoted the development of nuclear weapons. In great contrast to Pauling, Teller aligned himself with the national security state during the 1950s. By relying on political influence and Red Scare tactics, he largely neutralized his scientific opponents, Pauling among them. Within his framework of avowed anticommunism, Teller portrayed nuclear deterrence as an ethical response to atheistic and domineering communism and saw nuclear weapons as a fundamentally moral way to defend U.S. interests against the Soviets. With his efforts, he secured for himself a prized place within the national security state, winning funding for his weapons laboratory and other nuclear pursuits and gaining what many antinuclear scientists lacked: influence in policymaking circles.

During the 1980s, arguably no scientist was more famous than Carl Sagan, the astronomer who spoke to millions of people through his wildly popular books and TV series, *Cosmos*. Far more than a popularizer of science, he often spoke to the public about nuclear weapons just as fears of World War III ran rampant. At a time when scientists' role in the antinuclear movement had greatly diminished, Sagan's nuclear winter theory stood out both in terms of its claims—that the extinction of humanity was a possible outcome of a nuclear war—and in terms of its scientific reliability. Sagan's ability to connect to the greater public, combined with the decline of rabid anticommunism, allowed his ideas to be taken seriously by members of Congress. But nuclear winter's power as an antinuclear argument was severely undermined by conservative opposition as well as many scientists' concerns about what constituted the proper behavior of a scientist. Sagan's efforts thus reflect the political obstacles to scientific antinuclear activism as well as the ways in which the scientific community could restrain scientific dissent.

Some of the most active and influential scientists are not as well known to the general public, but this makes them no less deserving of attention. Working within the world of Washington politics often afforded scientists greater access to policymakers, though it limited the policies they could advocate. Scientists who advised the president and Congress are key to understanding the scientific divide: these men played by the rules, and most government figures and members of the scientific community found their methods of antinuclear activism acceptable. Throughout the Cold War, the distinguished physicist and Manhattan Project veteran Hans Bethe advised the government on nuclear policy, providing nuanced and pragmatic guidance on arms control, expert testimony on treaties, service at the Los Alamos nuclear weapons laboratory, and arguments to counter overly zealous pronuclear scientists. Though he possessed a deep moral conviction against nuclear weapons, Bethe's decision to work for disarmament and arms control as a government insider often forced him to support policies dedicated to maximizing U.S. nuclear capability.

Like Bethe, the physicist Herbert York appears at many significant moments in nuclear history: the Manhattan Project, the creation of Livermore laboratory, the furor over *Sputnik,* and numerous test ban debates. York's long career as both a weapons scientist and an arms control advocate makes him an important case study, as does his role in the ABM debate of 1969 and 1970. In addition, York served as an ambassador charged with negotiating an arms control treaty with the Soviets during the Carter presidency. While scientists had largely fallen out of favor in Washington by the 1970s, York managed to stay relevant to nuclear debates. Yet his influence depended heavily on his paradoxical identity of Pentagon weaponeer and arms controller.

Another group of scientists who merit analysis for their role in nuclear weapons policy are those who served as presidential science advisers during the Cold War. After the launch of the Soviet *Sputnik* satellite in 1957, the Eisenhower administration began to incorporate scientists into the cabinet with the post of presidential science adviser and the President's Science Advisory Committee (PSAC). Scientists suddenly found themselves with access to the highest echelons of policymaking, while policymakers were again concerned with the opinions of the country's most esteemed scientists. The nature of science advising had changed since the mid-1940s, however. When scientists in the late 1950s mobilized to take advantage of this new access, they no longer carried with them the heroic aura of atomic wizards. Instead, a new generation of scientists had entered the labs, as science underwent a "suburbanization" during the conformist 1950s, as characterized by one historian.[12] Furthermore, the Oppenheimer hearing had demonstrated that if government science advisers wished to oppose nuclear weapons, they had to make the case that neither arms control nor disarmament would harm the nation's offensive capabilities. Those scientists who favored arms control could not help but be aware of how the Oppenheimer hearing had redefined moral opposition to nuclear weapons as inappropriate and irrelevant.[13] At the very moment that nuclear weapons increased dramatically in destructive power, scientists' vocabulary of dissent became much smaller.

Despite these limitations, a number of scientists energetically took to advising the U.S. government on nuclear weapons policy. While far less famous than their Nobel-winning peers Bethe and Pauling, these men, specifically Killian, Kistiakowsky, Jerome Wiesner, Donald Hornig, and AEC chairman Glenn Seaborg, who variously served Presidents Eisenhower, Kennedy, and Johnson, had cabinet-level access to the Oval Office at a time when presidents sought scientific advice. If anyone could influence policy, they could. The historian Zuoyue Wang has described how these presidential science advisers brought technological skepticism to bear on many of the ludicrous nuclear fantasies of the age.[14] Yet their position presented a dilemma as well as an opportunity. As the scientists who were the closest to political power, they fundamentally served the president rather than the scientific community or the antinuclear movement and therefore faced political restraints (on rhetoric, advocacy, and arguments) that did not burden, for example, Pauling, Teller, or Sagan. Furthermore, as Hornig's tenure shows, a president could quite easily lose interest in scientific advice.

Some scientists blurred the line between government advisers and transnational activists. On April 13, 1955, the philosopher Bertrand Russell wrote to Albert Einstein just days before the legendary physicist's death. Russell insisted on sharing with Einstein an urgent manifesto he had composed that called attention to the increased menace of thermonuclear weapons. Einstein, in what was apparently one of his last acts, added his name to the document. The Russell-Einstein Manifesto implored scientists to take action to end the arms race. "Scientists should assemble," the manifesto read, "not as members of this or that nation, continent, or creed, but as human beings, members of the species Man, whose continued existence is in doubt."[15] Two years later, twenty-two scientists from both sides of the Iron Curtain heeded Russell and Einstein's call and met in Pugwash, Nova Scotia, to discuss disarmament. The Pugwash movement became a leading transnational organization of scientists, mobilizing international connections and technical expertise to bring together politically prominent Soviet, British, and U.S. scientists to discuss urgent nuclear issues in an unofficial atmosphere.[16] The British physicist Joseph Rotblat, the only scientist to quit the Manhattan Project for moral reasons, heavily influenced Pugwash with his philosophy and temperament. Unofficial and unfettered by governmental rules, Pugwash came to represent a segment of scientists who opposed nuclear weapons, and though its political influence waxed and waned throughout the Cold War, it merits analysis here.

Finally, the biophysicist Eugene Rabinowitch played an essential role in scientists' debates over nuclear weapons from the Manhattan Project into the 1970s. Months after World War II ended, Rabinowitch cofounded the *Bulletin of the Atomic Scientists* and became its leading editorial voice for nearly thirty years. Through the *Bulletin*, Rabinowitch invited scientists to contribute to the diffusion of informed ideas about the role of nuclear energy and science in general throughout the world. Under Rabinowitch's guidance, the *Bulletin* became an influential sounding board for scientifically based antinuclear sentiment. Convinced that humans would use nuclear technology only to destroy themselves, Rabinowitch hoped that the *Bulletin* would bring the rational and informed opinions of scientists to bear on the dilemmas of the nuclear age. Under his leadership, the *Bulletin* spoke out against McCarthyism, the Oppenheimer hearing, the H-bomb, and the arms race in general, often with an "evangelical fervor" for peace.[17] While the *Bulletin* had limited circulation, many elite figures in science and politics did read it. In addition, Rabinowitch participated heavily in the Pugwash conferences. In some ways, Rabinowitch was an outsider, but rather than embrace grassroots tactics like Pauling, he helped shape the understanding of the nuclear issue in the United States among scientists and policymakers through sophisticated analysis of the science and politics of nuclear weapons. Situated between activists and policymakers, Rabinowitch ultimately grew frustrated with each constituency and despaired of achieving nuclear disarmament.

In addition to investigating these scientists, the scope of *Redefining Science* broadens at times to examine pivotal moments in the Cold War when science and politics collided. The Oppenheimer hearing naturally warrants attention, as it marked the point when the U.S. government explicitly redefined science as technical recommendations for enhancing the nuclear deterrent and maintaining nuclear superiority over the Soviet Union. The debate over a nuclear test ban treaty during the late 1950s and 1960s demonstrates the ways scientists could—and could not—influence policy after the Oppenheimer hearing. The years of the Vietnam War saw the relationship between scientists and policymakers deteriorate, with scientists shifting their antinuclear efforts. And the debate over the nuclear freeze and the Strategic Defense Initiative (SDI) in the 1980s also initiated a substantial amount of scientific discussion in the public and political spheres, demonstrating the staying power of nuclear deterrence but also the emergence of disarmament as a moral cause. Ultimately, deterrence endured: the Cold War started to end when Ronald Reagan and Mikhail Gorbachev began to back away from mutually assured destruction, yet today U.S. national security is still premised on the possession of a large nuclear arsenal.

While Oppenheimer had presided over the splitting of the atom that resulted in the atomic explosions over Hiroshima and Nagasaki, the ruling in his AEC case fissioned not atoms but American science itself, unleashing a chain reaction that reshaped the scientific community. For almost fifty years, some of the nation's most influential scientists engaged in activism for and against nuclear weapons, while branches of the state concerned with national security constrained (and occasionally encouraged) their capabilities for activism. Furthermore, scientists' professional identity often hindered scientific activism, though some iconoclastic scientists transcended these barriers. In the aftermath of this fissioning, much of American science became increasingly militarized and politicized. In addition, a number of elite scientists went from being actively consulted on nuclear weapons to personae non gratae within policymaking circles, which occurred alongside broader cultural changes, especially the decline of the public's faith in the authority of the "great scientist"—the expert who took it for granted that the government and the public needed to hear his or her views on political, ethical, and social issues. Tracing the contours of scientists' role in the Cold War reveals much about dissent, authority, and expertise in an ostensibly democratic society that finds itself simultaneously in thrall to and skeptical of science and technology.

1

From "Highly Unreliable" to "Patriotic and Prompt"

Scientists Confront the National Security State, 1945–1957

N MAKING THE ATOMIC BOMB AND offering guidance on its use, scientists carved a political niche that, after World War II, made it seem natural for policymakers to consult them on atomic policy. By the mid-1950s, however, changes in the Cold War had drastically altered the relationship between scientists and policymakers and limited the type of advice science advisers could give. This transformation centered around Robert Oppenheimer, the emblematic scientist of the atomic age, who went from war hero to Red Scare victim after the 1954 security clearance hearing that dismissed him from government service. But looking beyond Oppenheimer's personal tragedy reveals bigger shifts in the dynamics of power. For the rest of the scientific community, the verdict was an ultimatum, redefining how scientists could give advice to the national security state. While U.S. scientists divided over the Oppenheimer hearing, predictions at the time that scientists would break entirely from the government can only be described as inaccurate. National security required keeping scientists on board while limiting their dissent against nuclear deterrence. By the late 1950s a new cohort of influential scientists came to the fore, eager to influence U.S. policy, even if it meant restricting their personal views and moral arguments against nuclear weapons.

Carving a Niche

Observers of all types hailed the atomic bomb at the moment of its use as a watershed invention in human history certain to change the course of civilization. Harry Truman claimed that on hearing of the use of the bomb against Hiroshima, he blurted out, "This is the greatest thing in history." From a distinctly different perspective, Japanese emperor Hirohito, speaking directly to his subjects for the first time, mentioned the "cruel bombs" that devastated Hiroshima and Nagasaki and concluded that "to continue the war further could lead in the end not only to the extermination of our race, but also to the destruction of all human civilization." In his survey of immediate reactions to the atomic bomb, the historian Paul Boyer found that Hirohito's perspective was not unique—that "in the earliest moments of the nuclear era," nuclear fears "had already found urgent expression."[1]

The daunting nature of atomic weapons certainly shaped visions of the postwar world. As has been repeated numerous times, on witnessing the test of the first atomic bomb at Alamogordo, New Mexico, Oppenheimer thought of Hindu scripture, in particular the apocalyptic verse "I am become Death, destroyer of worlds." To title his landmark history of the diplomatic significance of the A-bomb, Martin Sherwin paraphrased Oppenheimer's reaction in order to describe the military and political effects of the weapon: "A World Destroyed." Perhaps most tellingly, in the long history of violence that has produced countless weapons, "the Bomb" requires no other descriptors.[2]

But another reason the atomic bomb held such import for the postwar world was that its creators self-consciously endowed it with great significance long before its initial use. In 1939, hours after discovering that uranium would release enough neutrons during fission to create a nuclear chain reaction, the physicist Leo Szilard felt that "there was very little doubt in my mind that the world was headed for grief." That same year in Germany, Carl von Weizsäcker, working on the German A-bomb, reflected that "this discovery could not fail to radically change the political structure of the world." Niels Bohr, an idol to many physicists of the twentieth century, predicted that the weapon would be so terrible that it would end forever the human race's propensity for war, adding that the harnessing of atomic energy was "a far deeper interference with the natural events than anything ever before attempted." Bohr heavily influenced the thinking of Oppenheimer, who, not long after the war's end, justified atomic weapons as "the best argument science could make . . . for a more reasonable and a new idea of the relations between nations."[3]

The select scientists responsible for creating the A-bomb directly shaped perceptions of the weapon and in so doing carved a niche for themselves in the policymaking of the atomic age. When the Los Alamos physicist Robert Wilson felt pangs of doubt while working on the Manhattan Project, he convened a meeting to discuss the consequences of creating such a powerful weapon. To emphasize the bomb's image as a world-changing force, Wilson titled his meeting "The Impact of the Gadget on Civilization." The fact that a mere "gadget"—a wartime nickname Los Alamos scientists gave the A-bomb—could have an impact on "civilization" succinctly expressed scientists' vision of the bomb's magnitude: fairly straightforward to invent, quite difficult to control. In a November 1945 speech to Los Alamos scientists, Oppenheimer defended the bomb as the culmination of the quantum revolution in physics of the 1920s. Oppenheimer (no longer the lab's director) described the bomb as a momentous and crucial turning point in the history of science itself: "The real impact of the creation of the atomic bomb and atomic weapons [is] the fact that the very existence of science is threatened, and its value is threatened." On a more upbeat note, President Truman described the Manhattan Project as "the greatest achievement of organized science in history."[4]

Not everyone joined the chorus of voices proclaiming a new era. Many U.S. military officials and policymakers saw the bomb as a fairly conventional weapon, while those unfriendly to the United States simply scoffed at it. Unlike most of his fellow Manhattan Project engineers, David Greenglass (who passed atomic information to Soviet agents) did not even bother to wake up early for the Alamogordo test. "You gotta understand something," he explained to a journalist years later. "I knew it went off." According to legend, Joseph Stalin, who had been nonplussed when Truman revealed the bomb to him at Potsdam, had a similarly ho-hum reaction to his own atomic weapon. Stalin slept through the first Soviet A-bomb test in 1949, and when a phone call woke him to tell him of the successful explosion, the dictator muttered that he already knew and hung up. Mao Zedong attempted to belittle atomic weapons before his country developed them, describing the atomic bomb as "a paper tiger. It looks terrible, but in fact it isn't."[5] Reactions to the bomb reflected what was at stake in the atomic age. While enemies of the United States needed to be unimpressed with the bomb, it boosted the importance of U.S. scientists when the bomb appeared to have created a sea change in the course of history. If the public saw the bomb as momentous, it would seem more natural for scientists, as the creators of atomic weapons, to claim a role in guiding the nation's atomic energy policy.

Scientists and Early Atomic Policy

Such was the thinking of the atomic scientists who forged for themselves large roles in nuclear policymaking near the war's end and after. In his farewell speech at Los Alamos, Oppenheimer commented on the new world created by the bomb. "It is a new field," the physicist remarked, "in which the role of science has been so great that it is to my mind hardly thinkable that the international traditions of science, and the fraternity of scientists, should not play a constructive part." Oppenheimer was hoping to reinforce what had already tentatively begun: the active consultation of scientists by policymakers. Along with the Nobel Prize winners Enrico Fermi, Arthur Holly Compton, and Ernest Lawrence, Oppenheimer had been invited to serve as a scientific adviser to the spring 1945 Interim Committee that decided the most effective way to use the atomic bomb against Japan. These scientists joined Vannevar Bush and James Conant in rubbing shoulders with establishment luminaries such as James Byrnes, George Marshall, and Henry Stimson.[6] Other scientists endeavored to influence policy after the war with more civic-minded activism. Albert Einstein, Linus Pauling, Eugene Rabinowitch, Leo Szilard, Edward Teller, and other scientists took part in what became known as the Atomic Scientists' Movement, an attempt to shape U.S. atomic energy legislation. These efforts helped defeat the May-Johnson bill, which would have ceded control over atomic energy policy to the military, and helped pass the McMahon Act, which established the civilian Atomic Energy Commission to regulate, promote, and protect the U.S. atomic energy industry, including weapons.[7]

The Atomic Scientists' Movement had loftier visions than just the provincial goal of lobbying Congress for favorable legislation. Since the threat of atomic weapons loomed especially large in the shadow of Hiroshima, many scientists—including even the relatively conservative and aloof Oppenheimer—adamantly believed that only a world government with control over atomic energy could, in the long run, guarantee the survival of humanity. But the fragile ship of world government crashed and sank on the rough shoals of the Cold War. As tensions between the United States and Soviet Union heightened after 1945, nationalism triumphed over internationalism. U.S. officials cynically transformed Oppenheimer's proposal for UN control of atomic energy into a vacant piece of Cold War propaganda by insisting on conditions designed to lock in U.S. nuclear superiority and conceptions of national security.[8] The scientists who had hoped to guide atomic energy policy soon clashed with the anticommunists shaping U.S. policy and increasingly fell out of favor as paranoia replaced postwar optimism.

A growing public perception of theoretical physicists as the "weakest links" in the U.S. national security system painted scientists with a pink brush and proved particularly damaging to atomic activists. According to the historian David Kaiser, "Theoretical physicists emerged as the most consistently named whipping-boys of McCarthyism." These questions of character arose when atomic spy scandals involving Klaus Fuchs and Julius and Ethel Rosenberg came to light; the Soviet A-bomb, the fall of China, the Korean War, and Joseph McCarthy then encouraged a full-blown Red Scare well into the 1950s. In 1954 one scientist complained to the AEC that "exaggerated reports in the public press have led to the impression that scientists as a class are highly unreliable and that many are disloyal." Perhaps most troubling for scientists, some academic and government science institutions fell in line behind the Red Scare's manufacture of consent. The University of California (UC) at Berkeley instituted loyalty pledges for its faculty and fired many who refused to sign, while the AEC launched a new round of security clearance hearings to weed out alleged subversives.[9]

A categorization of all scientists as liberal-leaning activists would be inaccurate. The Manhattan Project's most famous scientists left Los Alamos after the end of the war, some of them to take up antinuclear causes. But more than enough scientists remained behind to staff the weapons lab and help build the nation's nuclear arsenal. A majority of scientists accepted, explicitly or tacitly, the policy of deterrence as the best means for preventing a nuclear war. While rank-and-file scientists may have powered big science forward in the years after World War II, the nation's elite scientists—mostly Manhattan Project veterans—wrestled over the direction of the ship. Men like Oppenheimer, Hans Bethe, and Teller engaged with the nuclear issue and were present during the 1950s as political conflicts reshaped power relations between scientists and the state.

The Oppenheimer Hearing

Though not really a participant in the Atomic Scientists' Movement, Oppenheimer had been politically radical during the Great Depression, when he supported a wide variety of Far Left causes and embraced communism as a fellow traveler.[10] Having purged himself of most of these leftist associations on joining the Manhattan Project, Oppenheimer emerged from the war as the premier government science adviser and perhaps the greatest beneficiary of scientists' newfound fame and cachet. But Oppenheimer also embodied scientists' fall from grace during the Red Scare, when the AEC revoked his security clearance after a 1954 hearing, completing a lengthy effort by his adversaries to oust him from government service. While Oppenheimer's tragedy marks the nadir of U.S. political life in the 1950s, his security clearance hearing also ushered in a new relationship between the national security state and elite scientists only slightly less influential than Oppenheimer.

In 1945 the destruction of Hiroshima and Nagasaki by atomic bombs elevated Oppenheimer to celebrity status. As the head of the Los Alamos lab that had produced the atomic bombs, the enigmatic and photogenic Oppenheimer expressed ambivalence about nuclear weapons and cultivated the mystique that allowed observers then and now to view him as the symbol of the atomic age and all of its dilemmas and contradictions.[11] The slender physicist was essential to the successful crafting of the first weapons of mass destruction but also worried deeply about war. As one who prided himself on having pondered Eastern religion, world literature, and human nature, Oppenheimer gave the impression that he would not wield his influence lightly. Even so, he could make boneheaded decisions—"I was an idiot," he later confessed to the AEC in an exasperated attempt to explain his concocted stories about espionage attempts during the Manhattan Project. At times Oppenheimer appeared to be a sort of pacifist, worriedly prophesying that "the time will come when mankind will curse the names of Los Alamos and Hiroshima" and denouncing the proposed Super Bomb (an early version of the hydrogen bomb) as a potential "weapon of genocide" that would "slaughter a vast number of civilians." Yet he eagerly advised military policymakers, and in place of the terrifying Super he comforted himself with the thought of a great many A-bombs, including an acceleration of the A-bomb program and tactical nuclear weapons.[12] Respected by many, Oppenheimer also advised the powerful: as head of the AEC's General Advisory Committee (GAC), he often met with congressional and military officials and rarely the president.

But in a drastic reversal of fortune, the AEC humiliated Oppenheimer in 1954 by upholding the decision of the previous year to revoke his security clearance (and thus his access to privileged government policymaking circles) after an infamous hearing.[13] In less than a decade, Oppenheimer went from the power elite of atomic energy circles to a martyred intellectual, exiled to the purgatory of Princeton's Institute for Advanced Study. Observers at the time, as well as scholars in years since, recognized that the hearing served as retaliation for a multitude of Oppenheimer's technical and political faux pas, including his initial opposition to the Super, his recommendations against U.S. air force atomic weapons and policy plans, and his alleged domination and intimidation of members of the GAC.

The hearing also resulted from the desire of several of Oppenheimer's enemies to punish him for his personal arrogance and the perceived insults they had received from him over the years. These transgressions included his bypassing of Teller for Bethe as head theoretical physicist of the Los Alamos lab in 1943, his public ridiculing of the AEC commissioner Lewis Strauss in front of Congress in 1949, and his continued "association," in the words of the AEC Personnel Security Board, "on what could not be considered a casual basis" with his friend (and known communist) Haakon Chevalier. Strauss, like a dark Wizard of Oz, used intimidation, coercion, and bribery to orchestrate the hearing and ensure Oppenheimer's dismissal. For his part, Teller damned Oppenheimer in his testimony by saying, "I would like to see the vital interests of this country in hands which I understand better, and therefore trust more." Teller had actually helped set the hearing in motion in 1952 by telling an interviewer with the Federal Bureau of Investigation (FBI) that the "H bomb would have been a reality at least one year ago if it had not been opposed by Oppenheimer" and that "he would do most anything to see subject [Oppenheimer] separated from [the] General Advisory Committee because of his poor advice and policies regarding national preparedness and because of his delaying the development of [the] H bomb."[14]

Menaced by the weapons they had made, the atomic scientists found that their agency, the AEC, had turned against them as well. Scientists had worked incredibly hard in the mid-1940s to see that atomic policy would not be dominated by the military, only to learn that the civilians who ended up running the AEC could be as militaristic as anyone in the national security state. This shift, with the hawkish Strauss eventually replacing the New Dealer David Lilienthal as chair of the agency (with Gordon Dean serving in between the two), reflected the increasingly belligerent policies of the United States that evolved during a decade that began with the Korean War, atomic spy scandals, McCarthyism, and National Security Council (NSC) Report 68.

Amid this changed political landscape, the Oppenheimer hearing served to get rid of Oppenheimer himself. But it was more than that, as the AEC chose to make an example out of Oppenheimer. Certainly, Oppenheimer was not the only scientist in the United States who could advise policymakers on nuclear weapons. Concerned about the elaborate lengths to which the AEC went to discredit Oppenheimer, I. I. Rabi, a physicist and Oppenheimer's close friend, drew attention to this exact point during the hearing, stating, "He is a consultant, and if you don't want to consult the guy, you don't consult him, period." Instead, the AEC went so far as to redefine what constituted proper science advice in the course of the hearing and its ensuing verdict. The AEC's insistence on making a spectacle out of Oppenheimer indicated that the agency wanted to do more than just get rid of him; the hearing served as a way of warning influential advisers not to give the AEC advice it did not want to hear. The AEC clearly feared that scientists could attain too much influence—that they might be "on top," not "on tap."[15]

The Oppenheimer hearing—the AEC's most notorious—was a farce, an injustice to Oppenheimer personally as well as an insult to the Bill of Rights that epitomized the Red Scare era, when the trampling of civil liberties took on the fervor of a national pastime. But while the hearing reflected and exhibited the Red Scare politics of paranoia, it also shaped the future of science-government relations by allowing the state to eliminate dissent by excluding certain views on nuclear weapons and certain scientists from policymaking. For those scientists who continued to advise the government, this ultimatum clearly defined the type of advice they could give.

The hearing made explicit the rules for future input and advice from scientists and demonstrated the costs of dissent from the state's militarism. Moral qualms such as reluctance to work on the H-bomb, the AEC believed, had hindered the pursuit of nuclear weapons development and thus deserved to be expelled from the science adviser's intellectual repertoire. Not that the AEC strictly forbade morality itself, but key aspects of the AEC's Oppenheimer verdict, presented in the Personnel Security Board's "Findings and Recommendation," expressed a deliberate intent to redefine morality to such an extent that it could not challenge the nation's commitment to increasingly powerful nuclear weapons. The board did not question Oppenheimer's "right" to his opinions regarding the development of the H-bomb, as "they were motivated by deep moral conviction." The problem arose, however, because Oppenheimer "may have departed his role as scientific adviser to exercise highly persuasive influence in matters in which his convictions were not necessarily a reflection of technical judgment, and also not necessarily related to the protection of the strongest offensive military interests of the country."[16]

While everyone had the right to express deep moral convictions, the document explained, "emotional involvement in the current crisis, like all other things, must yield to the security of the nation." The government certainly needed the advice of "competent technicians." But this advice had to reflect both "special competence . . . and soundly based conviction . . . uncolored and uninfluenced by considerations of an emotional character." Morality, in the government's eyes, was an emotional, unscientific feeling rather than an objective and rational mind-set. The AEC then defined the state's security interests in explicitly military terms. "In evaluating advice from a scientist which departs from the arena of his specialty," the commission declared, "Government officials charged with the military posture of our country must also be certain that underlying any advice is a genuine conviction that this country cannot in the interest of security have less than the strongest possible offensive capabilities in a time of national danger."[17]

As the agency destroyed Oppenheimer's reputation, it also established new guidelines for its future science advisers. In the process, the balance of power shifted away from H-bomb skeptics to thermonuclear advocates like Teller. Just as Teller's opinion mattered in the hearing, so it would also matter in the future. Most important, the hearing allowed the government to exclude morality from official discussions about nuclear weapons policy, including arms control and disarmament. Scientists, the state demanded, should recognize the threat to national security and give only technical advice that upheld the nuclear foundations of the national security state.

The AEC verdict directly addressed morality for a specific reason: the high-level debate over the H-bomb had been less about how to build a thermonuclear weapon and more about whether to build one. In his 1952 FBI interview, Teller had explicitly blamed Oppenheimer's opposition "on moral grounds" for thwarting the push for thermonuclear weapons. Many influential scientists besides Oppenheimer had objected to the Super, and they had, like Oppenheimer, often done so for moral reasons. The GAC majority report that recommended against a crash thermonuclear program, signed by James Conant, Hartley Rowe, Cyril Stanley Smith, Lee DuBridge, Oliver Buckley, as well as Oppenheimer, cast the Super as "a weapon of genocide," while the minority report, signed by Enrico Fermi and Rabi, went even further, describing the weapon as "necessarily an evil thing considered in any light," adding that "the use of such a weapon cannot be justified on any ethical ground. . . . Its use would put the United States in a bad moral position relative to the peoples of the world."[18] (Fermi and Rabi ultimately concluded, however, that if the Soviet Union went forward with the Super, the United States should follow suit.)

Moral misgivings about the Super were not limited to the GAC. In particular, the respected physicist Hans Bethe made clear in his personal correspondence how the H-bomb troubled his conscience. Indeed, the historian S. S. Schweber has characterized Bethe as a scientist who upheld his "moral responsibility" during the Cold War. After President Truman disregarded the GAC recommendation and announced a crash H-bomb program in 1950, Bethe wrote to Norris Bradbury, Oppenheimer's successor as head of Los Alamos, with the weapon clearly at the forefront of his mind. "The announcement of the President has not changed my feelings in this matter," he wrote to Bradbury in February 1950. "I still believe that it is morally wrong and unwise for our National security to develop this weapon." When asked if he would work on the Super itself, Bethe was blunt, writing that he could not "in good conscience work on this weapon." Less than two months later, Bethe wrote to Robert Bacher of the AEC and commented, "I still think that the moral argument is important and that one must point out on this occasion that one should not accept bigger and more powerful weapons of destruction without question." After trying to imagine a thermonuclear war, Bethe wondered "whether victory in such a war would mean anything and would still be preferable to submission."[19]

Bethe nevertheless agreed to work part-time at Los Alamos, though not on the Super. And when the Korean War began on June 25, 1950, he finally agreed to participate in thermonuclear research. For Bethe, morality did not end and begin with questions about nuclear weapons. He strongly believed that leading a moral life included upholding his civic obligations, including the defense of his country. But Bethe's agreement to look into the feasibility of the weapon (hoping it would prove impossible to make) did not mean he had resolved his moral dilemma. Teller, who had exerted much effort in order to get Bethe to Los Alamos, was still unhappy with his friend's lack of enthusiasm for the Super when he wrote to him in late November 1950. At first, Teller expressed pleasure that "our difference of opinion about general questions is becoming smaller and will eventually vanish completely." But, Teller continued, "I certainly feel that it would be awfully good if you might somehow rid yourself of this strong bias in the negative direction." Hinting that Bethe's moral judgment clouded his scientific thinking, Teller suggested that finding a common "basic opinion" on the Super "would be of the highest importance and would even get practical results with much greater rapidity."[20]

Bethe responded to Teller just over a week later. "I am sorry I can't change my negative attitude; I just don't like the gadget," he began. "Perhaps it is even a good thing that we take opposite points of view because then there is a motive for you to have new ideas and for me to investigate them in detail. In this way we are both doing what we can do best."[21] In this partnership, Teller would propose ideas about how to make a Super, while Bethe would root out any flaws in these theories. In the years before the Oppenheimer hearing, Bethe struggled to reconcile his moral sensibilities with weapons work and did not shy away from bringing his moral conscience to bear on his work as a weapons scientist. The Oppenheimer hearing, in contrast, told scientists to set aside questions of morality when giving the government advice on nuclear weapons. Of course, it was not morality per se but rather a morality that questioned reliance on thermonuclear weapons that gave the government pause. As long as scientists accepted nuclear weapons as the basis of defense, they could advise the state.

But if the hearing decreed that science advice had to conform to the AEC's demands, did elite U.S. scientists—who, aside from Oppenheimer, still had the power to choose or reject such work—accept this censoring? Of all people, elite nuclear scientists were not passive subalterns. They had power and could react to the state's decree. And though many of them initially doubted that they would continue to serve the state, many eventually did.

Scientists React to the Oppenheimer Verdict

In the years leading up to 1954, years that saw big science blossom in the United States, scientists had become more and more integrated into the national security state. This relationship had grown in spite of some trepidation about mixing politics and science. After the Oppenheimer hearing, scientists quickly recognized the significance of the ruling and interpreted it in light of previous concerns about the relationship between science and government.

Of all the emotions evoked by the Oppenheimer hearing, ambivalence was not one of them. Scientists who commented on the event generally reacted in two ways: they predicted the government would suffer by alienating quality scientific advisers, and they feared that the scientific community would split in two over the treatment of Oppenheimer. Over the years, Oppenheimer had endeared himself to many influential political figures, including David Lilienthal, James Conant, and George Kennan. Oppenheimer's leadership of the Manhattan Project, his thoughtful consideration of atomic policy, and his advocacy of world government had engendered among many physicists a feeling of respect, if not always affection. Even many of those scientists who, like the chemist Wendell Latimer, found Oppenheimer "very difficult to understand" owed their careers and prestige in some part to Oppenheimer's successful development of atomic weapons and large-scale physics during the Manhattan Project. Oppenheimer himself said that "the men who worked with me during those years hold chairs in many of the great centers of physics in this country."[22]

Not surprisingly, many scientists rushed to Oppenheimer's defense as soon as the hearing began. Sensing that the tribunal could have consequences beyond mere damage to Oppenheimer's reputation, several notable scientists predicted a major backlash against the government. In the *Bulletin of the Atomic Scientists,* the physicist F. W. Loomis worried that the treatment of Oppenheimer would "make [government] advisory positions so precarious that they will become unacceptable to men of ability and integrity." Those few who did accept government work, Loomis fretted, would be incapable of "honest expression of opinion," a situation "with grave consequence to the future of the country." Other observers echoed the fear that only unprincipled scientists would dare serve the government in the future. The sociologist Edward Shils, a close friend of *Bulletin* founders Hyman Goldsmith and Eugene Rabinowitch, predicted that because of the hearing, "only the mediocre and characterless among scientists will make themselves available for the purposes of an arbitrary government of demagogues and bureaucrats. Every honorable man will hesitate . . . to offer advice to a government which destroys those who turn out to be on the losing side of an argument in an advisory committee." Farrington Daniels, the chemist who had been director of the Manhattan Project's Metallurgical (Met) Lab in the summer of 1945, similarly worried that "men of high caliber" would no longer advise the government, while Hugh Wolfe, a physicist and participant in the Atomic Scientists' Movement, mourned in advance the disappearance of "the kind of responsible and able citizen who would be capable of making decisions on major questions."[23]

Scientists expressed such fears in private as well as in public and worried that, because of the conflict between Teller and Oppenheimer, the hearing—no matter the verdict—would cause a division in the scientific community. Bethe, slightly less prestigious than Oppenheimer but more universally admired by his peers, denied such a rift and consciously tried to prevent one. During the hearing (at which he testified in Oppenheimer's defense), Bethe wrote to one of Oppenheimer's lawyers about a conversation he had had with the physicist John von Neumann, a known Teller ally, and mentioned that "we agreed on almost every point."[24]

A letter from the mathematician Richard Courant to Bethe, written just after the hearing concluded, showed that not all observers shared Bethe's confidence that scientists remained undivided. "I am quite fearful that this case may lead to internal tensions and even to an internal split among the scientific fraternity," Courant wrote, "and I am very much concerned about this danger." Bethe quickly responded to calm Courant, protesting that "I do not believe there is any division, at least among physicists." He told Courant that even the faculty of the University of California Physics Department, which included Teller, was only "about evenly divided." Bethe deemed it "essential that a strong stand be made in [Oppenheimer's] case" in order to protect others, even if Oppenheimer himself was beyond saving.[25]

In contrast to claims of a split between scientists and the AEC, Bethe undertook efforts to take "a strong stand" and reform the AEC's security clearance procedures as best his influence would allow, in the process attempting to rehabilitate the relationship between scientists and the agency. In November 1954 Bethe wrote to the AEC commissioner Willard Libby and asked him to seek out the views of at least three individuals on "personnel security problems." Following Bethe's advice, Libby contacted the recommended scientists: Joseph Platt, Stanley Livingston, and Gregory Breit. First to respond to Libby's inquiry was Platt, an occasional consultant to the AEC from the University of Rochester. Platt told Libby that the AEC had made it "less easy" for the state to obtain scientific help, "and I feel this is a disservice to the nation which is not offset by any corresponding gain in personnel security." Platt doubted that "responsible physicists" would refuse to serve the government because of the Oppenheimer case but admitted that the "climate of cooperation has nevertheless deteriorated." Potential advisers could expect the AEC to apply to them the same criteria used to discredit Oppenheimer, causing them to fret that they had been on the "wrong" side of a scientific decision, made contact with an uncleared person, or befriended "political mavericks." Platt recommended an unambiguous statement from the AEC of the goals of the security program as well as an explanation of the grounds for determination of clearance.[26]

Similarly, Stanley Livingston of MIT described to Libby the "very disturbing" and "widening areas of misunderstanding and distrust" between the AEC and U.S. scientists. Although "scientists will not refuse their responsibilities" to the nation, Livingston assured Libby, "many of them have become disheartened and disillusioned" by security practices. Livingston warned of "a noticeable decrease in enthusiasm for work requiring security clearance."[27]

A final letter from the Yale scientist Gregory Breit urged Libby to reinstate Oppenheimer's clearance in order to "improve general morale." Otherwise, Breit feared a situation where "only those agreeing with official policies and those exhibiting a high degree of obedience in modifying their technical views will be acceptable for clearance." Oppenheimer was of course never reinstated, but neither was there a mass exodus from nor a vocal break with the AEC. To be sure, the official history of the AEC labels the effect of the Oppenheimer case as "permanent and damaging." Its authors found that "the Oppenheimer case had planted seeds of doubt. It was not likely that an agency that had destroyed the career of a leader like Oppenheimer could ever again enjoy the full confidence of the nation's scientists."[28]

At the same time as he attempted to reconcile scientists' concerns with the AEC's security system, Bethe acknowledged a divide in a letter he wrote to Teller about recent press coverage of the H-bomb debate. Transcripts of the Oppenheimer hearing had revealed to the nation the full extent of the secret discussion over thermonuclear weapons of four years earlier, and Bethe had become particularly upset with James Shepley and Clay Blair's 1954 book, *The Hydrogen Bomb: The Men, the Menace, the Mechanism,* that essentially credited Teller with single-handedly inventing the H-bomb. In doing so, the book implicitly endorsed the AEC's judgment that Oppenheimer had slowed the development of the H-bomb and explicitly denied the efforts of many scientists at Los Alamos who had worked to develop the weapon. Bethe implored Teller to set the record straight and in the process admitted that the scientific community had indeed split. Fearing his own correction would be "divisive," he wrote to Teller that "only you can give such an answer in a manner which will *unify* the scientific community again." In closing, Bethe expressed regret for the damage nuclear weapons had done to his personal relationship with Teller, whom he had known since 1928 as a physics student in Munich and with whom he had set sail for the United States in 1935. Bethe hoped that someday they could "again talk about the things we used to talk about meaning the things talked about before 1942."[29] As politics came to dominate physics during the Cold War, Bethe struggled to maintain a scientific community and defend it from dissolution into partisan conflicts.

The scientist who eventually replaced Oppenheimer as the AEC and military establishment's premier science adviser certainly saw a split—after all, he could take much credit for having caused it. Teller explained his actions many times after the hearing. "I want you to know that whatever I did in the Oppenheimer matter was done after a considerable amount of worry," he confided to one correspondent. "It was done not with the feeling of confidence that my action was correct but simply with the unhappy feeling that I did not know in what way to behave that would be better." Feeling the heat from other scientists, a sobered Teller reflected, "For me personally, there is one real gain in all this. I had an opportunity which does not come to many people, namely to find out what people really think about me."[30]

The hearing created scientific partisans on both sides who debated the split for years after. And the split, while very personal on one level, also symbolized the divide between scientists who believed in the right to dissent from U.S. nuclear policy and scientists who unquestioningly supported the arms race. While the President's Science Advisory Committee, created in the late 1950s, played a large role in developing a space program and nuclear arms control efforts, it inevitably became another scene of conflict between Teller and Oppenheimer partisans. In 1962 T. F. Walkowicz, a science adviser to the U.S. Air Force in the 1950s and "my friend," as Teller put it in his memoirs, sent a letter to the presidential science adviser Jerome Wiesner. Walkowicz attempted to convince Wiesner that "the Oppenheimer point of view" dominated the committee, which unfairly ignored "the Teller point of view." He doubted that the absence of the Teller "camp" on the committee could be explained by that camp lacking solid scientists. "American science is sharply divided," Walkowicz concluded, beseeching Wiesner to do something to repair "this dangerous crack in their own community." Walkowicz did not mention Teller's role in creating the crack, but his exasperation reflects the contentious and combative view that Teller's partisans took in viewing scientists with whom they disagreed.[31]

The Oppenheimer hearing undoubtedly changed the relationship between government and scientists and indeed caused some acrimonious divisions. Oppenheimer subsequently faded into martyrdom, while Teller would refuse to discuss the hearing in public interviews for years afterward. But while the Oppenheimer-Teller divide captured scientists' attention, the government was busy dividing scientists according to how they spoke about nuclear weapons and whether they accepted the principle of nuclear deterrence. In fact, fears that scientists would abstain from government work were well off the mark. Scientists had the ability to accept or reject the state's restriction of their role. While a few iconoclastic scientists refused a vision of amoral science and attempted to maintain their independence, numerous scientists, even those who supported Oppenheimer, resumed working for arms control from within the government not long after the Oppenheimer hearing.

Scientists Return

After weathering the storm of the Red Scare, scientists continued to inform and advise government debates over nuclear weapons during the late 1950s, but the state had altered their terms of service. The outcome of the Oppenheimer hearing had changed how government scientists who opposed nuclear weapons expressed themselves in the realm of politics, limiting advisers who objected to nuclear weapons to technical rather than moral reasons for arms control and disarmament. As the lone dissenter in the AEC's four-to-one decision to deny Oppenheimer security clearance, Henry DeWolf Smyth had written that the "[security] system itself is nothing to worship. It is a necessary means to an end."[32] Despite Smyth's plea, the system was worshipped rather than the values the system was supposed to protect. To maintain access to the government, a scientist had to approach opposition to nuclear weapons from a technical perspective. Such an approach may sound easy and even logical, as it did to many scientists who prided themselves on their dispassionate, objective dedication to knowledge. In practice, however, opposing weapons on technical grounds proved easier said than done, since strictly technical knowledge did not lead to a single interpretation. Rather, scientists and politicians could read the same technical information and come to vastly different conclusions. Faced with conflicting advice, Cold War policymakers chose to hear only advice that fundamentally accepted deterrence.

Scientists troubled by nuclear weapons—as Bethe had been—had to reconcile themselves to their presence at the heart of Cold War policy. Those who wished to work for nuclear disarmament and arms control from within the government had to make the case that limiting nuclear weapons would not harm the security interests of the nation. Scientists outside the government, for example, could simply argue that nations should not have nuclear weapons. Inside government circles, however, exceptions had to be made. Some nuclear weapons were necessary—the Soviets had to be deterred. And if some nuclear weapons were necessary, why not more? The logic of the arms race put antinuclear scientists on the defensive. Scientists who expressed objections to nuclear weapons faced a disadvantage because the AEC had restricted the arguments they could make; meanwhile, those who favored nuclear weapons could freely use morality to support their arguments.

Far from being silenced, thoughtful individuals such as Bethe continued trying to shape nuclear policy. Just as World War I drove chemists to the poison-gas laboratories and Pearl Harbor and the blitzkrieg sent physicists running to Los Alamos, the combined threat of H-bombs and *Sputnik* sparked a resurgence of scientists' influence in the government during the late 1950s. The dire prediction of the Nobel Prize winner and former Manhattan Project team leader Harold Urey that, after the Oppenheimer case, scientists "will be reluctant to serve the government in sensitive areas" was not realized, as just three years after the Oppenheimer hearing scientists eagerly served on Eisenhower's newly formed President's Science Advisory Committee. These top scientists hoped to show that their own predictions would not come true and that scientists of high quality would not fail to serve their country when called. Rather than force the state to atone for its treatment of Oppenheimer or renounce nuclear weapons, many scientists quickly adapted themselves to the state's new conception of scientists. They began to put the bitterness of the Oppenheimer fiasco behind them, looking forward optimistically and grateful for the leadership of a president who, whatever his past mistakes, recognized the importance of science in U.S. society. In a 1959 PSAC meeting with Eisenhower, the man who had given Strauss authority to initiate the Oppenheimer hearing, scientists fawned over the president, telling him they were "grateful [to him] for making science as important as baseball." Eisenhower had, they told him, "entirely changed [the] attitude of [the] country towards science," an occurrence that "seems almost too good to be true."[33]

Perhaps these scientists thought things might be different by the late 1950s, as the nation came to agree that scientists and science education were once again essential resources for the nation's security. The Cold War had entered a new phase: Nikita Khrushchev emerged as the Soviet leader after the death of Stalin and, in typically contradictory fashion, issued threats against capitalist nations alongside calls for coexistence. The arms race escalated, but so did hopes for some sort of easing of hostilities. The National Defense Education Act poured millions of dollars into science and engineering education after the *Sputnik* launch exposed a supposed gap between U.S. and Soviet technical accomplishments. Scientists, meanwhile, saw PSAC as a government body capable of balancing the relative hawkishness of the AEC, dominated as it was by men like Strauss and Teller.

Eisenhower himself appeared to recognize this impulse of scientists. In a television address titled "Science in National Security" delivered on the night of November 7, 1957, Eisenhower set forth his views on the role of science in society. He announced to the American people his intention "to put current scientific discovery at the service of your defense." An obvious reaction to the *Sputnik* launch, Eisenhower's speech explicitly linked science to U.S. military capabilities, including missiles, "atomic depth bombs," and nuclear-powered submarines. Science, then, would be a vital element in protecting and promoting anticommunism, as Eisenhower reminded the nation of the Soviet invasions of Finland, Poland, and Hungary. But the president cared about more than just bombs and missiles, as he revealed some concerns about U.S.

science as well. Later in the speech, Eisenhower stated that his "scientific friends" had urged him to address "the failure of us in this country to give high enough priority to scientific education and to the place of science in our national life." The president promised the resources necessary for improved science education and announced his willingness to promote scientific sharing and cooperation with allied nations. Finally, the president announced the creation of the cabinet-level office of special assistant to the president for science and technology, a post soon filled by James Killian of MIT. In addition, Eisenhower continued, the science adviser would lead the PSAC, "a strong Advisory Group of outstanding experts." He then emphasized that scientists and engineers, in offering their services to the government, "have been generous, patriotic and prompt."[34]

At a 1959 PSAC meeting, Eisenhower showed a willingness to embrace his advisers' visions for arms control and disarmament, as he hoped scientists would "be working themselves out of the job of devoting their talents to military weapons systems." Edwin Land responded by praising Eisenhower for turning around the country's attitude toward science. He then asked for the president's help in bridging scientists and the military. Scientists who discussed arms control with the military, Land stated, found themselves accused of being soft or indifferent to national security, even if they happened to be scientists who helped develop nuclear weapons in the first place. Eisenhower responded that "if the scientists can help to show concrete ways to make progress on arms control, he will be most grateful and glad to join in the process."[35]

But as scientists attempted to change U.S. nuclear policy, their advice continued to be framed within the rules set during the Oppenheimer hearing: to hold paramount in their concerns the ceaseless strengthening of the U.S. nuclear arsenal. A more typical meeting between Eisenhower, his science adviser Killian, and PSAC considered strictly "technical aspects" of nuclear weapons. An analysis of the ballistic missile program, for example, weighed the utility of the Nike-Zeus "active defense" system as a factor in missile defense against the merits of "dispersal, hardening and improved warning and reaction." Killian concluded that "passive tactics were cheaper than active, and should be a basic element in the protection of our retaliatory force."[36]

Under the new regime, political or moral advocacy had no place in scientific advice. When Bethe became a member of PSAC, he resigned as vice president of the Federation of American Scientists (FAS), an organization founded by Manhattan Project veterans hoping to prevent nuclear war. "It would be difficult to reconcile advocating a certain policy from the outside, as the Federation has to do," he reasoned, "and at the same time being an advisor so much on the inside of government."[37] While Bethe's decision to give up his external position was entirely conventional, his reasoning made it clear that even scientists who held deep beliefs about the danger of nuclear weapons thought it best to keep political views completely separate from and subordinate to their role as technical advisers. Members of the scientific elite had begun to adapt to the government's demands rather than deviate from them.

By the late 1950s, government science advisers who wished to maintain their influence had dramatically restricted their rhetoric since the robust moral and technical debate over the H-bomb; now that moral objections were taboo, only technical opposition to nuclear weapons remained acceptable. A 1959 letter found Bethe arguing for a nuclear test ban not on moral grounds but because it would lock in U.S. nuclear weapons superiority. Writing to Nelson Rockefeller, the Republican governor of New York, Bethe argued that while the U.S. nuclear arsenal was unlikely to get stronger, the Soviets had a great deal of catching up to do. "If nuclear tests are resumed," he explained, "the Russians are likely to benefit more from such a resumption than we are, simply because their nuclear weapons technology is not quite as far advanced as ours." Because the Soviets had been gaining ground in the arms race since 1954, Bethe declared himself "deeply convinced that U.S. security would be far better served by a well considered, reasonably monitored agreement on limitation of armaments to a low level than by an uncontrolled arms race."[38] Such was the content of a scientific argument for arms control, even from a scientist who held strong moral reservations about nuclear weapons in the first place.

In 1962 Bethe considered the same factors when he declared himself no longer in favor of a nuclear test ban. In a speech at Cornell University, where he was a member of the physics faculty, Bethe explained that his previous reasons for supporting a test ban had included a wish to maintain U.S. advantages in nuclear weapons. Because the United States no longer had a nuclear advantage over the Soviets, Bethe no longer saw any reason to support a test ban.[39] Bethe had previously been willing to support a test ban on the grounds that it would not harm U.S. national security. But if new circumstances meant that arms control measures hindered "the strongest possible offensive capabilities" of the U.S. military, as the Oppenheimer verdict had put it, he could no longer advocate such policies. Bethe's changing rhetoric from 1950 to 1962 shows how moral arguments against nuclear weapons differed tremendously from technical arguments in defense of arms control or disarmament.

The Oppenheimer hearing solidified the U.S. commitment to an arms race. But the government's decision to dedicate the nation to an arms race does not mean that scientists stopped trying to prevent one. Essentially unwilling to give up advising entirely, many U.S. scientists took the lessons of the Oppenheimer hearing to heart and continued to try to nudge government policy toward arms control and disarmament by supporting the nuclear deterrent rather than challenging it. The hearing did not come close to ending science-government interaction, though it did change the nature of the scientist-government relationship; as late as 1983, Teller complained that the Oppenheimer hearing was still having an effect on national security.[40] As a high-profile witness against Oppenheimer, Teller had only himself to blame. The Oppenheimer hearing and Teller's role in it had shaped the way that those scientists who wished to influence policy would interact with the government, the public, and other scientists for the remainder of the Cold War.

Not all scientists agreed to abandon moral arguments in return for government influence. The dramatic Cold War scares of the 1950s, including the advent of the H-bomb and the Korean War, mobilized the chemist Linus Pauling in particular. Where Oppenheimer was opacity, Pauling was clarity. He embraced the type of moral pacifism that so disturbed the AEC. But although Pauling had the freedom to discuss the ethics and morality of nuclear weapons, only government scientists like Bethe had a place at the policymaking table.

At the same time, the heightened Cold War tensions mobilized some scientists in the opposite direction—in favor of nuclear weapons. Edward Teller in particular manifested this contrarian spirit. The Oppenheimer hearing had changed only the relationship of scientists to government—it had not yet altered the public perception of science or irrevocably altered science's place in politics. Many scientists and politicians still believed that science and scientists had a role to play in solving the nuclear dilemma, even if they faced new constraints. The wreckage of this collision between scientists, social commitment, and nuclear weapons would have consequences not only on science-government relations but on science's role in society as well.

2

Linus Pauling's "Science of Morality"

Challenging Nuclear Weapons, 1950–1963

A ROUND THE TIME U.S. WEAPONS SCIENTISTS successfully tested the first thermonuclear device in 1952, other scientists began to reassess their role in the Cold War. As those who understood the complexities of nuclear physics, scientists had made themselves essential to the nation's defense. Consequently, U.S. Cold War science was not an objective, isolated endeavor but rather a contested form of expertise mobilized in the name of national security. Scientists did not confront the thermonuclear age in any single way. Activism reflected distinct—and often diametrically opposed—political views. As a government outsider, the chemist Linus Pauling practiced a brand of peace activism that embraced a scientific, humanistic approach to politics and society, which led him to a life-affirming, moral ideology that opposed nuclear weapons. Pauling's peace campaign proves that an overtly moral stand against nuclear weapons could effectively mobilize antinuclear sentiment, though it did not necessarily achieve concrete changes in official policy.

Morality sat at the heart of Pauling's beliefs about science and nuclear weapons. When Congress, the Atomic Energy Commission, and security officials confronted Pauling's antinuclear challenge, however, they did not do so on moral grounds. In the case of Robert Oppenheimer and other H-bomb skeptics, the government had excluded their views in part by making moral opposition to nuclear weapons subordinate to anticommunism and faith in the nuclear deterrent. But as Pauling's experience shows, pronuclear officials had more than one way to exclude an antinuclear scientist. While the AEC had primarily relied on a formal process to break with Oppenheimer, suspicions, insinuations, and up-front allegations of communist sympathies had also been effective against the physicist. In Pauling's case, conservative politicians relied even more heavily on Red Scare tactics, linking him (falsely) to communism and restricting his international travel. Because Pauling was not an establishment figure with powerful allies, the state could easily afford to silence him in this manner. When Pauling presented himself to the public as an expert who had the scientific authority to challenge the government's nuclear weapons policy, members of Congress responded by questioning his loyalty. At the same time, Pauling often clashed with his peers, causing influential scientists to question his objectivity and help contest his scientific authority.

Pauling is not as prevalent in the public memory as one might expect. Despite his peerless accomplishments in chemistry, he lacks the popular appeal of Albert Einstein or Benjamin Franklin. This may result from the fact that some scholars have dismissed his political activism and criticized the scientific claims he made about radioactive fallout in his campaign against nuclear testing as subjective and patently unscientific.[1] But no single scientist alone possessed the mantle of objectivity, as claims about fallout on either side of the debate could not be separated from their political implications. Pauling's campaign struggled against the Cold War consensus to determine who in U.S. society would hold the authoritative view on nuclear weapons. To Pauling, nuclear tests appeared blatantly illogical, as they aimed at enhancing national security but because of fallout resulted in physically harming the very people the weapons were meant to protect. The dangers of fallout and weapons tests brought into question the logic of nuclear deterrence, while the scientific aspects of fallout offered an opportunity for scientists like Pauling to play a public role. To dismiss Pauling and his test ban campaign as "unscientific" only reprises the debate over nuclear testing in the 1950s and does little to elevate the understanding of it.

The Roots of Activism

Like many of the influential scientists of the nuclear era, Pauling came of age scientifically during the quantum revolution in physics of the 1920s. Though a chemist, Pauling worked with physicists and studied under Arnold Sommerfeld in Munich, one of the epicenters of the quantum revolution. Pauling quickly grasped the significance of quantum theory and neatly applied its principles to the field of chemistry during the late 1920s and then revolutionized the understanding of the chemical bond, for which he eventually received the 1954 Nobel Prize in Chemistry. Thus, like many other politically active U.S. scientists, Pauling had become an esteemed scientist whose great achievements happened before World War II and, while quite scientifically productive through the 1950s (particularly in researching the structure of DNA and other biological molecules), had in some ways passed his scientific prime. As with Hans Bethe, Oppenheimer, Leo Szilard, and Edward Teller, Pauling could devote much of his time to causes outside the laboratory because he had already made his name as a scientist. Unlike these other scientists, however, Pauling had not participated in the Manhattan Project. At the California Institute of Technology (Caltech) in the late 1920s, Pauling and Oppenheimer had become close friends, and when the awkward physicist became involved with the bomb project, he invited his gregarious chemist friend to join him at Los Alamos. Pauling turned Oppenheimer down, however, because he suspected that physicists would dominate the project; in addition, the friendship had frayed after Oppenheimer had made a pass at Pauling's wife, Ava Helen. Notably, at this point no moral considerations prevented Pauling from working on atomic weapons, as he ended up assisting the military with explosives research during the war.[2]

Although Ava Helen may have indirectly kept Pauling away from Los Alamos, she played a much more direct role in shaping the social conscience that drove Pauling after the war. During the Great Depression, Ava Helen had encouraged Pauling to take a greater interest in social problems. As fascist movements took hold in Europe and the world approached war, Pauling began to see his life and vocation in a greater context. A social commitment was further solidified when he read J. D. Bernal's *Social Function of Science*, a Marxist polemic advocating the engagement of scientists in determining the social uses of their knowledge.[3]

Events closer to home also proved pivotal for Pauling. Living in Southern California during World War II, the Paulings witnessed Japanese internment firsthand, an event so enraging to Ava Helen that she joined the American Civil Liberties Union (ACLU) in order to oppose it. Pauling himself remained relatively aloof from the issue until, without giving it much thought, he apparently hired a Japanese American gardener, a decision that sparked outrage in the Paulings' Pasadena neighborhood. A vandal scribbled racist anti-Japanese graffiti on their house, and the family also received threatening phone calls. Pauling immediately became infuriated over the racist behavior of his neighbors and later said he had been politicized by the incident.[4]

After the war, Pauling exhibited a much greater awareness of political events, though Ava Helen still spurred him on. While Pauling often joked that he engaged in social causes merely to impress his wife, her influence went much deeper than that. Pauling recalled that "the humanistic concern she had was very great. I'm sure that if I had not married her, I would not have had this aspect of my career—working for world peace. It was her influence on me and her strong support that caused me to continue."[5] Pauling's subsequent dedication to political activism evinced a commitment far beyond the desire to simply please his wife.

Though he had played no role in the atomic bomb's construction and could not in any sense be considered responsible for it, the bomb's magnitude of destruction triggered in Pauling a sense of urgency and culpability. In addition to his fear of atomic war, Pauling possessed a touch of hubris—a natural self-assuredness that told him scientists could and should lead society to a better future. Endowed with these characteristics, which many Manhattan Project veterans shared at the time, Pauling participated in the Atomic Scientists' Movement. He gave talks to lay audiences on the atomic bomb itself, early efforts that soon blossomed into an embrace of the world government campaign. At this time, the public held scientists in such high esteem that even a chemist who had not been involved with the Manhattan Project could command a large audience to listen to his views on atomic weapons. In 1946 Pauling joined the Emergency Committee of Atomic Scientists, where he met Einstein, whose politically engaged pacifism Pauling tried to mimic. In these ways, Pauling shared a set of beliefs and a sense of purpose with other activist scientists, yet he also stood slightly out of place since he had not taken part in the Manhattan Project.[6] He consequently lacked connections to government circles and political institutions, which limited his influence but enabled him to take a different approach to scientific dissent against nuclear weapons. Being an outsider, however, put him in the position of speaking against the pronouncements of government figures, forcing him to convince his audience (both citizens and scientists) of official neglect, deceit, or incompetence in a pre-Watergate era when the U.S. government generally enjoyed an assumption of trust among the public.

More than anything, Pauling's overwhelming dedication to (some might say obsession with) social and political causes set him apart from other scientists and placed him even more outside the mainstream. In a consequential decision (which he would later recount casually), Pauling announced to Ava Helen that he would devote half his time to science and half to peace.[7] This simple mathematical formula launched a career in peace and social activism as eventful as his impressive scientific career. To be sure, the scientific credentials Pauling brought to the antinuclear movement cannot be overstated. In the opinion of Rosalind Franklin, the X-ray crystallographer whose photos led to the discovery of DNA's structure, Pauling ranked as the greatest chemist of all time, while a 2000 assessment in *Nature* stated that "Pauling ranks with Galileo, Da Vinci, Shakespeare, Newton, Bach, Faraday, Freud and Einstein as one of the great thinkers and visionaries of the millennium."[8] During the late 1940s and early 1950s, as other scientists shied away from activism, this intellectual giant became only more vocal. He first opposed the 1947 National Security Act, later the H-bomb, and then the Rosenberg execution. Pauling achieved his greatest public visibility during the fallout scare of the mid- to late 1950s, engaging in a high-profile push for a ban on nuclear testing. Science provided hard evidence for his arguments, offered him a model of rationality for the world, and allowed him to speak with a voice of authority in an age when the average American stood in awe of science. Most important, Pauling contested the government's decision, expressed in the Oppenheimer hearing, to forbid moral considerations from hindering the continuous development of a stronger nuclear arsenal.

The Science of Morality

In the years following World War II, Pauling framed his opposition to war, nuclear weapons tests, and the arms race as equal parts moral and scientific. His two Nobel Prizes, one for chemistry (1954) and one for peace (1963), manifested this duality, as his scientific view of the world told him that peace simply made logical sense. Pauling formulated a "science of morality," in his words, that relied on science to shape a moral code for society. "The more I studied issues about health, the more I looked around me at a world populated by humans who were in perpetual deadly conflict with one another, for no good reason," he recalled. This moral ideology offered a clear approach to the nuclear dilemma yet one that risked coming into conflict with the objectivity usually associated with science, since it so clearly grappled with contemporary political concerns. At the same time, Pauling's worldview made scientific geniuses such as himself central actors in the nuclear age. He explained, "I thought that people trained to think as scientists might make valuable contributions in searching for solutions to problems in society and in shaping the human future in a positive way. I came to believe that a science of morality is possible."[9]

Although Pauling was an iconoclast, he was far from alone in thinking that science offered powerful ways to improve human society. Szilard, who also marched to the beat of his own drum, had more than once proposed what he called *Der Bund*, a highly educated "spiritual leadership class" who would guide humanity away from its destructive tendencies.[10] More concretely, science and scientists had been improving human lives (or at least standards of living) after World War II, with treatments for cancer, disease prevention, improved health, and consumer goods. With a healthy dose of public adulation—"scientists" were *Time*'s Men of the Year in 1960—the assumption that their knowledge would benefit humanity became a central aspect of scientists' identity in the mid-twentieth century.

This science of morality, by which Pauling meant the application of scientific logic to moral concerns, led Pauling to oppose nuclear weapons and war in general and in particular nuclear testing that spread radioactive fallout. Pauling's crusade harmonized with mainstream antinuclear activists of the 1950s such as the Committee for a SANE Nuclear Policy (SANE), which also mobilized to protest nuclear fallout. After the U.S. nuclear testing program moved from remote Pacific isles to the Nevada desert, the radioactive by-products of nuclear explosions scattered into the atmosphere during nuclear weapons tests and menaced residents of the Southwest. When fallout drifted downwind and began to show up in milk and other foods, many Americans grew concerned that young children were at great risk, since the by-products strontium 90 (Sr90) and carbon 14 (C14) proved highly likely to bond to human bones. While historians have argued that criticizing fallout was a way for Americans to politely express their more primal fear of nuclear weapons, Pauling could not decouple the threat of fallout from the threat of nuclear war; one would not exist without the other.[11] The link between fallout and the arms race was thus both concrete and symbolic, and the fallout problem particularly offended Pauling's scientific and moral principles. In the mid-1950s Pauling, along with other scientists, including Ralph Lapp and Barry Commoner, began to take the lead in bringing scientific expertise to bear on the issue of nuclear fallout.

In his polemic *No More War!* (written over the course of two long weekends and published in 1958), Pauling outlined his science of morality. Although he became a popular public figure during the 1950s, his science of morality clearly fell far to the left of the U.S. political mainstream. He wrote that while "man has developed admirable principles of morality, . . . we are murderers, mass murderers. Almost all of us, even many of our religious leaders, accept with equanimity a world policy of devoting a large part of our world income, our world resources," he continued, "to the cold-blooded readying of nuclear weapons to kill hundreds of millions of people. I am an American, deeply interested in the welfare of my fellow Americans, of our great Nation. But I am first of all a human being. I believe in *morality*. . . . I believe that there is a greater power in the world than the evil power of military force, of nuclear bombs—there is the power of *good*, of *morality*, of *humanitarianism*."[12]

Pauling strove to get peers from around the world to endorse his views, at one point convening a gathering of scientists in Oslo to coincide with a North Atlantic Treaty Organization (NATO) meeting. More than sixty natural and social scientists, including several from the Soviet Union, gathered with Pauling to discuss disarmament. At the end of the conference, the participants released a statement on the "moral responsibility" of scientists that elaborated on Pauling's science of morality and the nuclear dilemma. The existence of nuclear weapons, the statement read, "demands a new understanding of moral responsibility." Nationalism was "obsolete, and loyalty to the whole of mankind is now a necessity." Scientists bore a special responsibility "to make plain the full significance of the revolutionary weapons development of the past decade," to give "factual information," and to provide "constructive proposals" in search of peace.[13]

This growing sense of morality and responsibility became an obsession with Pauling. While preparing articles and speeches, Pauling would jot his thoughts down on paper. Some of his notes read: "Great progress can be made following and built upon moral principles"; "Transformation of evil into good—i.e., possibility of decreasing suffering in the world"; "My ideas—Consistency not necessary in theory of values of morality or ethics (any more than in chemistry)"; and "The prime ethical postulate—We should take such actions as to preserve and increase the wonder of the universe & to decrease human (and other) suffering." In another unguarded moment, Pauling scribbled "I love this world. I believe that we can prevent this insanity" below a series of megaton calculations. In *I. F. Stone's Weekly*, he wrote, "I believe that war is immoral, and must be eliminated."[14]

On a fundamental level, Pauling's campaign against nuclear testing embodied his science of morality by relying on scientific data that supported moral arguments against nuclear weapons, as manifested in his 1958 article in the journal *Science*, "Genetic and Somatic Effects of Carbon-14." He buttressed his arguments against nuclear weapons testing with scientific proof of the effects of radiation on young people and children yet unborn, even "thousands of years" into the future. The half-life and radioactivity of the elements scattered by a nuclear test ensured, he argued, that earth would suffer the consequences of these effects for decades to come. By using children as a form of scientific data, Pauling's argument supported a moral interpretation of the nuclear weapons dilemma—otherwise, the death or deformation of millions of children simply would not have been a problem. But the argument also cloaked itself in the dispassionate language of science. Pauling rationally calculated the danger of fallout as "the predicted number of children born with defects caused by the mutations induced by the radioactivity."[15]

With no access to restricted information, Pauling culled information on bomb tests publicly released by the Atomic Energy Commission and used his own knowledge to interpret the numbers. His calculations published in "Genetic and Somatic Effects" convinced him that the AEC had grossly underestimated the threat posed by fallout. He calculated that the fission products in radioactive fallout from U.S. bomb tests "will in the course of generations cause the birth of 80,000 children with gross physical or mental defects, 300,000 to die at birth or in early childhood, plus 700,000 embryonic deaths. About one tenth of the defective children will appear in the first generation, and the others in later generations."[16] In Pauling's interpretation, science revealed the absurd cruelty of the arms race by objectively proving the government's willingness to sacrifice children in the name of national security.

Overall, Pauling dedicated more of his career to science than peace. But for the rest of his life after World War II, Pauling's professional interests reflected a concern for the well-being of humanity, including research into the causes of sickle-cell anemia as well as his vitamin-C crusade of the 1980s, which trumpeted the vitamin as a provider of perfect health and a possible cure for cancer. And at times during the 1950s and 1960s, peace appeared to become more of a priority than science. According to some accounts, Pauling's science seemed far less solid than his courage; several of his contemporaries accused Pauling of being more loyal to his political objectives than his scientific evidence. Pauling himself admitted that his scientific work at the time was not "wholehearted," and he willingly accepted that his activism raised eyebrows among his scientific peers. "I have not regretted my peace activism," he wrote late in life, "although this has damaged my reputation as a scientist among certain people and institutions."[17]

The wielding of scientific knowledge gave Pauling the confidence to challenge convention and agitate for disarmament. Yet his abrasive and smug personality may have worked against him at times, as he believed scientists—and only scientists—were smart enough to guide the world away from nuclear war. In the late 1950s, Pauling wrote to a *Newsday* reporter who had written an article on fallout. "The article seems to me to be thoroughly unsatisfactory, in that it repeats the meaningless statements made by AEC spokesmen and others," Pauling scolded the journalist, adding, "I think that you should have given some numbers. . . . It is too much to expect that it should be treated accurately by people other than scientists."[18]

Pauling's activities reflected the belief that scientists had special knowledge to bestow on the world in the hopes of a better life, a concept that shared much with the Atomic Scientists' Movement, which embraced the need for scientists to educate Congress and the public. In certain ways, Pauling's career in social causes can be seen as a direct continuation of this earlier movement, though Pauling differed greatly from the atomic scientists in his tactics and iconoclastic political behavior.

A Government Outsider

Pauling consistently held an oppositional stance toward the government regarding nuclear weapons and civil liberties. He publicly opposed the Rosenberg execution in 1953 and vociferously denigrated the Oppenheimer hearing a year later. With many others, Pauling joined the chorus in the *Bulletin of the Atomic Scientists* voicing support for his former friend Oppenheimer, adding his opinion that "many thoughtful scientists will conclude that it is dangerous to make an important contribution to the national welfare, and that they should not accept employment in government agencies, or, if they do, that they should be careful that their contributions are not important."[19]

By the mid-1950s, of course, Pauling had no illusions about being a government adviser. Because the state distinguished between appropriate and inappropriate types of scientists and arguments, Pauling's moral arguments and maverick behavior had consequences for his activism both negative and positive. Freedom from government restrictions allowed him on the one hand to rely far more heavily on moral arguments against nuclear weapons, though he naturally grounded these arguments in scientific reasoning. On the other hand, however, Pauling had no access to classified sources; his attacks on government policy simply consisted of AEC statements and other public information subjected to his own scientific analysis and criticism.[20]

The most well-known example of this method was his "Genetic and Somatic Effects" paper. The article served as a scientific challenge to and refutation of a 1956 paper, also published in *Science,* by the AEC commissioner Willard Libby that had argued that fallout posed little risk to humans. Libby had pioneered work on C14 during the 1940s, and his research had led to the development of radiocarbon dating techniques, for which he won the 1960 Nobel Prize in Chemistry. "Local precautions," Libby had concluded after looking into the threat of fallout, "should be entirely adequate and the worldwide health hazards from the present rate of testing are insignificant." "Genetic and Somatic Effects," by contrast, sounded a vibrant warning about the dangers of thermonuclear weapons tests, and it offered a distinct and original challenge to national security policy and the arms race. Pauling began the paper by explaining that Libby had previously claimed that fallout came from the "fission products" of a thermonuclear explosion, thus implying that as fusion weapons evolved, their risks would disappear.[21] But according to Pauling, a Russian paper provided evidence of the dangers of C14, a byproduct produced during the fusion segment of thermonuclear explosions. The heart of Pauling's paper consisted of calculations of the danger posed by C14 based on the amount of testing being conducted. The results offered great cause for concern: "It is concluded that 1 year of testing (30 megatons of fission plus fusion) is expected to cause in the world (estimated future number of births per year 5 times the present number) an estimated total of about 55,000 children with gross physical or mental defects, 170,000 stillbirths and childhood deaths, and 425,000 embryonic and neonatal deaths. . . . These numbers are about 17 times the numbers usually estimated."[22] Because information about how the H-bomb worked remained highly classified at this point, Pauling was quite literally making an educated guess.

Pauling framed the paper as the result of objective and scientific reasoning and later explained that his findings inspired in him an urgency to do something. "I was sort of stuck with it," Pauling recalled. "I felt that it was my duty to continue to work along these lines." Pauling saw himself as a crusader for justice supported by undeniable scientific evidence. "I gave over 500 lectures about radioactive fallout and nuclear war and the need for stopping the bomb tests in the atmosphere and the need for eliminating war ultimately. I didn't enjoy giving these lectures especially," he said.[23] Such an image contains some truth but also false modesty, as Pauling had consciously decided to dedicate half of his time to social causes.

Though he may have wanted to return to purely scientific work, his moral code and sense of self-importance compelled him to speak out. "I had a strong feeling about the morality of carrying out these problems," Pauling offered as an explanation of his *Science* article. The article did create a minor stir in political circles. In 1959 the Subcommittee on Radiation of the Congressional Joint Committee on Atomic Energy had taken Pauling's claims about fallout seriously enough to ask its advisers for an analysis of his *Science* article. But as an outsider, Pauling generally had no access to sources except those publicly available; his archives contain numerous newspaper articles glued to writing paper with notes and calculations scribbled all over them. Like any other ordinary citizen, Pauling had to get his information from sources such as the *New York Times*.[24] This restriction did not invalidate his views, but it did mean that government officials could dismiss his claims as uninformed. He had the freedom to say what he wanted but lacked the authority of being able to base an argument on "official" sources. In this way, Pauling could be fairly influential with the public but easily marginalized within government circles.

His fierce opposition to nuclear weapons obstructed him from influence in Washington, but government officials did not counter Pauling by attacking his moral message. Instead, Congress and the executive branch used Red Scare methods to dilute his influence; Pauling claimed that the FBI began keeping tabs on him as early as 1950. This oppositional relationship certainly suited Pauling's temperament, as he and the government wanted nothing to do with each other. Pauling's constant grappling with the moral dimensions of U.S. policy led him to question the entire Red Scare, including the blacklist, loyalty oaths, the Smith Act, and the McCarran Act. Such outspoken criticism from such a notable individual spurred the Red Scare apparatus into action. As with many critics of the Cold War, Pauling soon found himself slandered in the press as a Red. In 1952 the State Department began to restrict Pauling's travel abroad, telling him that "your proposed travel would not be in the best interests of the United States" and refusing to grant him a passport, essentially punishing the scientist for his leftist stand and making his scientific career more difficult. Only when Pauling won the Nobel Prize in Chemistry in 1954 was the State Department shamed into issuing him a passport so that he could travel to accept the award.[25]

The receipt of his passport was only a temporary reprieve in the government's campaign. The historian Lawrence Wittner has detailed the "high-level conspiracy" against Pauling, whom government officials feared as "a dagger to the heart." The AEC spread hostile information on the chemist provided by the House Un-American Activities Committee, and President Eisenhower obliquely tied his efforts to communism by describing them in a press conference as "almost an organized affair." Lewis Strauss and other AEC staffers made sure that various publications received information about Pauling's ties to alleged communist-front groups such as the American Association of Scientific Workers and the Hollywood Independent Citizens Committee of the Arts, Sciences, and Professions. Strauss also interfered with one of Pauling's research contracts, while J. Edgar Hoover sent a report to the White House further linking Pauling to communist-front activities.[26]

As Pauling increased his activism, anticommunists in Congress took further steps to stifle the chemist. Though the worst excesses of McCarthyism had peaked in 1954, the Red Scare continued into the early 1960s. Senator Thomas Dodd, head of the Internal Security Subcommittee, had built a reputation as a Democratic version of Joseph McCarthy, as he conducted a series of hearings in 1960 alleging that communists had infiltrated SANE and other antinuclear organizations. On June 21, Dodd hauled Pauling in front of the subcommittee to answer questions about the petition he had circulated against nuclear testing that had gained more than eleven thousand signatures—evidence, in Dodd's mind, that the petition had been organized by communists. The *Bulletin of the Atomic Scientists* described the hearings as "in effect a loyalty screening of Mr. Pauling." Harry Kalven, a law professor who wrote about Pauling's congressional appearance for the *Bulletin,* drew comparisons to the Oppenheimer hearing of six years earlier. Although both scientists suffered harassment for their leftist views, Pauling fared much better than Oppenheimer. Kalven wrote that Pauling "is so witty and effective in defending himself that one cannot down the impression . . . that he was having a very good time."[27]

The campaign against Pauling had an effect on public opinion. In April 1960, Pauling wrote to an ACLU lawyer about remarks in the *Arcadia (CA) Tribune* that apparently referred to him as "a man acting in a manner traitorous to the U.S. government" and "a stupid ass." And while Pauling showed no flagging of effort or spirit in his activism, the constant legal wrangling took its toll all the same. In September 1960, Ava Helen wrote to Dorothy Crowfoot Hodgkin to explain why she and Pauling had not been to any scientific meetings lately, telling her that because of the Dodd hearings, the couple had been "too distressed to really be of much use anywhere."[28]

In 1961 Dodd's subcommittee published *The Pugwash Conferences: A Staff Analysis,* hoping to discredit Pauling by virtue of his association with what virulent anticommunists considered a suspicious group of scientists. Most of the document consisted of material on the Pugwash conferences that brought together scientists interested in disarmament from both sides of the Iron Curtain. Dodd's document first attempted to portray the conferences as tools of Soviet propaganda and U.S. participants as unwitting dupes. "In most of the contacts that have thus far taken place," the tract began, "the free world scientists, although they have sometimes argued strongly, have not been able to compete with their Communist counterparts." The Soviets, the document explained, came to the Pugwash conferences with an imperialist agenda and hoped to exploit the conferences for subversive purposes.[29]

The Dodd subcommittee analysis explicitly highlighted Pauling's participation, noting that his "enlistment . . . added a certain amount of academic prestige to these conclaves." Failing to provide any direct evidence of Pauling's alleged communist sympathies, the Dodd document listed numerous instances in which Pauling was mentioned or praised by socialist and communist publications such as the *Daily Worker,* intimating that these statements provided evidence of a "predisposing framework"—communist sympathies, in other words—on Pauling's part. "During the past decade," the report concluded, "Pauling has appeared in the public eye with noticeable frequency as a crusader for distinctly political aims, and has shown a marked bias for Communist causes and a willingness to aline [*sic*] himself with Communist-held views having no scientific bearing or interest."[30]

Despite dozens of pages of allegations, the Dodd committee had no crimes with which to charge Pauling, and although the document linked him to Pugwash, the chemist had taken part in only two conferences by the time the Dodd report appeared.[31] Furthermore, linking Pauling to Pugwash in 1961 was especially misguided, as Pauling and Pugwash scientists had already grown tired of each other. Dodd's published smears can only be seen as an attempt to make sure that those in power would not take Pauling (or Pugwash) seriously. The direct influence of the Dodd document is unclear, but nuclear officials undeniably avoided Pauling and excluded his influence from the privileged circle of scientists dealing with nuclear weapons policy. The scientists who did influence policy at the time also failed to appreciate Pauling's claims about fallout. Discussing improvements in seismic detection methods to enforce a test ban during a meeting with the State Department, the Central Intelligence Agency (CIA), and the Pentagon, the presidential science adviser James Killian "pointed out that it would be dangerous to propose an agreement to ban atmospheric tests, since that would imply that the fallout hazard was real."[32]

Thus, Pauling stood as a public figure with the credibility of a Nobel Prize-winning scientist but also the stigma of being a leftist in the eyes of the government. Pauling returned the government's contempt in a noticeably bipartisan manner. He sued the Eisenhower administration for risking his life by exposing him (and the rest of the population) to fallout from nuclear tests; when John Kennedy succeeded Eisenhower, Pauling filed an identical suit against the new administration.[33] In 1963, after he won the Nobel Peace Prize, the White House arranged a meeting between the president and the chemist. Just before his meeting with Kennedy, however, Pauling picketed the White House with antinuclear activists angered by Kennedy's rush to complete nuclear tests before the Limited Test Ban Treaty (LTBT) took effect. Determined to belittle politics, Pauling refused to ask for access to government circles, nor was the government willing to grant influence to such a leftist. In this way, Pauling saw himself as following in Einstein's pacifist footsteps—indeed, the elder physicist personally admired and encouraged Pauling's activism.[34] Pauling saw himself as his own entity beyond government and helped generate substantial antinuclear sentiment in the 1950s and 1960s based not on access to policymakers but on his own moral and scientific authority, a challenge the government ultimately resisted. But the government did not act alone to limit Pauling's influence. His vision of science also ran afoul of those he saw as indispensable for his efforts to lead scientists away from militarism and toward morality: scientists themselves.

Pauling and His Peers

Pauling saw the superpowers as reprehensible for risking human annihilation during the Cold War. Because states would bear the brunt of his criticism, Pauling placed his faith in the public by embracing activism that encouraged grassroots dissent. Pauling's peace activism proved popular among ordinary protesters as well as more refined activists, including the Nobel committee, who awarded Pauling the 1963 Peace Prize. Such acclaim shows that Pauling's message of social commitment effectively moved people during the Cold War and that a scientific critique of nuclear weapons resonated with many people, scientists among them.

Pauling steadfastly maintained a belief that science and the scientific method formed the basis of a peaceful and moral society, and although he spoke to the public at large, scientists remained an essential constituency for his movement. Pauling's high-profile mixing of science with activism asked scientists to take a side—peace and morality or militarism and Cold War—

but his insistence on basing his crusade in a particular vision of "science" proved particularly galling to a number of scientists. Many aligned with or against him, while many other important scientists chose instead to avoid the issue altogether.

The Pauling Appeal

Even at the very start of his activism, Pauling saw himself as speaking for all scientists. This well-meaning but grandiose tendency was especially risky because he hoped to spark outrage and encourage activism among scientists, essentially enlisting the entire discipline of science behind his political movement. Delivering a sermon at a Unitarian church in August 1951, Pauling claimed that scientists had failed their moral and social obligations: "I deny that scientists have been guilty in making their discoveries. They have, however, failed in some part to do their duty as citizens."[35] Pauling spent much of his time in 1957 asking scientists around the world to sign his petition to stop nuclear testing. His appeal claimed an authority based on the idea that science revealed truth. When confronted with the objective assertions of scientists, he hoped that world leaders would halt the arms race.

As with all of Pauling's activism, his "Appeal by American Scientists to the Governments and People of the World" drew its moral authority from scientific evidence, reading in part: "Each nuclear bomb test spreads an added burden of radioactive elements over every part of the world. Each added amount of radiation causes damage to the health of human beings all over the world and causes damage to the pool of human germ plasm such as to lead to an increase in the number of seriously defective children that will be born in future generations." The third paragraph argued that continued testing would increase the likelihood of nuclear war, while the fourth claimed that a test ban would serve as a "first step" toward disarmament. The final paragraph made a declaration about the social responsibilities of scientists: "We have in common with our fellow men a deep concern for the welfare of all human beings. As scientists we have knowledge of the dangers involved and therefore a special responsibility to make those dangers known. We deem it imperative that immediate action be taken to effect an international agreement to stop the testing of all nuclear weapons." The petition traveled first to U.S. scientists and then around the world; eventually, more than eleven thousand scientists added their names before Pauling presented it to the United Nations on January 13, 1958.[36] Clearly, Pauling was not alone in his scientific objections to nuclear weapons.

Still, Pauling's presumption to speak for all of science rubbed some scientists the wrong way, feelings that came out in private and public. Helen Allison, a contributor to the *Bulletin of the Atomic Scientists,* addressed Pauling's campaign in the journal. "As a speaker," she began, "Pauling is humorous, personal, and very, very self-confident. He seeks to arouse the idealism of people, especially young people, to work for ends all sane men agree with—a test ban, disarmament, peace, freedom, survival." But Pauling, it seemed to Allison, posed more of a threat to the hallowed name of science than to the arms race. "To the more mature knowledgeable person," Allison continued, "his oversimplifications and unqualified absolutes tend to seem irresponsible." Allison described Pauling as more of a "crusader" than a "responsible" decision maker, which explained the "certain caution with which many of Pauling's scientific colleagues regard him." She noted that very few prestigious scientists deigned to sign his petition and concluded that although many admired Pauling, he nevertheless "cannot be regarded as the spokesman for the scientific community."[37] The debate over nuclear weapons evoked strong emotions because it very much represented the struggle over scientific identity in the mid-twentieth century.

Even late in life, Pauling adamantly maintained that a good portion of the scientific community did support his efforts. In a 1977 PBS interview, he stated, "Some scientists said that they considered me a spokesman for science in these matters [the study of fallout], as I was to some extent with respect to the bomb test treaty. There were many other scientists working on this problem. . . . I happened to be the one who stirred up feeling about it."[38] Undoubtedly, he had scientists who supported him, notably Barry Commoner of Washington University, an activist scientist in his own right. But a number of scientists refused to embrace Pauling's scientific vision. Instead of halting the arms race, Pauling's petition revealed that many scientists' professional identity resisted connecting science to specific social and political concerns.

At first, Pauling offered his appeal to U.S. scientists and received about two thousand signatures, which he submitted to the White House in the summer of 1957. Pleased with his success and cognizant of the internationalism of science, he expanded the petition to scientists worldwide. As always, Pauling mixed the moral with the scientific. To a Princeton scientist, Pauling explained, "I want tests stopped for two reasons. First, as a step toward disarmament, and second, because of the moral issues involved in injuring the nationals of other countries to any degree whatever."[39]

But in reality the scientific community failed to reflect the unity asserted by Pauling's petition. Although more than eleven thousand scientists did sign, many refused to do so. Remarkably, Pauling kept 103 notable letters of refusal in a safe in his office that reflected a very real division among scientists.[40] Pauling himself compiled a list of nine types of rejections. For the purposes of this analysis, three kinds of disagreement stand out: scientific objections, activist objections, and complete opposition to Pauling's crusade. (Of course, a few letters defy such strict categorization.) Such sources provide the opportunity to witness how scientists debated the role of science in politics and activism, the proper behavior of scientists, and the credibility, authority, and responsibility of scientists in the nuclear age.

Scientific Refusal

Some scientists begged off signing the petition but maintained that their refusal had nothing to do with the politics of the statement; instead, they simply lacked the right expertise, expressing a sort of agnosticism on the issue rather than outright disagreement. Referring to the Pauling petition as "a diadactic [sic] statement regarding knowledge which I do not possess," Milton Burton at Notre Dame told Pauling that "it is hard to get unprejudiced information. I know that political as well as scientific matters are involved in the decision. Scientists disagree on expressed interpretations of the data and on conclusions." He concluded that "I do not feel sufficiently well informed to arrive at a reliable scientific conclusion." Burton assured Pauling that he would make his decisions about political issues "more on the basis of moral and ethical principles than on any scientific basis," essentially telling Pauling that science and politics should not mix. The physicist David Inglis of Argonne National Laboratory agreed with Pauling on the need to stop tests but did not sign, explaining, "I find it hard to sign a statement implying that I have special knowledge about germ plasm, which I regret I don't have." Similarly, Robert Brode of the University of California at Berkeley, also a physicist, felt he could not sign for the same reason and urged Pauling to seek responses "from those who are competent to express an opinion on this matter." Stanford's Felix Bloch similarly claimed that a lack of expertise prevented him from signing, and added, "I would feel rather irresponsible in making a statement without such knowledge."[41] The phrasing of Pauling's petition, averring that the signatories "have knowledge of the dangers involved," clearly excluded those scientists who actually did not have knowledge of the subject matter. Yet scientists are generally not slow learners—surely, an interested but uninformed scientist could have looked into the subject, as Pauling himself had done at the dawn of the nuclear age. Still, this would not have guaranteed acceptance of the petition's claims.

Other refusals voiced more complex concerns about scientific credibility and how Pauling claimed the mantle of science. This group overtly worried about applying science to support a political point of view and saw Pauling as behaving unscientifically. In this way, Pauling's social commitment prevented him from gaining the support of some members of his core constituency. In addition, these letters revealed that many scientists' professional identity supported the government's view that opinions on nuclear weapons based in morality were inappropriate for scientists and that fundamental opposition to nuclear weapons lay outside the range of acceptable technical advice.

Percy Bridgman, a Harvard physicist, refused to sign the appeal because, he argued, "the danger of genetic damage from the tests alone is negligible." Although Bridgman admitted he would sign a statement on the need to abolish war, "I would be willing to sign only in my capacity as a citizen and not as a physicist." The Danish physiologist Brandt Rehberg excused himself from signing because scientists should speak on political matters only when they "have sufficient knowledge to enable them to form a real scientifically founded opinion on the matter. . . . I doubt, however, that all 2000 scientists who have signed your appeal have such a background knowledge that they may justly be called authorities on the subject." Such a "false authority," Rehberg wrote, could "weaken the confidence in general scientific statements. The number of signatures alone is not enough in such a case, and may be even harmful." Scientists, Rehberg concluded, "overstep their competence" when they mix science and politics, even though they have "the right" to express their opinions.[42]

Sam Goudsmit, a physicist at Brookhaven National Laboratory, told Pauling that the "scientific statements" made up "the weakest portions" of the appeal. "Though I fully agree," Goudsmit wrote, "that atomic war and really all destructive conflicts should be abolished, I see no reason to base this aim on scientific statements which lack objectivity." Goudsmit questioned Pauling's analysis of how much Sr90 enters the bone and accused him of relying on "unproven assumptions" and "scare data." He predicted that an exaggeration of the dangers would cause the public to lose confidence in scientists in general. Goudsmit did admit that "the other side" also promoted data favorable to their political interpretation but still deemed Pauling's appeal "thoroughly unscientific" and called for "arguments based on moral, economic, and historical foundations."[43] Goudsmit's mention of scare tactics echoes criticism of how the Atomic Scientists' Movement alienated many potential adherents by relying almost exclusively on fear to mobilize the public.

A scathing response came from an unidentified Cornell scientist who opposed bomb tests "as a man, not as a scientist." This scientist criticized Pauling's appeal exactly "because it purports to be scientific advice, from scientists, about a scientific matter." Offering a rebuke of Pauling's fundamental principles, he wrote, "The statement is anything but scientific because it is not quantitative. The assertions could equally apply, I suppose, to food preservatives, noxious gases from factories or refineries, even to toothpaste. . . . Scientists of all people have the duty to make precise statements, especially in a warning about such a grave matter." The author argued that nuclear war was a far greater threat than nuclear tests, and thus "your appeal will waste a significant scientific impact on what is today a peripheral subject." Similarly, the Nobel-winning physicist Edward Purcell of Harvard told Pauling that he could not agree with the scientific aspects of the statement "unless I abandon quantitative judgment entirely, as your second paragraph very nearly does." Purcell concluded that Pauling's statement was not "measured" enough, and "as scientists we ought to be the last to be drawn by our zeal into that form of excess."[44]

Finally, Pauling received a negative response from James Franck at the University of Chicago, known as Papa Franck for his mentoring of atomic activists such as Szilard and Eugene Rabinowitch during the Manhattan Project. He wrote Pauling that "in spite of the fact that I agree entirely with you, I cannot make up my mind to sign your appeal." Franck objected to appeals that, like Pauling's, "are written by scientists wearing the cloak of science. . . . Moreover, I believe that the task of science—to inform the public that danger is ahead—has been done. I doubt that we can help at this moment to see that the tests will be stopped internationally." In December Franck made up his mind not to sign because he feared that the petition might weaken the U.S. government in negotiations with the Soviets.[45] Just as the government insinuated that Pauling was disloyal to the United States, many of Pauling's peers told him he was disloyal to objectivity.

Activist Disagreement

Some scientists who refused to sign voiced no objections to the scientific aspects of Pauling's appeal. Rather, they objected to the petition itself as a form of protest. Some of these activist scientists complained that fallout was not the best reason to oppose nuclear weapons tests. A few refused to sign because of their official capacity, even when these positions would seem to be in harmony with Pauling's appeal, such as when the biochemist Paul

Doty of the Federation of American Scientists (FAS) declined to sign. The British physicist P. M. S. Blackett, at one time the president of the British Association of Scientific Workers, explained that he would not sign so that he would remain "uncommitted." Instead, Blackett mysteriously told Pauling, he hoped to "bridge the gap" between military realists and activists by learning to "talk the language of the strategico-military people."[46] The reluctance of scientists who would seem Pauling's natural allies demonstrates the great struggle scientists faced in trying to influence policy.

Bethe, who had worked so hard to reconcile scientists with government work after the Oppenheimer hearing, turned down Pauling's petition in May 1957. Although Bethe would soon become an integral member of the U.S. team dispatched to Geneva to negotiate a nuclear test ban with the Soviet Union, he wrote Pauling that he had listened to Libby of the AEC, who "convinced me that he and his collaborators have studied the problem of radioactivity very seriously, and that their conclusions are essentially sound." He thought that it was "quite wrong to put further emphasis on the radioactivity argument" and suggested that the sections of the petition about the dangers of proliferation might hold more appeal.[47]

Szilard, one of the more committed activists among scientists, refused to sign, as he put it, "for what seem to me to be good and valid reasons"— reasons that he failed to divulge. Yet Szilard proved very active at trying to stem the tide of nuclear weapons and above all knew how he wanted to engage people on the issue. At any rate, Szilard frequently refused to sign petitions, apparently a not uncommon stance among scientists. George Wald, the future winner of a Nobel Prize in Physiology and Medicine and a committed antiwar activist, wrote Pauling that "after a number of unsatisfactory experiences, I decided once and for all to sign no more petitions, but to speak for myself whenever I felt impelled." As for the appeal itself, the biochemist wrote, "I am of course against war, atom bomb testing, and so on; but I think there are circumstances under which I would be willing to put up with war, with or without atom bombs. I have lived a whole life joining in rejections of this or that; it is the particular disease of our time. I am about ready to try to find a few affirmations."[48] Finally, Wolfgang Panofsky, a Stanford physicist and advocate of arms control, questioned the political impact of the statement. Although Panofsky admitted that "no serious disagreement exists" about the biological effects of fallout, he suspected that a test cessation "would certainly not decrease the mutual suspicion and would increase the common uncertainty."[49]

Some refusals took issue with the more specific focus of Pauling's petition.

Harvard's John Edsall admitted "complete agreement" with the statement's objectives "and nearly all of its wording." Nevertheless, he wrote Pauling, "I believe the major reason for trying to stop bomb tests now is to help check the atomic armament race, serving as a first step to real disarmament." Fallout paled in comparison because, he believed, "the biological effects of nuclear testing . . . are quantitatively less important right now than medical x-rays and other problems." Instead, Edsall worried that scientific debate distracted from the true goal of convincing people that a ban on testing would not harm U.S. national security.[50]

Norman Goldberg of the FAS also disagreed with the emphasis of the proposal. He fretted that the wording "permits and perhaps encourages exaggerated and even incorrect interpretation of the danger." If the statement rested on the danger of fallout, Goldberg reasoned, some people might conclude that fallout is worth the health risk of defending national security. Theodore Puck of the University of Colorado, a geneticist, worried that Pauling's focus on fallout would "divert attention from the real issue of the necessity to give up warfare entirely." George Beadle expressed his feelings in a public statement, saying he wanted to "abolish all unnecessary radiation," whether it came from weapons tests, nuclear power, or medical uses. He argued further that the arms race would increase the chances of nuclear war. "In these respects I agree with the Pauling Appeal," he wrote. "I did not sign it because certain important issues raised in it go beyond science. In these I have no special knowledge or competence." Beadle, a geneticist, privately admitted to Pauling in a handwritten letter that "I have special competence and responsibility" to express views on fallout, and, he added, "Fallout is bad—no doubt about it." Yet Beadle could not sign, he wrote, because he did not feel that nuclear fallout was the primary reason to stop tests, as Pauling's appeal implied. Beadle assured Pauling that he was dedicated to stopping tests and could be more effective without signing.[51] Thus, the appeal revealed division among scientists who agreed that science supported antinuclear policies; in fact, many refusals came from scientists to the left of Pauling who wanted broader antiwar and antinuclear critiques. By trying to appeal to all scientists, Pauling risked alienating many.

Total Disagreement

Finally, a number of scientists simply disagreed fundamentally with Pauling's science, politics, and activism. James Conant, the establishment figure, president of Harvard, and former chemist, simply wrote that "I couldn't disagree with you more heartily. I, therefore, have high hopes that you will fail completely in your undertaking!!!" Vannevar Bush, the influential government official and prophet of big science, stated that "I do not join in petitions and the like. . . . I have not had the feeling that this was the very important way to get heard." Samuel Allison of the University of Chicago dismissed Pauling's appeal as "utopian" and feared it would "do more harm than good." Allison wrote, "Nobody pays much attention to round robin statements any more. On glancing at the (was it two thousand?) names on the appeal I recognized a mere handful as 'scientists (who) have knowledge of the dangers involved.'" Allison echoed Szilard, Wald, and Bush when he declared a preference for "direct, personally worded, and individual statements." Others sided more directly with nuclear deterrence. Frederick Seitz, the president of the National Academy of Sciences (NAS), blamed "the dictatorships" for the arms race and told Pauling that "the evil represented by the combination of Soviet imperialism and brutality far overwhelms, in my own mind, the evil associated with the tests." John Wheeler at Princeton's Institute for Advanced Study argued that although he would prefer peace, he believed nuclear weapons protected U.S. freedoms from the Soviet threat. David Griggs, a geophysics professor who often collaborated with Teller, opposed the unilateral nature of the appeal because he feared such a move would stunt U.S. nuclear weapons development. Other nations would, meanwhile, continue to develop weapons, which "might well tempt a nation bent on dominating the world to subjugate us with their newer and better nuclear weapons." Griggs then assured Pauling that scientists could conduct tests underground without any radiation escaping.[52]

One of the more virulent refusals came from Kenneth Pitzer of UC Berkeley's Chemistry Department. Calling Pauling's appeal "a most unfortunate action," Pitzer wrote that the risks of fallout were "very small" and that "any military defense involves some risks." Without tests, the quality of nuclear weapons would decline, threatening "human freedom in the world today." In closing, Pitzer tagged Pauling as an appeaser: "Just as the peace movements of the middle 1930's may have increased the probability of World War II, I am afraid that appeals such as yours may increase the risk of a future war."[53]

Using science to support a political goal proved difficult for Pauling, not least because he himself was a scientist. Taking his own findings into the realm of advocacy challenged the dominant scientific mores of the day. He attempted to practice both science and activism, but to many scientists the choice between science and activism was an either-or decision. One could advocate a political view or a scientific conclusion but not both. In this way, influential scientists kept themselves and others from taking part in the debate over nuclear weapons, inadvertently serving the government's purpose in limiting scientific dissent against nuclear weapons.

Despite the varying reasons behind their refusal to sign Pauling's petition, the refusers discussed here were rather uniform in other ways. Of those that can be identified, none were born after 1920, with seven born in the late nineteenth century (Pauling was born in 1901). Only six of these men did not participate in the Manhattan Project or some other wartime government endeavor, and seventeen of them were physicists, along with four chemists or biochemists, three biologists or geneticists, and one physiologist. While the refusers' statements should be taken at face value, it bears keeping in mind that scientists, like many Americans at the time, may have been hesitant to take a political stand because of the climate of the anticommunist 1950s. Oppenheimer and Pauling were just two people who faced retribution for their actual and alleged associations, including meetings attended and petitions signed. With McCarthyism a vivid memory, anyone asking people to sign a petition faced an uphill battle.

Pauling and the Antinuclear Movement

Undeterred by his conflicts with leading scientists, Pauling presented his petition to UN secretary-general Dag Hammarskjöld on January 13, 1958. In February 1961 he presented a second petition to the United Nations—this one on nuclear proliferation and signed by a far less impressive 720 scientists.[54] After the United States and Soviet Union signed the LTBT in 1963, the Nobel committee rewarded Pauling's years of activism with the Peace Prize, giving the embattled scientist a large amount of support, credibility, and publicity. Despite this recognition, however, Pauling continued to drive a wedge between leading scientific antinuclear advocates, as his personality led to or exacerbated clashes with scientists affiliated with Pugwash and the *Bulletin of the Atomic Scientists*.

Eugene Rabinowitch had left his native Russia after the Bolshevik Revolution of 1917 and arrived in the United States in 1938. Five years later he joined the Manhattan Project's Met Lab, where, working with Papa Franck, he did a great deal to draw scientists into the debate over atomic weapons. Just before the use of the A-bomb against Japan in August 1945, Rabinowitch had helped author the Franck Report, the Met Lab document that protested the use of the atomic bomb against Japan, arguing that doing so would make future international control of atomic weapons impossible and provoke an atomic arms race.[55] After the war, Rabinowitch continued his activism by cofounding the *Bulletin of the Atomic Scientists* as a forum for informed scientific debate over nuclear weapons, science, and politics.

Although the *Bulletin* included Pauling's name on its board of sponsors, Rabinowitch had refused to sign Pauling's petition in May 1957 for reasons that came down to conflicts over scientific identity. Rabinowitch echoed other scientists by siding with Libby: "I do not feel that I can sign it as a scientist," he told Pauling. "I am not convinced that a strong quantitative case for the cessation of testing can be made simply on the basis of the threat to health or genetic endowment of mankind. I have no reason to believe that Dr. Libby's figures are not approximately correct." Rabinowitch also feared that the appeal might accidentally convince Americans to willingly risk fallout in order to protect national security. Rabinowitch added that "I am personally sceptical [*sic*] . . . that the cessation of tests is likely to become a first step towards controlled nuclear disarmament."[56]

As editor in chief, Rabinowitch ran the *Bulletin* as a forum where scientists could debate their role in the nuclear age, examine arms control proposals, and explore science policy. In general, its contributors showed a preference for technical debate rather than impassioned rhetoric and endorsed the quiet and indirect influencing of policymakers' views instead of mobilization of the masses, a choice reflecting, perhaps, lessons learned during the Atomic Scientists' Movement. Although the *Bulletin* had published a favorable account of Pauling's appearance before the Dodd committee in 1960, by 1962 Pauling had begun to take issue with the *Bulletin*'s treatment of him and his peace campaign. A 1962 article by the geneticist Bentley Glass criticized Pauling as well as the nuclear enthusiast Edward Teller. Glass wrote that both men "are carried away by the conviction of the rightness of their opinions, and make extrapolations from the existing facts that are scarcely trustworthy, or are even lured into flat misstatements." He added that neither of the two had any particular scientific expertise on the matter of fallout, though Glass devoted most of his article to refuting at length Teller's pronuclear arguments. Glass concluded by expressing a common belief among scientists that their objective expertise could transcend the political aspects of policy debates, stating that "often scientists engaged in such [political] efforts have forsaken the scientific approach to the problem at issue." Instead, Glass suggested, the Pugwash conferences could serve as a "more hopeful" attempt at imbuing political action with "scientific integrity." Highly offended, Pauling wrote to the *Bulletin*, which published his response in the December 1962 issue, wherein he decried the "untrue and damaging statements" in the Glass article.[57]

Various demands and explanations went back and forth between June and September 1963, as the pages of the *Bulletin* filled with Rabinowitch's response, a comment from Glass, and then another response from Pauling. Such activity was not abnormal for Pauling, who defiantly confronted bad publicity and often filed successful libel suits. Indeed, Pauling bragged as much to Rabinowitch at one point, perhaps making a veiled threat.[58] During the melodrama, Pauling wrote to Bethe, the chairman of the *Bulletin*'s board of sponsors, to announce his resignation from the board. Pauling cited Rabinowitch's "half-hearted apology" and "damage done to me" during the Glass controversy as his reasons for leaving, concluding that "I am not willing to continue to sponsor Eugene Rabinowitch as Editor of the Bulletin." Pauling had essentially ousted himself from the *Bulletin,* further divorcing him from the scientific constituency that would seem to be his natural ally in the pursuit of disarmament.[59] While Pauling frequently claimed to speak on behalf of science, he often resembled a leader without a following.

Pauling's break with the *Bulletin* probably evolved out of a clash with the U.S. branch of the Pugwash organization, where Glass and Rabinowitch also ran the show. Pauling had attended the second Pugwash conference in 1958 and continued to take heat for it from Senator Dodd years later. Nevertheless, as with the *Bulletin,* he found himself out of place as more of a public activist among reserved insider types fond of thinking of themselves as quietly influencing geopolitics. On May 10, 1962, Pauling wrote to the secretary-general of Pugwash, Joseph Rotblat, turning down an invitation to a Pugwash conference. Sensing a conspiracy to exclude him, Pauling wrote Rotblat, "I judge that I am not going to be invited to the more important conferences, and I feel that for this reason, too, there is no need for me to attend the less important ones." That same day, Pauling wrote to Bertrand Russell, the British philosopher who had helped initiate Pugwash with his 1955 manifesto.[60] Pauling told Russell that he would not participate in Pugwash as long as the U.S. representatives included the "uncooperative" Rabinowitch and Glass and complained about Glass's "serious and grossly damaging attack upon me" that had appeared in the *Bulletin.* Pauling probably found a sympathetic ear in Russell, who had already begun to drift from Pugwash toward more radical, grassroots disarmament efforts.[61] Increasingly, many scientists appeared to send Pauling the message that grassroots activism was unwelcome among those who hoped to achieve arms control and disarmament.

The passage of time did little to heal Pauling's wounded ego. In 1967 he wrote to the editor of *Ramparts,* the radical New Left magazine, alleging that Pugwash had probably been infiltrated by the CIA or the State Department. In 1959, one year after his first visit to a Pugwash conference, Pauling claimed to have noticed a "change in policy," as U.S. participants "turned out to be less well-known scientists connected in some way with the government, especially with the military." Also of great significance to Pauling was the damning evidence that "I have not been allowed to attend most of the Pugwash Conferences since 1959." Finally, Pauling alleged that the U.S. Pugwash group's ability to raise one hundred thousand dollars in 1961 "with a major contribution made by the Ford Foundation" proved the CIA's secret influence over the organization. Such suspicions were not entirely baseless, as the CIA did direct the Ford Foundation's support of the Congress for Cultural Freedom, but there is no real evidence that Pugwash's Ford money was similarly tainted.[62] More important, Pauling's conspiracy charges missed the point. The scientists' antinuclear movement had been divided by infighting among Pauling and others. His strong personality and preference for direct action alienated many scientists, who preferred less controversial methods that the government found more acceptable.

Pauling also broke with SANE, the mainstream antinuclear organization that had helped carry the torch of disarmament during the late 1950s. After SANE conducted a purge of its left-leaning members following the Dodd hearings in May 1960 (the same hearings at which Pauling testified about his petition), Pauling made his disgust official. When SANE cravenly promised Dodd that it would question its members and drop them from the organization if they gave "unsatisfactory" answers, Pauling told SANE's leader, Norman Cousins, that he objected to the organization's "recourse to McCarthyism." Pauling also refused an invitation to join the board of SANE and prophesied that "SANE will be destroyed," an essentially accurate prediction. His break with SANE also had a personal aspect, as Pauling made clear in November 1960. Writing to SANE in order to distance himself from the organization, Pauling emphasized that he had dropped his connection to the organization because it refused to support him during the Dodd hearings.[63]

In contrast to his uneasy relationships with many U.S. scientists, the fact that some nine thousand scientists overseas signed his petition, as compared to two thousand in the United States, suggests that scientific opposition to Pauling's efforts might have been at least partly regional in nature. Americans were only just emerging from the Red Scare, where ordinary people had been permanently tainted for signing petitions. Meanwhile, Britain had a long-established antinuclear movement, and while British scientists participating in the antinuclear movement played a conventional role by providing it with technical expertise, advocacy of a policy position did not spark as much controversy as it did in the United States. Yet the scientific aspect of the movement in Britain did not command as much attention as Pauling did in the United States.

The Campaign for Nuclear Disarmament, Britain's largest antinuclear group, established a Scientists' Group in the early 1960s that informed and participated in CND activities. These efforts included a letter urging the U.S. government to abandon plans for a high-altitude thermonuclear test, while other efforts included a CND scientists' bulletin that reached a circulation of roughly fifteen hundred and a *Handbook on Nuclear War* that included sections titled "Effects of Blast on People" and "Protection from Fire."[64]

Most often the Scientists' Group provided information to other activists, as when the Committee of 100 direct-action group wrote to the scientists asking whether plutonium was being used at Capenhurst, the site of a nuclear fuel-enrichment plant. The CND scientists confirmed that "fissile material was being dealt with there." The group also received an inquiry from a local group about radioactivity in the water supply and the local authorities' reluctance to release data on the subject. In response, a Birmingham scientist "agreed to inform them that the levels were not dangerous and to urge that pressure be applied for the figures to be publicised." Other activists asked for a study on the potential effects of nuclear war on Britain, while a letter from the East Bay Women for Peace requested "figures for radioactive contamination of food." The scientists also informed the public about radiation threats, including Sr90 contamination of milk and the rate of leukemia relative to the amount of nuclear fallout. In these efforts, the Scientists' Group played a role roughly equivalent to the Committee for Nuclear Information in the United States, which promoted itself as politically neutral by providing objective technical information to the public.[65]

Opinions on policy flowed naturally from the Scientists' Group's efforts. One scientist from Edinburgh proposed a petition to Parliament in 1962 "about the dangers of nuclear tests to be signed by biologists." The scientists agreed to limit the petition to biologists, as it would deal strictly with "the biological uncertainty of fallout effects which were being soft-pedaled at the moment."[66]

The biologists' petition against nuclear testing provoked little outrage among British scientists, though it mingled scientific expertise with policy pronouncements. In Pauling-esque tones, it began: "As professional biologists, we are gravely concerned about the harmful biological consequences of testing nuclear weapons." Yet by identifying the signatories as "professional biologists" rather than the all-encompassing "scientists" mentioned in Pauling's petition, the Scientists' Group could avoid alienating (as Pauling had) those who supported the cause but could not claim expertise they did not have. The petition continued, carefully expressing a difference between what the British biologists knew and what they felt:

> We *know* that even a small increase in the level of radiation will have harmful consequences. The burden of suffering and death which must inevitably result will chiefly affect future generations, and its extent will not be known for many years; but these facts cannot absolve us from moral responsibility.
>
> Further, we *feel* that continued nuclear tests increase the danger of war by poisoning the political atmosphere, as well as by conditioning people to regard nuclear war as a feasible possibility rather than as a social and biological disaster of unprecedented and awesome magnitude.[67]

As the Scientists' Group shows, Pauling was not alone in believing that contesting the nuclear arms race was a scientist's duty. But contrary to his hopes, Pauling's use of science as a method of activism had not guaranteed the allegiance of all scientists, particularly in the United States. Nor did being a scientist create enough solidarity to allow other activist scientists to join Pauling without question. In the United States after the Oppenheimer hearing, there developed a split between scientists. But too much emphasis on the divisions between an "Oppenheimer camp" and a "Teller faction" distracts from noticing other influential splits. Antinuclear scientists had fierce divisions among themselves and found plenty to disagree on. In addition, Dodd and the State Department had done a great deal to challenge Pauling and harm his public image.

Still, the split over the Oppenheimer hearing and the role of Teller remained important. Pauling was not the only scientist on a crusade; as the so-called father of the hydrogen bomb, Teller exploited his personal connections and influence to secure for himself and nuclear weapons a prized place within the national security state. Both Pauling and Teller took it on themselves to mobilize science and scientists behind their opposing points of view, and while the rivalry between these two men played out as a battle for public opinion, on a deeper level the two waged a war that, in the end, influenced the direction of U.S. nuclear policy and helped redefine the place of science within a Cold War context.

3

Edward Teller's Flexible Response

Defending Nuclear Weapons, 1954–1963

A s THE U.S. SCIENTIFIC COMMUNITY GRAPPLED with Linus Pauling's attempt to push it in one direction, Edward Teller added another layer of tension by trying to pull it in the opposite direction. Teller, perhaps more than any Cold War scientist, helped shape U.S. nuclear weapons policy for decades, though a preference for heroes rather than villains and a neglect of U.S. conservatism in general have meant that historians until recently have often treated Teller as more of a foil than a subject deserving of focus.[1] Treating Teller as a punch line ignores his power during the Cold War; in fact, he had a great deal of influence over U.S. nuclear weapons policy. With vastly more access to policymakers than Pauling, Teller was essential to the formation of an alliance between pronuclear scientists and the national security state, and by framing the nuclear issue around the concepts of both loyalty and technical expertise, he helped enforce the redefinition of science.

The Case for Doomsday

As a founding father of the nuclear age, Teller was a well-known nuclear enthusiast often sought out by prophets and gadflies heralding the new world order. These characters included the eccentric thinker Herman Kahn, one of the earliest nuclear strategists at RAND, who made a name for himself by pursuing the unthinkable logic of the arms race. "Kahn's most notorious idea," according to his biographer, was the purposefully absurd Doomsday Machine that he described in his most famous tome, *On Thermonuclear War.* As the ultimate deterrent, the machine would, on sensing a nuclear attack, detonate enough fissile material to destroy human life on the planet.[2]

At his think tank, the Hudson Institute, Kahn remained enamored with the idea of the Doomsday Machine in August 1964, when he wrote to Teller and asked for his thoughts on it. After consideration Teller wrote to Kahn to tell him that the Doomsday Machine suffered from, in rare understatement, "impracticalities." Kahn rushed to assure Teller that the machines were actually quite practical, with Kahn's colleague D. G. Brennan adding that "rough calculations" suggested that "perhaps a million tons of U238" would be enough to create a Doomsday Machine. "Obviously," Brennan continued, "the political decision to undertake an effort of that magnitude is not likely to be forthcoming, but the point is that a society capable of undertaking the moon program *could* undertake a Doomsday Machine if it felt strongly about it." Still uncharacteristically playing the skeptic, Teller admitted that enough raw material probably existed for a Doomsday Machine. "But," he asked, "how many people in Russia or China or anywhere else could be persuaded to work hard and consistently on a project with a clear-cut aim that includes inescapable self-destruction? I would like to plea for some realism in evaluating the dangers with which we are faced."[3]

Kahn and Brennan would have been forgiven for expressing surprise at Teller's "plea" for "realism." After all, Teller was no stranger to outlandish ideas. Along with praising the mutative effects of nuclear radiation in the 1950s, Teller had also started a nuclear excavation program and showed a flair for the fanciful by brandishing a business card that read, "If your mountain is not in the right place, drop us a card."[4] But Teller was also rational and smart and knew how to pitch an idea. He got his viewpoint across in politics and could make exaggerated claims sound like realism to certain audiences, abilities that allowed him to cast doubt on the scientific claims of others. He shrewdly chose his audience and provided a modicum of logic, consistency, and scientific reasoning that fell somewhere within the bounds of contemporary political thought. Kahn may have been outrageous, but Teller was outrageous and influential.

As an established theoretical physicist at UC Berkeley, the public face of the H-bomb, the driving force behind the Livermore nuclear weapons lab, and adviser to all sorts of government entities, including the Atomic Energy Commission, the armed forces, and the occasional congressman, Teller challenged Pauling's antinuclear crusade.[5] While Pauling attempted to rescue science from militarization, Teller spent his time working to link science to U.S. national security and anticommunism, in the process growing increasingly closer to a resurgent conservative political movement. From this position, Teller played a unique role in the state's division of science between who did and did not support nuclear deterrence. To appropriate a term from the Kennedy administration's Cold War strategy, which offered varying ways of responding to a communist attack, Teller offered a "flexible response" to antinuclear challengers. When the occasion called for it, Teller could be subtle; when polemics were in order, Teller provided them. When scientific evidence appeared to challenge the nuclear deterrent, Teller refuted it in dry, technical terms. When scientific experts offered strategic reasons for arms control, Teller marginalized them as uninformed. While antinuclear scientists deemed the arms race a path to oblivion, Teller offered innovations in weaponry that would lead to clear victory in the Cold War. Teller thus actively helped conservatives in the U.S. government combat the scientists both inside and outside of Washington who challenged the arms race.

An Anticommunist Scientist

Like many of the Manhattan Project's most famous scientists, Teller was educated in Germany and eventually relocated to the United States. And like a number of other influential Cold War conservatives, Teller hailed from Eastern Europe and had experienced communist brutality firsthand. Born in 1908, Teller was raised a Jew in Hungary, where the maelstrom of World War I exposed him to several torrents of political upheaval. In his memoirs, Teller recounted the fear unleashed when communists under Béla Kun took over a defeated Hungary after the war. Kun's brief reign left Teller with such emotional scars that a profound fear of communists haunted him for the rest of his life. The communist takeover, in his words, "overturned every aspect of society and the economy," including his family, as his father was forbidden from practicing law because "a lawyer was a thoroughly worthless person in a 'good' society." The communist military even quartered two soldiers in their household. Outside the home, Teller found no relief. Posters appeared in streets and subways menacing the young boy. He recalled, "On one of them, a stern man with his arm extended and his fingertip as large as if it were half an inch from my nose, said: 'You, hiding in the shadows, spreading horror stories, you counterrevolutionary, TREMBLE.' The finger seemed to follow me wherever I went." When the communist government collapsed and the Jewish Kun was deposed, a wave of anti-Semitism accompanied the next regime's ascent to power. "During my first eleven years," Teller summarized, "I had known war, patriotism, communism, revolution, anti-Semitism, fascism, and peace."[6]

Despite the childhood turmoil, Teller did well in school. In 1926 he left Hungary in order to study chemistry and mathematics in Germany, and in April 1928 he enrolled at the University of Munich to study physics under Arnold Sommerfeld (who had also mentored Pauling). Teller and Sommerfeld never got along, so he finished his studies in Leipzig with Werner Heisenberg, where he relished living at the heart of the quantum revolution. In contrast to the joys of studying physics, the rise of Nazism made evident to Teller the need to leave Germany, and so he spent the 1933–34 academic year in Copenhagen, the home of Niels Bohr and, in Teller's words, "the first assembly point of the Diaspora of the German physicists."[7] Teller and his wife, Mici, then ended up in London in September 1934; one year later they arrived in Washington.

Just a few years after his arrival, Teller found himself working with his fellow physicists and Hungarian refugees Leo Szilard and Eugene Wigner, who had decided to petition the U.S. government to begin development of an atomic bomb. As the Manhattan Project came to life, Teller came to play a more significant role. In the summer of 1942 Robert Oppenheimer brought Teller and many of the nation's other elite physicists to Berkeley to probe the possibilities of an atomic bomb. At this meeting Teller first became captivated by Oppenheimer; he also conceived of using a fission explosion as a trigger for an even larger thermonuclear explosion. When the military decided to establish a lab for assembling the atomic bombs at Los Alamos, New Mexico, Teller began to recruit other scientists to work there. Teller was himself one of the earliest arrivals at the lab in March 1943. Despite this early enthusiasm for the bomb, Teller did not play a particularly active role at Los Alamos, spending most of his time theorizing about a thermonuclear "Super" bomb that would dwarf the power of the A-bomb.[8] Oppenheimer's refusal to give priority to the Super, combined with his selection of Hans Bethe over Teller as head of the lab's theoretical division, has made a future showdown between Teller and Oppenheimer seem all but inevitable. Teller himself lends credibility to this characterization, writing that this snub left him "a little hurt. I had worked on the atom bomb project longer than Bethe. I had worked hard and fairly effectively on recruiting, and on helping Oppie organize the lab during the first chaotic weeks."[9]

Teller's memoirs make it clear that he had a dispute with Bethe equal to or greater than his conflict with Oppenheimer. "Although I appreciated and enjoyed the differences between Hans and me," Teller wrote, "I was not happy about having him as my boss." Teller had already started to distance himself from the men who would become the U.S. scientific elite after the war. When Bethe asked him to calculate some implosion equations, Teller begged off, saying the work was "far too difficult [and] might not be completed in time to have any influence on a bomb that could be used during this war." In his memoirs Teller declared that "the incident marked the beginning of the end of our friendship."[10] These comments were a self-fulfilling prophecy; while at Los Alamos, he quickly lost almost all interest in the A-bomb and eventually worked out an arrangement with Oppenheimer that allowed him to pursue theoretical work on the Super, which stood no chance of being a factor in the war.

When the war ended, Teller anticipated that Los Alamos would begin concerted effort on the Super, but most scientists left instead to resume their prewar lives. Without a core of quality scientists around him, Teller reluctantly left Los Alamos, though he remained a consultant to the lab. In his memoirs Teller blamed Oppenheimer for scuttling work on the Super. Following the use of the A-bombs, Teller bemoaned, "Oppenheimer had seemed to lose his sense of balance, his perspective. After seeing the pictures from Hiroshima, he appeared determined that Los Alamos, the unique and outstanding laboratory he had created, should vanish. When asked about its future, he responded, 'Give it back to the Indians.'"[11]

Several of Teller's peers also resisted further military work, an attitude that Teller declared "thoughtless." Late in life Teller suggested that he simply held different—and more realistic—views from other scientists about weapons work and communism. Influenced by Arthur Koestler's novel *Darkness at Noon* as well as his interactions with communist scientists, Teller concluded that "Stalin, who could never catch up with Hitler, was still a close runner-up."[12] As the Red Scare began, Teller increasingly portrayed his rivals as naive about communism.

Like many Manhattan Project veterans, Teller advocated international control of atomic energy, supported the development of nuclear power, and did his part to defeat the May-Johnson bill. Teller also advocated a strong atomic defense—not unlike Oppenheimer. But Teller, who admitted to being a "monomaniac . . . who had several manias," saw communism as perhaps the greatest threat among equally urgent problems. Thus, when the Soviet Union tested an atomic weapon in 1949, Teller focused his energies on getting government support for the Super and in the process further refined an anticommunism quite distinct from that of those he saw as his antagonists, including Oppenheimer and Bethe. Teller actively pushed for the Super at a time when many scientists objected to it; he raged in frustration when Oppenheimer told him to "keep your shirt on." Instead, Teller began to find common cause with other scientists who shared his conservative, anticommunist beliefs, such as the Berkeley physicist Ernest Lawrence. In short, at the beginning of the Cold War, Teller underwent a political awakening. At the time he described himself as, "like most immigrants, a Democrat." But soon, he wryly recalled, he came to grasp "the idea that there were two political parties in the United States." By 1951 Teller had absorbed a conventionally conservative view of geopolitics, decrying, for example, the "shrill" voices arguing for a pacifist solution to the Korean War. In response to criticism of the United States for acting too belligerently, he penned a poem for the *Bulletin of the Atomic Scientists* that mentioned "the Chamberlain umbrella" and asked:

> Will the people have the dash
> That Britons had when their world seemed to crash
> Before a small man with a small mustache?[13]

Teller's personal political beliefs were drawing him away from the postwar nuclear establishment centered around Oppenheimer, who, as the chair of the AEC's General Advisory Committee, was recognized as the leading science adviser in the nation.

During the 1954 Oppenheimer hearing, Teller permanently split from the liberal scientific elite. As the most prominent and outspoken (but by no means only) critic of Oppenheimer, Teller quickly became notorious for his testimony in the AEC security clearance hearing. In 2001 Teller recounted how his actions separated him from the scientific community that had provided him with meaning and friendship for his entire life. After the rise of Hitler had forced him to take refuge in the United States, "everything had been unfamiliar except for the community of theoretical physicists." Even two decades later, "the community of my fellow scientists was the only place that afforded me complete comfort, and had done so since my arrival. Now, at forty-seven, I was again forced into exile." Teller's first meeting with his friend Robert Christy at Los Alamos after the Oppenheimer hearing left a lasting memory: "I hurried over, reaching out to greet him. He looked me coldly in the eye, refused my hand, and turned away. I was so stunned that for a moment I couldn't react. Then I realized that my life as I had known it was over. I took Mici by the arm, and we returned to our room upstairs. Our last exile had begun."[14]

These somewhat melodramatic recollections indicate that the division of the scientific community became the defining feature of the rest of Teller's life. But Teller omitted from his memoirs his role in encouraging this division and how he used it to build his own faction of scientists in favor of nuclear weapons development and the arms race. Although Teller liked to act as though he was the victim of the Oppenheimer hearing (and indeed his personal reputation was in shambles), his reputation suffered only in the eyes of those he had already repudiated. At the same time, his testimony proved a boon to his career, as it impressed the power brokers in the AEC and military who had maneuvered to remove Oppenheimer from power. Teller consequently emerged in the late 1950s as perhaps the government's foremost science adviser. With Oppenheimer discredited, Teller exhibited the zeal for weapons work demanded by the AEC's verdict, and he would spend the rest of his life working to meet this demand for ever-stronger offensive—as well as defensive—nuclear capabilities.

Teller recognized how his actions against Oppenheimer had left science riven, but rather than suffer in silence or help heal the divide, he quickly mobilized to win scientists to his side. The physicist Luis Alvarez, who had also testified against Oppenheimer, wrote Teller a revealing letter describing the Oppenheimer hearing as just one step in a campaign to sway U.S. scientists. After the hearing Alvarez went to Los Alamos, where he tried to convince other scientists that Teller had done the right thing by testifying against Oppenheimer. There he first called on the Berkeley professor and former Manhattan Project physicist Robert Brode, "and I talked two hours, with the 'Bible' in my hand"—an obvious reference to the hearing transcript. Alvarez showed Brode sections he had marked, "and [Brode] said several times to me that it was abundantly clear to him that Robert was a security risk, and that it was clear, without any evidence from the H-bomb business." Alvarez told Teller that Brode "agrees with me now, that you are an innocent bystander, and in no way a Judas," and urged Teller to get more copies of the transcript to scientists at Los Alamos in order to show that he had been right and Oppenheimer wrong.[15] An active campaign to perpetuate and exploit the schism dividing U.S. science had begun.

Although Teller would craft a narrative that he had been ostracized by many of his peers, in reality he stood on one side of a divide in U.S. science, unpopular with the opposing side but with plenty of allies of his own, and outside the scientific community many Americans supported Teller, including a resident of Toledo, Ohio, who sent the physicist a telegram in October 1954. Signed "A human being," the telegram read: "Thank Heaven for a person with your integrity. You know your position, and do not attempt to decide the future of this U.S. With all the subversives, who have wormed their way into gov't. projects as 'experts' it is a joy to read of you. All the American people owe you their futures, and hopes. Bless you for your honesty."[16] Like this letter, Teller's own views came to echo those of Senator Joseph McCarthy's anticommunist crusade as the 1950s and 1960s progressed. Yet Teller also offered a uniquely optimistic slant on the nuclear age.

The Peaceful Uses of Nuclear Weapons

Because Teller had yoked his career, political beliefs, and identity to the development of nuclear weapons, the momentum that Pauling helped gather for a nuclear test ban in the late 1950s threatened to quash more than just his scientific ideas. When Teller managed to meet with President Eisenhower on June 24, 1957, the subject of Pauling's petition against nuclear testing arose. Apparently, Eisenhower recognized that "the Pauling comment may be quite invalid but . . . so many nations and people are reading in the press these fearsome and horrible reports that they are having a substantial result."[17] Because challengers like Pauling threatened to unmoor science from national security, Teller thus had to take every opportunity to silence them.

In response, Teller sought to expand the nuclear weapons establishment as well as give those weapons a more positive reputation. He solidified his commitment to the militarization of science by successfully pushing for the establishment of a second nuclear weapons lab in Livermore, California (later Lawrence-Livermore National Laboratory), and during the 1950s Teller was also eager to show that nuclear explosives had "peaceful uses." One of his pet projects at Livermore was a nuclear excavation business named Project Plowshare, giving him a personal interest in opposing a nuclear weapons test ban. His list of "suitable projects" for Plowshare included using thermonuclear explosions to create "harbors, channels and canals." Expecting opposition on account of a fear of fallout, Teller argued that the Plowshare program ensured that it would be "possible to release large energies in a safe way even rather near to populated areas."[18]

Teller knew that he had to provide concrete proof of Plowshare's viability, and this meant finding some place on earth willing to host a nuclear explosion—one that would presumably benefit from the changed landscape. Teller soon decided that Alaska would be the perfect place to show off Plowshare's potential. In 1958 he sent a memo to Washington's Democratic senator Henry Jackson, explaining that the Plowshare team could demonstrate the benefits of nuclear excavation, though he urged discretion since "the [Atomic Energy] Commission seems to be quite anxious not to influence real estate values or upset anybody by speculation."[19]

The memo outlined grand uses for Plowshare, including "shattering water impermeable layers" of earth to turn deserts into oases. Teller also saw "extensive possibilities of using nuclear explosives for mining purposes" that "might increase our oil reserves very greatly." With even more grandeur, the memo explained how a Plowshare explosion in Alaska (code-named Project Chariot) would even help atone for use of the A-bomb during World War II. Because creating a harbor would jump-start coal exports, a resource Japan needed, "it would be satisfying if the first peaceful application of nuclear explosives would benefit the same Country which had first suffered from the atomic bomb."[20]

Teller then began a prolonged campaign to seduce Alaska into hosting a thermonuclear blast. One week after President Eisenhower signed the Alaska Statehood Act on July 7, 1958, Teller left for the new state "with the hope that the elation about statehood will help along other reasonable plans," a clear reference to Plowshare. One year later, after returning from another trip, Teller told the president of the University of Alaska, "I just cannot stay away from your state for any length of time." All these efforts in the forty-ninth state came to nothing; local activists and University of Alaska scientists mounted a steadfast opposition that halted Project Chariot.[21]

Although no nuclear excavations took place, Teller's dream of a nuclear-powered earthmoving business endured. The program's lack of profit never bothered him in the least, since Plowshare's true value lay in providing a way to continue weapons experiments and subvert the arms control measures being pursued by the Eisenhower administration in the late 1950s. After representatives at the 1958 Geneva test ban negotiations proposed a test cessation, Teller told National Aeronautics and Space Administration (NASA) missile engineer Hans Mark that "I am beginning to think quite seriously of putting under Plowshare a shot with the exclusive purpose of scientific experiments" that would provide data showing the impossibility of enforcing a nuclear test ban. In a letter to the chair of the AEC's GAC, Teller directly linked Plowshare to the prevention of a test ban, writing that "the demonstration of the peaceful use of nuclear explosives will help to stop the threat toward ban of all nuclear explosives."[22]

The Role of Scientists

Like Pauling, Teller saw science as necessary and useful for society, and his science always matched his politics. As the A-bomb was originally an anti-Nazi endeavor, for the anticommunist Teller the H-bomb directly countered the aggressive tendencies of the Soviet Union. But Teller worked to hide the connections between his scientific and political positions in order to claim the objective high ground. Since the late 1930s, Teller's scientific work had been rooted in his conscience: he helped Szilard get the U.S. government interested in building an A-bomb, and at Los Alamos in 1945 Teller again felt compelled to act on his conscience when Szilard began circulating a petition urging a demonstration of the bomb as an alternative to military use against Japan. Szilard's petition emphasized the role of scientists in determining how the bomb should be used and argued that a demonstration would avoid bloodshed and uphold moral responsibility. In his memoirs Teller wrote, "Those reasons made good sense to me, and I could think of no reason that those of us at Los Alamos who agreed shouldn't sign it." Yet Teller chose not to sign after Oppenheimer counseled instead that he place his faith in the leaders of the nation.[23]

Curiously, instead of simply notifying Szilard of Oppenheimer's command, Teller fashioned his own reasoning in his response to Szilard. "The accident that we worked out this dreadful thing should not give us the responsibility of having a voice in how it is to be used," he wrote. "This responsibility must in the end be shifted to the people as a whole and that can be done only by making the facts known." Teller constructed a new vision of scientists somewhere between passive bystanders and political activists. "That was our job as scientists," he explained later, "a point that became clearer when I became aware of the great progress the Soviet Union had made on a nuclear explosive. The responsibility of scientists is to describe and demonstrate what is possible, to disseminate that knowledge as fully as possible, and, with everyone else in our democracy, to share the decisions that are necessarily connected with knowledge." Interestingly, Teller did not see himself as simply coming to a different conclusion about the implications of atomic energy on society.

Time and again Teller would argue that, in contrast to Pauling's "morality of science," scientists' "special responsibility" extended only as far as informing the public and those in power of the technical and scientific possibilities of nuclear weapons. Voters and government officials would decide how to act on these possibilities.[24]

Predictably, Teller framed these thoughts as a contrast to Oppenheimer's. He had felt betrayed when he learned that Oppenheimer had been an adviser on the wartime committee to examine the use of the bomb, especially because Oppenheimer had told him that scientists should leave the decision making to men like Harry Truman, Henry Stimson, and General George Marshall. "When Oppenheimer had advised me that, as scientists, 'we' should not participate in the decision making," he wrote, "he had already acted contrary to his advice. The result was that I became convinced that, as scientists, we have a clear responsibility to participate in decisions by making new knowledge and new possibilities available for discussion." Teller repeated his thinking in a 1960 letter to a Fordham University official about a proposed talk, "The Role of a Scientist." He explained, "I frequently have been faced with the argument that a scientist is responsible for the way in which the result of his work is used. I disagree with this. I do not believe that the scientist has such a responsibility. However, I do believe that the scientist has many other responsibilities," namely, seeing that new facts and discoveries become public knowledge.[25]

These carefully chosen words sound straightforward, but they tellingly echo the Cold War redefinition of science, framing the discipline as neutral, emotionless, and apolitical. Teller would use such words (or some variation of them) again and again during the Cold War to obscure his great influence. Indeed, Teller spent much of the Cold War trying to shape policy and dictate the end uses of science by dreaming up new weapons systems, imagining ways that the Soviets might attack, proffering reasons not to trust the Soviets, and enumerating the flaws of countless arms control proposals. Teller's career reflects a larger problem for science during the Cold War—that there was essentially no such thing as objective, neutral knowledge, no such thing as ordinary information about nuclear weapons that could be simply passed on to the public, since both sides in the nuclear debate used science to support their point of view.

Teller's stance was, essentially, pronuclear. To be sure, some Manhattan Project physicists expressed a sense of responsibility—often bordering on guilt—for Hiroshima. Robert Wilson recounted that "the news of the tremendous suffering and damage and loss of lives . . . was an epiphany that has changed my life ever since," while Szilard embarked on a restless crusade for world peace. But one Oppenheimer biographer rightly points out that "the idea that the Manhattan Project's scientists were collectively wracked with guilt over Hiroshima and Nagasaki is a misconception." Teller sought to appeal to those scientists who saw Los Alamos as a patriotic accomplishment by ignoring the bomb's negative image and arguing that scientists should let the proper authorities decide on the end results of scientific knowledge. Teller naturally left it unsaid that this abdication of responsibility would undoubtedly result in military applications of science. At the Oppenheimer hearing, the AEC had demanded that scientists devote themselves to the strongest military capabilities of the United States; the national interest was defined in explicitly military terms, and the state had made it clear how it would use the knowledge its scientists produced. To ignore the end result may have sounded like objectivity, but it was in reality the tacit acceptance of the militarization of science, especially because Teller knew exactly what the state would do with scientific knowledge.[26]

As a scientist Teller counted on and believed in the image of science as truth, just as Pauling did. Because Pauling and other scientists had cultivated an image of thoughtful, responsible, scientific leadership, Teller had to negate his rivals' political efforts while still retaining the same scientific credibility. But as a vocal and politically active scientist, Teller often faced accusations of having violated his own claim to scientific objectivity. In response, Teller formulated a philosophy that justified his actions and revealed his vision in a letter to an author who had recently interviewed him. Scientists had the right to express political opinions, he explained, but should not support these opinions with "scientific authority," nor should they "pose as the high priests and augurs on whom society must depend if wise decisions are to be reached."[27] In stating this philosophy, Teller ostensibly set himself apart from scientists like Szilard and Pauling, who believed their scientific expertise explicitly gave them the authority and responsibility to address social problems.

Although Teller's vision sounded quite neutral, it was anything but, as he constantly relied on his scientific expertise to give credence to his political arguments. Teller spent little time on work—scientific or otherwise—not explicitly connected to national defense. A letter from the physicist Freeman Dyson to his parents, written after a 1958 visit to Livermore, gives a glimpse of scientific work at the lab. In the days leading up to a nuclear test moratorium, "Livermore was wildly exciting." The scientists there "were throwing together everything they possibly could to give it a try before the guillotine came down. Everyone was desperate and also exhilarated." Teller, according to Dyson, was "in very good spirits" as he worked on theoretical ways of "cheating the test-ban," which would discredit the verification measures being suggested at Geneva. In crafting an image of scientists divorced from responsibility for the applications of their knowledge, Teller simply wished to distance himself from the scientists associated with disarmament and arms control. In 1957 Szilard attempted to get his friend Teller involved in the first Pugwash conference, but Teller turned him down. "I am not confident that scientists are in any better position than other people to make reasonable recommendations about questions like the stability of the world," he wrote Szilard.[28]

Teller admitted on several occasions that he did engage in politicking, but only because he maintained truly objective scientific views. In a letter to Ferenc Nagy, Teller told the former Hungarian prime minister that his opponents' claims that he mixed science with politics did not disturb him. "People will pay close attention to what I say," he explained, "only as long as my statements are connected in some way with my scientific and technical knowledge. I am afraid that if I deviated from this course in the near future I would lose what little effectiveness I have." Any influence he had within government circles "is almost entirely due to the fact that they respect my scientific objectivity." This was false modesty, of course; Teller had found the perfect audience that supported his nuclear mission. But like Pauling, Teller claimed the mantle of scientific objectivity and attempted to apply it to his solutions of the dilemmas of the nuclear age. Objectivity, Teller argued, was the norm for a true scientist. "The majority of the scientists are indifferent to politics," Teller later wrote to Nagy. "Of the minority which are engaged in politics, practically all are dedicated to a line of appeasement."[29] Such a stance implied that a politically active scientist was a seditious scientist, and conflating objectivity with being apolitical echoed the AEC redefinition of science.

For Szilard, individuals and nation-states needed to soberly confront the dangers of nuclear war. For Pauling, scientists needed to lead the way to a peaceful, humanistic society. And for Teller, science needed to protect U.S. society from the communist threat. Teller's actions reflected the mind-set not of a man calmly in control of policy but of a man constantly striving to steer policy in the direction of his interests. The state continued to rely on scientists to improve and expand the nuclear arsenal, but despite the new rigidity enforced by the Oppenheimer hearing, the H-bomb had created a whole new awareness of the nuclear threat among scientists and grassroots activists.[30] Teller thus constantly worried about opposition from politicians, scientists, and the public, waging a scientific and political campaign in order to maintain his privileged space in the state. Like McCarthy and other partisans of the era, Teller divided the world in two: on the one side stood the patriotic advocates of a strong nuclear defense, and on the other side stood those who opposed weapons development. Though political arguments dictated his activism, Teller attracted a broad audience because of his scientific credibility—a science that supported nuclear deterrence, as the redefinition of science demanded.

Teller's Scientific Arguments

Most antinuclear activism in the 1950s and early 1960s centered on the harmful effects of nuclear fallout released into the air during nuclear weapons tests and eventually coalesced around support for a nuclear test ban, even becoming a significant issue during the 1956 presidential election. Ever vigilant against criticism of nuclear weapons, Teller and his fellow physicist Albert Latter wrote and published *Our Nuclear Future* in 1958 in order to counter the "fallout propaganda" that was making Teller "more and more unhappy."[31]

On a public level, Teller and his rivals differed over the role of expertise, the interpretation of complex scientific data, and the danger of fallout. In 1958, for example, Teller engaged in a lengthy argument with one scientist over whether 0.0003 roentgens of fallout was a "negligible" amount.[32] In his writings, talks, and correspondence, Teller reassured the public that fallout was almost entirely safe and that nuclear tests would benefit humanity in two ways. First, testing would protect innocents by helping develop a clean, fallout-free bomb, and, second, testing would enhance the nuclear weapons that protected the United States from communism. Teller offered two further claims that negated the need for test ban: that civil defense worked and that the science supporting a test ban was unsound.[33] Facing the public's fears of fallout, Teller calmly answered them by swearing on his own scientific credibility that nuclear fallout caused no more harm than a common chest X-ray.[34]

To promote the idea that fallout was safe, Teller wrote to a Pentagon official. He described Pauling's views as "distorted" and contradicted an article from the *Washington Post* suggesting that fallout might result in as many as one million leukemia victims. This estimate Teller dismissed as "a pure guess," adding that while "there are some mutations induced by low-level radiation . . . the estimates given are unreliable." Teller may have been on relatively safe ground when he noted that not all mutations are harmful (though most are). But in a misleading overstatement, he suggested that fallout might actually help the human race evolve: "The implied assumption that all mutations are harmful is incorrect. Without mutations adaptability and evolution would be impossible." Teller advised the Pentagon to concentrate on three other facts: that radiation from fallout was "considerably less" than other sources of radiation, that "different types of radiation have entirely similar effects," and that "many avoidable sources of radiation, such as high altitude radioactivity, wrist watches, etc., are not being considered by people like . . . Pauling and that therefore their bias against nuclear explosions rather than radiation is obvious."[35]

In 1960 Teller gave his correspondent Henry Kissinger a quick lesson on fallout. He described C14's radiation as "so weak that its biological effects need not be taken at all seriously," as it would cause only an "infinitesimal" increase in the mutation rate. In yet another variation on the safe-fallout theme, Teller told the Senate Committee on Foreign Relations (CFR) that because the city of Denver was situated at a high altitude and consequently had a thinner atmospheric shield against the sun, "people in Denver are in greater danger" of exposure to radiation than those exposed to fallout from nuclear tests.[36]

During the test ban debate of the 1950s, Teller proposed to many people (including AEC chairman Lewis Strauss) that instead of a test ban or moratorium, the United States should restrict only the amount of radioactivity released into the atmosphere. A limit on released radiation would allow work to proceed on so-called clean bombs—thermonuclear weapons of heightened efficiency that would release little or no radioactive fallout. With typical optimism, Teller counterintuitively claimed that the problem of fallout could be solved by more testing and new weapons. Clearly, Teller also had other interests at stake. "The main problem which we have to put before the public," he told Strauss, "is the local fallout because this is the only worry and the only real worry, and because it is closely connected with Plowshare."[37] A comprehensive test ban (CTB) would ruin Teller's plan for a nuclear excavation business, whereas a ban that limited the amount of radiation released would keep the program alive. And if Plowshare lived, the development of nuclear weapons could continue.[38]

Such weapons would help protect innocent civilians, Teller claimed, whether they were used in testing or in war. In a letter to Stuart Symington (D-MO), Teller gave his pitch for clean weapons to the influential senator who had been the first secretary of the air force. "In a limited war," Teller wrote, "radioactivity from a dirty bomb is likely to be carried over countries which are not participating in the conflict. There would be every moral reason and considerable political reason to assure the neutral countries that we at any rate are not hurting them." While testing produced "negligible" amounts of radioactivity, numerous weapons used in war could create a hazardous amount of fallout. Teller therefore wanted to "limit the harmful effects of nuclear weapons to the enemy's fighting forces. I feel most unhappy about hurting anyone who is not directly participating in the conflict." Because a clean bomb had not been developed yet, of course, the AEC needed to continue further testing—so to ban testing would actually be immoral.[39]

Teller explained the morality of testing in a meeting with President Eisenhower. After the meeting a National Security Council staffer wrote that Teller's argument "reopens the issue of nuclear testing, in my opinion, from both a technical and moral point of view." Refusing to make clean nuclear weapons when esteemed scientists believed they could be built would be a "crime against humanity." If the United States stopped work on a clean bomb but the Soviets did not, "we may face a situation in the future in which world opinion would inhibit us from using our . . . weapons, while the Soviet Union would not be restrained from using their . . . weapons."[40] Yet while Teller argued that "clean bombs must be developed to save the innocent bystander," he believed that nuclear weapons primarily served as deterrents: "Without atomic weapons there would not be any means by which to stop Russian aggression."[41]

As yet another reason to oppose a test ban, Teller offered the concept of civil defense. Teller contacted Senator Henry Jackson in 1956 with what he described as "another maverick idea." He argued that civil defense could work, and "we can look into the future with a considerable amount of optimism." He assured the senator that "it is possible to construct deep shelters, readily available to all the endangered part of our population for a fraction of the cost of our present yearly defense budget," able to "stand up under anything except a direct hit by an H-bomb." Teller optimistically added that "the number of casualties would, of course, be great; but the nation as a whole could survive the attack."[42]

Finally, Teller frequently challenged the science behind detection and verification in order to damage the test ban under discussion in the Eisenhower administration. During his second term, Eisenhower desired a test ban but refused to consider proposals not enforced by completely reliable verification systems. Teller exploited Eisenhower's need for absolute certainty and easily sabotaged test ban proposals by bringing their verification measures into question. He scoffed at, for example, pro–test ban scientists who "are so confident about the soundness of their seismological judgment and about the effectiveness of our proposed network that they seem to expect to detect whenever a fly lands on the Ural Mountains."[43]

Confronting the Appeasers

Despite Teller's array of scientific arguments, politics clearly defined the scientific divide over nuclear weapons, as he spent much more time criticizing his opponents' politics than their science. Teller saw nuclear politics in personal terms and simplistically reduced the opposing sides to patriots and appeasers. This split fell along the same lines that dominated the national political discourse and fierce arguments over foreign policy during the 1950s, including Alger Hiss and the "fall" of China.

While Teller was not the only scientist with a divisive view of science's role in society, he more than anyone else encouraged the scientific divide that defined nuclear policy debates during the 1950s and 1960s. His rhetoric in personal correspondence reflects his divisiveness; he became especially fond of the right-wing tactic of branding his political opponents as appeasers, a phrase loaded with connotations of weakness, femininity, and naïveté. He stated in 1958 that test ban talks in Geneva "remind me of the procedures of Munich in 1938" and that the country was "giving in." A letter to Senator Clinton Anderson (D-NM) in 1960 described arms control talks as "a trend which may lead to an agreement similar to that of Munich in 1938. As Munich has led to World War II, so a new surrender may lead to a third world war."[44]

In 1958 Soviet premier Nikita Khrushchev challenged President Eisenhower to begin a nuclear testing moratorium. Although fearful that the Soviets would cheat a moratorium, Eisenhower also felt that a testing pause could serve as a sort of practice test ban, allowing the President's Science Advisory Committee and other officials time to work on verification measures to enforce a formal test ban. During the testing pause, Teller struggled to stave off a permanent test ban. Writing to Los Alamos director Norris Bradbury "with the greatest of disappointment" after learning of the moratorium agreement, Teller lamented, "You know how greatly I am worried about the consequences of the recent policy decisions and I am anxious to do everything to put our developments in the strongest possible position because I am afraid even that will not be strong enough."[45] The United States began its moratorium at the end of October, and the Soviet Union followed suit just a few days later; these test pauses continued into the Kennedy administration until the Soviets ended theirs in September 1961.

As the director of the Livermore lab between the late spring of 1958 and June 1960, Teller articulated a lasting and influential pronuclear standpoint that embraced deterrence for the present and development of new nuclear weapons for the future, claiming that nuclear weapons not only kept the peace but also promoted essential U.S. values. He wrote to the new AEC chairman John McCone as the moratorium continued: "You know that I am deeply worried about the issue of the test moratorium. The reason for my worry is the fate of our Nation and the fate of the Free World." Months later, Teller wrote to McCone again: "If weapons work is discontinued in Livermore many of the best people in the Laboratory will leave," as they would no longer be able to fulfill their "unique mission." Because the culture of Livermore was built around nuclear tests, a prohibition on these essential exercises meant that new weapons scientists would not be properly trained.[46]

Most often, however, instead of casting his own efforts in a positive light, Teller preferred to attack his opponents—in particular Pauling, the scientist most associated with a test ban. Teller opposed Pauling on a scientific level by trying to counter Pauling's conclusions with conclusions of his own, rebutting rational argument with rational argument. The embodiment of this approach came during their 1958 debate that aired on the San Francisco Bay Area's PBS affiliate, KQED. For years after, Teller considered himself the victor and sent a transcript of the program to people who wrote to him and implored others to seek it out when he ran out of copies.[47]

Teller, who had more of a sense of humor than Pauling, recognized a shared iconoclasm between the two. While hiking in 1960, Pauling had slipped off a cliff that overlooked the Pacific Ocean and spent a terrifying night with nothing but his grasp of a tree branch preventing his fall. Upon Pauling's rescue, Teller dashed off a brief letter to the chemist. "Dear Linus: I was happy to read in the paper that you are safe and that the Pacific Ocean has been now properly instructed in the theory of the chemical bond," Teller chuckled, referring to Pauling's scientific expertise. "The particular purpose of this letter is to welcome you to the most exclusive club of controversial scientists out on a limb."[48]

Such humor was most likely wasted on Pauling because of Teller's otherwise relentless and occasionally mean-spirited attacks against him. In most circumstances, Teller preferred to deploy the politics of anticommunism, painting Pauling as an appeaser rather than merely scientifically incorrect. To one correspondent, Teller described Pauling as "immoderate," adding that his logic "is the same that was taken at the time of Munich in 1938. His point of view will lead to either surrender or delay in our resistance." In another letter, Teller railed, "It seems that only Pauling and his friends talk and those of us who believe that the days of Munich are being repeated seem to shut up."[49] Pauling apparently did not even deserve the right to voice his views. When the American Chemical Society (ACS) invited Pauling to give a talk in 1963,

Teller appealed to the organization as a scientist: "It certainly is inappropriate to give Linus Pauling a free chance to make propaganda in the Chemical Society," he wrote. "[The] Chemical Society is not the right forum and I also find that Dr. Pauling has gone in his pronouncements beyond limits of really good taste." Although it is unclear whether Pauling gave the talk, he did threaten to resign from the ACS that year.[50]

When Teller was not tarring antinuclearism as a form of appeasement, he was busy making common cause with politicians who felt the same. Teller heartily endorsed the efforts of Senator Dodd, who had taken on SANE, Pugwash, and Pauling. Meeting Dodd, Teller told him, "was a great privilege." To his many contacts, Teller echoed the senator's line, sending a copy of a Dodd speech to a friend in an attempt to give it wider distribution; the speech had alleged that "the Communists have unquestionably succeeded in infiltrating this [test ban] movement . . . providing it with much of its guiding philosophy and stock of arguments." Teller deemed the speech "excellent" and wrote to yet another correspondent that communists supplied SANE with its "propaganda."[51] In June 1960 Teller arranged to have twenty-five thousand reprints of Dodd's speech distributed by a member of the Air Force Association.[52]

Though rooted in his childhood experiences, Teller's anticommunism effortlessly transformed into a badge of status among the conservatives of an era still in the shadow of McCarthyism. From behind his shield of anticommunism, Teller attacked prodisarmament scientists in his correspondence with influential people, waging the battle as a public relations campaign aimed at scientists and policymakers whom he saw as his constituency. For Teller, the redefinition of science had to be constantly policed. During the 1960 presidential campaign, Teller wrote to a scientist at Oak Ridge that Kennedy's proclivity for "appeasement" had convinced him "to vote for Nixon." That same year he warned another correspondent about "the enormous dangers to which our policy of appeasement exposes all of us." To Harry Truman he alleged: "Many people in this Country are doing their utmost to repeat all the mistakes of Munich." In 1964, even as U.S.-Soviet tensions began to ease, Teller complained to Herman Kahn: "I do worry somewhat about increased emphasis throughout the Country on moves that are politely termed 'détente' but could be impolitely called 'appeasement.'"[53]

Teller did display a less virulent side. As he had during the Oppenheimer hearing, Teller refused to accuse his opponents of disloyalty but rather charged them with the lesser crime of naïveté. He expressed as much in a letter to Congressman Francis Walter (D-PA) about "the dangers of Communism."

The main threat, as Teller saw it, was not internal subversion but rather the military strength of the Soviet Union. Teller recommended that "we should counteract our opponents within the United States with the greatest possible patience."[54]

A zeal for anticommunism often overcame his own advice, however, as he continued to attack his opponents with virulent denunciations. Among his opponents, the members of PSAC merited extra attention because these scientists conformed to the dictates of national security by accepting deterrence and making strictly technical recommendations, and they had the president's ear. Teller had reason to be nervous: Eisenhower had wanted PSAC in part as a counter to the hawkish recommendations of AEC scientists.

PSAC and the presidential science adviser James Killian provided the administration with advice on arms control, science policy, and, most important, the technical aspects of a nuclear test ban. Though Killian invited Teller at least once to participate on a PSAC panel, Teller instead sought to counter the influence of these advisers. Bethe, an early member of PSAC, suffered much of Teller's abuse. Although in Teller's words the two "used to be really good friends"—indeed, Bethe had signed a 1941 letter to Teller, "Love, H. Bethe"—by 1962 Bethe's "methodical and unimaginative approach and . . . his passion for working with the appeasers has caused confusion and is going to do still more damage." Teller confessed to Lewis Strauss that Bethe "has been misled by his wishes," and he hoped that "this mistaken advice will not lead us into a really terrible situation," an implication that PSAC scientists would render the United States impotent against the Soviet threat.[55]

Teller consciously waged this name-calling campaign in order to influence the national security priorities of the state. In the early 1960s, Teller began to link himself more and more to the fortunes of rising Republican politicians, especially New York governor Nelson Rockefeller. He initiated fairly regular correspondence with Rockefeller (and Rockefeller's associate Henry Kissinger) to advise the aspiring presidential candidate on science and national security issues. In 1962 Teller provided Kissinger with a list of scientists for Rockefeller to consult on "questions of scientific development." Predictably, Teller began his list with a scathing denunciation of Oppenheimer, despite the latter's removal from power eight years earlier. "Without any doubt he is by far the most clever on the side of the opposition," Teller complained, and is "the source of many of the[ir] opinions." Teller clearly reinforced the idea of an Oppenheimer divide in the scientific community, while also maintaining his conspiracy theory, first expressed during the H-bomb debate, that Oppenheimer controlled scientists' opinions.[56]

In the same letter, Bethe again suffered Teller's acid critique. "He is the scientific mainstay of the opposition," Teller told Kissinger. "He talks with an appearance of considerable authority. Actually he is relatively easily influenced and his opinions are none too stable." I. I. Rabi, a vocal scientist critic of Teller, was dismissed as "a complete opportunist." He described James Killian as "strongly biased" and scientifically uninformed. Revealing that he sought to influence scientists just as much as he claimed Oppenheimer did, Teller described Edward Purcell as one who "could be won over to our side." George Kistiakowsky, Killian's successor as Eisenhower's science adviser, was "a rather frivolous individual." Wolfgang Panofsky, a PSAC member, "is thoroughly convinced of the general line of Oppenheimer and Bethe" and "is one of the strongest among our opponents," while Freeman Dyson "is under the influence of our opponents but he has withstood this influence remarkably well." University of California at Los Angeles geophysicist David Griggs, who had testified against Oppenheimer and questioned the technical reliability of a test ban, "is the strongest proponent of the anti-Oppenheimer group. He is apt to make rather extreme statements which turn out to be correct in a great number of cases."[57]

Such claims carried weight because of Teller's access to individuals as well as classified information. To his credit, Teller consistently opposed secrecy restrictions all his life, but as long as the information remained secret, Teller used his proximity to it to his advantage. He made a show of telling people that he had knowledge of secret information but in the interests of national security could not reveal it. For example, when a member of the ACS suggested that Teller publicly debate Pauling, Teller pondered the challenge. But while he had "some relevant specialized knowledge in the field, I cannot use this knowledge in any complete manner because of security restrictions." In an interview given during his campaign against the 1963 Limited Test Ban Treaty, Teller claimed that his biggest reservations about the treaty were classified. Even when he could not reveal information, he allowed his access to such information to appear as a mark of credibility.[58]

To Hans Bethe, he argued: "I would be very happy if I could share your opinion that we are ahead of the Russians in tactical weapons. *From what I know* I have not the slightest reason to conclude that we are. I am most eager to hear from you why you are so optimistic on this score." To Eugene Rabinowitch, Teller complained that he could not properly rebut a paper by Jay Orear written in support of a test ban because of security restrictions. "I never know precisely what has been declassified and what has not," he explained. "It seems clear to me that I should not discuss methods of evasions openly." Teller then wrote to Orear to convince him that under a test ban, the Soviets could still hide tests and evade detection. "I have said repeatedly," he thundered, "that I cannot tell you how tests can be hidden without violating security regulations. I can assure you that I have studied the question carefully." He then encouraged Orear and Rabinowitch to obtain security clearances and participate in government research.[59]

Although Teller had been among the journal's founding members, he, like Pauling, split from the *Bulletin of the Atomic Scientists.* In the eyes of its editors, the *Bulletin* offered a diverse sounding board for opinions on the nuclear age. In Teller's view, however, the journal pushed a purely political line. When *Bulletin* editors changed the wording in an article of his, Teller took it as a personal affront, asking "whether the *Bulletin* is practicing these editorial changes with all its authors."[60]

In late 1959, after reading the *Bulletin*'s annual report, a "deeply disturbed" Teller wrote again in order to complain about the journal's mission statement, which described its "primary purpose" as "explor[ing] and expos[ing] the danger of nuclear war, the consequences of testing nuclear weapons, and other dangerous implications of science in human affairs; and to discuss methods to meet and control these dangers, and to approach a stable peace." The reference to the consequences of testing especially peeved Teller, who peppered Rabinowitch with seething questions. "Do you mean that nuclear testing is dangerous in itself because of fallout or some other reason?" he asked. "Or do you mean to say that nuclear testing is indirectly dangerous by causing international tension?" Teller suggested that testing created a positive geopolitical stability by strengthening the free world and accused the *Bulletin* of being biased. To Eugene Wigner in early 1960, Teller confided, "I am greatly worried about the Bulletin. They have a really harmful influence," adding that its editorial standards were "one-sided." Later that year, Teller bluntly told Rabinowitch that his *Bulletin* was "a partisan publication."[61]

A Well-Armed Lobby

Although he often refused the title, Teller's public image as the "father of the H-bomb" demonstrated to many his unwavering scientific and anticommunist credentials. Teller consequently had access to important government figures and did not shy away from approaching them. While both he and Pauling had attempted to sway many minds to their respective points of view, Teller cultivated connections to those already more inclined to support his pronuclear views. Because Teller was making a case for nuclear weapons, many government officials did not receive his arguments with the skepticism they generally reserved for antinuclear scientists' views. Since his anticommunist, pronuclear arguments fitted in nicely with the militaristic bent of U.S. policy during the 1950s, Teller had easy access to political officials; he also attempted to bend specific aspects of the rewards and education system to reflect his own views.

The armed forces warmly received Teller. At one point he wrote to the air force commander in chief about weapons development, endorsing "any system, with practically no regard to its expense." Missile defense especially excited Teller, who theorized about both a U.S. system and ways of overcoming a Soviet system. He expressed the "great danger" of the Russians developing an anti–intercontinental ballistic missile (ICBM) as a reason for U.S. antimissle research, discussed planning requirements for long-range nuclear weapons development with the navy, and served on the Science Advisory Board of the air force, which he described as "the only group of scientists who are giving effective and sane advice to our Government."[62]

Teller approached not only military officials but also lawmakers, concentrating his efforts on those who occupied important committee seats. In Congress he advised Senator Jackson, a member of the Preparedness Subcommittee and the Joint Committee on Atomic Energy and served on Jackson's NATO Committee on Scientific and Technical Personnel. During 1957 JCAE hearings, Jackson paraphrased Teller's "Denver" argument as a question when he interrogated Shields Warren, a scientific witness, who had argued that fallout produced harmful mutations. Jackson asked Warren, "Have there been any studies made of the situation as in Denver where people live at 5,000 feet as distinguished from people living at sea level? I was told that these mutations do not occur as anticipated." In response to the senator's 1958 request, Teller sent Jackson a memo on Plowshare and also denounced current test ban proposals, particularly the lack of a "rascal-proof plan for policing."[63]

In 1962 Jackson asked Teller to recommend scientists for service on the PSAC, and Teller again took the opportunity to castigate his opponents and promote his allies. John Wheeler, Teller wrote, "would be my first choice. I doubt that he would be strong enough to balance the present overwhelming opinion on the PSAC, but he would be a good influence." The Ford researcher Montgomery Johnson "is generally respected, but of course is not considered as a real first runner in those circles in which you have to be of the opinion of [Kennedy science adviser Jerome] Wiesner and Bethe in order to be taken seriously." And Griggs "has been one of the strongest opponents of

Oppenheimer in 1954. For all the above reasons he is thoroughly unpopular with the present members of PSAC. In fact, I suspect he is the only one who is more unpopular than I am." In Teller's mind, this made Griggs "the best candidate." Ardor did not always produce results for Teller; none of those he recommended became members of PSAC, not least because the committee naturally reflected the preferences of the president above all others.[64]

Teller continued to devote much of his time to lobbying Symington, a member of the Preparedness Subcommittee whom he once described as "our only hope" for stopping a test ban. These efforts sometimes involved straightforward scientific education, as in early February 1958, when Teller sent Symington a primer (evidently requested) on the scientific concept of parity as well as the "screw-nature of the neutrino." But even basic science could be essentially political, as when he wrote a long letter to Symington in March 1958 with a detailed explanation of the dangers and nondangers of radiation. At other times Teller attempted to influence Symington more directly. In April 1958 Teller asked Symington for a chance to testify in a closed session in order to bring out "the weak points" of Bethe's analysis of a test ban. Not all of Teller's attempts worked, of course. In 1959 he wrote to a correspondent, "I was just in Washington and did my best to see Senator Symington. This unfortunately did not work out. I am quite unhappy about it because the Geneva [test ban] discussions are in a critical state."[65]

Teller meanwhile grew closer to Republican figures, providing them with scientific information to ensure that they took a hard nuclear line. Teller praised the conservative William F. Buckley and his *National Review* for "defending my viewpoint." Teller also buttered up Rockefeller during his 1958 run for governor of New York. "If it would be technically feasible I would almost be tempted to move to New York to deliver a vote on the right side," he flattered the candidate. In early 1960 Teller and Kissinger discussed Rockefeller's decision not to run for president, with Teller lamenting, "I am most unhappy about it."[66]

As a Republican Teller hoped to impart to the party his sense of urgency on nuclear weapons. Critiquing a report of Kissinger's in 1957, Teller complained that the GOP was "underplaying . . . the fact that the Russians have caught up with us in military strength." He even warned Kissinger that "we are obviously losing the arms race," and the nation should prepare "our own people and our allies for the necessary use of nuclear weapons in limited engagements."[67] Teller did not offer evidence, leaving it unclear whether his assertions were based on his gut or actual data, but he spoke with the authority of a nuclear insider who could therefore be trusted.

Teller's views also had influence inside the AEC, and these views could sometimes make their way to the highest levels. At a meeting between Eisenhower and the NSC, Lewis Strauss drew on Teller's arguments when he critiqued an arms control proposal suggested by Harold Stassen, Eisenhower's disarmament adviser. Strauss vigorously denounced Stassen for lowering the proposed number of annual on-site inspections in the Soviet Union and as justification mentioned Teller's assessment that dozens of inspection stations would be required to monitor Soviet nuclear testing.[68]

While U.S. and Soviet diplomats and scientists debated a test ban in Geneva, Teller wrote a letter to Warren Johnson, chairman of the AEC's GAC, in order to poke holes in the ongoing negotiations. First, he argued, the conference did not consider explosions under one kiloton, which could not be distinguished from earthquakes. Second, the proposed detection method was "dubious." Third, no detection proposal was made for shots more than thirty miles up in the atmosphere. Finally, the experts had not even considered testing in "interplanetary space," which would make "evasion indeed quite possible." Such an experiment would involve sending a weapon and an observation "object" not less than ten million miles into space. Naturally, "the Russians could apply this method sooner than the other side."[69]

In a different letter, Teller offered to resign from the AEC's GAC because he felt his position as director of Livermore created a conflict of interest. (He later resigned his Livermore directorship as well, in order to "oppose without hindrance the test-ban treaty that was soon to be pursued by President John Kennedy," according to the historian Gregg Herken.) Teller nevertheless often coordinated his efforts with the AEC. When writing *Our Nuclear Future* with Albert Latter, Teller had a draft of the manuscript vetted by Libby, who advised the duo on fallout-related matters, including "rain scavenging," how fallout "almost exclusively" comes down in rain; the calcium-to-radioactive-strontium ratio; and the chemical similarity of active and nonactive strontium. Teller also continued to supply Strauss with ammunition to use against test ban advocates, advising the AEC chair that "a test moratorium would have disastrous consequences . . . [and] would be a powerful tool in the hands of the Russians to deprive us of this last advantage." Strauss used such information to weaken Eisenhower's confidence in test ban verification methods and undermine his trust in the Soviet Union.[70]

An ardent Republican by this time, Teller also reached out to Richard Nixon, supporting the former presidential candidate in his ill-fated 1962 run for California governor and pressing Kissinger to enlist Rockefeller's support for him as well.[71] After Nixon lost, Teller looked for an ascending star on which to hitch his ambitions. In 1963 Teller thanked Kissinger for setting up a meeting with Rockefeller, adding that he planned to do what he could to get Rockefeller nominated in 1964 as the Republican presidential candidate. Teller then ventured beyond science advice when he urged Kissinger to prod Rockefeller to attack the right wing of the Republican Party for its opposition to civil rights and for its isolationist foreign policy. The Kennedy administration, on the other hand, he denounced as "wrong in its policy of appeasement." During congressional debate over the 1963 test ban, Teller sent Kissinger some statements against the treaty to pass on to Rockefeller.[72]

A year later, Teller was invited to serve as science adviser for the Republican presidential candidate Barry Goldwater and found himself tempted to take the position despite his previous alliance with Rockefeller. But with Rockefeller and Nixon out of the running for the 1964 nomination, he signed on with Goldwater after Rockefeller gave him his blessing.[73] Teller's position amounted to naught after Lyndon Johnson easily trounced Goldwater in the general election, but had the nuclear enthusiast Goldwater won, Teller would likely have been a cabinet-level presidential science adviser.

Teller's status as an esteemed scientist also allowed him to participate in the distribution of awards representing the authority and imprimatur of the scientific and government establishments. In the early 1960s, still smarting from the snubs of his former colleagues, he tried to use his ability to influence awards to craft an image of himself as nobly atoning for his role in the Oppenheimer hearing. As a winner of the AEC's Enrico Fermi Award in 1962, Teller was invited to suggest nominees for the next recipient. In his memoirs, written nearly forty years later, he explained his choice. "I, like countless other scientists, was saddened by the onus that the security hearing had cast over Robert Oppenheimer," he wrote. An "unparalleled" leader, Teller's former friend deserved "government acknowledgement" of the great miracles he had performed at Los Alamos. Such recognition "would help to heal the schism that had developed in the scientific community." He nominated Oppenheimer for the 1963 Fermi Prize, which, to Teller's "delight," he received. "Unfortunately," Teller admitted, "the schism persisted without change." The idea that Teller hoped to reconcile with Oppenheimer and rehabilitate his own image has persisted in recent years.[74]

Evidence from Teller's personal papers, however, reveals a different story about the Fermi Prize. Teller actually nominated three men for the 1963 prize: Oppenheimer, Hyman Rickover (who oversaw development of the nuclear submarine), and Szilard. Teller wanted Szilard to win the award more than Oppenheimer, since he had been trying to get the prize for his close friend and fellow Hungarian since 1960. That year he wrote to Wigner, another

Hungarian friend, telling him, "It would be of special value to Szilard to receive the Fermi prize." Teller was unsure why, but he knew the desire was not for financial reasons or want of recognition. "Right now he seems to want it and he appears to have his heart set on this special thing. I may be wrong, but this is my impression," he explained. It is also possible that Teller felt indebted to Szilard, who had recently helped arrange for Teller's mother and sister to leave communist-controlled Hungary for California. Szilard, at any rate, was an eccentric and inspired arms control advocate, showing that Teller did not as a rule avoid or scorn those who held opposite political views. In addition, while Teller may have wished to appear as though he had influence over the distribution of prizes, the reward system was too dispersed for him to single-handedly control it. Ultimately, the liberal establishment figures McGeorge Bundy and Arthur Schlesinger Jr., along with AEC chairman Glenn Seaborg, exerted the most effort to see the prize awarded to Oppenheimer, as they and many other Democrats saw him as an unfairly martyred man.[75]

Teller took a direct approach in his efforts to shape the education of scientists and engineers by establishing a school of applied sciences affiliated with the University of California at Davis and located on the grounds of the Livermore lab. In 1964 Teller helped create the Hertz Fellowship for graduate students in the applied sciences. Money for the fellowship came from the Hertz Foundation and rewarded graduate students at MIT, the University of Chicago, Caltech, and the new Department of Applied Sciences at UC Davis-Livermore so that, in Teller's words, "we can stay in closer touch with them." At first, Teller personally interviewed each candidate and continued to conduct interviews for decades. He also helped select the recipients of the Hertz Prize, the first of which went in 1966 to the men who developed lasers. In 1977 the Hertz Building at Livermore was dedicated with an address by Teller's old friend Rockefeller, and that same year Greg Canavan won the second Hertz Prize for his "outstanding work on shielding missiles against laser radiation." After winning the prize, Canavan joined the Los Alamos lab. Teller himself pointed out that of twelve hundred Ph.D. scientists at Livermore, thirty-five of them were former Hertz Fellows. In his memoirs, however, Teller disputed the idea that Hertz Fellows only developed weapons; rather, he argued, they were bright scientists who worked in all sorts of settings. He was undoubtedly correct about this, but in 1960, when Teller began to set up the school for applied science at Livermore, he directly linked its mission to national security. "If this plan should turn out to be feasible," he wrote to AEC chairman McCone, "it will be an important contribution to the continued vigor of the Livermore Laboratory."[76]

Teller's constant vigilance against antinuclear scientists, as well as his role in fierce political debates, has led to some caricature; numerous authors, for example, have referred to Teller as "the real Dr. Strangelove." And while Teller brought much scorn on himself, he suffered in his own way. Throughout his youth, Teller had amused himself and his friends by writing whimsical poetry in his native Hungarian. In 1952, however, after painful—and highly personal—battles over the H-bomb and the Korean War, Teller lost the passion and never wrote poetry again. And like other scientists, Teller felt hostility from the general public because of his vocation. In a 1956 letter to a fellow scientist, Teller unburdened himself, expressing the need for a "reorientation in values" in the United States. While athletes earned tremendous admiration, the public seemed unaware of scientists' "considerable contributions," he wrote. Teller bemoaned that those responsible for creating the high standard of living in the United States were largely dismissed by the public as "at best . . . harmless eccentrics." Teller saw science as a lonely pursuit, perhaps rooted in his own self-image as a scientific pariah. "The scientist must either not give a hoot what people think of him," he concluded, "or he must conceal his interest and work in solitude; and naturally this atmosphere does little to encourage entrance into the field." The letter then took a personal turn for Teller. "My son, Paul, is thirteen," he wrote. "Some of my interest in science has rubbed off on him, and with me he is enthusiastic in his curiosity. But he conceals this curiosity from his teachers and his classmates." Teller asked, "If my son were a really good quarterback, would he be ashamed to let his classmates know about it? The result of all this is that we are flooding the market for quarterbacks while the field of science goes begging." In the Soviet Union, a nation that Teller otherwise feared, "a scientist is very nearly the most revered man in the community."[77] Teller wrote this letter before the National Defense Education Act flooded colleges with funding for math and science education. Instead, public esteem for scientists had given way to Red Scare suspicions, which helps explain Teller's need to remake science in a way that would harmonize with public opinion, validate his political beliefs, and create a more conservatively aligned scientific community.

While the state redefined science in light of the demands of national security and the Cold War, many scientists mobilized as well, as too much was at stake for them to sit back and be neutral. Pauling's grassroots campaign, which imagined a consensus identity for scientists, motivated many scientists and activists outside of the government. But his movement failed to achieve disarmament in part because scientists bristled over Pauling's attempt to define their professional identities. Teller's counterattack expressed the anticommunism of the time and fell more in line with the requirements of the national security state.

The choice of audience was crucial. While Pauling aimed at the vast constituency of some imagined scientific community, Teller aimed primarily at the political and military elites most inclined to favor his views. In 1958, after Pauling and Teller participated in their KQED debate, the air force distributed a film of the debate to each of its air divisions, along with a memo explaining the air force's reasons for showing the film. The memo acknowledged the air force's "great stake in Dr. Teller's position" but emphasized that hearing both sides would help "all audiences in making up their minds." In case anyone in the audience did not make up their mind in the right way, a set of "summing-up remarks," required to be read aloud, followed the film. While Pauling worried about potential mutilations of the unborn, the statement began, he ignored "the $5,000,000,000 we spend annually on war veterans for their mutilations because we did not keep up our military power in relation to enemy efforts, which drew us into wars." Then came an analogy that might have made Teller envious: "Not long ago people avoided eating a vegetable called the 'love apple' because it was said flatly to be poison. Today, we eat it all the time and know it as the common tomato. Somebody tested and proved the poison claim false." After having compared nuclear weapons to tomatoes, the remarks went on to say that "in this debate, we have one side pleading for cessation of testing, testing which could lead to possible discoveries of staggering import beneficial to the human race. This is paying homage to panic rather than progress, which is hardly scientific."[78] Teller's views resounded across a broad spectrum, from hawks in Congress to weapons labs and to the military—in short, the national security state itself.

The way Pauling used science proved, in one sense, self-defeating. While science gave Pauling credibility, it also left him open to scientific counterattacks, from the air force's cartoonish analogies to Teller's more sophisticated discussion of radiation effects. Many scientists, meanwhile, rejected Pauling's claims because as scientists, they did not see all the evidence their professional standards demanded. Politicians in Congress and officials in the State Department dismissed Pauling as a communist, while the armed forces naturally embraced Teller's message. Teller had the benefit of being an insider, with all the attendant credibility and connections. Because the militaristic, conservative members of the government already believed Teller, he could contradict Pauling with the imprimatur of sources based on access to all sorts of classified information. Pauling could answer Teller's claims, though he could not back up his responses with official information, getting his data from the *New York Times*.

As the conflict between Teller and Pauling shows, scientists, politicians, and the military have long sought to use "science" to support a specific point of view. Scientists were not just the victims of a Cold War consensus. Instead, they actively struggled over the meaning of science. In this conflict, Teller supported U.S. nuclear policy and cast doubt on those scientists who opposed it. During the debate over the landmark 1963 nuclear test ban treaty, this conflict between scientists erupted into public view and altered the course of Cold War geopolitics.

4

"Crucified on a Cross of Atoms"

Scientists and the Test Ban Treaty, 1957–1963

T HE SCIENTIFIC BATTLE OVER A TEST ban, started by Linus Pauling and joined by Edward Teller, culminated in the first major arms control treaty of the Cold War, but its significance extends beyond even this momentous shift. The 1963 Limited Test Ban Treaty catalyzed the transition from aggressive confrontation to détente between the superpowers, shifted the focus of the Cold War from Europe to the Third World, and—ironically—escalated the arms race.[1] Because the test ban hinged on scientific expertise, debate over the issue provided the first major test of the redefinition of science by the Atomic Energy Commission and the subsequent division of scientists into two camps: those who worked with the state for nuclear deterrence and those outside the state and opposed to it. Moral arguments for a test ban, such as Pauling's, remained beyond the boundaries of debate, while government science advisers argued over the test ban in terms of national security and scientific reliability. But technical arguments in favor of a test ban were countered by Teller's equally technical arguments against a test ban, showing the limits of basing antinuclear sentiment on a strict scientific and technical foundation.

The test ban debate took place in an era when the public and the government looked to scientists for truth and guidance, but scientists were not a single-minded entity. Those involved in debates over nuclear weapons were but one subset, a subset that was in turn diverse, made up of those in and out of government, for and against nuclear weapons for a variety of reasons. Conflicting ideas between these groups about the relationship between science and politics affected the ultimate shape of the test ban treaty, rendering it effective at stopping fallout but ineffective at stemming the arms race. Although restricted in their arguments, pro–test ban scientists in the United States achieved their goal of a test ban largely because of their technical expertise. This test ban, however, was not the comprehensive prohibition of nuclear tests that most scientists in favor of arms control and disarmament had hoped for. The LTBT that emerged after a grueling debate reflected scientists' efforts yet was also truly "limited" in every sense of the word.[2]

The differences between a comprehensive ban, which might have put a brake on the arms race, and the limited ban that actually emerged, which only moved the arms race underground, show how the technical debates in which scientists engaged directly resulted in the test ban's limitations. This mild version of success, then, came at a great price: the very nature of their influence had opened scientists up to challenge. Technical arguments for arms control were countered by other scientists, while opponents of arms control easily negated the transnational basis of the movement by questioning Soviet credibility. Furthermore, the debate exacerbated existing divisions in the scientific community and severely damaged scientists' status as authoritative and objective experts in society. Famous scientists split over the test ban issue and publicly confronted each other in congressional hearings, conflicts that reflected deep political divisions in the scientific community. Society relied heavily on scientists for objective truths, but government officials expected science to offer a consensus view on nuclear weapons rather than the continual argument, counterargument, and refinement that characterize the scientific discipline. Simply put, at the beginning of the test ban debate, the government turned to scientists for answers; by the end of the debate, the government (and the public, to a certain extent) had begun to look elsewhere for answers to the dilemmas of the nuclear age.

Pugwash's Path to Protest

While Pauling campaigned for a test ban from outside the government, using petitions, lawsuits, and public advocacy to push for the measure, the

Pugwash scientists took a less oppositional approach and tried to influence nuclear policy more subtly. These scientists, many of them unconcerned with the fallout threat, believed that a test ban would help slow the arms race and prevent a thermonuclear war. Their venture consisted of transnational activism that promised to use scientists' elite status to bring about disarmament.

While he was serving as the editor of the *Bulletin of the Atomic Scientists,* Eugene Rabinowitch also played a major role in Pugwash. During World War II, Rabinowitch had worked on the Manhattan Project at the University of Chicago's Metallurgical Laboratory, where, after the defeat of Germany, he began to reconsider the need for the atomic bomb. He consequently joined Leo Szilard and James Franck in arguing for a demonstration in lieu of military use of the atomic bombs on Japan. Rabinowitch penned most of the Franck Report intended for Secretary of War Henry Stimson, only to watch the report get "lost somewhere in the higher echelons in Washington." Despite this frustration, Szilard and Rabinowitch's work on the Franck Report helped launch the Atomic Scientists' Movement.[3]

The Atomic Scientists' Movement and antinuclear sentiment in general waned with the rise of the Cold War in the late 1940s. But amid the tumultuous waters of the Red Scare, Rabinowitch maintained a steady ship. After his work on the Franck Report, Rabinowitch devoted much of his professional life to mobilizing scientific opinion against nuclear weapons. Not content with merely editing the *Bulletin* and being "undoubtedly the most distinguished encyclopedic authority in Photosynthesis" research, Rabinowitch embarked in 1957 on the Pugwash venture.[4] With Joseph Rotblat and the financial support of left-leaning railroad magnate Cyrus Eaton, Rabinowitch arranged for the group's first meeting in Pugwash, Nova Scotia, bringing together scientists from ten countries, including the United States, Britain, Japan, and the Soviet Union. Rabinowitch thought scientists were ideally suited to confront the challenges of the future because "the detachment to which the study of science has accustomed one helps to avoid errors into which partisanship often leads the most astute political leaders and observers."[5] In tune with the redefinition of science, Rabinowitch characterized true science as divorced from political opinions.

At Pugwash conferences the assembled scientists discussed "the scientific and technical implications of atomic energy," paying special attention to "the political problems which are the background to international negotiations."[6] The relatively unstructured and informal private meetings attempted to create a cooperative atmosphere for the enlightening exchange of views from each side of the Iron Curtain. The scientists at Pugwash considered their first meeting in 1957 so successful that they initiated annual meetings and even took to describing their efforts as a "movement."[7] Pugwash participants hoped to encourage disarmament in three ways: by influencing governments, by forming a channel of communication between scientists, and by educating public opinion. Dialogue between East and West, Rabinowitch believed, could encourage trust and cooperation between the Cold War superpowers. Immediately, Pugwash participants engaged in discussions about adequate verification for a test ban. Nine of the first eleven Pugwash conferences, first held in the West and later in Warsaw Pact nations, dealt with aspects of a test ban in some measure.[8]

Pugwash helped revive scientists' role in geopolitics. Soviet scientist Lev Artsimovich, a Pugwash participant, declared, "Diplomacy is an antiquated vehicle. Our role is to remove obstacles from the path of this antique chariot."[9] While official U.S.-Soviet relations remained fraught with tension in the late 1950s over incidents in the Suez, Hungary, Berlin, and even outer space, the Pugwash conferences helped develop trust across the Iron Curtain, bypassing suspicious officials and connecting scientists who shared common understandings.

Although inspired by the moral urgency of the Russell-Einstein Manifesto, Pugwash scientists decided at the outset that their influence on disarmament would be technical—specifically by providing scientific analysis of inspection and verification systems enforcing a nuclear test ban treaty. This decision may have reflected an internalization of the lessons from the Oppenheimer hearing or perhaps a renewed belief in the inherent power of scientific authority. Whether politically shrewd or naive, the decision to emphasize technical information fitted within the bounds of political acceptability under the Cold War consensus and redefinition of science. As early as their second meeting in 1958, Pugwash scientists discussed technical aspects of inspection under a test ban, and the fourth conference in 1959 aimed to jump-start the stalled official test ban negotiations under way in Geneva.[10] Pugwash scientists felt comfortable working on a test ban because the Russell-Einstein Manifesto encouraged international agreements. "Any agreement between East and West is to the good in so far as it tends to diminish tension," Russell had written.[11] But the elusive test ban proved to be a fateful choice because, in order to come to fruition, any treaty would require Senate approval in the United States, opening the agreement up to political as well as scientific debate.

Science Advisers and the Test Ban

Pugwash activism began at almost the same moment as the creation of the President's Science Advisory Committee. Though fear of thermonuclear war spurred them, PSAC scientists hoped to take advantage of the Eisenhower administration's newfound sentiments in favor of scientists and a test ban and ultimately influence U.S. nuclear policy. At first, this seemed unlikely, as the Eisenhower administration's relationship with scientists had gotten off to a rocky start. Eisenhower's tacit approval of the Oppenheimer hearing had offended many scientists, especially given the president's close friendship with Lewis Strauss, the man who had colluded with the FBI to ensure Oppenheimer's humiliation. Later in his administration, Eisenhower would express a commitment to a nuclear test ban but retained Strauss as his primary atomic energy adviser.[12]

Judging by the distinct pronuclear slant of Eisenhower's first term, Strauss did seem an appropriate nuclear adviser. The New Look, Massive Retaliation, and Brinkmanship strategies all relied on the nuclear arsenal as the basis of U.S. military and diplomatic policy. As late as January 1956, Ambassador to the United Nations Henry Cabot Lodge and Secretary of State John Foster Dulles linked U.S. nuclear weapons to world peace, telling Eisenhower that "the greatest single factor in the world today for peace is our atomic superiority."[13]

International events and public opinion eventually convinced the Eisenhower administration of the wisdom of pursuing a test ban.[14] Although government officials doubted the dangers of fallout, many expressed hope that a test ban would lead to more concrete disarmament efforts. The menacing bleeps of *Sputnik* in 1957 initially spurred fears of Soviet ICBMs sporting thermonuclear warheads, but scientists, grassroots activists, and Eisenhower himself all hoped to turn this threat into an opportunity by increasing their efforts for a test ban. Scientists' status as the brain trust of nuclear knowledge meant that when nuclear weapons were involved, government officials still instinctively turned to them for advice. When Eisenhower reached out to scientists beyond those vetted by Strauss and the AEC, he found them surprisingly eager to join PSAC. As one PSAC member put it, "Eisenhower now had a group of scientists who had a loyalty only to him," while scientists saw PSAC as a way to influence policy. Hans Bethe, an early PSAC member, excitedly wrote to Rabinowitch at the *Bulletin*, "We now have a mechanism to get the ideas of scientists directly to the government."[15]

PSAC initially advised Eisenhower on space exploration and defense matters, and although the test ban debate increasingly intruded on his work,

Eisenhower's first science adviser, James Killian, remained reluctant to enter the disarmament field. But "inevitably," he wrote, PSAC was "drawn into the debate about nuclear tests and their detection." The Oppenheimer hearing had eliminated morality from the language of science advisers, but expertise and objectivity remained powerful tools on which scientists could rely, especially since the debate over a test ban hinged not on the moral implications of thermonuclear war but on the narrow technical aspects of nuclear test detection. Specifically, the enforcement of a comprehensive test ban relied on the ability to detect nuclear explosions hidden underground. Thus, at a 1958 NSC meeting, Killian was told that "the President expressed the hope that we could advance rapidly in our discovery of detection devices."[16] Meanwhile, the Soviet Union announced a unilateral test moratorium in March of that year. Eisenhower, emboldened by world opinion against testing as well as the counsel of PSAC but also eager to neutralize the Soviet propaganda advantage from their moratorium, subsequently announced that the United States would also begin a unilateral nuclear test suspension on October 31, 1958. The Soviet Union, claiming the right to catch up to Western advantages attained during their own moratorium, actually exploded a few nuclear weapons just before starting another moratorium on November 4.[17] With all nuclear testing finally paused, Eisenhower faced continuous pressure from the AEC and the Department of Defense (DOD) to resume tests, while Killian and PSAC raced to hammer out a viable detection system.

Killian and his successor, George Kistiakowsky, provided the respected pro–test ban views of scientists to counter test ban opponents in the AEC and DOD. As Bethe recalled, "Eisenhower had confidence in Killian and later in Kistiakowsky." The science advisory committee had the president's confidence, but advisers could not oppose nuclear weapons on the grounds of the harm the weapons might do to others; instead, they had to prove that arms control measures would not harm U.S. national security. The restriction to technical advice was often made explicit; during a meeting with Eisenhower, Killian "pointed out that this [test ban] is a controversial subject on which the observations of his group are limited to technical aspects only and must of course be balanced against other considerations." Eisenhower's science advisers had internalized the amoral stance mandated by the Oppenheimer hearing. At one NSC meeting, after Bethe reported on detection, Eisenhower questioned whether the Soviets could disguise tests as earthquakes. According to the memorandum of discussion, Bethe told him that "we really knew too little about this problem to provide the President with a clear and categorical answer." After Eisenhower twice insisted, Bethe offered the president a 90 percent certainty.[18] Bethe's reluctance to put forward a clear and unambiguous answer reflects the very nature of the scientific method, in which rigorous experimentation and careful analysis precede any conclusion. The president genuinely wanted a test ban, and his science advisers tried to provide him with one. But restricted to technical interpretations, Eisenhower's advisers could give him only the rough estimates of an ongoing scientific analysis, not moral boldness. Purely scientific advice thus provided no quick or easy answers to the dilemmas of the nuclear age.

Morality was not most scientists' main concern, at any rate. As U.S. science advisers limited themselves to technical arguments, Pugwash scientists attempted to use PSAC as a conduit to influence U.S. nuclear weapons policy. Thus, they too adopted technical arguments, despite the moral urgency of the Russell-Einstein Manifesto that had inspired their movement. Sources indicate that Pugwash had access to PSAC in the late 1950s, but the group's influence on policy appears only sporadically. Jerome Wiesner, a member of PSAC, went to a Pugwash meeting in 1958 and on his return immediately reported to PSAC and the president. Wiesner's Pugwash experience reaffirmed his belief—and helped him convince PSAC—that a test ban would not risk the nation's security. Wiesner tellingly wrote, "I thought my best arguments were technical, that no amount of Soviet testing would reduce the value of the American weapons." For the most part, however, Pugwash scientists had a hard time getting through to the administration. In late March 1960, Rabinowitch visited Kistiakowsky "with a hard sell of the Pugwash conferences," but Kistiakowsky told him, "I am not at all sure about the value of these conferences." Six weeks later, Wiesner also urged Kistiakowsky to support Pugwash, but "I reserved judgment," he noted. Nevertheless, the organization alerted its contacts within the U.S. administration to the genuine desire among Soviet scientists for a test ban, as well as the fact that the Soviet government was divided over the issue. Later in 1958, the U.S. Pugwash participant Victor Weisskopf wrote to Killian conveying information from the third Pugwash conference, including the Soviet delegation's assertion that they were "very much devoted to the cause of the atom bomb test stop" and that "there is a bitter fight within the USSR government between the test supporters and the test stoppers, and that the stoppers have a[t] present a slim lead which might break at any time."[19]

Nearing a Test Ban

While Pugwash scientists worked behind the scenes for arms control, official scientific delegations from East and West had met in Geneva in an attempt to reach agreement on the technical aspects of a test ban. The 1958 Conference of Experts gave scientists a specific negotiating task for the first time in "vital diplomatic negotiations," in the words of two scholars who studied the conference. The "international scientific congress" had been convened to examine four methods of test detection in order to determine the minimum threshold of a test ban. Dulles had selected U.S. delegates who represented a range of opinions on the wisdom of a test ban and instructed them to treat the conference as "a purely scientific technical job." But the balanced nature of Western scientists at the Conference of Experts only proves that scientists were divided over a test ban and that the Eisenhower administration hoped to placate its congressional critics on both sides of the aisle. Despite this mixing of science and politics, however, the Conference of Experts reported agreement on scientific findings related to a test ban.[20]

But the tentative nature of scientific conclusions was brought to the fore when, in January 1959, U.S. scientists returned to the negotiations in Geneva and admitted that new information indicated that underground tests would be harder to detect than previously realized. Data from the Hardtack nuclear test series had shown that nuclear tests in outer space and at high altitude could possibly evade detection and that underground tests would be difficult to distinguish from earthquakes. U.S. scientists concluded that they had underestimated their ability to distinguish between underground tests and earthquakes by a factor of ten. The Soviet delegation apparently felt betrayed by this reevaluation of test-detection data, even though the revision of original estimates happens frequently in science. Likewise, although U.S. scientists saw the need to be "as careful and as conservative as we could," according to the U.S. delegate James Fisk, Western scientists were baffled when Soviet scientists reached different conclusions about the Hardtack data. The attempt to maintain objective standards of science in such a politically charged atmosphere ensured that the results of the Geneva conference were, according to one account, "almost grotesque."[21]

As the U.S. and Soviet governments took tentative steps toward a test ban in Geneva, public pressure for the measure increased. Much of the international sentiment in favor of a test ban consisted of opposition to radioactive fallout mobilized by Pauling. Instead of concentrating on fallout, however, PSAC and Pugwash scientists followed three arguments for a comprehensive test ban: a test ban would maintain U.S. nuclear superiority, most tests could be detected, and the Soviets could be counted on to adhere to the treaty. None of these three arguments contained the moral sentiment implicit in the fallout issue, but prodisarmament scientists saw their claims and influence contested nevertheless. This challenge directly threatened a comprehensive test ban, which depended on the U.S. government's confidence in scientists' claims about detection reliability. Arms control opponents challenged the scientific basis of a test ban by using scientific evidence to rebut scientific arguments, mirroring the traditional manner in which unresolved scientific debates progress. Kistiakowsky recalled that "there was a continuous running battle" between PSAC and AEC scientists, and the DOD also opposed a test ban.[22]

Teller Mobilizes

Teller was by far the primary opponent of the test ban; Kistiakowsky dubbed him "the most dangerous scientist in the U.S."[23] Using his connections to influential figures, Teller provided scientific ammunition for test ban opponents and tirelessly waged his own war against the ban to protect the nuclear weapons establishment around which he had constructed his professional identity.

Teller naturally opposed a test ban on scientific grounds. Although he was not the only scientist opposed to a test ban, he was by far the most effective. He often dismissed fears of fallout by attempting to make increased radiation seem normal, such as when he declared that living in a brick house—a perfectly safe choice—exposed a person to more additional radiation than fallout from a nuclear test. Relying on his own scientific expertise, Teller drew from his extensive arsenal of tried-and-true pronuclear arguments, including his claim that fallout produces less radiation than living in an elevated city like Denver, "where cosmic radiation has a greater intensity." Never one to shy away from bold statements, Teller even suggested that radiation might hold some benefits. "A living being is a most complex thing," he wrote. "Damage to a small fraction of the cells might be beneficial to the whole organism. Some experiments on mice seem to show that exposure to a little radiation increases the life expectancy of the animals." Most effectively, he played on fears of the Soviets by telling Congress about methods the Soviets might use to cheat a test ban. "We already see strong possibilities, effective possibilities of hiding tests," he menacingly claimed. In March 1960 Kistiakowsky spoke of the United States and Soviet Union when he told PSAC that the "real stumbling block is the mutual distrust of the two sides," a disconnect he attributed to Teller.[24] Teller's prophecies of Soviet evasions undermined the trust between U.S. and Soviet scientists that had been built up by Pugwash conferences and drove the superpowers further apart, all in the name of additional testing, anticommunism, and an increased arms race.

Teller's scientific evidence told him that the Soviets could merely move testing underground, where it would be nearly impossible for U.S. seismologists to distinguish low-yield nuclear explosions from earthquakes. But he also made it his mission to devise more theoretical ways in which the Soviets could evade a test ban. By far his biggest success was with the decoupling theory that hypothesized that the Soviets could muffle explosions in extremely large, deep holes (called Latter Holes, after Teller's colleague Albert Latter, who conceived of them). Teller delighted in thwarting his opponents; when Latter won the AEC's Ernest O. Lawrence Award in 1964 (which came with a gold medal and a cash prize), Teller wrote to congratulate him and chuckled, "Would it be proper to say that you found a pound of gold in the 'big hole'?"[25] Tactics like this frustrated proponents of a test ban on both sides of the Iron Curtain. Soviet Pugwash scientist J. Riznechenko later regretted that the "U.S. delegation dragged in the big hole to disrupt the [Geneva] conference."[26] At a meeting in England, Killian recalled, "Latter said to me in casual conversation that whatever advances might be made in detection technology, the West Coast group led by Teller would find a technical way to circumvent or discredit them."[27]

The claims Teller made were not disingenuous, but they were quite cynical. His arguments ranged from the plausible to the exaggerated, all in the hopes of deflating his rivals' support for a test ban and making concrete progress on arms control more difficult to achieve. His machinations increased pressure against a comprehensive test ban from Congress and the Pentagon and left the technical basis of test detection vulnerable to a scientific onslaught. Furthermore, the inability of the United States to be consistent about verification confused the Soviet Union.[28] Eisenhower, predisposed not to trust the Soviets, vacillated as well. In a June 1957 meeting with Eisenhower, Teller impressed the president with visions of clean nuclear weapons that would produce no fallout. Eisenhower, according to the meeting memorandum, responded that no one could oppose clean nuclear weapons. He worried, however, about "an extremely difficult world opinion situation," and he did not want the United States to be "crucified on a cross of atoms." Teller responded by bringing the scientific reliability of verification into question and voiced concern that the Soviets might secretly continue testing and developing bombs, while the United States, scrupulously honest, stopped testing and was defended only with weapons that world opinion would not allow it to use.[29]

Eisenhower eventually began to resist Teller and the AEC to some extent. "Because I did have in Dr. [Ernest] Lawrence [and] Dr. Teller," Eisenhower wrote to Strauss, "I rather think it might be a good idea for me to pick two or three scientists who represent a contrary view and ask them in for a visit." Strauss advised the president to resist the urge.[30] Nevertheless, Eisenhower sought out his physicist friend and test ban advocate I. I. Rabi, who gave him advice that conflicted completely with Teller's. In an October 1957 diary entry, Eisenhower wrote that Rabi had told him that with about six inspection posts in the Soviet Union, "any significant explosion could be detected." His entry further revealed that he had begun to grasp the notion that scientists could dislike each other. "Incidentally," he wrote, "I learned that some of the mutual antagonisms among the scientists are so bitter as to make their working together almost an impossibility. I was told that Dr. Rabi and some of his group are so antagonistic to Drs. Lawrence and Teller that communication between them is practically nil."[31] Eisenhower later told Killian straightforwardly that "he had never been too much impressed, or completely convinced by the views expressed by Drs. Teller [and] Lawrence . . . that we must continue testing of nuclear weapons."[32]

Teller did not stand alone in his campaign against the test ban. Connections to Strauss and the Joint Chiefs of Staff (JCS) facilitated much of his influence. At an April 1957 meeting between the State Department, the AEC, and Harold Stassen's disarmament office, Strauss took it on himself to correct what he saw as mistaken assumptions about the feasibility and desirability of a test moratorium. While Stassen believed that a moratorium would entail only "limited risk," Strauss saw "substantial penalties in acceptance of such a policy." He predicted that a moratorium would cost the U.S. weapons program a year of development, a setback made all the more costly because, he assured Stassen, weapons scientists were "now in a position to make a family of weapons which would not produce as much strontium 90." Such an advance, he added, would be impossible "without a vigorous testing program."[33]

The opinions of the JCS also carried substantial weight in test ban discussions. At an NSC meeting in January 1958, the JCS and Strauss presented a united front against Stassen's latest disarmament proposals. His plan recommended a detection regime consisting of between eight and twelve inspection stations in the Soviet Union, along with reciprocal inspection stations in North America. The JCS declared their "opposition" to the Stassen plan, after which Strauss added that a test cessation "would have rather severe repercussions" on weapons programs, including "clean" nuclear weapons. Even without Teller, Strauss and the Joint Chiefs could provide vocal ammunition against a test ban, though they relied heavily on Teller's scientific expertise to support their opposition.[34]

John McCone's replacement of Strauss as AEC chair did not interrupt the commission's line of thinking regarding a test ban. At a January 1959 meeting between State, science advisers, and the DOD, McCone argued that the reliability of seismic science and detection methods "necessitates more tests" rather than a test ban. A DOD representative supported McCone's claim, stating that the Pentagon "would not support an agreement which would outlaw tests beyond the reach of detection." Instead, McCone suggested, a restriction solely of atmospheric testing would satisfy "world public opinion" concerned about fallout. Ten months later, Deputy Secretary of Defense Thomas Gates complained that with the test moratorium, "the Soviet Union is getting just what it wants for nothing." Yet another Pentagon official added that the DOD's "historic position" had been "to oppose suspension of testing." Although the DOD supported the administration's policy on a test ban, it did "not want to be committed to suspend tests." McCone emphasized that the AEC held the same position.[35]

As the Geneva talks went on, Teller continued to do what he could to upset them, acting as "a formidable one-man anti-PSAC," in the words of one historian.[36] At a meeting with the State Department and Killian's office, Teller pointed out many "loopholes," including that explosions below one kiloton would be indistinguishable from earthquakes and that no method had been discussed for detecting nuclear tests at extremely high altitudes or in outer space. Meanwhile, Strauss continued to play on Eisenhower's suspicions of the Soviets, telling him to "refus[e] to be victimized by Russian duplicity."[37]

Such pressure worked; Eisenhower could not bring himself to ignore Teller's and Strauss's claims.[38] Even more damaging to the test ban, Eisenhower felt obligated to share these doubts with the Soviets. Wiesner wrote that Teller's visions of clean bombs convinced Eisenhower in 1960 to tell the Soviets that the United States could end the test moratorium at any time. Pugwash scientists attempted to negate Teller's efforts at their conferences. In selecting scientists to invite, Bernard Feld of U.S. Pugwash suggested one scientist for his "unofficial, Anti-Teller, more 'radical' technical view."[39] Nevertheless, Teller's doubts had turned several of Eisenhower's advisers against a test ban, and Eisenhower himself worried about trusting the Soviets. Without the scientific unanimity of his experts, Eisenhower did not push as hard as he could have for a test ban. Feld later lamented that the test ban "opposition . . . was more effective than the test ban proponents."[40]

At the end of Eisenhower's second term, the superpowers had come tantalizingly close to a test ban treaty, albeit an atmospheric one. What had begun as tentative talks had resulted in scientific conferences, moratoriums, and, by 1960, an agreement in principle to ban all tests in the atmosphere as well as those belowground that registered more than 4.75 on the Richter scale. This proposed threshold ban actually sidestepped the technical disagreements over inspection and detection that confounded a comprehensive ban. Most government scientists and officials in the United States, Britain, and the Soviet Union nevertheless endorsed the threshold ban, until the U-2 affair in May 1960 caused Khrushchev to withdraw from test ban talks.[41] His test ban aspirations thwarted by Teller at home and fateful events abroad, the president turned bitter. Frustration bubbled over in his famous farewell address, when, after warning about the military-industrial complex, Eisenhower said, "Yet, in holding scientific research and discovery in respect, as we should, we must also be alert to the equal and opposite danger that public policy could itself become the captive of a scientific-technological elite." With the U.S. scientific community divided over a test ban, the president's ambiguous words accurately reflected the state of U.S. science.[42]

The day after the address, Kistiakowsky approached Eisenhower at a farewell party and asked him to elaborate on his comments. In a memo sent to PSAC members, Kistiakowsky recounted that the president had expressed "concern and forebodings" over the state of U.S. science. Especially worrisome to Eisenhower were colleges and universities, institutions that while supposedly dedicated to "free intellectual inquiry . . . were influencing research people on their staff to abandon basic science for the sake of higher monetary rewards." Eisenhower also expressed a fear that scientists were "being hoarded by the military-industrial combine." Kistiakowsky noted in his memo that Eisenhower's sentiments resembled those of many PSAC members. Years later, the PSAC scientist Herbert York bluntly asked Eisenhower which scientists he had in mind when he had issued this warning. Eisenhower, in York's words, "answered without hesitation: . . . 'Teller.'"[43]

Scientists and the Test Ban Treaty

The debate over a nuclear test ban did not cease with the Eisenhower administration. In September 1961 the Soviet Union ended its nuclear test moratorium with a series of high-yield nuclear explosions; the United States responded two weeks later by ending its moratorium. The resumption of tests, however, served to only reanimate the test ban debate for the Kennedy administration. The clash of scientists that had occurred under Eisenhower had failed to quell the greater public's belief that science would provide needed truths about nuclear weapons. Ruth Adams, the managing editor of the *Bulletin of the Atomic Scientists,* wrote to Feld, saying that after the Soviet Union resumed nuclear tests, "our mail has tripled from readers seeking advice and what they call nonpartisan facts." Sharing the era's faith in science, Kennedy relied, as had Eisenhower, on science advisers for test ban expertise. Even before his inauguration, Kennedy sent his deputy national security adviser, Walt Rostow, along with Wiesner, his choice for science adviser, to Moscow for a Pugwash meeting in late 1960. An early Pugwash veteran, Wiesner allowed the organization to play a more prominent role in U.S. disarmament policy and encouraged the Kennedy administration to sign a test ban treaty in August 1963. But the test ban opposition again mobilized and used science to turn the test ban from what many considered a first step toward disarmament into what one antinuclear scientist described as an "arms control disaster."[44]

Much like Kistiakowsky had for Eisenhower, Wiesner acted as Kennedy's counter to the anti–test ban hawks and reflected a hearty embrace of science by the White House. According to one Kennedy administration official, Wiesner "was a driving force to do something about the test ban negotiations."[45] With a friend of Pugwash as the president's science adviser, the organization's views could finally be brought to bear directly on U.S. policy. After attending the 1960 Moscow Pugwash meeting, Rostow and Wiesner reported directly to the State Department about Soviet willingness to work with Kennedy for a test ban. But with Wiesner's direct access to the White House, Pugwash's influence appears to have gone even further. Wiesner's informal contacts with the Soviets provided him a great deal of otherwise inaccessible information, as he explained in a 1987 letter: "I developed very good relationships and a good rapport with Soviet scientists [at Pugwash meetings]. . . . While working as science advisor to President Kennedy, these contacts were very important to me in my effort to achieve a nuclear test-ban."[46]

Kennedy and Wiesner also appeared to share a moral concern about nuclear weapons. One rainy day, as the two sat in the Oval Office, Kennedy asked Wiesner to explain how fallout returned to earth. "And I told him," said Wiesner, "that it was washed out of the clouds by the rain, that it would be brought to earth by rain, and he said, looking out the window, 'You mean, it's in the rain out there?'—and I said, 'Yes'; and he looked out the window, looked very sad, and didn't say a word for several minutes."[47]

Despite the very human concerns about fallout shared by Wiesner and the president, arguments for the test ban remained purely technical. One

Wiesner letter to Kennedy reviewed the need for atmospheric testing and justified a test ban strictly in national security terms: "I believe that our most important task is to maintain an extremely effective deterrent and that we have the capability to do so without conducting atmospheric tests." Instead of atmospheric testing, he suggested "aggressive use of underground testing, imaginative laboratory work, and possibly even space testing if it should prove necessary."[48] Wiesner thus gave Kennedy what was essentially advice on military capabilities—a far cry from standing by the window and worrying about rain. Though technical views were a necessity in such a debate, antinuclear scientists could hope for at best limited arms control measures, since deterrence and the buildup of weapons could not be questioned.

Still, Pugwash could have some influence. When Khrushchev wrote to Kennedy in 1962 about a test ban treaty, he mentioned the scientists' movement by name, praising Pugwash's suggestion of using "black boxes" to monitor seismic activities in order to eliminate the need for manned observation within the Soviet Union. Kennedy, surprisingly, failed to see Pugwash scientists in the same light as Khrushchev. "None [of the scientists] represented the United States Government or had discussed the matter with responsible officials," Kennedy replied to Khrushchev. "All were speaking as individuals and none were seismologists. Their agreement does not signify anything other than that this area was an area which justified further study."[49]

Meanwhile, the test ban negotiations at Geneva continued to idle. Pugwash held an elite meeting in 1963 in London specifically to discuss "the nuclear test ban deadlock." The meeting included Eisenhower's former science adviser Kistiakowsky, who had at one time doubted the value of the conferences. Kistiakowsky had remained on PSAC after the change in administration but had joined Pugwash when he grew frustrated with "the ineffectiveness of diplomatic efforts in the field of disarmament."[50] In London the Pugwash scientists discussed the need to convince the U.S. and Soviet people about the uselessness of further testing as well as the potential problem of the U.S. Senate's ratification of a treaty. The scientists also shared a great deal of information about methods of detection and inspection, including the results of various seismic experiments and the number of inspections each side desired. Lev Artsimovich, who had regular contact with Khrushchev, told Kistiakowsky that the Soviets would accept five annual inspections even after the United States had suggested just three. Scientists passed this information on to Kennedy administration officials, though with no discernible result. Perhaps more significantly, the exchange foreshadowed the upcoming battle in the United States over the test ban, which emphasized suspicions of the Soviet Union's motives. At one point Riznechenko said to the U.S. scientists, "We are not working on anti-spoofing [counterintelligence]. Why are American seismologists and those close to them work[ing] so much on spoofing? . . . Latter and Teller for instance. Why are US [scientists] suspecting USSR seismologists? We are honest!"[51]

Teller's Test Ban Assault

While scientific efforts continued, events outside the sphere of science drove the United States and Soviet Union toward a test ban. In particular, the near disaster of the Cuban Missile Crisis spurred mutual desires on both sides of the Iron Curtain for an arms control agreement.[52] Yet this newfound urgency resulted in an atmospheric, not a comprehensive, test ban. The scientific approach to the test ban debate directly affected this shift from a comprehensive ban to one that did little to slow the arms race, primarily because of Teller's ability to provide opponents of a test ban with technical claims that a comprehensive test ban was scientifically shaky and that the Soviets could not be trusted.[53] In August 1963 the United States and Soviet Union signed the LTBT in Moscow. As the conference began, the Soviets made it clear that they were not willing to discuss a comprehensive test ban.[54] Underscoring the irrelevance of science, the chief negotiator Averell Harriman included no science advisers as official members of the delegation. The seismologist Frank Press made the trip, but when a comprehensive ban disappeared as an option, he returned home.[55] The treaty that was signed prohibited testing in the atmosphere, outer space, and underwater, moving tests underground. Pro–test ban scientists still hoped the treaty might lead to future disarmament and slow the arms race. But the treaty had to leap one final hurdle: the U.S. Senate, where the test ban's opponents would make their final stand.

The test ban eventually passed, but to the chagrin of many scientists who wanted genuine arms control, Senate ratification required the U.S. government to pursue an increased weapons development program. This hitch negated the arms control aspects of the treaty, leaving scientists to praise only the ban's reduction of fallout, even though many of them had originally doubted the dangers of fallout. Three factors worked against the pro–test ban scientists in the Senate: scientific opposition to the treaty, nationalist suspicions of the Soviet Union, and scientific divisions that harmed scientists' reputation as objective authorities. In July the Kennedy brain trust held a meeting to discuss the "pros and cons of the test ban" after Harriman had worked out the atmospheric agreement in Moscow. A memo drafted by CIA director John McCone (replaced as AEC chair by Glenn Seaborg) argued that although Teller "would protest the treaty . . . I did not think the protest would be particularly well received by either the public or the Congress."[56] But McCone's prediction proved drastically off base, as Teller's charisma and forceful arguments buttressed strong opposition to a test ban within Congress.

As he had during the Eisenhower administration, Teller flexed herculean might in opposing the Kennedy administration's test ban. When the hearings began, he announced to his frequent correspondent Henry Kissinger, "I hope to amend or to defeat the test ban treaty." At the start of his campaign, Teller continued to voice his distrust of the Soviets and argued that only a strong nuclear deterrent would stop them. Long before a treaty had been signed, Teller had turned his attention to the Senate, maintaining consistent correspondence with the senators who would likely decide the fate of a test ban, including those on the Committee on Foreign Relations and the Preparedness Subcommittee of the Committee on Armed Services. On a visit to Washington in the summer of 1962, Teller visited Senator Stuart Symington of the Preparedness Subcommittee, who took him to see his fellow subcommittee member John Stennis (D-MS). After the visit Symington asked Teller to compose "a statement on the need for continued testing." A short time later, Teller declared to Stennis, "I stand ready at any time to appear before your committee and make the required statements on the need for further nuclear testing." When the hearings finally began, Teller wrote to Henry Jackson, also on the Preparedness Subcommittee, telling him of the "extremely serious difficulties" in improving U.S. defense under the test ban.[57]

These objections had been crafted to poke holes in arguments in favor of a comprehensive test ban, but even the atmospheric measure signed by the superpowers offended Teller. Accordingly, in addition to lobbying behind the scenes, Teller also played a public role in the hearings. Although he was adept at the use of media and other outlets, his ability to nearly dominate the hearings—even taking into account the eventual passing of the treaty—demonstrated most clearly the great effects of his rhetorical and demagogic skills as well as the arms control scientists' logical but fateful decision to seek arms control through a treaty.

Whereas science advisers had influenced Eisenhower and Kennedy, Teller had a comparable influence on conservative members of Congress and the military. After years of consulting with dozens of congressmen and military officials, Teller knew he had many allies in the government. The Preparedness Subcommittee held hearings on the test ban treaty, as did the Committee on Foreign Relations. Teller played three roles in the hearings: an adviser to test ban opponents, a warrior-witness against the test ban, and an omnipresent force that framed many of the questions to which other witnesses had to respond. Many witnesses in the hearings reflected Teller's influence either openly, as when General Maxwell Taylor acknowledged Teller as one of his advisers, or tacitly, as when witnesses regurgitated Teller's arguments as their own.[58] When attempting to dismiss the significance of the treaty's fallout reduction, air force general Curtis LeMay, Los Alamos director Norris Bradbury, and navy admiral Arleigh Burke all recycled Teller's "Denver argument" that downplayed fear of fallout. Burke, for example, argued that "the difference [in natural radiation] of living here [in Washington] and in the Rocky Mountain area, is a greater difference than an increase of contamination in the air caused by a reasonable amount of nuclear explosives."[59] During the CFR hearings, Senator Bourke Hickenlooper (R-IA) echoed Teller's claims about radiation when he questioned Seaborg. "We could take any number of examples," Hickenlooper began, "where a little bit is not necessarily proved to be harmful and a little bit of some things are actually beneficial. . . . It runs in my mind that we do have evidence in some kinds of life that a little stepped up radiation has actually increased the strength of the recipient."[60]

Teller himself spent hours in front of both committees passionately testifying against the test ban. Echoing the words of government scientists, Teller asserted that he would limit himself to "technical factors." As before, Teller used his own scientific expertise to debunk the scientific arguments in favor of a test ban, though he went further in his comments. Teller claimed that the treaty would prevent the United States from achieving an antiballistic missile system and added that, in his judgment, the Soviets already had one. He cast doubt on U.S. scientists' ability to detect Soviet tests, calling existing detection methods "castles of sand." He thundered that the Soviets had surpassed the United States in weapons development and promised that the treaty would hinder U.S. weapons development as well as bury useful Plowshare projects. He narrated scenarios in which the Soviets would hide tests, including "small clandestine experiments in the atmosphere" and "bigger shallowly buried literally legal underground experiments," both of which "may endanger U.S. security."[61] Teller even predicted that the treaty would leave the United States powerless to use its nuclear arsenal in times of war. Certainly, not every senator believed Teller, but both committees gladly listened to him. William Fulbright (D-AR), chairman of the CFR, told Teller, "I had no idea you would be such an interesting witness as to keep us in session all day. . . . This is unprecedented, as far as the length of the session is concerned."[62]

Most important, the senators found Teller's arguments plausible enough that they posed his claims as questions to other witnesses who testified. Policymakers like Secretary of Defense Robert McNamara and scientists including Harold Brown of the DOD, Bradbury, York, Seaborg, and Kistiakowsky found themselves having to answer questions about Teller's objections to the treaty, including ABM development, Soviet advantages in high-yield weapons, detection methods, and the Plowshare program.[63] During his testimony, Kistiakowsky was asked by Fulbright, "Dr. Teller stated categorically the Soviets are ahead of us in their anti-ballistic missile defense because of their 1961–62 test series. Would you care to comment on that?"[64] By adopting Teller's concerns as their own (even if not endorsing them), the senators essentially allowed Teller to ask the questions during the hearings, forcing the discourse to focus on his objections and casting enough doubt on the test ban to limit it severely in several ways.

Test ban opposition also came in the form of fears of Soviet mendacity, something that the Pugwash movement had worked hard to overcome. Symington cast doubt on the transnational exchange of Pugwash by accusing Soviet scientists of "lying" to Wiesner at the 1960 Pugwash conference and "planning [tests] all the time."[65] Most senators and witnesses throughout the hearings took it for granted that the Soviets would cheat the test ban, and Teller encouraged the idea that the Soviets wanted a test ban only because they held an advantage in weapons development. The CFR hearings began with numerous references to the number of treaties the Soviet Union had violated, leaving Secretary of State Dean Rusk to resort to the argument that the "treaty is not standing upon the foundation of trust."[66] Instead, pro–test ban witnesses argued, any Soviet violation of the treaty would not threaten U.S. security, as underground testing, permitted by the treaty, would ensure preparedness.[67] The scientists who had reached across to their Soviet counterparts quickly jettisoned their arguments about transnational trust in favor of more pragmatic claims about the treaty's ability to allow—indeed promote—weapons development, essentially the opposite reason they had originally wanted the treaty.

Finally, the conflicting views of Teller and other scientists shattered long-held beliefs about the nature of science. Teller made a convincing-enough case against the test ban that some senators believed that scientific opinion had divided over the ban, despite York's testimony that "the majority [of scientists] agrees with me rather than Dr. Teller. . . . [T]hey are in favor of proceeding with the test ban."[68] Scientists worried so much about Teller's influence that they publicly challenged his knowledge and questioned his personal motivations. Kistiakowsky, worried that Teller would raise a "red herring," testified in order to refute his predictions of clandestine Soviet outer-space tests.[69] Still more scientists testified or wrote to Fulbright in order to question Teller's qualifications. The Federation of American Scientists accused Teller of making "misleading" statements, and Bethe directly attacked Teller's competence, writing to Fulbright that Teller "is not an expert" on antimissile defense.[70]

This dispute within the scientific community baffled the senators, who held unrealistic expectations about the extent to which scientific information could produce a consensus. During the Preparedness Subcommittee hearings, Symington, referring to a disagreement between Livermore director John Foster and Teller, commented, "Now what is a mystery to me is how two people who have worked together and been so close together in this field can nevertheless be so far apart in conclusions. I am not asking this in humorous fashion. I think in a sense it is the crux of this whole problem." Jackson, also confused, asked Los Alamos director Bradbury about the division of scientific opinion:

> What I am getting at is, do we have enough back of us to come to a conclusion? All science is a matter of prediction, isn't it? I mean, you try to predict out of a given number of cases or situations, based on certain things happening, that in the future certain things are apt to happen. And it will vary by the degree of the experience back of you. Now I realize you do not have too much experience back of you in all of these elements we are talking about. But do you have enough to come to a reasonably certain conclusion that a certain thing will happen in a given set of circumstances?

Bradbury's answer could not have satisfied Jackson: "I think the answer to the question is 'Yes.' Dr. Teller's answer to your question would be 'No.' Dr. Foster can make his own answer. . . . We all look at the same set of facts, and we come to different opinions about their relevance, interpretation, and importance." Scientists were accused of being subjective, not the objective manifestation of reason and empiricism that they were in their laboratories. Senator Robert Byrd (D-WV) joked with Curtis LeMay that nuclear weapons tests were more reliable than the scientists who devised them; LeMay concurred.[71]

As the hearings dragged on, Fulbright grew increasingly peeved by scientists' differing views. "One of the most unexpected developments, at least from my point of view," he told the former AEC commissioner Willard Libby, "has been the wide divergence of views among the acknowledged experts, particularly in the basic scientific areas in which you operate. I thought that these intellectual giants would arrive at some sort of common conclusions. But I find they differ, just as much as politicians do, and this has been very puzzling to me." Near the end of the hearings, Fulbright became downright irritable. "It is good to have someone who isn't a scientist occasionally discuss these matters," he complained to one witness, "not that I didn't like the scientists."[72]

Teller's campaign did not defeat or amend the test ban treaty as he had hoped. But it is clear that his influence in military and government circles greatly weakened the test ban that eventually emerged. Teller's scientific claims, his influential connections, and the mistrust of the Soviets he encouraged had their biggest influence on the JCS. The JCS made their acceptance of the LTBT contingent on government acceptance of their four "safeguards": "comprehensive, aggressive, and continuing underground nuclear test programs"; financial and experimental upkeep of the U.S. nuclear laboratories; a well-funded readiness program to restart atmospheric testing at a moment's notice in the event of Soviet treaty violations; and drastic improvements in verification and intelligence. The safeguards bore the distinct imprint of Teller, and indeed the JCS admitted that Teller heavily influenced their views.[73] Other observers noted the closeness firsthand. In a letter to the prime minister, the British science adviser Solly Zuckerman reported that at a June 1963 NATO speech, Teller's anti–test ban fury was "clearly music to the ears of the American Chiefs of Staff." Although some senators disputed Teller's testimony, none dared oppose the JCS and happily pledged allegiance to the safeguards. By the time the test ban easily passed the Senate (80 to 19) in September 1963, the Kennedy administration had also accepted the JCS safeguards.[74] The safeguards ensured that nuclear testing actually increased after the test ban, adding fuel to the arms race fire; LeMay had directly assured the senators that the U.S. military budget would increase after the treaty because of the safeguards. The Pugwash scientist Bernard Feld had these developments in mind when he called the treaty an "arms control disaster."[75]

Teller's efforts must not be overestimated, of course. Although he had campaigned tirelessly against a test ban since the mid-1950s (efforts that rewarded him with the hostility of former friends and colleagues), he failed to prevent the ratification of the LTBT, and the survival of his Plowshare project was far from guaranteed. He appeared to have been defeated. Even his longtime foe Linus Pauling was honored with the Nobel Peace Prize in recognition of his efforts for a test ban. Teller's secretary apparently cried when she heard Kennedy praise the LTBT's ratification.[76] Perhaps Teller consoled himself by realizing that his Far Right arguments had enabled the intense nuclear development mandated by the JCS safeguards.

Although the test ban struggle brought many scientists together in common cause, the debate revealed science to be a house divided, damaged the belief in scientific objectivity, and weakened the authority of science in society. In the Eisenhower and Kennedy years, when scientists opposed each other in public, politicians ended up believing those who supported their political point of view. At one point in the hearings, Symington demonstrated this change when he brought up the disagreement among scientists. He then told Teller, "I am more inclined to go along with you and Dr. Johnny Foster than I am with Dr. Brown." And Symington was perhaps even more confused than he let on (or perhaps simply made his decision on reasons other than science), as he ended up voting *for* the treaty.[77]

Scientists received a great deal of credit for the achievement of a test ban, despite the arduous struggle to bring it into being. The *New York Times*, observing the confusion caused by the scientists' role in the Senate debate, described the LTBT as "coming into the world like an unwanted child." Yet scientists still spoke with authority. In expressing their support for the treaty, the *Times* editorial staff quoted Bradbury: "If now is not the time to take this chance, to count on this hope . . . what combination of circumstances will ever produce a better time?" In late 1963 British prime minister Harold Macmillan also looked to scientists for guidance in the nuclear age. A telegram of greeting from Macmillan to the Pugwash conference under way in Yugoslavia praised the scientists for helping bring about a test ban and asked them to "help the politicians as they have done before."[78]

Yet the test ban treaty, long fought for by scientists, eventually came to be seen as a missed opportunity. The LTBT did little to slow the arms race but still provided Americans with the calming illusion that the superpowers were taking steps to make nuclear war less likely. Near the end of his life, Feld wrote that "the treaty was fatally flawed." Attending a Pugwash meeting in Czechoslovakia just after the treaty's ratification, scientists noticed that the achievement of a test ban threatened to divide the organization. Many U.S. Pugwash scientists complained that their organization had become too official, risking its free and open exchange, while others hoped to broaden the movement's goals beyond "symbolic" arms control agreements like the test ban. Frank Long of the Arms Control and Disarmament Agency told Feld that Pugwash was "attaining an increasingly quasi official status," a path that could lead only to irrelevance.[79]

The test ban years also marked the zenith of PSAC's influence on policy.

Kistiakowsky remarked that PSAC's decline began under Kennedy, when PSAC and the presidential science adviser "largely lost their influence in matters of national security." When Lyndon Johnson became president, Bethe added, "The whole of PSAC deteriorated and there was not very much contact between the science adviser and President Johnson. And still later even less between the science adviser and President Nixon, until Nixon abolished the whole committee."[80] Even Teller lost some influence, though he continued to make bold assertions about nuclear weapons and regained influence in the Reagan administration.

After the test ban, scientists continued their efforts to influence politics, though they could no longer claim to be apolitical. In 1962 Leo Szilard founded the Council for a Livable World, which raised money for Senate candidates who endorsed nuclear disarmament. In 1964, much to the chagrin of his old Republican friend Eisenhower, Kistiakowsky helped found Scientists and Engineers for LBJ, where he ended up debating Teller, who was campaigning for Barry Goldwater. Kistiakowsky grimaced, "My name was so frequently used in this campaign that I have clearly lost the status of a pure scientist."[81]

In their analysis of scientists' role in the test ban debate, historians have argued that scientists allowed their hopes for international cooperation to interfere with their technical expertise and objectivity, hampering, rather than helping, U.S. diplomacy. But instead the opposite is true—their strict observation of the technical boundaries of their positions hindered the antinuclear arguments they could make. Limited to technical advice and confronted by nationalist fears, government science advisers failed to develop arguments effective enough to challenge the advocates of nuclear weapons. Just as transnational resources opened different doors for antinuclear protesters, moral messages effectively swayed public support in favor of the disarmament movement. In the 1950s and early 1960s, Pauling had mobilized a significant number of Americans against fallout, arguing that nuclear testing was immoral because it harmed the people, including children, it was meant to protect. Even Teller at one point told Congress that it would be immoral to stop testing because he was close to developing a clean bomb—one that would produce no fallout at all. Such an invention, he claimed, would save innocent people at home and abroad.[82]

In contrast, in order to retain influence in the government, science advisers and Pugwash participants had the burden of arguing that fewer nuclear weapons made the nation safer. Ever since the Oppenheimer hearing, the state had explicitly demanded a brand of science advice that spoke the language of deterrence and weapons development, where only nuclear weapons promised salvation. Although the test ban proved a dramatic turning point in scientists' relationship with the state, scientists remained determined to influence policy. This goal proved difficult, however, as few policymakers in the late 1960s were interested in listening to them.

5

To "Sail Before the Wind of Time"

Scientists and Disarmament after the Test Ban Treaty, 1963–1972

THE SUCCESSFUL RATIFICATION OF THE TEST ban, initially cause for celebration, soon became cause for concern among scientists interested in arms control and disarmament because the fight over the treaty had revealed the limits of what scientists could achieve after the government's redefinition of science. Weighing in on the test ban debate had challenged, rather than reaffirmed, scientists' role in policymaking, and the rise of détente after 1963 threatened to make the transnational connections of Pugwash scientists superfluous. But while redefining science had changed how scientists could give advice to policymakers, it did little to dampen their willingness to do so. Rather than end their political activity, many scientists in Pugwash and on the President's Science Advisory Committee expected to build on the success of the test ban by taking on other Cold War problems, including settlement of the German question, nuclear nonproliferation, international cooperation, and aid to developing countries. And when the Vietnam War became the biggest obstacle to peace in the world, scientists even felt emboldened to try to solve that conflict as well. Having internalized the Cold War redefinition of science, however, meant that scientists' efforts at confronting these new challenges proved ambiguous at best and left them as distant from political influence as ever.

Fallout from the Test Ban

When the U.S. Senate ratified the Limited Test Ban Treaty on September 24, 1963, Eugene Rabinowitch had mixed reactions. As editor of the *Bulletin of the Atomic Scientists* and one of the leaders of Pugwash, he saw the implementation of the treaty as validating his years of antinuclear activism. It pleased him that after nearly two decades of nuclear tension, the United States and the Soviet Union had finally reached agreement on some form of arms control. At the same time, he recognized that the treaty might very well put an end to the antinuclear movement without eliminating nuclear weapons at all. Rabinowitch hailed the signing of the LTBT, even moving the *Bulletin*'s symbolic clock back a few minutes from nuclear midnight. "Not that the treaty is a significant step toward disarmament," he cautioned; "it is not." Having earlier dismissed the problem, Rabinowitch continued to ignore the issue of fallout and focused instead squarely on the prospects for disarmament. Although he praised the LTBT as "welcome news" and "an encouraging event," he believed that its value was entirely symbolic. The treaty did not outlaw underground tests, encouraging the arms race to accelerate. Rabinowitch believed that such partial, almost token, gestures fell far short of the ultimate goal of disarmament.[1]

On a deeper level, Rabinowitch also worried that arms control agreements like the LTBT might render much of his life's work irrelevant if they distracted people from crucial problems yet to be resolved. If the test ban relieved people that fallout would no longer poison the air, they might forget that the superpowers continued to stockpile enough nuclear weapons to kill nearly everyone on earth. Five years before the LTBT, Rabinowitch predicted that a test ban would "become a first step to nowhere," leaving the world "where it was before—a house divided, with nations jealously maintaining their capacity for mutual destruction." The antinuclear movement, he feared, "will find itself deflated without a new worthwhile, realistic goal."[2] In many ways, Rabinowitch's fears were realized.

The signing of the LTBT signified the moment when East and West backed away from the "eyeball to eyeball" confrontation of the Cold War and proceeded toward a stabilizing détente.[3] The year 1963 also changed the fate of the antinuclear movement, as "nuclear apathy" grew in the United States. Moving tests underground made the nuclear threat harder to perceive, while protest against the Vietnam War soon drew away many protesters from the antinuclear movement, leaving only "a dwindling band of older activists" to carry a torch for nuclear disarmament.[4]

Many of these remaining stalwarts could be found at Pugwash conferences during the 1960s. Stoic though these activists may have been, previous accounts have argued that the LTBT was particularly damaging for Pugwash and its adherents, describing the group of scientists as "languishing" during the late 1960s and early 1970s.[5] Rather than languishing, however, Pugwash spent these years actively and anxiously attempting to reformulate its goals and maintain its influence within policymaking circles. In a contentious and difficult process, Pugwash members pushed and pulled the movement in different directions, toward ideas as disparate as disbanding entirely or broadly expanding its aims.

After the signing of the LTBT, Pugwash scientists claimed for themselves a fair share of the credit and greeted the test ban with "exhilaration."[6] The *New York Times* reported in September 1963 that the eleventh Pugwash conference in Dubrovnik, Yugoslavia, opened with an "air of amity" due to the recent signing of the treaty.[7] A Brazilian scientist at the conference described participants as "full of optimism" and "euphoria," while others "expressed unanimous satisfaction" with the treaty and "expressed hope" that further disarmament measures would follow.[8]

As the euphoria subsided, however, Pugwash appeared to lose some focus. Rabinowitch and his fellow Pugwashites expected an avalanche of more meaningful disarmament measures to follow, but instead the LTBT threatened to bury their movement. Freed from their test ban obsession, the scientists at Dubrovnik recommended everything from a joint U.S.-Soviet flight to the moon to proposals for nuclear safeguards and seismic-detection measures to prevent underground testing. Still another observer claimed that the problem of the division of Germany "appeared to be at the heart" of the conference.[9]

The achievement of a test ban left Pugwash with no specific objective, and the organization slowly began to reconsider its mission. This introspection reached the Pugwash Continuing Committee, the body of scientists who organized the conferences, including Joseph Rotblat, the secretary-general of the committee; Bernard Feld, the chair of the U.S. Pugwash Committee; and Rabinowitch, a member of the committee since its creation. These men found themselves questioning the meaning of their efforts on a fundamental level and confronted the worst possible fate: irrelevance. They feared that Pugwash risked losing its autonomy, of becoming "unofficially official," rather than "officially unofficial," in the words of one Soviet scientist. Bertrand Russell, who had inspired Pugwash, began to leave scientists behind in order to participate in disarmament efforts based on civil disobedience. "I suspect," Rabinowitch wrote to Feld, "that these conferences have appeared to [Russell] for some time to be much too tame (and perhaps not sufficiently anti-American) to suit his impatience (and taste)!"[10] With their honorary chairman bolting for different ventures, Rotblat, Feld, and Rabinowitch knew that they had to reinvigorate their movement in order to keep it alive.

Proud of creating an innovative approach to confronting the Cold War, Pugwash scientists feared becoming a part of the status quo in the quest for peace. In 1961 the social critic and author of *The Lonely Crowd* David Riesman commented on Pugwash. He wrote that while "talk of disarmament has become fashionable . . . an intellectual never wants to be fashionable, but rather to be ahead of fashion." Rabinowitch wrote one year later that the U.S. government should "sail before the wind of time with a stronger will and a firmer hand at the tiller than it has now." Never one to count on the government, Rabinowitch fully expected scientists to navigate the world through the atomic age. After the Dubrovnik conference, Rabinowitch asked Feld, "Did we act ahead of official thinking, or merely endorse what is already agreed upon . . . on the official level? The purpose of the Pugwash Conferences," he declared, "is to stay far ahead of governmental thinking and to influence it, rather than to endorse it!"[11]

But in which direction would the ship of Pugwash sail? All agreed that Pugwash should aim to end the Cold War and encourage peace. Opinions differed widely, however, over how to achieve this goal—after all, with détente approaching, the leaders of the superpowers seemed to be ending the Cold War all on their own. The leadership of Pugwash ultimately divided over the issue; Rotblat wanted to retrench on disarmament, while Rabinowitch wanted to take Pugwash in new directions, especially toward expanding international cooperation and development.

In 1962 Rotblat wrote, "The urgency of the disarmament problem makes it, at present, a topic of priority." That same year the Pugwash Continuing Committee "recommended that disarmament be the main topic of all future Pugwash conferences," because otherwise a "dissipation of interest" would dampen the "pioneering" nature of the conferences. Although Pugwash meetings continued to vary in their focus, Rotblat attempted to keep Pugwash on the disarmament track after the test ban, as he understandably thought that the LTBT would make further arms control even easier. In this spirit, the Continuing Committee devoted the 1964 conference to disarmament in order "to restore to Pugwash its role as a source of new ideas and mutual understanding in the disarmament field."[12]

Rotblat could not ignore the Pugwashites who wanted to address international cooperation in science, the problems of developing nations, the population explosion, and the social responsibilities of scientists. But a "consensus," in Rotblat's words, among Pugwash scientists decreed that disarmament and world security demanded "the most urgent attention and should, therefore, occupy the bulk of the Pugwash effort." In practice this meant that at a typical Pugwash conference, three of the five sessions concerned disarmament, while the other two addressed any of the various other issues. Rotblat apparently preferred to keep development and cooperation separate, "so that he would be free to proceed with Pugwash's historic focus of attention on disarmament."[13]

Despite this alleged consensus, Pugwash began to spread in different directions. Of the ten conferences between 1964 and 1971, only two focused exclusively on disarmament and world security. Six of the conferences framed disarmament as merely one of the problems related to cooperation and development. Still, in the eyes of the media, at least, Pugwash remained a disarmament organization. In the years following the test ban, the (fairly scant) coverage of the movement highlighted Pugwash's recommended disarmament proposals, including a ban on the sale of uranium, a nonaggression pact between NATO and the countries of the Warsaw Pact, the postponement of the deployment of NATO ships armed with nuclear weapons, and the creation of nuclear-free zones around the world. In 1966 the *New York Times* repeated Rotblat's assertion that Pugwash discussions would soon result in a comprehensive nuclear test ban.[14]

The anticipated comprehensive test ban never materialized in the years following the LTBT, nor did the expected avalanche of disarmament measures. For Rabinowitch, the wind of time blew in a different direction. Serious nuclear arms control, almost within the world's grasp, seemed to be slipping away when China exploded a nuclear device in 1964. Rabinowitch soon began to argue that disarmament could not be achieved by pursuing disarmament. By focusing Pugwash's attention on more fundamental dilemmas, he hoped to eliminate the forces that drove nations to arm themselves. Disarmament would come as nations learned to cooperate and develop without recourse to war or ideology.

Back in 1958, in a letter to the social critic Gilbert Seldes, Rabinowitch complained that the idea of a test ban had "been permitted to assume much more than its proper share of importance." Because a test ban was a concrete, tangible goal, scientists had rallied to the cause. But Rabinowitch had refused to go along with the crowd. At Pugwash conferences, Rabinowitch called for cooperation above all else, since disarmament would only soothe the fever of the "world's sickness" without attacking its causes. Two years later, Rabinowitch penned a draft memo in which he contemplated taking disarmament off the Pugwash agenda, ostensibly because the American Academy of Arts and Sciences had begun a bilateral disarmament study with the Soviet Union, but more because he grew weary of the "endless, frustrating, all-or-nothing disarmament negotiations."[15]

By the end of 1963, this attitude had taken hold to some extent within Pugwash. The U.S. scientist Matthew Meselson wrote that Pugwash, after the Dubrovnik conference, "had lost considerable initiative in its attempts to find ways of securing peace." Détente and the LTBT "left Pugwash scientists not so far ahead of the general level of thinking in these matters as they used to be." Meselson concluded that the organization needed to "alter the nature of its Conferences" in order to "maximize its leverage and relevance to the international problems which remain to be solved."[16]

With a limited test ban out of the way, Rabinowitch seized his opportunity to push Pugwash in new directions. The problems of the world in the 1960s, he argued, could not be solved by disarmament measures, policy decisions, or anything scientists or intellectuals could devise. Instead, the world needed "a change of mentality, for the replacement of obsolete attitudes." Such a revolutionary shift would occur once international cooperation—previously only a "sideshow" to disarmament—rose to the top of Pugwash's agenda. Long a proponent of internationalism, Rabinowitch developed a plan for cooperation with two components. First, the developed nations of the world would assist each other on prohibitively expensive scientific programs such as space exploration, which would encourage the Cold War powers to cooperate while simultaneously advancing scientific discovery. Second, he wanted the developed countries of the world—especially the United States and the Soviet Union—to launch joint programs to aid developing nations. This cooperation would produce two tangible results. All nations, and especially those in the process of industrializing, would see material results. Furthermore, by working together, the United States and Soviet Union would learn to coexist and thus trust each other. Only then could meaningful disarmament take place.[17]

Rabinowitch seemed to have a point. Rotblat found the pace of disarmament so slow in September 1966 that he considered disbanding Pugwash and asked the Continuing Committee to explore why Pugwash should continue. He told the committee that he "recognized the undeniable successes, but there were also many shortcomings, such as insufficient influx of fresh blood, lack of public support for Pugwash, and inactivity of many of the national groups." Rabinowitch, on the other hand, considered Pugwash a viable vessel for his mission of cooperation. The fourteenth Pugwash conference in April 1965, held in Venice, focused on international cooperation, while the fifteenth conference, held in Addis Ababa, Ethiopia, had the theme "Science in Aid of Developing Countries." At the Addis Ababa conference, eighty-six scientists represented thirty-one countries, with more than half coming from Africa, Asia, and Latin America. Conference proposals included a "massive" training program for science teachers funded by developed countries, the encouragement of scientists from developed countries to work in underdeveloped areas, and a call for international cooperation in scientific research and conservation programs in developing nations.[18] After the conference, Rabinowitch conducted an extensive survey of the participants, and despite some complaints about the overrepresentation of large developed countries and political biases, most participants embraced the idea of further conferences on and in developing nations. In 1966 Rotblat encouraged the formation of a Pugwash committee on development in order to "absorb the inevitable frustrations growing out of efforts at arms control," of which Rabinowitch became chair.[19]

As Rabinowitch looked toward a new future for Pugwash, the organization's present posed real problems. Pugwash had always boasted about its access to policymakers, but this access appeared to be dwindling. An October 11, 1964, *New York Times* editorial praised Pugwash, hailing its recommendations as "important because policymakers in Washington, Moscow, and other world capitals pay serious attention to the results of Pugwash meetings." Although this may have been true during the test ban era, President Lyndon Johnson made a point of turning a cold shoulder to Pugwash. On September 13, 1964, Paul Doty and Jerome Wiesner cabled national security adviser McGeorge Bundy from Karlovy Vary, Czechoslovakia, requesting a message of greeting to the conference from President Johnson. As president, Kennedy had sent greetings to the Pugwash conferences, a gesture that Johnson continued for an early 1964 conference in India. But by late 1964, the situation had changed. Refusing Doty and Wiesner's request, Bundy replied that Pugwash would survive without the "banality" of a "repeated official blessing from on high."[20]

The actual reasons for snubbing Pugwash lay in the interplay of domestic politics and the administration's fear of criticism. In a handwritten note to

Bundy, the acting director of the State Department's Office of International Scientific Affairs explained that a message to Pugwash might harm the president during an election year "because of congressional criticisms of Pugwashery." Despite his eventual landslide, Johnson pessimistically predicted a difficult challenge from Goldwater in the 1964 election, though there is little evidence to suggest that he could have seriously expected to be attacked for support of the little-known Pugwash conferences. The *Congressional Record* reveals no comments on Pugwash during either 1963 or 1964, while in 1962 Senator Jennings Randolph (D-WV) had praised Pugwash, emphasizing his endorsement of the 1962 conference's statement that "full disarmament is realistic and urgent."[21]

In 1961, however, the Senate halls had echoed with attacks on Pugwash in particular and disarmament in general, when Senator Thomas Dodd had used the Internal Security Subcommittee as a soapbox for his "personal anti-Communist crusade," in the words of the *New York Times*. This campaign had started with his 1960 hounding of SANE and Linus Pauling and continued the following year with severe criticism of Pugwash. A staff analysis by the Internal Security Subcommittee alleged that the Pugwash conferences "have been exploited by the Communist apparatus as a propaganda devise [*sic*]." According to Dodd, communist scientists arrived at Pugwash conferences as "captive[s] of an inflexible political dogma" and hoped "to shape and exploit the conference in a manner which will best serve the ends of Soviet imperialism." Dodd also ripped Pugwash for its connections to the unabashedly pro-Soviet Cyrus Eaton, the industrialist who had helped fund the conferences.[22]

For years, the U.S. Pugwash group had been distancing itself from Eaton's "moronic mentality" and his "particularly embarrassing" support, in the words of Pugwash participants. Just after the first conference, the U.S. Pugwash group attempted to rename the organization the Conferences on Scientific and World Affairs because of the "odious" connotations of the term *Pugwash*. The name change never entirely caught on, but the presence of Eaton became more muted over time. At any rate, Dodd's charges appeared to cause little damage to public perceptions of the movement. Rabinowitch claimed that although one oppositional editorial appeared in a local paper during the 1961 Stowe, Vermont, conference, its author celebrated Pugwash by the conference's end.[23]

Nevertheless, Dodd's accusations in 1961 might have made an impression on Johnson, the vice president at the time after an influential tenure in the Senate. In fact, Johnson and Dodd had encountered each other years before. As Senate majority leader in 1959, Johnson welcomed Dodd to the Senate and immediately enlisted his support against Clinton Anderson, who opposed Johnson's position on a filibuster rule. Returning the favor, Johnson placed Dodd in charge of the Internal Security Subcommittee.[24]

Johnson famously feared domestic anticommunism. In 1965 Jim Thomson, a China specialist from the State Department, mentioned Dodd by name in a memo to Bundy, expressing fear of a McCarthy-esque reaction if the United States failed to stand up to communist aggression in South Vietnam. While U.S. Pugwash representatives asked for presidential messages of support, the Johnson administration ignored the requests, possibly because they feared the wrath of Dodd or other rabid anticommunists. Johnson himself claimed that he would be "destroyed" if Dodd ever accused him of being soft on communism. Congressional opinion of Pugwash nevertheless remained relatively positive (when it existed at all) through the 1960s. In 1966 Senator Stephen Young (D-OH) hailed Pugwash as "an outstanding example of peaceful cooperation" and even praised Eaton without any apparent harm.[25]

Along with fears of anticommunist backlash, Johnson believed that science properly belonged not in the realm of nuclear weapons policy and geopolitics but in the domestic sphere as part of the Great Society, where the progress of science would elevate the standard of living of all U.S. citizens.[26] Scientists' desire to advise the president on geopolitics quickly annoyed Johnson, causing hostility toward Pugwash and PSAC. Whereas the Eisenhower and Kennedy administrations had relied fairly heavily on the expertise of scientists, the Johnson administration began to spurn the advice of its scientific experts regarding nuclear weapons. Although the Office of Science and Technology (OST) remained friendly to the antinuclear scientists, a gap grew over time between scientists in general and the Johnson White House, as the president's Vietnam policy and personal philosophy on the role of science combined to alienate scientists, while at the same time many scientists began to break from the foreign policy and defense establishments.

Donald Hornig, who had replaced Wiesner as Kennedy's science adviser and chair of PSAC in late 1963 and retained his position after Kennedy's assassination, pressed Johnson to support Pugwash. In 1965 he drafted a statement to send to the spring Pugwash meeting, but the White House turned down the idea. Later that year, Hornig tried again with identical results. Hornig had at the very least casual interest in the Pugwash conferences, going so far as to request the reports of the individual working groups from the Addis Ababa conference.[27] Pugwash veterans continued to serve on PSAC, although their overall numbers declined during the Johnson presidency. But when they served, they appeared to advocate the ideas of Pugwash. Between 1964 and

1965, six scientists served on PSAC who had attended at least one Pugwash conference before Johnson became president. Although the individual scientist retained much personal initiative, it appears that these Pugwash veterans brought Pugwash ideas to the PSAC table. In late September 1965, Pugwashites Frank Long and George Kistiakowsky wrote to Hornig, discussing their meetings with Soviet and British scientists on "the South Vietnam problem." Hornig encouraged the scientists to continue such meetings and stressed the "value of such informal contacts."[28] Paul Doty, a regular Pugwash attendee, conducted a PSAC study of Western European affairs, while Long explored initiatives with Eastern Europe in applied science and technology. Wiesner, who still served PSAC as a consultant, and Long had begun to support Rabinowitch's initiatives in cooperation and development. Long also suggested that Hornig create a panel on "international science" that would "search for new directions for improvement of scientific relations between the U.S. and USSR with emphasis on the development and use of nongovernmental channels."[29]

As the president's science adviser, Hornig's agenda ultimately reflected the president's concerns rather than those of Pugwash. Although he pursued several policies reflective of Pugwash concerns, the demands of the Johnson administration gradually pulled Hornig and PSAC further from the influence of the organization. Hornig initially supported transnational communication between the United States and the Soviet Union in hopes of preventing the development of antiballistic missiles and also worried about the plight of developing countries. In 1966 Hornig traveled to London to give a talk called "The Role of Science and Technology in Aid to Developing Countries," a title nearly identical to the theme of the 1965 Addis Ababa Pugwash conference.[30] Another problem he attempted to solve was the "brain drain" problem: the migration of physicians from the Philippines to the United States that left the Filipinos with precious few doctors. Hornig proposed extending aid to the Philippines for development, and in 1968 the brain drain also ranked high on the agenda for the Pugwash conference in Nice, France. As background to a PSAC meeting on industrial and agricultural uses of nuclear power, the committee received a copy of a paper presented at a 1967 Pugwash conference.[31]

But on matters of military and strategic importance, Hornig and the Johnson administration broke ways with Pugwash. In a list prepared for Johnson describing the work of the OST, Hornig put "military technology and its interaction with strategic problems" at the top of the list, ahead of disarmament and arms control. Hornig, like Pugwash, supported the idea of a comprehensive test ban, though he paradoxically supported conducting nuclear tests in order to develop verification techniques with which such a test ban could be enforced.[32] In 1968 Hornig prepared a memo describing PSAC's accomplishments in honor of its tenth anniversary, and although arms control made the list, "military technology" achievements outnumbered any other category.[33]

Scientists and Vietnam

By 1965 scientists could no longer ignore the worsening situation in Vietnam. And while for the most part the Johnson administration refused to pay attention to Pugwash, the White House did occasionally express interest in what the scientists had to say about Vietnam. When Johnson's press secretary Bill Moyers's office requested a memo from the National Academy of Sciences on the Addis Ababa conference, Wilton Dillon responded with an assessment of how the suggestion of a bombing pause affected the Soviet Pugwash delegation and included the conference's statement on Vietnam. Dillon also attached a memo on Pugwash's goals for cooperation and development.[34] For the most part, however, the war threatened to overwhelm Pugwash by creating tension between U.S. and Soviet scientists, and while Pugwashites ultimately adapted their goals to include finding ways to end the war, this abrupt shift drew attention and energy away from Rabinowitch's move toward cooperation.

The war first intruded on the 1965 Venice conference, where it cast a "heavy shadow" over the proceedings, taking up much of the participants' efforts despite not being on the agenda. After a great deal of debate over possible solutions, the conference issued a relatively tame statement that denounced the use of gas by the United States in Vietnam and urged the United Nations to intervene to end the war. Rabinowitch later dismissed the statement as "hardly worth the effort," but Pugwash's reaction to the war had already begun to obscure other goals of the movement. Although Rabinowitch intended for the Addis Ababa conference to begin a new era in cooperation, Vietnam and disarmament occupied the bulk of a *New York Times* editorial about Pugwash; nothing was made of the conference's discussions of developing nations. Unlike other issues, Vietnam produced bickering at Addis Ababa. Working Group Five on security problems in developing countries quibbled endlessly over the wording of their statement, debating whether to advocate the withdrawal of troops from "Vietnam" or "North and South Vietnam."[35]

Vietnam ended up on the official agenda for the fall 1966 Pugwash conference in Sopot, Poland. One working group was devoted exclusively to the

Vietnam conflict, and most conferees skipped a trip to the opera to attend a special session on the war. Despite missing the opera, the delegates witnessed plenty of Sturm und Drang at the special session, as Soviet speakers "bitterly attacked" U.S. involvement and expressed "horror and indignation" over the war. But the heated debate produced little in the way of recommendations. Although the conference made news by condemning the war, in Rabinowitch's opinion the meeting offered only empty speeches, not tangible results.[36]

As with their movement against nuclear weapons, Pugwash scientists hoped that the free exchange of opinions between scientists would solve the problem of Vietnam. But in doing so, scientists moved beyond the nuclear and technical expertise that had defined them in the test ban debate. Furthermore, the war in Vietnam risked destroying what Pugwash stood for: the belief that through calm scientific discussion, problems could be solved, nationalism could be transcended. In different circumstances, Vietnam might have served as the ideal laboratory for Rabinowitch's experiments with transnational cooperation and developing nations. Instead, the Vietnam War represented transnational relations at their worst, with U.S. and Soviet scientists sniping at each other as subjects of rival states rather than citizen-scientists of the world.[37] Pugwash participants deemed their previous efforts successful because influential scientists had been freed, to a large extent, from the political restraints of official diplomats. But Soviet attacks on U.S. policy at Pugwash put U.S. scientists in the awkward position of being asked to defend positions they did not necessarily support. At the same time, the Vietnam War tested Pugwash's claims to represent a broad movement of scientists concerned with more than disarmament. Scientists might have felt at home discussing nuclear weapons' payloads and inspection measures, but when it came to Vietnam, they spoke with less authority, in large part because science advice had been redefined as exclusively technical judgments about nuclear weapons.

The year 1966 might have been Pugwash's worst. Along with the upheaval of Vietnam, Rotblat had questioned the reasons for continuing the conferences. Frederick Seitz, president of the National Academy of Sciences and earlier a colleague of Rabinowitch's at the University of Illinois, wanted to put an end to NAS participation in Pugwash. Rabinowitch himself bemoaned "amateurism, [and a] lack of proper preparation and follow-up" at conferences. Though he praised the "informal and multilateral discussion," the debates over Vietnam proved how tenuous these benefits were.[38] Battered over Vietnam and divided over pursuing disarmament or cooperation,

Pugwash nearly dissolved. Rabinowitch noticed that although more countries than ever had a role in Pugwash, they had begun a shift toward "more regional problems." Instead of trying to end the Cold War, Pugwash participants wanted to focus on their own respective corners of the globe. This move reflected a "weakening of forces directed at international integration, and of a renewed trend toward international anarchy." Nationalist priorities would make cooperation all but impossible. "This central hope is becoming obscured," he lamented, "and the great vision of the world community is receding." Still, Rabinowitch contended that ending the Cold War "remains the basic challenge of our age; it is the life and death problem of the human race." Pugwash must continue, despite its "disappointingly slow" progress.[39]

Other Pugwash scientists noticed this slow decline. David Inglis, a Pugwash veteran since 1960, noted the "frustrations" caused by Vietnam. "I believe Pugwash will make more progress when that's over," he wrote. But rather than wait out the storm of Vietnam, Pugwash confronted the problem of the war head-on. At the 1967 conference, Pugwash delegates ceased attacking each other and managed to agree on specific proposals to end the war. Other Pugwash efforts went even further. In 1967 two French Pugwash scientists became "unofficial negotiators" between the United States and North Vietnam. Apparently encouraged by Henry Kissinger, himself a veteran of Pugwash, to exploit their personal acquaintance with Ho Chi Minh, Raymond Aubrac and Herbert Marcovich embarked on a secret mission for the U.S. State Department. Because Marcovich was organizing a Pugwash symposium in Cambodia, the scientists could journey there on "Pugwash business." Through Cambodia they reached Hanoi in July 1967. According to various accounts, the Frenchmen brought back assurances that the United States could assume that North Vietnam would not use a bombing pause to supply its combatants in the South. This so-called San Antonio formula may have softened U.S. reluctance to begin negotiations. Although the San Antonio plan had little immediate impact, negotiations finally began outside of Paris less than a year later.[40]

In an imitation of Aubrac and Marcovich's maneuver, Eaton, whose fortune funded the early Pugwash meetings and who often attended later ones, made his own trip to North Vietnam. In Hanoi he met with Xuan Thuy, the head of the North Vietnamese negotiating committee in Paris. In a letter delivered to the 1969 Pugwash conference, Eaton listed Xuan's demands, hoping that perhaps the delegates could do something about them. As the war dragged on, even U.S. Pugwash scientists began to advocate broader critiques of the war. A 1968 Pugwash report by Paul Doty decried the effects of the Vietnam

War (and the Soviet invasion of Czechoslovakia) on nonproliferation efforts, thundering "End the Vietnam War. Get out of Czechoslovakia," and the statement from the 1969 Pugwash conference advocated the complete withdrawal of U.S. forces from Vietnam as a "necessary condition for the establishment of peace."[41] Although Pugwash scientists had placed a premium on being an avant-garde force in the world, their approach to Vietnam placed them squarely in the mainstream.

Edward Teller likewise had little original thought to offer to the Vietnam debate. Frequently harangued during the war years by student radicals who claimed he had advocated waging a limited nuclear war against North Vietnam, Teller saw the conflict in fairly partisan terms. In the 1960s he supported U.S. intervention in Vietnam because "the chance for the people of South Vietnam to live in freedom was being lost." After Richard Nixon became president and took over the war effort from Johnson, according to Teller, "stupid decisions were no longer made," though the war remained essentially unwinnable. "Even in retrospect," he wrote, "I do not know how we should have answered the hard questions posed by this conflict."[42]

Rabinowitch, for his part, tried to convince his peers that the war, while regrettable, was a distraction from bigger problems. Back in 1965 he had devoted a great deal of space in the *Bulletin of the Atomic Scientists* to discussing the war, including an article titled "Focus on Vietnam" in June. On New Year's Day 1966, Rabinowitch proposed in the *Bulletin* that the United Nations or the World Court arbitrate an end to the war. Two years later, Rabinowitch again attacked the Vietnam War and the Johnson administration in a scathing editorial. The war, he argued, diverted world attention from the challenges of peace and developing nations, wasting precious energy and resources on "struggles for political and economic domination or ideological supremacy." Recognizing that the war risked further nuclear disaster, Rabinowitch angrily moved the *Bulletin*'s clock forward to seven minutes to midnight.[43] While he opposed the war, however, Rabinowitch preferred not to use Pugwash as a method of ending the conflict. Vietnam distracted governments and the public from the possibilities of cooperation, Rabinowitch believed, and apparently it distracted Pugwash as well. Slowly, Rabinowitch began to grow frustrated with the organization. In 1968 and 1969 he published no articles about Pugwash in the *Bulletin*.

Just as Pugwash attempted to end the Vietnam War, U.S. science advisers also worked to bring the conflict to a close. But also like Pugwash, and indeed U.S. society as a whole, government science advisers found that the Vietnam War tore at the strands of cohesion in their community. As late as December

1964, PSAC meetings did not address Vietnam, but the advisory committee's role changed as soon as ground troops were introduced into Southeast Asia. An April 1965 PSAC meeting considered the topic "War in South Viet Nam," a discussion that continued at meetings on June 7 and 8. By February 1966, PSAC had moved on to the theme "Scientific and Technical Support for Military Operations in Viet Nam," and scientists' role in the war continued to fill PSAC's agenda at meetings in May 1966, May 1968, and June 1968.[44]

Hornig's tenth-anniversary memo pledged PSAC to develop new weapons technology for use in Vietnam. But as the Johnson White House began to mobilize its scientific resources for the military campaign, many U.S. scientists voiced opposition to the war. Although PSAC had always worked on defense and military technologies, Vietnam forced Hornig into an awkward position. As an array of scientists increased their criticisms of Johnson's Vietnam policy, Hornig found himself trying to keep the scientific community from revolting against the White House while simultaneously trying to enlist scientists for the war effort. A *New York Times* article in late May 1967 had described Johnson's growing disconnect from the intellectual community, and Hornig wrote to Johnson about the article, warning him not to "discount the interest and influence of the scientific community. . . . They are among the most worried and hard to deal with in connection with Viet Nam and we continue to need their support." A few weeks later, an OST scientist terminated his government contract in protest of the war, while elsewhere Hornig had to defend himself against charges of denying a spot to William Taylor on PSAC's Innovation in Education Panel because of his opposition to the war.[45]

In order to bridge the growing divide between the administration and scientists, Hornig tried one last time to convince Johnson to send a presidential greeting to Pugwash in 1967. Hornig assured Johnson that doing so "would help improve your image in the intellectual world." As before, no message was sent. But even as he tried to convince Johnson to reach out to scientists, Hornig played his own part in driving the two sides apart. The same year that Pugwash recommended an immediate and unconditional bombing halt followed by peace negotiations, Hornig formed the Ad Hoc PSAC Vietnam Group, whose contribution to solving the "problem" of Vietnam would be through the "application of technology [capable of] improving our ability to secure and hold areas and hamlets."[46] Clearly, by this point Pugwash and the OST were working at cross-purposes; government scientists, having been redefined as purely technical advisers, could offer only military technology as a means of ending the war.

A 1967 letter to Hornig from Sidney Drell, the chair of PSAC's Ground Warfare Panel, reflects the active role government science advisers took in pursuing weapons technology during the Vietnam War. Expressing a mindset that new weapons would help end the war (not dissimilar to many scientists' feelings about the A-bomb during World War II), Drell asked Hornig that "technology be given a chance to show what it can offer for improved border security." At the time, Drell and other top U.S. physicists consulted for the Institute for Defense Analysis as part of a group known as the Jasons. Their attempts to use technology to end the war came from their belief that the Rolling Thunder bombing campaign was ineffective and needlessly cruel. With new "sensor technology," Drell wrote, Vietcong movements into Cambodia could be better observed and "blocked with a commitment of resources far less than would be required of us to extend the actual fighting base across the Cambodian border or across the DMZ [demilitarized zone]."[47] While emphasizing the strictly technical had allowed scientists to take part in the test ban debate, a similar approach to Vietnam obscured the larger moral issues at stake in the war.

As the war further transformed into a quagmire in 1968, Hornig found himself working more and more for the war effort rather than the peace effort. He defended the war, "regrettable as it is, [as] vital to the interest and security of this Nation and the World" and assigned Drell's panel to work on problems associated with "pacification/revolutionary development." He then promised Johnson "an intensive effort on Viet Nam" that included improving war technology in Vietnam because "some brands of [the] latest technology make us look pretty silly." One of the OST's accomplishments during this period was the "Snoopy" helicopter that carried a television camera for use at Khe Sanh.[48]

Even though Hornig continued to work toward closing the distance between the Johnson administration and scientists, the damage had been done. In March 1968 Kistiakowsky resigned his position as an adviser to the Pentagon in opposition to the war. While Kistiakowsky remained a PSAC consultant, his move reflected heavy disenchantment among the academic community with Johnson. In the spring of 1968 PSAC counted just two Pugwash veterans among its members, and one of those, Seitz, served as president of the NAS and automatically sat on the committee. Instead, representatives of industry and business dominated the committee, including an executive of Ford Motor Company and two industrialists.[49]

With the Johnson administration oblivious to Pugwash and ever more consumed by the war in Vietnam, scientists' avenues for influencing U.S.

Cold War policy narrowed as the 1960s progressed. After the high point of scientists' influence in 1963, cooperation between scientists and the White House was tested. Hornig had sympathy for Pugwash and shared many of the organization's goals regarding development, and while Pugwash goals harmonized with OST policy at some points, Vietnam stifled this potential partnership. As for science advisers' antinuclear goals, disarmament had gradually disappeared from the OST's agenda—just as Rabinowitch had predicted. Indeed, PSAC's overall influence declined severely after Wiesner left the post of chief science adviser.[50]

Scientists and the Nonproliferation Treaty

Although arms control and disarmament was no longer part of PSAC's purview, progress was still made on that front. While at least one Pugwash scientist complained in 1967 that the conferences had grown stagnant and that "the pros have caught up with us," Bernard Feld anticipated in 1968 "exciting and fruitful" advances in disarmament building on the nuclear Nonproliferation Treaty (NPT) that pledged each signatory power to pursue realistic disarmament proposals "in good faith." Furthermore, nuclear weapons states vowed not to provide nonnuclear powers with nuclear weapons, while nonnuclear adherents promised not to pursue nuclear weapons development.[51]

Concern about nuclear proliferation had begun simultaneously with the development of atomic weapons during World War II. The movement for international control of atomic weapons after the war had attempted to prevent proliferation before it started, though the Baruch Plan submitted by the United States to the United Nations failed at this endeavor. Eisenhower's Atoms for Peace program, a bald propaganda attempt aimed at downplaying the U.S. embrace of nuclear weapons, made a token nod at nonproliferation by promising to make nuclear power universally available, and Kennedy had hoped to achieve nonproliferation with a comprehensive test ban, though the LTBT fell short of this goal. When Johnson replaced Kennedy, a nonproliferation treaty became "the number-one arms control priority" of his administration, according to AEC chairman Glenn Seaborg. The successful Chinese A-bomb test in 1964 gave added impetus—urgency even—to this effort.[52]

While the United States and Soviet Union agreed in general terms that nuclear proliferation was highly destabilizing and menacing, the nations disagreed over whether nuclear sharing—especially with America's NATO allies—counted as proliferation. The State Department initially hoped to exempt the transfer of nuclear weapons to allies from any nonproliferation agreement in order to retain West Germany in the alliance. The Soviets, for their part, objected to any agreement that would allow West Germany to acquire or even house nuclear weapons in any form. A government committee, led by Roswell Gilpatric, deputy secretary of defense under Kennedy, took the opposite view, downplaying NATO's importance and recommending to Johnson that nonproliferation take priority, even at the risk of fraying the alliance.[53]

By 1966 the United States and Soviet Union had reached basic agreement on what became the first two articles of the treaty. Article I prohibited the transfer of nuclear weapons between any nations whatsoever, while Article II forbade nonnuclear signatory states from developing nuclear weapons. Article III addressed inspection measures to verify compliance, an issue that the U.S., Soviet, and European negotiators struggled with at length. While these articles eventually satisfied the nuclear powers, the nonnuclear nations, led by Sweden's Alva Myrdal, felt cheated. From their perspective, they were being asked to forgo the security of nuclear weapons without the superpowers sacrificing anything at all. The French defense minister, sympathetic to these dissenters, described the treaty as an attempt "to castrate the impotent." The nonnuclear nations accordingly exacted a "ransom," in Seaborg's words, in the form of Articles IV and V that pledged the nuclear powers to assist any nation that signed the treaty with the development of peaceful nuclear energy. Because this pledge extended the treaty to developing nations with no real potential for a nuclear weapons program, Seaborg described it as "out of hand." The nonnuclear states also forced Article VI on the superpowers, which obligated the nuclear states to make genuine efforts at disarmament. The NPT was signed in Moscow, Washington, and London on July 1, 1968, with the U.S. Senate ratifying it by a margin of eighty-three to fifteen on March 16, 1969.[54]

Scientists had little to do with the NPT's creation, not necessarily because of Johnson's disconnect with scientists or their relatively low status in his administration but mostly because, unlike the LTBT, the treaty did not hinge on important scientific questions. The test ban debate had sparked dispute (some of it contrived) over how "real" the fallout threat was as well as the reliability of verification measures. In contrast, Seaborg explained, there was "no technical fix for the proliferation problem." Instead, the nuclear powers had to convince other nations that nuclear weapons were an unwise, unnecessary, and dangerous pursuit. Policymakers had no real need for technical experts to advise them on nonproliferation; at Senate hearings held by the Committee on Foreign Relations, Seaborg and Teller were the only scientists to testify.

The treaty inspired little controversy in the United States, as nearly everyone opposed proliferation—Teller did not even mention it in his memoirs.[55]

The lone scientific issue affecting the treaty concerned how to monitor nonproliferation. Article III identified the methods used to detect the diversion of nuclear materials from peaceful uses to weapons purposes, known as safeguards. As AEC chair, Seaborg did the most to analyze this concept and explain it to government officials. While the Soviets and Americans planned on implementing safeguards established by the International Atomic Energy Agency (IAEA), several European nations objected. The members of the European Atomic Energy Community (EURATOM), Belgium, France, Italy, Luxembourg, the Netherlands, and West Germany, preferred their agency's own established safeguards, claiming that outside inspectors might steal industrial secrets. The Soviets, however, dismissed such a solution as self-policing. To break the impasse, Seaborg helped convince Johnson to put U.S. facilities under IAEA safeguards, demonstrating the nation's willingness to submit to universal standards. Another compromise allowed EURATOM inspections to take place with IAEA oversight. Seaborg exerted so much effort in resolving the safeguards controversy that Secretary of State Dean Rusk once referred to the NPT as "Dr. Seaborg's treaty." Even so, the dispute over safeguards was not really about the mechanics of inspection or detection but rather about political posturing, as Seaborg admitted that either IAEA or EURATOM standards would have sufficed.[56]

Seaborg's experiences in the Johnson administration did not match those of other scientists, as he suffered neither the indifference shown to Hornig nor the antagonism directed toward PSAC. At the beginning of his tenure in office, Johnson enthusiastically told members of PSAC, "You just tell me what it is I should do. Don't you worry about how to get it done. That's my job and I'll take care of it." But three years later, he berated them: "You people just come in here and tell me what I ought to do. You never stop to think how hard it is for me to do it, and you never take the time to help me with it."[57] In contrast, Johnson and Seaborg remained on good terms, with the chemist carrying out some relatively important tasks, including official visits to Australia, Brazil, India, Pakistan, and Israel in order to gently (and ineffectually in the last three cases) discourage these nations from going nuclear.[58] One reason for Seaborg's warmer reception in the White House might have been personal: unlike many PSAC scientists, Seaborg never questioned Johnson's Vietnam policy but rather supported his efforts and decades later continued to blame the "insistence" of the president's advisers for Johnson's "gradual ensnarement" in the conflict.[59]

On a deeper level, Seaborg avoided clashing with Johnson because neither he nor the AEC represented science or scientists in the administration. Instead, the AEC was charged with making and testing nuclear weapons and with promoting nuclear power in the United States, meaning that in a professional sense, Seaborg spoke for the nuclear weapons and power industries. When the Gilpatric Committee was being formed, Seaborg had maneuvered to get the president of the New England Electric System appointed in order to defend the nuclear power industry against claims that it might contribute to proliferation. Seaborg's official reports on AEC activities on the first and last days of the Johnson presidency contain nothing about arms control but a great deal on nuclear testing, the Plowshare program, and nuclear power.[60] The AEC had, of course, fully aligned itself with the national security state and nuclear deterrence by the time of the Oppenheimer hearing of 1954, and having a scientist at its head did nothing to change that. This situation caused cognitive dissonance for Seaborg, who had contributed to the Franck Report in 1945 and been a member of the GAC during the Super debate of 1949 (though unlike the rest of the committee, Seaborg advocated unconditional development of the bomb). But as AEC chair, Seaborg often found himself in the awkward position of promoting weapons and policies that made him privately uneasy. During one discussion about a comprehensive test ban, Seaborg actually argued against such a treaty on the grounds that it would prevent important nuclear tests from taking place. Such a stand reflected the "personal dilemma" he faced as AEC chair. "At all times then and since," he wrote later, "I have strongly believed that judicious arms control agreements, most especially a comprehensive test ban treaty, are essential to secure a tolerable future for humankind. Yet, in my official position, I felt obligated to point out the technical need for certain types of tests. This was especially true when, as in this case, it was national policy to develop major new weapons—there is no way to do this without testing." As the AEC had intended in 1954, a scientist—even the agency's own chair—stifled his moral beliefs in order to support weapons development and deterrence.[61]

The NPT, meanwhile, reenergized Pugwash, even though its scientists had played no real role in the treaty's creation. After much debate, the organization issued a public statement in support of the NPT and began a critique of the next step in the arms race: antiballistic missiles.[62] Rabinowitch, however, grudgingly acknowledged the NPT, even moving the Bulletin clock back to ten minutes to midnight, but he refused to be impressed by arms control measures that simply froze the status quo. "The importance of the treaty is mostly symbolic," he wrote, echoing his interpretation of the test ban treaty nearly six years earlier. The NPT, he explained, would not lower the number of nuclear weapons, nor would it prevent the current nuclear powers from increasing their arsenals. The treaty would also do little to stop a nation from acquiring nuclear weapons should it choose to do so. The NPT, like the LTBT before it, was nothing more than "a first step." The great powers "must proceed without delay to the next one—the dismantling, gradually, of their own oversized military establishments. Otherwise the hope raised by the treaty will prove futile."[63] Rabinowitch likely anticipated that a revival in symbolic yet tangible goals like the NPT would further drive Pugwash away from cooperation and back toward the tired field of arms control.

Scientists under Nixon

Despite the schism between scientists and the Johnson administration, many politically engaged scientists saw a Republican presidency in 1968 as an even greater evil. A number of former science advisers thus exerted their influence in an attempt to defeat Richard Nixon's presidential bid. Wiesner agreed to head a scientific advisory panel for the Democratic candidate Hubert Humphrey's campaign, while Rabinowitch wrote to the *New York Times* endorsing Humphrey and blasting Nixon for "stemming the flood of change." Feld went even further, framing the election as a "life-or-death" decision between Humphrey and Nixon, whose plans for a nuclear buildup "would place us squarely on the road to national and international disaster." Kistiakowsky also penned a letter to the *Times* endorsing Humphrey. Hans Bethe became a founding member of Scientists and Engineers for Humphrey in 1968, despite receiving a form letter from the Republican and former AEC chair Lewis Strauss inviting him to join his organization for Nixon and Agnew.[64]

As the election drew near, Bethe penned a letter to Drell in October 1968 regarding a planned TV discussion between Drell and Humphrey. Bethe urged Drell to emphasize arms control in the discussion rather than Johnson's Great Society pet projects. Bethe's primary arms control interest was ratification of the NPT, but he also mentioned ABMs and multiple independent reentry vehicles (MIRVs). Hoping to prevent these advances in weaponry, he told Drell, "The experience has been that it is very difficult to eliminate a weapon once it has been introduced, but that it may be possible to avoid introducing it." Refusing to introduce a weapon was what Bethe and other scientists had hoped—and failed—to do with the H-bomb back in 1950. "So the time to act is now," he wrote, "and Humphrey is the only likely candidate to act constructively." On arms control as well as research money for science, Humphrey was clearly preferable to Nixon.[65]

After Nixon won the election, scientists found themselves predictably distant from the new administration. Nixon appointed Lee DuBridge of Caltech as his science adviser, and although the choice "delighted" Kistiakowsky, DuBridge fared no better in elevating scientists in the policymaking realm. Certainly, DuBridge seemed less likely to do so: in 1958 he had written to Rabinowitch expressing a desire to stay out of political causes. "I am one of those," he wrote, "who feel that things would have been better if [scientists] had stayed out of the so-called civilian control of atomic energy fight in 1945–46, for I think a better bill . . . had been proposed than the one which was finally passed."[66] (Given the AEC's actions since the mid-1950s, this was not an unreasonable statement.) With no interest coming from the president, DuBridge eventually grew "disaffected" with Nixon and resigned amid complaints from the scientific community that the White House had failed to adequately fund U.S. science. Nixon replaced DuBridge with the electrical engineer E. E. David, but this did little to placate the administration's scientific critics. In early 1972 *Physics Today* railed that no Nixon administration official was qualified to speak for the scientific community. Feeling "less than useful," David resigned in January 1973, and later that month Nixon abolished PSAC altogether, claiming budgetary restrictions. A *New York Times* editorial conjectured that Nixon's decision hinged on "the large number of prominent scientists who opposed him on the Vietnam war and on many other issues," including the supersonic transport and ABMs.[67]

With the Nixon administration escalating the Vietnam War, increasing numbers of scientists chose to distance themselves from work with military applications entirely. A 1969 declaration by MIT scientists stated, "Through its actions in Vietnam our government has shaken our confidence in its ability to make wise and humane decisions. There is also disquieting evidence of an intention to enlarge further our immense destructive capability." Criticizing the "small group that helps to conceive these policies" and the "handful of eminent men who have tried but largely failed to stem the tide from within the government," the MIT scientists declared that "it is no longer possible to remain uninvolved." They proposed turning research away from military technology and toward solving environmental and social problems. They also hoped to organize scientists and engineers for political action, harnessing "their desire for a more humane and civilized world." This cry came from politically inclined scientists who called for a research strike on March 4, 1969, and in the aftermath formed activist groups including the radical Science for the People and the more moderate Union of Concerned Scientists. Calling for an end to exploitative science that fed on social, racial, and sexual inequality, many scientists (often younger and not physicists) formulated an ethos that declared their independence from militarism but also one that diminished their public authority as objective experts.[68]

As the 1960s drew to a close, and with science being drawn into the decade's civil wars, Pugwash had only just survived. Confronting Vietnam had made little impact; disarmament remained the group's focus, while issues of cooperation and development ranked a distant second. Pugwash had extended its reach somewhat, but it did not completely transform. Most important, the group's ultimate goal continued to be the influencing of governments. But during its crisis years, Pugwash had become estranged from the governments it hoped to influence. In the Nixon White House, scientists had essentially no role within the administration, making it nearly impossible for Pugwash or any scientists to influence policy. Although Kissinger and Nixon preferred to keep disarmament negotiations, and foreign policy in general, under their own control, Kissinger had attended seven Pugwash conferences as either a participant or an observer. Yet in 1963, when Pugwash's "black box" proposal attempted to break the deadlocked test ban talks, Kissinger had written to the *New York Times* in order to distance himself from the group.[69]

Pugwash carried on nevertheless and continued to make occasional news; its plan for an end to the arms race made the front page of the *New York Times* in 1969. Far from a slow news day, the article on Pugwash shared the headlines with the Supreme Court's order to use busing to enforce school integration and the placement of the Black Panther Bobby Seale in chains at the Chicago Seven trial. Meanwhile, in recognition of his many years of service, Rabinowitch was elected president of Pugwash in 1970. His address to the annual conference tried to steer Pugwash toward cooperation in the pursuit of world peace. The danger of nuclear war "had abated," he asserted, "even if it is by no means permanently eliminated." Instead, "Pugwash has a more creative role to play—that of exploring and implementing constructive cooperation between all parts of mankind." Pugwash must work on "narrowing the gap between the rich and the poor nations," which was "the key to the future of mankind." As always, Rabinowitch closed on an optimistic note. "In approaching the end of my involvement in Pugwash," he announced, "I know that I will, at best, see some light at the end of the tunnel."[70]

Rabinowitch's optimism was misplaced. A Canadian student at the conference asked the scientists if all their talk achieved anything at all. After the conference, Rabinowitch wrote to Rotblat, explaining that "my last ambition in connection with Pugwash is to help initiate a viable Pugwash program in development." He then warned Rotblat about the fate he had feared for Pugwash since 1963: "becoming utterly institutionalized and ritualized as a series of friendly annual social affairs with no pioneering in critical problems of man's future—and development is in my mind, the most important one of them."[71]

But Rabinowitch felt that he spoke to deaf ears. He wrote in late 1970 about the "recalcitrant attitudes when it comes to discussing development at Pugwash." Although some scientists agreed on the urgency of development (notably Wiesner and Long), Rabinowitch believed the Soviet members of Pugwash stifled true advances. The "backwardness" of Soviet delegates, Rabinowitch wrote, as well as disapproval from "their bosses in the Kremlin," prevented progress on a development program. The Soviets, "sensitive about soiling their pure white Marxist clothes," did not want to deal with development because doing so would imply that coexistence with capitalism was possible. After venting his frustrations, Rabinowitch announced that he was "rotating out" of the Continuing Committee in early 1971. Later that same year, he suffered a heart attack, and less than two years later he died.[72]

The First Step Is the Easiest

The technical approach to arms control, shaped by the redefinition of science, had resulted in a series of arms control achievements by the early 1970s. Taken individually, these agreements seemed to promise a path to disarmament, but the cumulative effect painted instead a picture of an eternal cycle of first steps. Initially, when a nuclear test ban became a political issue in the 1956 presidential election, many antinuclear scientists had jumped on the idea and predicted that the test ban would be the crucial first step toward disarmament.

During the presidential primary campaign in the late summer and fall of 1956, the Federation of American Scientists endorsed a nuclear test ban "as a preliminary step toward complete and universal enforceable disarmament."[73] The Democratic candidate, Adlai Stevenson, had proposed a nuclear test moratorium during the general election as "a beginning, a starting point, a way to get off the dead center of disagreement" over the "means of taming the nuclear weapons."[74] Such language permeated the test ban debate. Rabinowitch, not personally disposed toward a test ban, nevertheless begrudgingly listed some justifications for a test ban, including that "the test ban could be a relatively easy first step toward controlled disarmament." When the superpowers signed the LTBT in 1963, Rabinowitch echoed his earlier sentiment in an editorial titled "First Step—to Where?" In moving the *Bulletin's* famous Doomsday clock a few minutes back, he explained that "the limited test ban is a first step," hopefully, though not certainly, "toward progressive disarmament and readjustment of the threatening deployment of the two camps."[75]

As the years passed after the test ban treaty, disarmament, rather than appearing one step closer, seemed as far away as ever. The NPT in 1968 had renewed a familiar hope; a *Bulletin* article in June of that year by the Indian physicist Indu Shekhar Mishra argued that "an effective treaty will be the first major step toward nuclear disarmament." And when the U.S. Senate ratified the NPT in March 1969, Rabinowitch hailed the treaty in these exact terms, first announcing that the Doomsday clock would be set back by three minutes, to ten minutes to midnight. Then, perhaps forgetting what he had written about the test ban treaty, he declared, "The great powers have made a first step. They must proceed without delay to the next one—the dismantling, gradually, of their own oversize military establishments. Otherwise the hope raised by the treaty will prove futile."[76]

Apparently, the hope did prove futile, as by the 1970s scientists continued to search for that elusive second step. A June 1972 *Bulletin* editorial by Feld praised the agreements that came out of the Strategic Arms Limitation Talks as "only the first step" in what would be further disarmament. The concept reached the level of cliché: Rabinowitch reprised his old metaphor in an article just a few pages later, writing that "the chief importance of the Moscow [SALT] agreements is that they represent first steps toward" stabilizing the arms race.[77]

Détente also threatened to make Pugwash irrelevant. Rotblat resigned as secretary-general in 1973, reasoning that with détente in full swing, Pugwash was no longer the only East-West communication channel. A 1974 paper by the Polish Pugwash group declared that the Cold War "has been completed."[78] In a historical oddity, nuclear protest in general declined during the era of détente, just as many arms control measures arrived, including the establishment of nuclear-free zones and limits on strategic arms, in addition to the NPT.[79] These achievements failed to buoy scientists' hopes, as they found it especially painful that arms control agreements had failed to bring peace; a joint statement by the U.S. and Canadian Pugwash groups castigated the movement's impotence. Pugwash had been "foolishly complacent" in believing that détente would lead to disarmament. Instead, atmospheric tests by the Chinese and French, India's successful nuclear test, and underground tests by the British, Soviets, and Americans were a collective "rude awakening." They predicted that "a new cycle in the arms race is about to begin."[80] In many ways, Rabinowitch's skepticism about the pursuit of disarmament proved correct, as many antinuclear activists felt they had gotten nowhere, despite the many treaties signed.

Yet scientists may have influenced peace and the Cold War despite their own pessimism about their efforts. Although none of the treaties and meetings and first steps led toward disarmament, they did stabilize the arms race to some extent, locking in the nuclear stalemate until political conditions within the Soviet Union brought the Cold War to an end, after which nuclear arms reductions followed. Instead of failure, prodisarmament scientists were perhaps successful in a very different way than they envisioned or even realized.

The close of the 1960s and the beginning of the 1970s saw Pugwash and PSAC decline in influence. For scientists engaged in transnational efforts to influence policy, the rise of détente made these efforts superfluous. The primacy of the Vietnam War, meanwhile, left scientists with little influence, as their identity had been redefined as strictly technical, and even nuclear agreements such as the NPT were settled with little input from scientists. Members of Pugwash perversely had to look forward to the end of détente to play an influential role again. In a 1981 interview, Feld, the head of Pugwash after Rotblat, explained that during détente, Pugwash "seemed less and less interesting, because there were a lot of channels for discussion. Now that we're back in a period of freeze, this becomes important again." In reality, however, scientists' efforts to bring about arms control and disarmament did not stagnate during the era of détente. In particular, the physicist Herbert York offered a new perspective on nuclear weapons during the 1970s. A Pentagon scientist, York's mainstream approach to politics brought him impressive influence in Washington, as he became a diplomat, leading negotiations over an arms control treaty with the Soviets at the highest levels. The 1970s saw scientists reach new heights—and face new challenges—in the struggle against nuclear weapons.

6

The Dilemmas of Herbert York

Opposition in the Mainstream, 1952–1981

I N LATE 1973, THE NUCLEAR PHYSICIST Herbert York learned he was on
Richard Nixon's enemies list. "I am amused by it all," he wrote to a friend
on hearing the news, "but not particularly proud of it, because I am well
aware a great many other deserving people . . . were omitted for reasons
which reflect neither well on me nor badly on them."[1] After wagering with
friends that Nixon would serve out his second term, his losses included a
hundred dollars and two bottles of champagne. Settling up one of these bets
took him to Moscow, where he presented the eminent Soviet physicist Peter
Kapitza with a fake newspaper emblazoned with the headline "KAPITZA
WINS BET, YORK HUMILIATED."[2]

At the moment he found himself on Nixon's list, York stood squarely in
the mainstream of politically active U.S. scientists. A longtime government
science adviser, former chief Pentagon scientist, and first director of the
Livermore nuclear weapons lab, York had for years made recommendations
on both weapons development and arms control to presidents, Congress, and
the Department of Defense. In 1969 York had actively opposed the Nixon

administration's antiballistic missile program, perhaps the reason he ended up as one of the president's enemies. A year later, he published a book, *Race to Oblivion,* that denounced the arms race and counseled government and the public alike that there was no technological solution to the arms race. Because the arms race was "wondrously absurd and exceedingly dangerous," he wrote, the public was willing and eager to believe the "hard-sell technologists" who promised technological salvation from the Soviet threat. Scientists themselves frequently bought into this myth as well, creating "self-righteous extremists who have all the answers." In York's view, the belief that only scientific and technical experts could solve the nuclear weapons puzzle was dangerous. The only solution to the arms race was political, he argued, consisting of negotiations with the Soviets and "a sensible, reasonably self-interested diplomacy and foreign policy."[3]

By the early 1970s, it made sense to speak of a mainstream of scientists' thoughts on nuclear weapons. For decades, conservative scientists like Edward Teller had promoted an ever-increasing array of ever-more technologically advanced weapons: H-bombs, ICBMs, submarine-based missiles, ABMs, MIRVs, and more. In the late 1960s, more radical leftist scientists (some of them in organizations such as Science for the People and the Union of Concerned Scientists) challenged the fundamental concepts of science itself, exposing sexism, racism, and elitism in the scientific discipline.[4]

Reflecting his mainstream nature, York expressed total confidence in the ability of the U.S. government to solve the problem of nuclear weapons. His responsibilities in the Pentagon took him frequently before Congress, and although his personal politics were transforming him into a critic of the arms race, he was no radical. He later wrote that his years in Washington gave him "an even stronger confidence in its [the U.S. government's] validity and in its ability to produce the right policies, given accurate inputs and enough time." He nevertheless saw a tremendous need for "good inputs" from experts and officials within the executive branch, especially in the realms of science and technology.[5]

As far as antinuclear scientists were concerned, Charles Schwartz, a physicist at UC Berkeley, embraced a radical leftist critique. Schwartz described the diversity of views on government science advisory committees as varying only "from hawkish to super hawkish." (York actually agreed with this statement.)[6] Elsewhere, in correspondence with York, he hoped for a mass movement with truly radical antinuclear goals. The arms control "experts" were almost exclusively oriented "towards working within the government and its associated elite channels." Schwartz expressed disdain for working within the system; conferences, congressional testimony, and expertise like the kind York practiced had the effect of telling the public, "These are very complicated matters . . . so all you worried but unqualified people should just quiet down, trust the experts, trust the system to work things out best."[7] York had for years warned people against blindly trusting experts, yet in his pursuit of arms control he relied heavily on his authority as a respected physicist and member of the nuclear weapons establishment.

York could have such a dialogue with Schwartz and find many areas of agreement in the 1970s, but it had not always been so. During his most formative years in science, York was in many ways a typical weaponeer. York's "odyssey," as he put it, from the Manhattan Project to comprehensive test ban negotiations, made him into an arms control advocate. But he never completely shed the duality of one who both designed weapons and sought to limit them. In one of his books, York identified seven dilemmas about the arms race, three of which stand out. First, he identified the paradox that the bomb was essential in preventing war yet risked "the end of all civilization, if not mankind"; second, that scientists have "special knowledge" about nuclear weapons, but their solutions to the nuclear problem were "often naïve and based on false notions"; and third, that more nuclear weapons made for a stronger deterrent, but this made the potential failure of deterrence drastically more dangerous.[8] These dilemmas manifested themselves in York himself as well—he made this quite explicit when he titled his autobiography *Making Weapons, Talking Peace*. As a politically active and influential scientist after the chaos of the Oppenheimer hearing, the Red Scare, the H-bomb, the test ban, and Vietnam, York continued to struggle with the contradictions and dilemmas involving science and nuclear weapons. But unlike many who preceded him in scientific activism, York gained influence into the 1970s after so many others had been discredited or alienated. While the Vietnam War had weakened the links between science and the state, excluding many scientists from government advising, York helped sustain the alliance that joined science with national security by critiquing nuclear weapons from a patriotic, technical perspective that still supported the basic premise of nuclear deterrence.

From the A-bomb to the H-bomb

York's early years as a scientist gave no indication of the future dilemmas he would wrestle with. He grew up in Rochester, New York, reading biographies of Galileo, Columbus, Pasteur, and the French astronomer Camille

Flammarion. His teen years coincided with the Great Depression, which had left his father and several other relatives unemployed. In his writings he never mentioned any sort of personal politicization occurring during the 1930s other than becoming a Roosevelt Democrat and an "avid newspaper reader" who enthusiastically followed the New Deal. This was in contrast to Robert Oppenheimer, who was radicalized by the Depression, and a number of Jewish physicists overseas alarmed by the rise of Hitler. Unlike many other scientist activists of the postwar era, York was not a refugee from Europe and was a bit younger than the more famous names of the Manhattan Project. Yet he was undoubtedly part of the World War II generation, as he listed the formative events of his youth as Munich, Pearl Harbor, Auschwitz, Yalta, and Hiroshima.[9]

York studied science as an undergraduate at the University of Rochester, and on graduating in 1943 he moved to Berkeley to study at Ernest Lawrence's Rad Lab at the University of California; Lawrence had been a "remote hero" of York's ever since he learned about the cyclotron, which Lawrence had invented. At the Rad Lab, he joined the Manhattan Project and worked to develop techniques for the mass production of U235. As uranium production ramped up, he moved to Oak Ridge, Tennessee, where he put those techniques into practice, which helped produce U235 for the Hiroshima bomb. Whereas scientists at Los Alamos and Chicago spent time reflecting on the significance of the atomic bomb, York did not think much at all about the morality of the weapon. This mind-set resulted perhaps from his youth but certainly from the influence of his mentor and "father figure" Lawrence, who discouraged such thoughts. After the atomic bombs fell on Japan, York, in typically low-key fashion, simply uttered, "We did it." To him, the A-bombs signified the end of World War II rather than the beginning of the Cold War, so he accordingly closed this chapter in his life and looked forward to the next one.[10]

With the war over, York left Oak Ridge and spent the next four years as one of Lawrence's graduate students at UC Berkeley. Despite the tumult of postwar discussion, anxiety, and protest over the A-bomb, York stayed above political debates, with the famously conservative Lawrence telling him, "Keep your nose to the grind-stone" and out of politics, even though Lawrence was himself very involved in nuclear policy discussions. As a graduate student, York took classes with Oppenheimer, whose "intellectual arrogance" turned him off. Instead, he learned nuclear physics from Emilio Segrè and in due course married, had a child, and received his Ph.D. in 1949. In his reserved fashion, he described his relationship with his wife in just a few sentences:

after their "first big date," he wrote in his memoirs, "things developed nicely from there. We were married in Berkeley's First Congregational Church in September 1947, and we have lived 'happily ever after' ever since."[11] After earning his Ph.D., he managed to stay on as a faculty member at the Rad Lab, where he was quite content. Working closely with Lawrence naturally guided York toward weapons development rather than considering the political implications of nuclear weapons, as many other scientists were doing at the time.

Despite Lawrence's restrictions, political events in the late 1940s insinuated themselves into Rad Lab discussions. The Berlin Airlift, the Soviet A-bomb, and the fall of China—these Cold War crises eroded in York's mind the sense of invulnerability that had graced the United States since the end of World War II. For nuclear scientists and government officials, including Lawrence, in late 1949, these events directly affected the heated debate over whether to begin a crash program for the Super. With the Rad Lab already involved in making tritium and free neutrons for the development of a thermonuclear device, discussion of the weapon could not be confined to its scientific aspects.

Once President Truman ordered crash development of the Super in January 1950, the Rad Lab doubled its efforts. York joined the H-bomb project in the spring of 1950, having missed most of the controversy over the decision to build it. To him, the decision mainly meant a boost to his career and his interests. "New horizons had suddenly opened up before me, and I was anxious to explore them," he wrote in his memoir. Discussions over the H-bomb in his circle mostly emphasized "the impact that it would have if only the Russians went down this road and not us," he recalled in a 1987 interview. "I never thought of it as anything other than a plausible answer to the growing problems that we were facing externally." York took to the H-bomb project with enthusiasm. Frequently at Los Alamos, he worked on ways to measure the unprecedented temperatures that would be created by the George shot, an elaborate experiment to ignite a small thermonuclear explosion. It was here where he came to know Teller, whom York fondly described as full of "infectious" and "youthful enthusiasm." He heard about the Teller-Ulam innovation directly from Teller himself and—with a shudder—recognized that it would produce a true thermonuclear explosion. After the George test succeeded in May 1951, York looked forward to returning to pure scientific research.[12]

Inside the Scientific-Technological Elite

Like so many elite nuclear physicists during the Cold War, pure research was not in York's destiny. Instead, York was instrumental in the creation of the second national weapons laboratory in 1952, very much playing the role of weaponeer. In this way, York had a front-row seat for the development of the H-bomb, Teller's rise to power, and the escalation of the arms race. More than just an observer, York epitomized the "scientific-technological elite" that Eisenhower would warn about in his farewell address. Yet by the time Eisenhower made that statement, York would agree wholeheartedly with the president.

The origins of the second national weapons lab lay in Teller's years of dissatisfaction with Los Alamos, dating back to his demands immediately after World War II that the lab dedicate itself to Super research or frequent atomic tests—demands that the Los Alamos director Norris Bradbury refused. In the years since, Teller had deemed the staff of Los Alamos too slow and unprepared for serious H-bomb research.[13] Lawrence joined Teller's campaign for a second lab and asked York whether the country needed such an institution. Asking around, York's inquiries convinced him that a second lab was indeed needed, though he later admitted that he had talked mostly to people sympathetic to Teller. According to York, many scientists saw the need for a second lab because China's entry into the Korean War and the Sino-Soviet alliance indicated that the struggle with communism would be a long one. Since Lawrence could staff this lab with people already on his payroll, the Atomic Energy Commission easily approved the second lab, and in a surprising moment Lawrence approached York and simply told him to "run it."[14]

Although York held the position of lab director, Lawrence and Teller very much shaped the new institution. While both men were happy to have the second lab, they differed over the philosophy that would guide Livermore. Lawrence wanted few concrete goals, while Teller wanted the lab to undertake a crash program to develop the Super. (Los Alamos had begun work on the Super, but Teller had since refused to work there.) The AEC ordered vague plans, leaning more toward Lawrence's view, but Livermore was clearly a weapons lab when it opened in September 1952. One of York's earliest memories from the lab dated to November 1952, when he and Teller "witnessed" the 10.5-megaton Mike test by watching the explosion's shock wave register on Livermore lab equipment. For York, the successful thermonuclear test gave him a feeling of "awe and foreboding." But given the lack of communication with the Soviets, he saw no way it could have been avoided.[15]

With Livermore working on thermonuclear weapons, Teller had the influence and respect he felt he deserved since cutting ties with Los Alamos. Though not officially in charge, Teller served as a member of the lab's steering committee, offering ideas, advice, and inspiration. York also got a sense of Teller's broader influence when in 1960 an AEC commissioner told him, "I don't just admire Edward, I *worship* him."[16]

Although no single man dominated the lab, Livermore did manifest Teller's spirit of nuclear ambition and optimism and very much fueled the arms race. The ruling philosophy at Livermore was not to wait for requests or instructions from the government; rather, researchers were encouraged to push the technological extremes to produce the smallest, lightest, cheapest, and most explosive nuclear weapons possible. Only after development would they work on selling them to the government. "We were completely confident that the military would find a use for our product after we proved it, and that did indeed usually turn out to be true," York wrote. At one point, York even proposed a 20-megaton nuclear test, but Eisenhower refused the request, stating, "Absolutely not; they are already too big. . . . [T]he whole thing is crazy; something simply has to be done about it."[17]

Some of Livermore's first weapons included the Polaris, a submarine missile, and the Davy Crockett, a nuclear mortar shell. The strategy of pushing the limits of weaponry, the lab leadership believed, would best maintain U.S. nuclear supremacy and the intellectual stimulus required to keep scientists at the lab motivated. Because of this, York later wrote, "The laboratory leadership had to engage in a continual effort to sell its ideas, to anticipate military requirements, and to suggest to the U.S. military ways in which its new designs could be used to enhance preparedness and better support our general nuclear strategy." The arms race that York would later declare absurd grew out of clear, if paradoxical, logic: nuclear weapons seemed to be the safest, surest, and cheapest way of maintaining U.S. security.[18] Yet this security, achieved so easily in the short term, carried tremendous risk to all humanity.

The escalation of the arms race, very much driven by Livermore's philosophy, pushed Eisenhower in the direction of arms control. This shift cohered with the global movement alarmed by nuclear fallout from massive testing, but Eisenhower's initial advisers on a nuclear test ban included Lawrence and Teller, neither of whom was inclined to support arms control. Teller not surprisingly was totally hostile, demanding full speed ahead on weapons development. Initially, York saw no benefit to a test ban, but he did support "mutual restraints of some kind." Observing his mentors' role in the test ban debate taught York that U.S. leaders would have to overrule opposition to arms control and disarmament. "They cannot simply repress it or hope to convert it," he counseled later. After all, the government had asked these same men to build the most potent arsenals possible and could not reasonably expect them to later renounce these weapons. Tellingly, even York was not above using scare tactics to build support for his weapons lab; in the late 1950s, he would menacingly play the beeps of *Sputnik* as he made his pitch for more funds.[19]

Despite his closeness to Teller and Lawrence, York did not wholly absorb the hawkish attitudes of his mentors. "Among the group at Livermore and Berkeley," he wrote, "I was always more open to the notion that we ought to negotiate, that not only are we providing a solution, b[ut] we are creating a problem at the same time." In conversations with Lawrence and Teller, York "always thought we ought to try harder, we ought to be doing more. Maybe we could figure out some way to limit nuclear weapons." Working closely with Teller at Livermore, York "came to understand" his older colleague's worldview but ultimately rejected Teller's "extreme views" about nuclear weapons development and his "total hostility" to negotiations with the Soviets.[20]

Leaving the University of California for Washington led him to more liberal views on nuclear weapons (possibly the first time anyone became more liberal by *leaving* Berkeley). Joining the President's Science Advisory Committee in the late 1950s and working for President Eisenhower and his science adviser James Killian very much altered York's views on the nuclear weapons that he had helped develop at Livermore. "I talked with other people," he told an interviewer in the 1980s. "The people I talked with, instead of being Teller and Lawrence, were [Hans] Bethe and Killian. . . . I really was changing my views with respect to the utility of [arms control], and concluded after some months that it was a good idea."[21]

When he left Livermore, York also left behind Lawrence, his mentor, and Teller, his strong-willed colleague, a break that could not have been easy for York, though his many writings reveal frustratingly little about such personal matters. When he heard news of Lawrence's death from colitis in 1958, York recalled that he simply "put nuclear physics and the Radiation Laboratory off in a quiet corner of my mind." Teller, meanwhile, claimed to have no hard feelings about York's evolution into an arms controller, writing in his memoirs that even though York favored a test ban, "the issue never came to a head between us as Herb left [Livermore]." York never indicated anything to the contrary until an interview decades later, when he said, "My support of the Test Ban, after I got to Washington, was regarded by a number of people at Livermore, particularly Teller, as being a major act of disloyalty on my part."[22]

A pivotal moment in his transformation came at a 1957 meeting between Eisenhower and his science advisers in Puerto Rico. When the president asked whether he should consider a nuclear test ban, everyone voted yes except for York, who chose to abstain. "Here we are a bunch of physicists," York told the group. "What do we know about this as in the best interest of the United States?" he asked. Jerome Wiesner later pulled York aside and told him, "First of all, the President can ask anybody anything he wants. And second, there isn't anybody else to ask."[23] From that point on, York felt empowered to weigh in on political debates over nuclear weapons.

From PSAC to the Pentagon

The 1957 flight of *Sputnik* so alarmed the United States that the Eisenhower administration almost instantly transformed U.S. science and its relationship with the government. York found himself caught up in these dramatic changes that, as he put it, exposed him to people with "considerably broader and more complex" views on world and national security. As a member of PSAC, York served on five panels involving space exploration, missile development, and arms control and disarmament. York did not exactly fit in with the other members, who largely resented York's close connection to Teller. "Evidently," York reasoned, "they wanted someone from inside the current nuclear weapons establishment."[24]

Although a Democrat, York warmed to the president after meeting him and found that they agreed about imposing limits on the nuclear arms race. In particular, York used data and evidence to counter critics of Eisenhower's who decried the (imaginary) missile gap with the Soviets. This new cadre of government advisers within PSAC, including York, most of whom "regarded nuclear testing as pernicious," marked a "sea change at the White House level" in attitudes about nuclear weapons.[25]

The early 1950s, disrupted by the Red Scare and increasing Cold War tensions, had been notable for the number of ways in which scientists inclined toward arms control had been increasingly excluded from policy circles. York's mentor Lawrence had done much to convince him that scientists had no place in the political sphere, and he had been initially uncomfortable passing judgment on the test ban and other political questions. But Wiesner and other PSAC members convinced him otherwise. "I quickly came to realize that he and the others were right about this peripheral issue," York wrote, "and I approached the substantive questions with a new seriousness." But the presence of scientists in policymaking created another dilemma for York. In his mind, scientists had long sounded the warning about nuclear war based on their expertise. "Physicists and physicians understand better than others the thermonuclear horror that is always only thirty minutes away from happening," he wrote. Their warnings are "correct and soundly based." Scientists' solutions to the problem, however, had too often been to bureaucratize the problem—York mentioned the Arms Control and Disarmament Agency (ACDA) as an example—leading to little progress. Instead of a plethora of experts and paper pushers, York suggested that the president needed to take charge of nuclear weapons policy.[26]

Following a year of working with PSAC on test ban monitoring and missile-gap analysis (and even a critical moment when he advised Eisenhower to allow Francis Gary Powers's ill-fated U-2 flight to proceed), York made the jump to the Pentagon, recently expanded because of the *Sputnik* scare. The new secretary of defense, Neil McElroy, was sworn in just days after *Sputnik* took orbit; in this frenzied atmosphere, he established the Advanced Research Projects Agency (ARPA) and the Office of the Director of Defense Research and Engineering (DDRE) to counter the perceived problems with U.S. defense technology. After consulting with Lawrence and Killian, McElroy appointed York as ARPA's chief scientist. Under York ARPA managed defense projects that had been ignored or stalled by interservice rivalries, especially ABMs, rockets, and a space program.[27]

ARPA served as a short-term answer to the problems manifested by the *Sputnik* launch; the DDRE offered a long-term answer. York soon became the head of DDRE and assumed authority over appropriations and expenditures for, in York's estimate, about eighty thousand projects, from better shoes for soldiers to lasers. Everything in the defense establishment involving research, development, testing, and evaluation fell under York's purview, but he felt his most important work at the DDRE involved merging the army space program into NASA.[28]

While working at Livermore had given York one view of the military-industrial complex, his position at the Pentagon revealed even more sinister dangers. Visiting the North American Air Defense Command in 1960, York learned about the development of Launch on Warning, the automated nuclear retaliation to a registered threat. Alarmed that nuclear war could be initiated by computers, York then visited the headquarters of the Strategic Air Command, where he learned the U.S. plan for waging a nuclear war. There York was thoroughly exposed to the concept of mutually assured destruction, which he labeled "absurd" and "seriously wrong." But as before, York saw no simple way out of the nuclear dilemma.[29]

York served only a brief time at the Pentagon; in 1960 he suffered a heart attack and found himself sharing a VIP hospital suite with the outgoing vice president, Richard Nixon. (The aspiring presidential candidate had been admitted for a knee injury and infection suffered on the campaign trail; Nixon later blamed the time spent recovering for his sallow and unhealthy appearance during his infamous debate with John Kennedy.)[30] Although York likely could have served whichever candidate was elected, he planned on leaving government after the election. He remained at the DOD until Robert McNamara was sworn in as secretary of defense and was soon replaced at the DDRE by Harold Brown, a close colleague from Livermore.[31]

By 1960 York had transformed noticeably from the pusher of technology he had been at Livermore. He later summarized his beliefs about nuclear weapons at this point in his life: defense of the U.S. population is impossible, no technical solution exists to the national security dilemma, and a political solution is the only real hope for ending the arms race. But he still embodied a duality that reflected the paradox of nuclear weapons. That is, he worked for both weapons development *and* disarmament, for military preparedness *and* the search for political solutions to the arms race. York himself pointed out this seeming contradiction:

> In my mind the two sides of the security equation are inextricably linked. In making decisions to develop and deploy the weapons needed to maintain a stable balance, we must take into account the way such actions will affect the nuclear arms race. And conversely, when working out plans for controlling or eliminating nuclear arms, we must bear in mind how the resulting action will affect the "correlation of forces"—to use the Soviet term. Most important, in all cases we must base our thinking on the facts as they are in the real world, not on how we might wish them to be. . . . Given my long history of involvement— some might say complicity—in creating the nuclear weapons world we all now must live in, I have felt obliged to maintain an active interest in and involvement with both sides of the problem.[32]

This statement describes more than it explains; throughout his life York prided himself on his balanced approach to both sides of the nuclear issue. Referring to his later role in arms control policy under Jimmy Carter, York said that he was "enthusiastic about helping the new administration push ahead. But the military balance was also getting out of hand. So I also supported a number of activities in the Defense Department designed to redress the imbalance."[33] By keeping nuclear weapons development and disarmament in mind simultaneously, progress in either realm would be measured, productive, and not too disruptive to the geopolitical situation—somewhat like York himself. At any rate, other influential scientists, such as Oppenheimer, Bethe, and Andrei Sakharov, had, at various times, also pursued the seemingly contradictory goals of arms development and arms control.

Once he left government service, York became the first chancellor of the University of California at San Diego (UCSD) in 1961. But this new job did not hold York's interest for long; bored with the duties of chancellor, York contracted a serious case of "Potomac fever" and began to miss Washington politics. He resigned as chancellor on the fateful day of November 22, 1963, with the result that no one paid attention to his departure. Although he stayed on campus, he felt the role of aging prestigious professor did not suit him and continued to yearn for more consulting and advising in the "national security world."[34]

He got his chance in 1964 when he rejoined PSAC, where his responsibilities included Third World technical assistance and service on a nonproliferation committee that recommended a nonproliferation agreement, a comprehensive test ban, and nuclear-free zones. But by the time of his return, the committee had outlived its "golden age." Torn between Johnson's vision of using science in support of the Great Society, on the one hand, and his desire to win the Vietnam War, on the other, science in the Johnson White House quickly fell out of favor. York explained: "Our failure to help him win [the Vietnam War] contributed to his disenchantment with us and our kind." For his part, York never had any doubt that Vietnam was a lost cause, leading him to become "disaffected with Lyndon Johnson and the war" and "disgusted with what I would call the phoniness of it all," especially "the false optimism based on entirely erroneous judgment about what was happening." About half of PSAC felt the same, according to York, but Johnson dismissed their concerns as merely the irrelevant views of strictly technical advisers. The Vietnam War "demoralized me," York later admitted. "It was such a gross mistake and misuse of American power. It discouraged me. I sort of turned away from dealing with those people, the pros at the top of the Defense Establishment. But I never turned away completely."[35]

By 1969 York had little access to Washington circles with Nixon in power, their shared hospital stay years earlier notwithstanding. No longer on PSAC, he instead served as graduate dean at UCSD, with a brief stint as acting chancellor during the student rebellions of the late 1960s. To try to satisfy his desire to influence national security, he first created the interdisciplinary Program on Science, Technology, and Public Affairs and then the Institute on Global Conflicts and Cooperation, apparently requested by the state of

California in order to balance out UC's image, tarnished from its role as over-seer of the Los Alamos and Livermore labs.[36]

The ABM Debate

Having seen both sides of the nuclear weapons issue, York continually worried about the influence of what Eisenhower described as the scientific-technical elite in his famous farewell address. "[Eisenhower] had in mind, and I know this from talking with him later," York recalled, "[missile designer Wernher] von Braun and Teller as people who are just out there selling and selling, and telling you that if you don't do what they're telling you you ought to do, you are going to be doomed. The hard-sell technologists are what he had in mind."[37] In a 1964 article in *Scientific American,* York wrote that "there was no technical solution to the problem of security vis-à-vis the Soviets," and he called for "arms control restraints." The article, according to York, "very much annoyed" the DOD. York's congressional testimony for the Limited Test Ban Treaty in 1963 and against ABMs at the end of the decade put, in his words, "a measure of dissent between me and . . . the majority of the Defense Establishment."[38] He also wrote a book supporting the General Advisory Committee's recommendation against the H-bomb in 1950, stating that "it was not only right, it was right for the right reasons."[39] And in 1973 he told an aide to Senator George McGovern (D-SD) that "for the long run, I think we've got to attack the notion of deterrence itself. . . . There has got to be a better way."[40] By 1976 York had moved far from where he started, telling a peace organization staffer:

> My basic position is that the development and deployment of nuclear weapons have turned out to be a horrible mistake that must somehow be undone. We and four other nations have created and built systems whose basic purposes are to achieve certain policy goals by threatening to set in motion a chain of events which would kill a half billion people in a single day. That is not a theoretical statement or speculation about what might be done or what ought to be done; it is a literal description of what has been done; it is a description of a means which cannot be justified by any conceivable ends.[41]

York publicly emerged as a force for nuclear disarmament and arms control during the 1969 debate over ABMs. Missile defense, as an idea, had developed in lockstep with missiles themselves during the German bombing campaign against Britain during World War II. But in reality, practitioners of missile defense had little to show for their efforts. Still, although the massive power of nuclear weapons suggested there could be no viable defense against them, the United States pursued defensive measures during the Cold War all the same, from civil defense volunteers watching the sky to bomb shelters and duck-and-cover drills. And for those prone to see salvation in technology, ABMs seemed irresistible. Although the concept remained popular for decades, the technology behind ABMs never really changed: powerful radars would detect incoming warheads and determine their course, at which point nuclear warheads would be launched into the path of these missiles, totally destroying them. By 1956 von Braun had begun to develop the Nike-Zeus interceptor missile as part of the army's ABM effort. Working at ARPA in 1958, York supported a "full-scale, high-priority" effort "to develop and deploy" this system, and when he moved to the DDRE he continued to approve ABM research but advised against deployment because the system was too easily overcome with countermeasures.[42]

ABMs never totally lost their allure to the Pentagon, even though the fundamental concerns about their efficacy were never addressed. After the tumultuous years of the test ban, the Vietnam War, and détente, the controversy over ABMs briefly promised to return scientists to political relevance. The approach of antinuclear scientists had changed in some ways since the early 1960s, however. During the test ban debate, scientists had largely argued that fewer nuclear weapons would make the United States more secure and that technology could enforce a reliable test ban. In contrast, the ABM dissenters challenged the reliability of science and technology, while also arguing counterintuitively that defensive missiles made the United States less secure. Led by York, scientists attempted to make the case that the solution to the arms race relied not on technology but rather on diplomacy and clear political reasoning. Initially, this promised to reduce scientists' role in nuclear weapons debates because, it seemed, scientists were not the diplomats and politicians that would achieve these breakthroughs.

Debate over ABMs began around the time of the ratification of the LTBT in 1963, sparked mostly by the decision of the Soviets to deploy ABMs around Leningrad in 1962 and Moscow in 1964.[43] Thwarted in his attempt to stop the LTBT, Teller quickly mobilized to counter criticism of ABMs, which had become the next evolutionary step in the arms race. During test ban hearings, Teller had named ABMs as one reason not to sign a test ban, arguing that the treaty would hamper U.S. development of defensive weapons. Among several arguments in its favor, Teller pitched missile defense as protecting the nation from a plethora of imagined future threats coming from China, including "big nuclear explosives" delivered "from ocean-going vessels" that could be detonated in "any big city in the world." "If this situation should arise," he declared, "it will be possible for the Chinese to blackmail either us or our NATO allies." No technology could prevent "an all-out Russian attack," he wrote, but missile defense would protect the major cities of the North Atlantic against the "crude missiles that the Chinese are likely to possess. It seems to me reasonable, in fact almost necessary, to insure ourselves against independent Chinese blackmail."[44]

In 1967 Teller continued to reference the Chinese threat as well as tensions within NATO in his advocacy of ABM development and deployment. But he also made clear that ABMs would be of value against the Soviet Union. At a public discussion, Teller's audience applauded when he stated, "The Russians are not given to adventure. If we have an Anti-Ballistic Missile system which will call into question the efficacy of their attack, this in itself will greatly contribute to deterrence." Elsewhere, Teller presented a further argument for ABM deployment: "Such a measure would be the best procedure to shield the United States from the consequences of nuclear proliferation."[45] Teller's lobbying paid off as usual; the Johnson administration decided in 1967 to deploy an anti-Chinese ABM system that briefly ignited public debate over the issue.[46] The system, dubbed Sentinel, consisted of roughly one thousand missile launchers capable of neutralizing a Chinese nuclear attack dispersed around twelve missile sites. Although McNamara described the system as "light," as planned it was apparently much larger than the system the Soviets had to defend themselves against a U.S. attack. After the army bought property near Boston, Chicago, and Seattle for ABM construction, residents of the neighborhoods around the sites rose up in protest.[47] Ultimately, the ABM program spun its wheels until the Nixon administration took over.

While a number of government scientists argued against Sentinel, Nixon as well as members of Congress pushed for a new ABM system to defend against Soviet missiles. The Soviet Union had recently deployed new SS-9 ICBMs, leading the DOD to estimate that in 1975 or 1976 a preemptive Soviet attack could destroy all but forty of the U.S. Minuteman missiles. Furthermore, ABMs could easily protect the Soviet Union if the United States counterattacked with its remaining missiles. Nixon accordingly changed Sentinel to Safeguard, intended for deployment around U.S. Minuteman silos to protect against a Soviet nuclear attack. Aside from the origins of the imagined missiles, however, Safeguard barely differed from Sentinel. The missiles would now be located away from cities, and the radars were to be upgraded to observe missiles launched from the USSR and China as well as other locations. But the basic equipment remained the same: missiles and radar. Specifically, the components included a long-range nuclear interceptor missile (named Spartan), a fast short-range nuclear interceptor missile (Sprint), two types of radar, a computer, and a command-and-control system. Safeguard resembled Sentinel in another dubious way: it appeared unlikely to work. To be sure, protecting missile silos was easier than protecting cities, according to York, because "only those warheads heading for impact within, say, two thousand feet of their well-protected targets had to be intercepted." But other protection measures "seemed more promising and much cheaper," including "mobility, deception, proliferation in numbers, and superhardening."

Critics of ABMs found the logic of the system wanting, explaining that the U.S. deterrent (nuclear submarines, bombers, and ICBMs) had so many warheads that it could never be taken out all at once, ensuring a retaliatory capability. Additionally, the Soviets would eventually build enough missiles to easily overcome Safeguard. Finally, the essential question asked was whether ABMs would even work. York found the question hard to answer because it was "a contest between two technologies; offensive weapons and penetration aids versus defensive weapons and discrimination techniques." Although nature eventually yielded its secrets to the scientist, there was no guarantee that humans could devise a technology to intuitively combat another technology. There existed far too many ways to confuse the defenses, as well as what York called the hair-trigger–stiff-trigger problem: an ABM system had to be able to sit for years and still be fired instantaneously when needed, yet it must never go off by accident.[48]

At congressional hearings in 1969, each presidential science adviser except Nixon's testified against ABMs; other expert scientific witnesses included York, Bethe, Wolfgang Panofsky, and Sidney Drell. They argued that the components of ABMs were poorly designed and even if fixed would provide protection against only a narrow range of threats over a limited period of time.[49] York was at this point situated at UCSD and, in his own words, a government "outsider" working with the Federation of American Scientists. Along with Bethe and Kistiakowsky, York petitioned to address Congress, and on March 11, 1969, he gave testimony against ABMs. Among the many technical reasons to oppose the system, York believed that the lack of real testing made any deployed system vulnerable to "catastrophic failure in which at the moment of truth either nothing happens at all, or all interceptions fail." He further argued that ABMs were dangerous because they might make people believe in a technical solution to the arms race, but technological advances must not divert from the search for a political solution:

Perhaps the worst arms control implication of the ABM is the possibility that the people and the Congress would be deceived into believing that at long last we are on the track of a technical solution to the dilemma of the steady decrease in our national security which has accompanied the steady increase in our military power over the last two decades. Such a false hope is extremely dangerous if it diverts any of us from searching for a solution in the only place where it may be found; in a political search for peace combined with arms control and disarmament measures.[50]

Here York offered a different argument for arms control: technology would not save the nation; it would not help win the Cold War. This was not the strictly technical advice of previous advocates of arms control, but it was also not the strong moral objections offered by true outsider scientists (despite York's use of the term). Instead, it was a scientist arguing against technology. Science had been so subverted into militaristic aims that one of its practitioners—one who had helped create nuclear weapons—argued against it. York pointed out the difference between designing technology and judging its merits: "If you want to know how to get to the moon, ask a rocket expert; if you want to know who should pilot the spacecraft, ask experts in space medicine and psychology; if you want to know what ought to be done after getting there, ask a geophysicist. But if you want to know whether someone should go there in the first place, ask any sensitive informed person."[51]

After a meeting with national security adviser Henry Kissinger, York testified in front of Congress again in the spring of 1969. York's appearance had little effect, however. Testifying against ABMs alongside the baseball player Jackie Robinson, York noticed that the House subcommittee basically slept through his testimony. But he persevered and provided testimony again in front of the Senate Foreign Relations Committee in July 1969.[52]

A joint statement from the time coauthored by York emphasized the "promising opportunity . . . to bring the strategic arms race to a halt by mutual agreement with the Soviet Union" on ABMs. The deployment of ABMs would quash the diplomatic progress made during détente, which was the true game changer in the Cold War. But York still relied on scientific expertise for his arguments, as the statement went on to criticize the technical aspects of ABMs, describing the Safeguard system as "poorly designed for the purposes it is to serve" and one "we could have little confidence in." The ease of penetrating or confusing an ABM system gave the scientists "grave doubts whether an ABM system would work as planned." A litany of further problems followed: there was no way to test the system in conditions that truly resembled the fog of nuclear war, U.S. ICBM sites did not need such extensive defenses, the Soviets might see the initial deployment as the last chance to strike, China was simply not a large-enough threat to merit ABMs, and "tax reduction, checking inflation, coping with pressing social needs, and possibly also other military requirements, have a far stronger claim on our resources at this time."[53]

In contrast, Teller found himself on the opposite side of the issue from his old colleague and relied on tried-and-true tactics in support of nuclear weapons. As he had during the test ban debate, he challenged the credibility of both his ABM opponents and their arguments by questioning their objectivity. In a letter to Sharon Weldon, a graduate student in political science who was studying arms control, Teller wrote, "It is my opinion that these technical arguments happen to be fallacious and are to a great extent motivated by political, rather than by technical considerations." Bethe, by now a member of the old guard of arms control scientists, also wrote to Weldon, explaining that his reasons for opposing ABMs "were both technological and strategic. . . . Technologically, we believe the system to be ineffective. Strategically we think it will greatly stimulate the arms race." Bethe notably added that "there are no moral reasons against ABM."[54]

Bethe continued to critique nuclear weapons from a technical perspective. In congressional hearings he discussed the Sentinel ABM system, stating that its components "are well designed, and . . . will work as designed," a significant divergence from York's view. Despite the system's functional reliability, he continued, "I am worried about the possibilities of penetrating the system." Objects as simple as thin Mylar balloons could be coated with metal, which would allow "the balloon [to] reflect the radar waves so that the balloon appears to the radar like a reentry vehicle." Other decoys, including chaff and radio waves, could also easily deceive the system. But Bethe's objections did go beyond the strictly technical and into the strategic. Turning to the presumed aggressor, China, Bethe questioned the logic of Sentinel. As China's missile supply grew, Sentinel would become less effective. "They need to deploy only a small number of ICBM[s] to penetrate our defenses," he stated to Congress. "It is for your committee to judge whether a few years of protection against the Chinese missile attack is worth the price of the Sentinel System." Bethe reminded his audience that any Chinese attack on the United States would be "totally suicidal, without accomplishing much of military value against the United States. . . . [And] China has not shown any suicidal tendencies in its military policy toward other nations."[55] In tune with York's beliefs, Bethe implied that the solution to nuclear threats lay less in technological advances and more in a sober assessment of U.S. adversaries.

An August 1969 Senate vote on ABMs resulted in a tie, and although Vice President Spiro Agnew broke the deadlock in favor of Safeguard, deployment was essentially halted until a year later, when the supporters of deployment regained momentum. Appearing before Congress one more time on August 3, 1970, York expressed his concerns about the increasing automation of the arms race. In the case of ABMs, York predicted that policymakers would not have complete confidence in the system, which would lead the defense establishment to push for a Launch on Warning doctrine. This system would in turn have to be controlled by computer because the time to make a decision would be so short. "The decision will have to be made on the basis of electronic signals," York stated, "electronically analyzed, *in accordance with a plan worked out long before by apolitical analysts in an antiseptic and unreal atmosphere.* In effect, not even the President, let alone the Congress, would really be a party to the ultimate decision to end civilization."[56] Far from a savior, the mechanized technology of the arms race in the 1970s would become the faceless initiator of the apocalypse. These words, advising against overreliance on technology, from the mouth of a onetime weapons scientist, harmonized to some extent with the disaffection many Americans felt with science and technology in general during the late 1960s.

But the absence of moral arguments against ABMs meant that when the political or strategic environments changed, those weapons became acceptable as alternatives to even newer, more destabilizing weapons. In 1978 Bethe wrote to York about the MX program, an expansive ten-thousand-mile network of roads and shelters for ICBMs on mobile launcher vehicles. "I am appalled by the concept of the MX," he wrote. "Surely if we go in this direction, the Soviets can and probably will do so as well." Bethe recognized the pattern of the arms race, where new systems only created new threats. But his technical opposition to nuclear weapons put Bethe in a pattern of accepting whatever happened to be the previous generation of weapons. "I remember when the multiple warheads were first conceived and introduced," his letter to York continued. "From the beginning it seemed to me highly destabilizing, and . . . we [PSAC] pretty well agreed that this was so. After the brief interval during which MIRV gave us superiority, we now must be afraid of it in the hands of the Russians. Do we want to repeat this, on an even larger scale with MX?" Given this logic, the formerly scorned ABM seemed like a good option. "It looks to me that the ABM defense of selected missile sites is still very preferable to the MX," he wrote. "It may even be cheaper."[57]

Eugene Rabinowitch criticized ABMs as well, challenging not their tech-nological aspects (although it remained unclear whether these missiles would work) but the system's dependence on psychological—and hence unpredictable—factors. "I doubt whether anybody (and least of all, scien-tists) can predict the psychological consequences of various steps in the arm [sic] race," he wrote to York. Should the Soviets develop an ABM defense, "will this increase their bellicosity or make them more accommodating? If the Americans deploy an objectively insufficient ABM defense, will it nev-ertheless have a determining effect on Soviet aggressiveness?" These "psy-chological problems make rational argumentation about ABM deployment very difficult," he ended. "I have no conclusions to offer, except that I am against spending tens if not hundreds of billions of dollars on an undertaking of doubtful efficiency."[58] Whereas technical objections to nuclear weapons failed to halt the arms race during the test ban era, the ABM debate proved that arguing against technology also made it difficult to challenge the arms race. Scientists made their influence felt during the ABM debate, to the point that ABMs all but disappeared. Yet this success depended on challenging the reliability and efficacy of technology itself.

Ultimately, sentiment turned against ABMs. Public and congressional opinion opposed further military expenditures at the end of the Vietnam War so much that Nixon pursued an arms control treaty in order to help his reelection bid. With that in mind, the Nixon administration negotiated an ABM treaty with the Soviet Union, reaching agreement in 1972. The treaty limited each signatory to deployment of two ABM systems, a token amount that effectively made ABMs a nonfactor in nuclear strategy; the United States set up just one system, at the Minuteman site near Grand Forks, South Dakota, but shut it down in 1975.[59]

York's experiences with ABMs reinforced his belief that political change happened from the inside rather than the outside of government circles. He even came to regard his time dissenting outside of political circles with some regret. "I now look back on that [as]—I won't say, 'a mistake,'" he told an interviewer in 1987, "but the next thing to it. I would have been able to have a much more positive influence over the course of events if I hadn't taken such a public position. . . . I didn't like being an outsider. But I didn't do anything to stop it, either." Elsewhere, he elaborated, "If a person wants to help resolve a serious structural dilemma like the nuclear arms race, the best way to do so is by joining the mainstream, the establishment." For almost forty years, of course, York had been a part of that establishment, his self-described phase as an "outsider" notwithstanding. While "dissidents and outsiders" could have some influence, true change was achieved only by "those who join the main-stream." "Persuasion, persistence, and patience are more powerful tools than placards," he explained. "Serious study, including a real attempt to under-stand how things got the way they are, will produce better results than protest songs." While his status as a university administrator during the tumultuous 1960s influenced these views, he wrote that this lesson was also reinforced by visits to the Soviet Union in the late 1970s and early 1980s.[60] Although York professed to have the greatest confidence in all the representatives of the American people, he also believed that change ultimately depended on the president. And in 1976, after the election of Jimmy Carter, York was able to again become an influential insider when Carter appointed Harold Brown, York's close friend from his Livermore days, as secretary of defense.

The Scientist as Diplomat

Even before Carter's election, York had perhaps anticipated a return to gov-ernment service, as he discussed with Brown in May 1976 his preferences for working within the executive branch. Although he would not "design or promote new weapons," he wrote to Brown, he would be pleased to work as a special assistant "for the purpose of either (1) being implicitly or explicitly responsible for relating new weapons technology to overall national secu-rity issues, including especially arms control, or (2) improving the over-all quality of the defense establishment." After Brown's appointment, York got his wish. Consulting for the DDRE, the office he once headed, York advised the Pentagon on nuclear weapons systems, including the B-1 bomber and the MX missile, helped negotiate the prohibition of antisatellite technology, and attended frequent meetings with the secretary of defense.[61]

   According to York, Carter tried the hardest of any president on nuclear arms control and disarmament but accomplished the least. The détente of the 1960s and 1970s had encouraged coexistence between the superpowers and resulted in a series of agreements on nuclear weapons: the LTBT under Kennedy; the Outer Space Treaty and NPT under Johnson; SALT, ABM, and a Threshold Test Ban under Nixon; and a Peaceful Nuclear Explosion Treaty under Ford. Eager to do his part to stem the tide of nuclear weapons, Carter embraced a comprehensive test ban as part of an ambitious arms control agenda that included proceeding with SALT II talks, notification of test mis-sile launchings, demilitarization of the Indian Ocean, and large reductions in nuclear weapons. According to Carter, bringing the arms race under control was the "best tool for improving our relations" with the Soviet Union. At the same time, however, the obstacles to arms control seemed daunting. The Soviets, by the late 1970s, had caught up quantitatively with the United States in terms of nuclear weapons, and, in York's opinion, "there was legitimate reason to believe that they were going to go further than that."[62] Arms control agreements, according to York, would not at this point have locked in any sort of strategic advantage for the United States.

Nevertheless, progress on arms control was not out of the question. While the LTBT had simply moved testing underground, where it actually increased, a complete test ban would eliminate all nuclear tests on earth and, it was hoped, hinder the creation of new nuclear weapons. Like many scientists, York had always felt that the LTBT was inadequate. "I hope the present partial nuclear test-ban will be followed by a second and more significant step," he wrote to the editor of *Science* in late 1963.[63] By the 1970s his idea of a "more significant step" had evolved into a comprehensive test ban, although as of 1973 he was "pessimistic" about achieving one during the ongoing SALT negotiations.[64]

York served on an expert panel reviewing the reasons for and against a CTB in 1977. The panel decided that a CTB would aid efforts at nonproliferation and would fulfill Article VI of the NPT that pledged the superpowers to make genuine efforts at true nuclear disarmament. On the downside, a ban on testing might make the U.S. nuclear stockpile less reliable and might discourage the nation's brightest scientists from pursuing work at the national weapons laboratories. These fears had been used to challenge the LTBT in 1963, but this time York could assure the Carter administration that the nuclear establishment's worries were "exaggerated." When official CTB negotiations between the United States and the Soviet Union began in Geneva in July 1977, York was working for Frank Press, Carter's science adviser, and informally in the Pentagon, where most of the DOD opposed a CTB.[65]

In late 1978 Paul Warnke, the head of ACDA and chief negotiator at the CTB talks, resigned. At the start of the new year, York was asked to replace Warnke as chief negotiator, which came with the title of ambassador (a childhood dream of York's). At the time, influential scientists like Bethe supported a CTB, as did Jeremy Stone, head of the FAS. But York was less certain: "I reached basically negative conclusions" about a CTB, he wrote, since U.S. leadership might not have confidence in a nuclear stockpile that had not been tested. Yet he accepted the assignment because he still believed a CTB was "in the best interests of the United States and the world" and because the nation's elected officials decided to pursue one. York's promotion came about so quickly that he had to abandon a course he was in the middle of teaching at UCSD.[66]

York's arrival in Geneva marked a brief renaissance in the influence of scientists on U.S. nuclear weapons policy. Since the 1940s U.S. scientists had endeavored to affect nuclear weapons policy as directly as possible, primarily by advising congressmen, the armed forces, and the executive branch. After the formation of PSAC, the science adviser became a cabinet-level position. Kennedy's science advisers had informally discussed a test ban with their Soviet counterparts, helping to achieve an arms control breakthrough in 1963. And although Johnson had alienated scientists and Nixon had downgraded the science adviser's status, here was York, just a few years later, a physicist, conducting arms control negotiations at the highest level. York's mainstream approach had finally given him the access to policymaking and a chance to negotiate with the Soviets, which had been his own prescription for ending the arms race and the Cold War.

Yet York's room for maneuver faced severe restrictions. He later wrote that the negotiating positions for each participant nation had been tightly controlled by their respective governments; neither Moscow nor Washington nor London had allowed their representatives much flexibility. Furthermore, with the Joint Chiefs of Staff and Department of Energy hostile toward a test ban, the instructions York received from Washington rarely amounted to anything helpful.[67]

At Geneva previous negotiations had left only the details of the treaty to work out. In particular, York spent his time focusing on the Separate Verification Agreement, which would implement a system to monitor each nation's adherence to the treaty. Disagreement over the need to monitor and inspect seismic events and ensure that no one was cheating the treaty had derailed the test ban negotiations during the Eisenhower administration and had caused the Kennedy and Khrushchev administrations to accept only a limited—rather than a comprehensive—test ban. But York was optimistic that an agreement could be reached, and presumably his scientific background gave him some authority during negotiations over complex technical matters. York was not the only optimistic participant: during a meeting with the chairman of ACDA's General Advisory Committee, Thomas Watson, the lead Soviet negotiator, A. M. Petrosyants, expressed "hope" that York's appointment would "accelerate" the negotiations. When Petrosyants told Watson that the Soviets were "in favor of cessation of testing," even though it would stunt nuclear weapons development, Watson assured Petrosyants that "a great many nuclear scientists like Dr. York . . . adhered to a similar line of thinking." The parties proposed that national seismic stations (NSS), essentially black boxes equipped with seismometers, be placed on U.S., British, and Soviet territory and discussed on-site inspections for suspicious events, periodic renewal of the treaty, and a ban on so-called peaceful nuclear tests.[68]

To York's disappointment, verification issues—especially the NSS—plagued the CTB talks, as they had the test ban negotiations almost twenty years earlier. The United States and Soviet Union disagreed over the method of data transmission for the NSS, with the Soviets objecting to the use of satellites. The Soviets also objected to the notion of mandatory on-site inspections, so York's team agreed to refer to them as voluntary in name only. Other roadblocks that were never resolved during York's tenure included establishing the acceptable reasons for conducting an on-site inspection, with the Soviets demanding that only seismic data be used to justify a visit, while the Americans insisted that other factors be allowed to trigger inspections. In addition, the two sides haggled over whether the NSS equipment in one country should be made by that same country or by the other.[69]

The British surprisingly threw a wrench into the negotiations by rejecting the NSS at first and then rejecting the proposed locations (chosen by the Soviets) for NSS on British territory. Apparently, the Ministry of Defence objected to the treaty just as much as the DOD and hoped to scuttle the talks by denying Soviet requests and emphasizing the prohibitive cost of implementation. Margaret Thatcher's rise to the post of prime minister added another influential voice of opposition to the CTB talks. The Soviets further complicated matters by insisting that Britain host an identical number of NSS as the United States, even though British territory was much smaller.[70]

More than a year into the negotiations, York despaired of reaching a settlement, writing that "the overall scene external to the negotiations, in both its international and its domestic aspects, effectively prevents very much real progress."[71] At the time, the Cold War was very much in flux. In addition to the U.S. military and DOD's opposition to the CTB, delays and problems during SALT II negotiations also slowed CTB talks. Various foreign policy crises, including the revelation of a Soviet battalion in Cuba and the taking of U.S. hostages in Iran, made negotiating with the Soviets look like a sign of weakness in the eyes of a revitalized Cold Warrior class in the United Sates. The final straw was the Soviet invasion of Afghanistan that quickly ended détente. York nevertheless saw value in continuing to talk—he had claimed for years, after all, that only negotiations could end the arms race. Without the end of détente, York suspected that a treaty would have been signed but that the U.S. Senate still would not have ratified it based on the disapproval of the JCS. These factors led York to declare that dealing with Washington during negotiations was even more frustrating than dealing with the Soviets.[72]

York visited Moscow in 1980 in an attempt to move the talks forward, but "bad luck in timing" set negotiations back, as the United States registered a possible violation of the threshold test ban treaty just as York arrived. York then returned to Geneva, where he learned of Ronald Reagan's lead over Carter in the presidential race. Reagan's stated opposition to a CTB made future negotiations unlikely, and his election victory turned the U.S. representatives in Geneva into lame ducks. The Carter round of CTB negotiations had been a failure, York wrote later—a failure that was "very overdetermined."[73] After Carter was voted out of office, York commented that the CTB negotiations were left "about at the halfway point." In 1981 his pessimism remained, as he assessed the CTB as "specifically unfinished, and without good prospects." He eventually mentioned a feeling of "desperation" about the treaty. By the late 1980s, he had reversed course almost entirely on a CTB, telling an interviewer, "I'm no longer sure about the role of the Test Ban in moving toward a better world." Because the CTB "arouses the most hostility within the Defense Establishment . . . it becomes hard to do anything," and because testing was no longer "the driving edge" of the arms race in the 1980s, a CTB "would have very little influence on the arms race."[74] (The United States eventually signed the CTB in 1996, though it has yet to be ratified by the Senate.)

Living with Paradox

After Reagan's inauguration in 1981 forced him to give up his post as ambassador, York continued to suffer from Potomac fever until his death in 2009. During the 1980s he pushed for a "no first use" nuclear policy, advocated for the human rights of scientists in the Soviet Union, and established the Institute on Global Conflict and Cooperation at the University of California, where he fed a captive graduate student audience his many anecdotes about science and politics.[75] There he hoped to "see a new generation come and take over. Try and do things better. . . . There's a new generation of experts. I want new people in there." Proud of his career, York stated that his generation had handled the nuclear weapons dilemma "as well as we could. We managed to get through without a nuclear war. On the other hand, we didn't eliminate the possibility. So I don't think we did so badly, and that we created something which is stupid and awful. I think that we handled things in a way that's far from perfect. But other people could have done a lot worse. I don't have any apologies either for me or my generation." There may have been a hint of defensiveness in his comments, as he once admitted that, in reference to the younger generation, "a very wide gap separates us."[76]

It is telling that near the end of his life, he was, as the institute's resident scholar-diplomat, educating political scientists rather than physical scientists, for York had spent most of his life wrestling with the contradictions of the nuclear age and the Cold War and far less on pure science. Nuclear weapons presented humanity with dangerous dilemmas: security at the risk of war and peace based on mutually assured destruction. York recognized these dilemmas and offered thoughtful ways to try to nudge the United States toward peace and away from nuclear war.

The greatest paradox York faced was himself: a weapons developer who pursued arms control. This duality gave York tremendous credibility among policymakers, since, as the former head of a weapons lab and chief Pentagon scientist, his pronuclear credentials were unimpeachable and allowed him to make the case for arms control. But this also limited his antinuclear ambitions. In the most direct sense, of course, he was busy promoting more efficient nuclear designs. But as one who prided himself on recognizing what was possible in politics, he refused to succumb to the utopian antinuclearism of, for example, Linus Pauling. York dreamed of a world without nuclear weapons, as Pauling did, but York's methods involved patient discussions and negotiations with the powerful and influential elites who ruled the superpowers. Pauling, a peace activist at heart, was more likely to circulate a petition or march with a placard. "A person who pretends to be an expert in one field and goes off preaching in another, undermines his credibility in everything," York stated. "I generally don't look with favor at people going off and making big preachments about things they don't know about."[77]

While the national security state very much excluded Pauling from decisions about nuclear weapons, it very much included York in policymaking circles. His views did not fundamentally challenge the state but rather harmonized with relatively mainstream political opinions. In correspondence with York about a CTB, Bethe expressed similar feelings about his role as a science adviser on nuclear policy. "The important thing of course," Bethe wrote, "is to move toward a test ban in a manner which can gain political acceptance. . . . Politics is the art of the possible."[78] But while York did everything by the book, he was still not necessarily more successful than Pauling in pushing the superpowers toward disarmament. Far from a radical, York's challenge to nuclear weapons was ultimately absorbed by the state. Although York had access to policymakers, and even negotiated an arms control treaty, this very influence actually reinforced the power structure of Cold War America and the centrality of nuclear deterrence.

York's life suggests that he very much internalized the views of the state.

It might be too much to suggest that he lived under a sort of false consciousness, but his own personal belief system seems to show that he defined himself in a way that would be the least challenging to the authority of the state.
Although York would probably have disagreed with this characterization, his
own words reflect this mind-set:

> It is almost never true that a ripe new idea is pushed only by a few active out-
> siders and unanimously opposed by those in the mainstream. Well before a
> new idea matures, the mainstream will itself become divided on the matter,
> and insiders as well as outsiders will be searching for ways to introduce the
> changes the new ideas call for. And when they finally succeed, it will be the
> insiders who work out the details and who control and elaborate all the other
> actions that, in the end, are necessary to make the changes effective. Thus, even
> in those cases in which dissidents play an essential role, and revolutionary sit-
> uations aside, it is the insiders who ultimately determine the shape, extent, and
> effectiveness of the final result.[79]

Although York was an independent thinker and a thoughtful advocate for
peace and disarmament, he also privileged access to elites above challenges
to the system. Even York's modest stab at dissent from outside the system
caused him consternation later in life. "In retrospect it's the part of my career
that I'm least happy about," he admitted. "I think that integrated over my
whole life, I would have done more for the general good and my country, if
I had not taken a public-dissenting stand"—this even after he helped stop
ABMs.[80] In this way, he shows the effectiveness of the Cold War state in controlling dissent not by repression but by enabling its citizens to internalize
the correctness of the dominant political system.

Not every scientist held the political establishment in such high regard. As
York and many of his fellow Manhattan Project veterans faded from the arms
control scene in the early 1980s, the new generation of activists that York
had envisioned rose to challenge nuclear weapons. This group included Carl
Sagan, a scientist who came of age in the counterculture of the 1960s. Sagan's
scientific conception of the world after a nuclear war would create an altogether new and dramatic challenge to nuclear weapons.

7

"An Elaborate Way of Committing National Suicide"

Carl Sagan and Nuclear Winter, 1980–1989

D URING THE EARLY 1980S, ANTINUCLEAR ACTIVISTS awakened from their slumber and swarmed across North America and Europe. In the United States, protesters rallied around a general antinuclear fervor, including but not limited to calls for a nuclear freeze, an arms control proposal that would instantly halt the arms race. Scientists participated in this revived antinuclear movement, including some a generation removed from the old guard of the Manhattan Project and the Atomic Scientists' Movement. No one exemplified these new voices better than the astronomer Carl Sagan, who moved politicians and the public alike to oppose the escalating arms race.

While the Pentagon and the executive branch tried to ignore this nuclear dissenter, as they had done with previous antinuclear iconoclasts, many members of Congress enlisted Sagan and his scientific theory as allies against the policy of nuclear deterrence. Surprisingly, while a substantial segment of the government had begun to look beyond the arms race and welcomed a scientist who challenged nuclear weapons, an equally substantial segment of the scientific community helped neutralize Sagan's efforts by emphasizing the apolitical definition of science established during the Red Scare decades earlier.

Mission to Mars

Carl Sagan arrived at the Senate Caucus Room in Washington on December 8, 1983, to participate in a forum convened by Senators Edward Kennedy (D-MA) and Mark Hatfield (R-OR). The public face of astronomy had come to speak on the severe disruption a nuclear war would inflict on the global climate, a disastrous effect he and his colleagues had dubbed "nuclear winter." In so doing, Sagan culminated a journey that had begun more than a decade earlier and millions of miles away—on Mars. As part of the NASA team controlling the *Mariner 9* mission to the red planet in 1971, Sagan followed the spacecraft's journey into Mars orbit. "We arrived at the planet—I say 'we,' but it was an unmanned spacecraft," he explained at the forum; "the spacecraft arrived at the planet and permitted us to watch what was happening on Mars."[1] Sagan vicariously returned to Mars in 1976 when the *Viking* spacecraft landed on the planet's surface to collect samples, run experiments, and take pictures. "I personally spent in a certain sense a year on Mars in the course of that mission," Sagan later recalled. Although the experiments dashed Sagan's hopes by finding no signs of life, the photographs provided him a particular thrill. At one point, he fashioned a large panoramic photo of the Mars horizon into a cylinder with the image facing inward and placed it around his head. With this crude but effective virtual-reality device, Sagan took himself to Mars. *Rolling Stone* journalist Timothy Ferris came along for the "ride"; the two men took turns gazing at the Martian landscape, silent and awestruck.[2]

Sagan also spent a great deal of time analyzing the data sent back from the probes. During its orbit of the planet, *Mariner 9* had encountered a "global dust storm" and recorded the odd combination of a warm atmosphere but a cool planetary surface. With little else to pass the time as they waited out the storm, Sagan and his colleagues began to crunch numbers, hoping to explain the oddity. The *Viking* mission confirmed that during a dust storm, "the temperature [on Mars] drops considerably," leading Sagan's group to conclude that "fine particles in a planetary atmosphere" cooled the surface temperature. Intrigued, the scientists wondered if a similar temperature drop could occur on earth. Computer models soon showed that a volcano could theoretically cool earth's surface if a major eruption released enough particulate matter into the atmosphere.[3] Soon enough, the scientists realized that the explosion of nuclear weapons could also cause a similar effect through the deposit of tremendous amounts of dust and, through the burning of cities and forests, smoke and soot into the atmosphere. After further calculations, the Sagan group estimated that nuclear war could trigger "a dense hemisphericwide pall of sooty smoke" over the northern half of the globe and "quick freezes" in the South, leaving the planet "in the cold and the dark." Alarmed by the findings, Sagan journeyed to Washington, where he told Congress, "There are no sanctuaries in a nuclear war." Indeed, the extinction of mankind was a possibility. During hearings on nuclear winter, when Sagan projected a slide onto the wall portraying the postnuclear war United States and Soviet Union engulfed in flames and blanketed by soot, he intoned, "One cannot tell from this figure who started the war. And it hardly matters."[4]

Today, nuclear winter is no longer in the headlines, but Sagan's antinuclear campaign does not deserve such a fate.[5] While the conservative and hawkish executive branch did fiercely resist his efforts, the planetary astronomer received an enthusiastic reception in Congress, where the theory had substantial influence on debates over arms control and provided scientific evidence for challengers of nuclear deterrence and the arms race. The concept of nuclear winter played a part in the breakdown of the deterrence consensus in the 1980s, as the bare facts of science repudiated the Cold War logic that had upheld deterrence since the 1950s.

Sagan probably expected objections from hawks and conservatives; more surprising were the scientific opponents who attacked him when the theory appeared. Openly conservative scientists like Edward Teller and S. Fred Singer naturally disputed his claims, but Sagan also faced criticism from less partisan peers like George Rathjens and John Maddox, the editor of *Nature*. Many of these opponents cared less about Sagan's science than his presentation of the science to the public and his subsequent political stands. These critics believed that using his science to make a political argument tainted his results and, by association, science itself. Sagan's failure to adhere to the strict and conservative mores of the scientific discipline alienated many scientists and resulted in the theory being excessively muted and disputed. While Sagan argued that science spoke urgently to the world, many scientists asked him to keep quiet, stressing that science should not seek out public or political influence. This view of objectivity reinforced old Cold War power structures that kept science from challenging deterrence.

Science in the Counterculture

Sagan's activist roots ran deep and reflected his coming of age amid the 1960s counterculture. Although his introduction to activism came when his graduate school adviser required him to canvass for the Democratic Party, he took quickly to liberal politics. By the mid-1960s he was traveling to Alabama to teach science seminars at the Tuskegee Institute and speaking out against the Vietnam War. Sagan also turned down projects funded by the military, stating, "I certainly don't want to be a party to this crime," and as the anonymous "Mr. X" he praised the mind-expanding powers of marijuana in the early 1970s. (His 1977 Pulitzer Prize–winning book, *The Dragons of Eden*, was "obviously written under the inspiration of marijuana," according to one biographer.) Despite these countercultural leanings, Sagan refrained from speaking out against nuclear weapons during the late 1960s, even as debate raged over antiballistic missiles. One study of Sagan explains, "The safest scientific foes of militarism were those who, like [Hans] Bethe, Linus Pauling, and others, were already famous. Sagan probably didn't feel famous enough to take the risks they did. Not yet."[6]

Observers of Sagan, from wives to biographers to former colleagues, discuss his reverence and love for science as almost religious in nature. Sagan himself described science as "informed worship." Though an outspoken atheist, Sagan looked to science to fulfill personal and philosophical aspects of life for which many other people turn to religion, including the search for meaning in and understanding of the world as well as moral guidance. As a planetary astronomer, Sagan knew the vastness of the universe, in addition to humanity's isolated and powerless place in it. Because "we're on our own . . . nothing can save us," he liked to say. In an existentialist rationale, Sagan suggested making life meaningful by trying to accomplish something worthwhile, such as ending poverty, hatred, or inequality.[7]

Sagan insisted equally on being scientific and encouraging scientific rigor in other realms of life, including religion and politics. To Sagan, this meant a steadfast reliance on solid evidence and a willingness—eagerness even—to be proven wrong. He told an interviewer in 1976 that science is "littered with dead theories," which he interpreted as a sign of progress, proof that scientists have to correct their theories and admit their mistakes. "I'd like to see politicians willing to admit that their ideas have been wrong and now they'll adopt a new one which will work better," he explained.[8] Sagan passionately and aggressively defended the objective reputation of science by relentlessly attacking pseudoscience such as "evidence" of unidentified flying objects.

Perhaps this conspicuous skepticism was necessary because at various times in his life he had entertained some fairly wacky ideas, including UFOs.[9] He had also pondered whether the moons of Mars were actually disguised alien vessels, theorized that "balloon animals" floated above Venus, and enthusiastically endorsed and promoted the radioastronomer Frank Drake's equation predicting the number of advanced civilizations in the Milky Way galaxy, $N = R \times f_p n_e f_l f_i f_c L$.[10] Thus, when Sagan did enter the nuclear weapons debate, he took care to appear as scientific as possible, supporting his claims with technical evidence and engaging with the people who criticized and tried to disprove his arguments. But Sagan was a stubborn opponent and easily took scientific evidence to be a jumping-off point for political advocacy.

The public first became aware of Sagan as part of the team organizing the NASA missions to other planets in the 1970s. A combination of lofty visions, media savvy, and non-nerd demeanor drew journalists to him, while his good looks and verbal flair ensured him a wide audience, including his role as essentially the in-house astronomer on Johnny Carson's *Tonight Show*. Though he published prolifically in the scientific literature—by one estimate he averaged a paper per month over his forty-year career—Sagan suffered criticism from some scientists who dismissed him as a mere popularizer. Because the scientific discipline often devalued its members who communicated frequently with the public, Sagan faced an enormous risk in trying to combine scientific study with public debate. The ability to speak about science in a way the public understood boosted his celebrity but made him less of a "real" scientist in the eyes of many of his peers. His fervent participation in the search for extraterrestrial life also led some scientists to see him as less than serious. Undeterred, Sagan reached the crest of his fame as host and creator of the PBS series *Cosmos* in 1980. An estimated 150 million viewers soared across time and space with Sagan as their guide, making *Cosmos* the most watched PBS series of all time up to that point. In 1996 he claimed that a half-billion people in more than sixty countries had seen the series, while *Nature* stated that the book based on the television series "was the best-selling science book ever published in the English language." Fans of Sagan described him as a "science missionary" who explained to the public the intellectual and political relevance of science.[11]

Cosmos aired during the great reawakening of antinuclear movements across the United States and Europe. As a popular celebrity with an intellectual's mind-set and liberal politics, Sagan was poised to move into the antinuclear movement—a move that had hampered Pauling's scientific career and reputation. But Sagan claimed he could not separate his science from his activism, seeing the two as indivisible. Thanks to *Cosmos*, Sagan had come to be seen as such an authority on science that the Carter administration asked him to provide a passage for the president's farewell address in January 1981. Thus, the president read, in words unmistakably Sagan: "Nuclear weapons are an expression of one side of our human character. But there's another side. The same rocket technology that delivers nuclear warheads has also taken us peacefully into space. From that perspective, we see our Earth as it really is—a small and fragile and beautiful blue globe, the only home we have. We see no barriers of race or religion or country. We see the essential unity of our species and our planet, and with faith and common sense, that bright vision will ultimately prevail."[12] The success of *Cosmos* and the Carter endorsement may have convinced Sagan that he had finally become "famous enough" to take on U.S. militarism and nuclear weapons.

The Nuclear Winter Theory

Sagan's antinuclear essays and actions spoke to scientists, the public, and governments simultaneously, drawing from the logic of science and the humanism of the counterculture. He soon came to focus on a specific antinuclear argument: nuclear winter. But this theory did not come from thin air. In a way, people in the 1980s already had Armageddon on the mind. Members of the Reagan administration had casually voiced millennial musings, while Jonathan Schell's popular 1982 book, *The Fate of the Earth*, argued that nuclear war would result in a global holocaust. And scientists had begun to study for the first time the long-term effects of a nuclear war. A 1982 Congressional Committee on Science and Technology had explored the concerns of "scientists worldwide" that a nuclear war could disrupt the global environment and the balance of life on earth. Representative Al Gore Jr. (D-TN) saw the distinct possibility that the superpowers could "bomb all humanity back to the Stone Age" until they "destroy humanity."[13] The scientific statements during this hearing presaged some of the dire forecasts of nuclear winter, which Sagan and his team elaborated on and popularized to a new level of public consciousness.

The concept of nuclear winter hatched from the confluence of three scientific endeavors. First, Sagan and his colleagues' analyses of dust storms on Mars and volcanic eruptions showed that particulates in the atmosphere could drastically cool the planet. Second, in 1980 Luis and Walter Alvarez presented evidence that a tremendous collision between an asteroid and earth resulted in an altered and hostile climate that drove the dinosaurs to extinction; this theory strengthened the case that severe climate change could cause mass extinctions on earth. Third, a 1982 article by Paul Crutzen and John Birks in an environmental science journal explained that smoke from fires caused by nuclear explosions could blot out sunlight for a significant period.[14] Realizing the political implications, Sagan and his colleagues Richard Turco, Owen Toon, Thomas Ackerman, and James Pollack—a group soon abbreviated as TTAPS—used the one-dimensional model from their volcanic studies to calculate the specific temperature drops that would follow various levels of nuclear wars. Making their study unique, TTAPS took into account the burning of cities, which contain enormous amounts of materials that, when burned, turn into thick, dense smoke. They found that airborne smoke, dust, and soot would absorb and reflect enough sunlight to cause temperatures on land to plummet to between −15° and −25°C (5° and −13°F). Calculations for different nuclear war scenarios showed that particles and fallout could spread to the Southern Hemisphere and "encircle the earth" in as few as one or two weeks. The cold, darkness, and radiation would threaten human survivors and other living species by halting photosynthesis and food production. Perhaps most alarming was the evidence that such a scenario could be triggered by a threshold as low as one hundred megatons. At the time of their study, the cumulative yield of the seventeen thousand nuclear warheads on earth equaled twelve thousand megatons.[15]

The Search for Peer Review

As a lifelong opponent of pseudoscience and the self-appointed protector of the scientific method, Sagan knew that the nuclear winter hypothesis required rigorous peer review. But because the urgency of an activist equally possessed him, he was also anxious to present nuclear winter to the greater public. In early 1983 he had already begun to plan a conference at which he would dramatically announce the theory. Cognizant of the potential for controversy, Sagan made a conscious effort to balance his desire for publicity with attempts to boost the theory's scientific credibility by subjecting it to peer review, or at least something resembling it. Rather than go public immediately, Sagan put the conference on hold and sent a long paper summarizing the work to numerous colleagues. He also convened an unconventional meeting with scientists to review the theory in person, achieving something close to, yet in some ways still far from, conventional peer review.

Sagan arranged for between seventy and one hundred physical and biological scientists to attend two meetings over five days in late April 1983 at the American Academy of Arts and Sciences in Cambridge, Massachusetts. The conveners would proceed with the public conference only if the nuclear winter data "held up" to this scrutiny. First, forty physicists and ten biologists heard the TTAPS presentation and commented on the paper draft. The scientists "generally agreed with the conclusions of the report" regarding reduced sunlight and severe climate changes, though they did suggest "minor adjustments."[16] One sympathetic observer later explained that the physicists "had numerous questions about details but very little quarrel with the findings. Several of the scientists went home resolved to try the scenarios on *their* atmospheric models." Next, the remaining scientists examined the "consensus results" of the first group and found "general agreement" on the "devastating" and "previously unforeseen" effects, including possible "extermination" of humans and many wildlife species.[17] With this positive response, planning for the conference recommenced.

Though no doubt pleased with the approval at Cambridge, Sagan continued to seek out review from his peers. In particular, Sagan sought approval from his colleague at Cornell University Hans Bethe, who served on the conference's Scientific Advisory Board. In the summer of 1983 Bethe gave TTAPS a serious critique of the science behind nuclear winter. Bethe liked the theory, but he questioned their choice of model, suggesting that a different model "could reduce the results [of nuclear winter] substantially." Nonetheless, Bethe praised the overall hypothesis as "very good indeed" and "a very important piece of work."[18] Bethe's enthusiasm, tempered by slight concerns about the one-dimensional model, foreshadowed the mixed scientific reception nuclear winter eventually received.

Elsewhere, Bethe gave Sagan some straightforward suggestions, ranging from simple edits to more scientific advice. While listening to Sagan review his findings in November 1983, Bethe recorded in his notes, "Generally in agreement w/ Sagan. Have read report," and noted that the Livermore and Los Alamos laboratories had substantial interest in conducting three-dimensional calculations that would incorporate an analysis of data from forest fires. Bethe, who had decades of arms control advocacy behind him, counseled Sagan that he "should emphasize *most likely* result, not worst case, if we want to persuade govm't." The *we* indicates that Bethe felt himself to be actively involved in the endeavor.[19] But Sagan chose to disregard Bethe's advice about not emphasizing the worst-case scenario, a decision that later earned him criticism. Sagan argued that because nuclear winter presented such a cataclysmic threat, the worst-case scenario should be taken seriously as long as the scientific evidence did not convincingly rule it out.

Although Sagan continued to handpick the reviewers, he did attempt to run the theory by some potentially hostile critics. And he undoubtedly knew where to expect criticism: from Edward Teller, whom Sagan contacted in the spring of 1983. Whether offering a preemptive olive branch, initiating the inevitable confrontation, or aggressively challenging Teller's authority on nuclear weapons, Sagan clearly recognized that it would enhance the credibility of nuclear winter if it withstood this fierce critic's glare. Thus, at roughly the same time as the Cambridge peer-review meeting, Sagan sent Teller a 145-page draft of the TTAPS team's work and requested "detailed criticisms." Sagan sent more material to Teller on June 24.[20]

Later that summer Teller sent Sagan a not entirely hostile response. "There is no question that the effects of smoke and dust are of great importance," he wrote. But because the TTAPS one-dimensional model was an "incomplete step in evaluation," he preferred calculations on a two-dimensional model performed at Livermore laboratory, "which gives (as you expect) much milder results, which are nonetheless severe." Teller concluded by stating, "I believe you and I can agree that serious extensive efforts to clarify this question need to continue. There is a particularly important duty for technical people to make information available when it becomes sufficiently reliable."[21] The absence of hostility did not, however, amount to an endorsement. Sagan would later assert that Teller urged caution only when scientific evidence appeared to support an antinuclear view; when science supported nuclear weapons, Teller never hesitated to trumpet his views. But Sagan would soon learn that scientific critics besides Teller counseled patience on nuclear winter as well.

While TTAPS continued to refine the science behind nuclear winter, Sagan began to hash out his views on the political aspects of the theory. Just as he had with the TTAPS paper, Sagan sought out the views of various experts but this time those of the foreign policy and national security establishments. George Kennan, the creator of the Cold War containment strategy and long-time skeptic of the value of nuclear weapons, was one who fitted the bill, so in November 1983 Sagan sent Kennan a draft of his upcoming article in *Foreign Affairs* on the policy implications of nuclear winter.

"I think the article very powerful," Kennan wrote to Sagan. "It will be the crowning phase of an effort on your part, and . . . probably one of the great landmarks of the anti-nuclear movement. I cannot tell you what a great thing I feel you have done." Kennan especially liked how Sagan challenged the fundamental beliefs of deterrence and the arms race. "You have provided what we all lacked and which no scientific layman could have provided: the clear and irrefutable demonstration of the enormity of the danger presented by these vast nuclear arsenals. I hope it will receive the widest possible distribution." Kennan congratulated Sagan "from the bottom of my heart" and urged him "not to rest until every intelligent person in the NATO and Warsaw Pact countries has understood what you have had to say."[22]

Such readership seemed to be the goal, as scientists and nuclear policy experts around the world apparently were drenched in a paper deluge of Sagan's drafts on nuclear winter. By the time Sagan and Turco gave the subject a book-length treatment in 1991, their acknowledgments had become massive in scale. The authors thanked 28 readers, including McGeorge Bundy, Robert McNamara, Freeman Dyson, Richard Garwin, Jeremy Stone, and Frank Press, in addition to an unspecified number of reviewers who preferred anonymity. Following that list was a roll call of 114 scientists, politicians, and others who "helped" by aiding "our understanding of nuclear war, nuclear winter, and their implications, or by stimulating our thinking on these issues." This list included Bethe, Luis Alvarez, Helen Caldicott, Daniel Ellsberg, Newt Gingrich, Barry Goldwater, Al Gore, Kennan, George Kistiakowsky, Richard Perle, William Proxmire, Joseph Rotblat, Brent Scowcroft, and Teller. Such lengthy lists at the very least give evidence of extensive review, of having carefully thought, rethought, written, and rewritten again. When Sagan received criticism of the nuclear winter theory, he often told his critics that the TTAPS paper had been reviewed by more than 100 scientists.[23]

As the spring of 1983 turned to summer, the TTAPS team continued to incorporate the many suggestions and criticisms of their peers. After attending the Cambridge peer-review meeting, twenty scientists, led by the Stanford biologist Paul Ehrlich (author of *The Population Bomb,* a Malthusian warning of overpopulation in the 1970s), had been inspired to draft a companion paper to TTAPS elaborating on the biological consequences of nuclear war, including the effects on plants, animals, and humans.[24] Upon completion, both groups of scholars submitted their papers to the peer-reviewed journal *Science* and prepared to announce the results at a conference on Halloween 1983. In order to maintain an objective outlook, the organizing committee "decided that political discussion," including the implications for disarmament and arms control, "should not be a part of the proposed conference."[25] But just before the conference, Sagan addressed the mainstream public; this jumping the gun would dog the nuclear winter theory in the eyes of many scientists who believed that science and public advocacy should not mix.

Going Public

As one who saw an urgent need for the public to be informed of and familiar with science in general (often dismissed as a popularizer), Sagan endeavored to reach those who would never even notice a scientific conference. Accordingly, he published an article on nuclear winter in *Parade* that reached millions of ordinary Americans on the Sunday before the conference.

Sagan began the article by explaining the effects of a two-megaton nuclear weapon on "a fairly large city." He described how "buildings would be vaporized," their occupants "reduced to atoms and shadows." A weapon detonated at ground level would leave a crater large enough that the landscape would resemble the moon. Such was the power of one weapon; meanwhile, the superpowers possessed some fifty thousand nuclear weapons with a total yield of thirteen thousand megatons—"enough to obliterate a million Hiroshimas." Sagan then explained the fallacy of the nuclear weapons strategy, including limited nuclear wars. Military experts agreed, he wrote, that any nuclear war would quickly escalate. The world's nuclear weapons "now sit quietly and inconspicuously, in missile silos, submarines and long-range bombers, faithful servants awaiting orders." Once unleashed, carnage would devour earth: Sagan cited a recent World Health Organization study estimating that more than two billion people—"almost half the humans on earth"—were imperiled by the direct effects of nuclear war.[26]

But nuclear weapons had destructive effects beyond their immediate explosive and radioactive impact, and these long-term effects would threaten the roughly two billion survivors of a nuclear war. Sagan then introduced his readers to nuclear winter. Before continuing, he paused to warn his audience. "Some of what I am about to describe is horrifying. I know, because it horrifies me," he wrote. "We must steel ourselves to contemplate the horrors of nuclear war." He estimated that ten thousand tons of dust entered the atmosphere for every megaton burst, and with a baseline model of five thousand megatons, tremendous amounts of dust, smoke, and soot would blot out the sun. In the Northern Hemisphere, "an unbroken and deadly gloom" would persist for weeks. The temperature would suffer a massive drop to well below 0°F, and crops, farm animals, and other food supplies would disappear. "Most of the human survivors would starve," he asserted.[27]

The apocalyptic troika of coldness, darkness, and fallout would unleash "a severe assault on our civilization and our species," with disease rampant, hospitals destroyed, and health care all but impossible. One of the theory's more controversial aspects was the claim that nuclear winter had a threshold—

that a certain number of megatons was necessary to trigger nuclear winter. TTAPS considered this a reasonable assumption based on the fact that no nuclear winter occurred after the first two atomic bombs fell on Japan in 1945. But Sagan believed this threshold to be very low, around a modest one hundred megatons.[28]

The authority of science supported nuclear winter, Sagan wrote. More than one hundred U.S., European, and Soviet scientists had "carefully scrutinized" the results and agreed on the "global consequences." Science, and not just Sagan, predicted "subfreezing temperatures in a twilit radioactive gloom" for months after a nuclear war. He also summarized the claims of the Ehrlich group: that many plants and animals would go extinct, and humans might follow.[29] Despite all of this support, however, Sagan's repeated emphasis of the solidity of the hypothesis gave the sense that he *doth protest too much*. The extraordinary peer-review conference, the refusal to let the peer-reviewed articles speak for themselves, and the popular presentation of the material conflicted with the usual process of the scientific discipline. Sagan claimed that the urgency of the nuclear winter threat demanded no less, but another interpretation was that Sagan was bypassing tradition and using science for political ends, a move that violated the norms of the scientific discipline, where the search for nature's truths means more than any political or social cause, no matter how worthy.

Sagan also jumped the gun in another way: on the morning of the conference, he first met with members of Congress to brief them in private on nuclear winter. With the public, the government, and the scientific community thus alerted, the World after Nuclear War: The Conference on the Long-Term Worldwide Biological Consequences of Nuclear War began at the Washington, D.C., Sheraton Hotel on October 31, 1983. Upwards of five hundred participants and one hundred media representatives from twenty nations attended the conference. To emphasize the global implications of nuclear winter, the conference featured an innovative "Moscow Link," a live discussion of nuclear winter with scientists in the Soviet Union. Sponsors of the conference included the Sierra Club, the Wilderness Society, the Federation of American Scientists, and the American Institute of Biological Sciences.[30]

The conference's organizers aimed to showcase the scientific credibility of nuclear winter as much as express the dire threat it posed. The Stanford biologist Donald Kennedy opened the conference by declaring himself "neither a likely technical resource for an arms control conference nor a promising candidate for cheerleader at a peace rally." But the "serious scientific analysis" of the TTAPS report had moved him to action. When Sagan spoke, he described to the audience the "witch's brew of radioactive products" that a nuclear war would release into the atmosphere, including fallout, smoke, soot, and dust. He mentioned the "general agreement" that "a period, lasting at least for months, of extreme cold in a radioactive gloom" would follow a nuclear war and that the destruction would spread to the Southern Hemisphere. He closed by pointing out the appropriateness of the Halloween setting for the conference, as nuclear winter would make real the sinister themes of fire, winter, and death reflected in the holiday's pagan origins.[31]

In the questions following Sagan's talk, a physicist asked Sagan about peer review of his "new and startling" claims, and from a scientific perspective this issue lay at the heart of nuclear winter's credibility. Was the TTAPS team planning on consulting scientists or, for example, the National Academy of Sciences for their views? In his answer, Sagan defended the TTAPS work as having endured criticism from "individuals of many different political persuasions, including representatives of the government weapons laboratories." Sagan added that the TTAPS and Ehrlich papers had both passed peer review by *Science*.[32]

Ehrlich followed Sagan and presented the possible long-term biological consequences of nuclear winter, emphasizing that the results reflected "the consensus of a large and distinguished group of biologists." He added that the findings were "robust"—not sensitive to assumptions about initial conditions. In other words, it was difficult to conceive of a nuclear war that would not lead to a biological catastrophe. The climate would kill "virtually all land plants" in the Northern Hemisphere, and most animals would die, leaving "rats, roaches, and flies the most prominent animals shortly after World War III." The extinction of *Homo sapiens* was a distinct possibility. On Tuesday an astrogeophysicist brought the conference to a close, reemphasizing the strong scientific integrity of the nuclear winter theory. "We are together, basically, regarding the physical and biological matters discussed at the Conference," Walter Orr Roberts stated, though he did add that this consensus did not extend to the political implications of the theory.[33]

After the conference, Sagan next appeared in the December 1983 issue of the journal *Science* as coauthor of the two peer-reviewed papers on nuclear winter. TTAPS introduced the idea of nuclear winter and set the terms of the ensuing scientific and political debate. After presenting possible "nuclear exchange scenarios," the TTAPS paper stated that dust, fires, soot, and smoke caused by thermonuclear conflagrations would significantly alter the global climate. In the ensuing weeks after a war, temperatures would drop, various ecosystems could shut down, agriculture would decay, and people far removed from the conflict would suffer or even starve. The second article, "Long-Term Biological Consequences of Nuclear War," emphasized the wide array of support for its argument in its list of authors, led by Ehrlich but including Sagan and eighteen other coauthors. It elaborated on the terrible plight of the 2.3 billion humans who would survive a nuclear war, ominously concluding that "the possibility of the extinction of *Homo Sapiens* cannot be excluded."[34]

With the scientific work established, Sagan's movement turned overtly political in the new year. On New Year's Eve 1983, Sagan gave a talk at the Cathedral of Saint John the Divine in New York that mapped out the next phase. Sagan began by lyrically (if not entirely accurately) describing the evolution of human society from hunter-gatherer times, "when all life on the planet was in a nearly perfect ecological harmony, and when the uranium was still in the rocks." But as 1984 began, "the uranium is no longer entirely in the rocks." The eighteen thousand nuclear warheads on the planet threatened human existence with a cataclysm of war and nuclear winter. As his New Year's resolution, he vowed to "work to elect those who are committed—not to some vague and fence-straddling generalities, but to specific and consistent proposals for major and verifiable mutual reductions in the world inventories of strategic weapons." Referencing George Orwell and Stanley Kubrick, he concluded, "Let us convert 1984 from a codeword for a government-managed nightmare, to a year in which we start freeing ourselves from the trap that we have carelessly and foolishly set for ourselves. I would like 2001 to dawn on a world that will truly initiate a new millennium, liberated from the danger of nuclear annihilation of the human species." As he hoped, public officials heard his message, including Representative George Miller (D-CA), who placed Sagan's speech in the *Congressional Record*. Miller added that nuclear weapons had made the world "substantially less secure than we were at the end of the Second World War."[35]

Freed from the moratorium on political statements at the Halloween conference, Sagan directly addressed the policy implications of nuclear winter in *Foreign Affairs*. He began the article with a statement about nuclear winter's scientific credibility: "Apocalyptic predictions require, to be taken seriously, higher standards of evidence than do assertions on other matters where the stakes are not as great."[36] He then framed his argument as having been thoroughly vetted by readers from all across the scientific and strategic communities. A footnote thanked Kennan as well as many others, including Bethe, Bundy, Dyson, Garwin, Averell Harriman, McNamara, Joseph Rotblat, Herbert

Scoville, Teller, and Albert Wohlstetter. The article briefly summarized the findings of the TTAPS and Ehrlich papers, though it extended the argument at some points. For example, to offer a possible death toll, Sagan estimated not only the world population of four billion but also potential as yet unborn generations, arriving at an unfathomable (and preposterous) prediction of five hundred trillion fatalities.[37]

The policy implications of nuclear winter lay at the heart of the *Foreign Affairs* article, as the theory made traditional nuclear strategy all but obsolete in Sagan's view. Four specific claims stood out in future nuclear winter debates. First, a nuclear first strike would be "tantamount to national suicide for the aggressor—*even if the attacked nation does not lift a finger to retaliate.*" Second, the nations of the Third World were at risk, even if they avoided any involvement in a war whatsoever. Third, nuclear winter made civil defense pointless, as any survivors would be unable to live in the destroyed biological and agricultural environment. Finally, nuclear winter rendered useless technological defenses such as ABMs and the Strategic Defense Initiative, since many experts agreed that even a working missile defense would be far from impenetrable. Sagan suggested ways out of the trap of "apocalyptic threats and doctrines" that had created a working version of Herman Kahn's "Doomsday Machine," including confidence-building measures, the de-MIRVing of missiles, and reductions of as much as 90 percent of world nuclear arsenals. "It is nowhere ordained," Sagan optimistically concluded, "that we must remain in bondage to nuclear weapons."[38] Soon, opponents of nuclear weapons around the world would rely on nuclear winter to challenge the concept of nuclear deterrence. Such a combination of scientific authority, environmental alarm, and quasi-millennial prophecy created a powerful antinuclear argument, one that soon appeared in scientific journals, newspapers, magazines, foreign policy quarterlies, and government publications.

Initial Reactions: November 1983 to August 1984

Sagan aimed his campaign at three different constituencies: the public, scientists, and politicians, though his actions and rhetoric addressed all three at once.

The Public

Among the public, nuclear winter added a scientific edge to the widespread nuclear scares of the early 1980s, including the Three Mile Island meltdown,

Schell's *Fate of the Earth*, and ABC's television movie *The Day After*. Around the world nuclear fears had escalated since the end of détente in 1979 and especially after the Reagan administration's belligerent rhetoric about "winnable" nuclear wars and the "evil" Soviet empire. The phrase *nuclear winter* seamlessly worked its way into mainstream discussions of nuclear weapons already influenced by the theory's wintry cousin, the nuclear freeze, a proposal to halt nuclear weapons production in the United States and Soviet Union.

The *New York Times* greeted the theory of nuclear winter with harsh skepticism in an editorial following the Halloween conference. Noting the nearly simultaneous appearance of the concept of nuclear winter and *The Day After*, the *Times* asked, "Why this deluge of restating the obvious?" Surely, everyone already knew that "nuclear disaster is hazardous to human health." Deterrence remained the best way to prevent nuclear war: "Deterrence works because it is based on horror. . . . There's no visible alternative to deterrence, no matter how ghastly the ways nuclear war would kill." Nuclear winter and other "profiles in apocalypse" had some value if they convinced the Reagan administration that nuclear war was neither winnable nor survivable. But, the editors incorrectly noted, nuclear winter "should not be confused with science; it has not yet been published or properly checked." Roughly ten months later, another *Times* editorial repeated this skepticism, especially of claims that nuclear winter required rethinking nuclear strategy. "Not even a new dimension of terror can undercut policies based on deterrence," the editorial argued. But the *Times* expressed a slight change in stance, stating that if the theory proved that soot would devastate the climate, "nuclear winter would . . . mean the end of civilization. That prospect has to make a difference eventually, however successful the policy of nuclear deterrence has been so far, and however invisible the alternatives."[39]

Not everyone agreed with the editorial board. In a review of the published proceedings of the Halloween conference, *Times* science reporter William Broad asked, "So what?" about nuclear winter. "So everything," he answered. Nuclear winter "undermines military strategy and doctrines of targeting and communications—and thus the concept of deterrence that has dominated superpower relations for a third of a century." He hailed the theory as "a remarkable testament to the power of free scientific inquiry."[40] Even unexpected sources noticed Sagan's work. In 1984 Pope John Paul II invited Sagan to brief him on the concept of nuclear winter. Despite being an avowed and intense atheist whose popular novel *Contact* pitted science against religion, Sagan accepted the invitation. (Sagan had refused an invitation from the Reagans to dine at the White House.) After the meeting the pope released a statement warning the world of the danger of nuclear winter.[41]

Nuclear winter also made its way into more mainstream areas of popular consciousness. In a survey of reactions to *The Day After*, broadcast on November 21, 1983, a reporter quoted a high school teacher whose class had told him that "the program was too much like a soap opera. . . . They've been reading about the phenomenon of 'nuclear winter' and they felt the film was inaccurate in showing that the bombs would be so survivable."[42] Sagan would likely have appreciated that his theory had inspired such skepticism about survival.

In an open letter to Reagan and Soviet leader Yuri Andropov, the International Physicians for the Prevention of Nuclear War included nuclear winter as one of the reasons nuclear weapons had put "all human life . . . in critical condition."[43] While grassroots U.S. antinuclear groups remained ambivalent about nuclear winter, in Britain the Christian Campaign for Nuclear Disarmament relied on the concept as evidence that the threat of nuclear weapons "has grown worse," referring to the hypothesis as laying bare "the probably catastrophic consequences of a nuclear war for our environment and all living things, and therefore the risks which the nuclear powers are taking with God's creation."[44] To coincide with the third European Nuclear Disarmament (END) Convention in Perugia, Italy, the editors of *ENDpapers* reprinted Sagan's "Nuclear War and Climatic Catastrophe" in the summer of 1984 "for the attention of the Perugia delegates."[45]

An Uncertainty Principle

The scientific reaction to the nuclear winter hypothesis was undeniably mixed but contained more positive assessments than previously recognized. Bethe had been so impressed with nuclear winter that he initiated a Los Alamos study on the subject in the summer of 1983.[46] The Los Alamos study would follow Bethe's vision by using a three-dimensional model that exceeded the capabilities of the TTAPS one-dimensional model and in the coming years would yield results supporting the possibility of nuclear winter.[47]

In the meantime, however, other scientists pounced aggressively on nuclear winter's uncertainties. S. Fred Singer, a professor of environmental sciences and a consultant to the White House science adviser, challenged the theory on scientific and political grounds. In the *Wall Street Journal*, Singer linked nuclear winter to a freeze and facetiously wondered if the reason Soviet scientists believed in nuclear winter was because a freeze would be good for Soviet objectives. Like most opponents of nuclear winter, Singer hammered the theory's uncertainties, writing, "The range of uncertainty is so great . . . that the prediction isn't particularly useful." Singer suggested that the greenhouse effect disrupted by nuclear debris—which Sagan argued would keep warmth out—might actually prevent the remaining warmth from escaping. He criticized TTAPS for using Mars to guide their calculations, since "Martian dust has different physical and optical properties than smoke and soot," and even claimed that the immense burning after a nuclear war would help keep earth warm. In addition, the immense particulate matter in the atmosphere would force itself to be rained out. Finally, Singer argued that nuclear winter failed as a deterrent because the threshold might make a "small nuclear power" feel free to launch a single tactical nuclear bomb.[48] Sagan responded that his opponents who complained of the theory's uncertainties missed the point. Humans frequently took precautions in the face of uncertainty, he often explained, pointing to flood insurance as evidence of rational approaches to improbable—but still dangerous—events.[49]

The *Bulletin of the Atomic Scientists* printed a special fifteen-page supplement on nuclear winter in April 1984. The editors endorsed Sagan's view on urgency, stating that "on an issue so vital to the planet, a worst-case analysis is the only prudent approach." Except for this supplement, however, the *Bulletin* hardly mentioned nuclear winter at all. One exception was the geophysicist Joseph Smith's review of the published proceedings of the Halloween conference. Smith instantly cast doubt on the theory, asking, "If we cannot accurately forecast the weather a week in advance, what is the meaning of 'nuclear winter'?" This attempt to shrink the nuclear winter debate down to a guess about the local weather was grossly misleading. While estimates of exact rainfall and temperatures are often off-base, scientific estimates about seasonal temperature ranges prove quite reliable. At any rate, although he made clear his admiration for the "moral indignation and plain guts" of the nuclear winter scientists, Smith also questioned their objectivity. "The more uncertain a prediction," he wrote, "the more likely an emotional discussion." He deemed Sagan's article "convincing when the assumptions of the models are accepted" but rejected a specific threshold as unlikely, based on his inability to find a single meteorologist who supported the idea. "This valuable book," he summarized, "should further develop an emotional climate about the problems of nuclear war. Readers, however, might wish to reserve judgment about whether the present concept of nuclear winter might turn out to be a metaphor rather than a reliable basis for planning military and civil defense."[50] Smith's language directly echoed the distinction between emotional and objective science enforced by the Atomic Energy Commission since 1954.

Scientific reaction to nuclear winter made for heated debate; the pages of the world's premier science journal, *Nature,* show how far the theory spread in scientific discourse. The journal's editor John Maddox heaped heavy skepticism on the theory in his initial editorial on nuclear winter, asking that Sagan's conclusions "be plainly stamped with the label QUALITATIVE for fear that their apparent precision may prove spurious." In ensuing commentary, he declared that it was "too soon" to draw conclusions about the climatic consequences of nuclear war. The TTAPS paper, he wrote, "is less than convincing," as was demonstrated by "the pardonable simplicity" of its calculations. Maddox feared for the good name of science when he counseled that "there is the strongest case for asking that the prospect of a nuclear winter should not be made into a more substantial bogeyman than it is by those who earnestly wish to avert the prospect of nuclear war as such. By clouding the case with disputable predictions, they are in danger of weakening it."[51]

As Maddox had predicted, his editorial fired but the first salvo in a "prolonged and contentious argument" over nuclear winter that played out across the pages of his journal. In the ensuing months, scientists from Finland to Australia argued over a disparate array of topics related to nuclear winter. Two scientists claimed that their "study of frost rings as indicators of climatically effective volcanic eruptions" suggested that the effects of nuclear war could be "grave indeed." Others who offered their two cents discussed the importance of meteors, volcanoes, World War II fire bombings, sunspots, forest fires, and atmospheric humidity as sources of data. Alan Robock analyzed "long-term seasonal cryospheric interactions with . . . sea ice/thermal inertia feedback" and found reason to believe that nuclear winter "might persist longer than previously calculated." When Singer contended that a nuclear war would cause mere "patch clouds which thin out rapidly—hardly a cataclysmic nuclear winter," other scientists argued back that "the cooling need not be down to $-40°$ C nor last for several weeks or more to produce devastating agricultural damage."[52] With so much at stake, scientists eagerly awaited the results from nuclear winter studies under way by the NAS and the International Council of Scientific Unions (ICSU).

Adversary

In the meantime, Sagan and his allies had to deal with the longtime nemesis of disarmament, Edward Teller. Although Teller had in the past spoken of his belief that scientists should make information known to the public and let the government decide on a course of action, he now counseled Sagan against publicizing his information. "My concern is that many uncertainties remain and that these uncertainties are sufficiently large as to cast doubt on whether the nuclear winter will actually occur," he wrote in a letter to Sagan. Teller then turned to his familiar Red Scare trope of appeasement, telling Sagan that "you are more concerned with frightening the American public than with giving them an accurate assessment of the nuclear war situation. . . . If the American public is sufficiently frightened, it will call for surrender to Soviet demands in a time of crisis. This is, of course, the path followed by Britain prior to World War II with dire consequences."[53] Teller had earlier used similar rhetoric to good effect against Linus Pauling, but with the Red Scare long over, such epithets failed to stick.

Sagan joined Teller's challenge. In one instance, he took particular offense that Teller had dubbed him a "propagandizer." Sagan countered, "You yourself told me that Nuclear Winter was the only serious unanticipated consequence of nuclear war you were aware of." Sagan made a conscious point of appealing to Teller's respect for the scientific discipline, stating his refusal to stoop to "*ad hominem* arguments," as "they seem inconsistent with the method of science. . . . These are values you share. You have repeatedly stated that we must follow the truth wherever it leads." He also reminded Teller of the lengthy TTAPS draft he had sent in 1983: "You have yet to reply. Do you not think it better to state your scientific objections explicitly before making vague public pronouncements?" Teller fired back that "a propagandist is one who uses incomplete information to produce maximum persuasion. I can compliment you on being, indeed, an excellent propagandist—remembering that a propagandist is the better the less he appears to be one."[54]

And thus a scientific duel began, waged across the pages of scientific journals and eventually in the halls of the U.S. Capitol. In *Nature* Teller deemed it his "important responsibility" to inform the public about the uncertainties surrounding the possibility of nuclear winter and argued that fallout in uninvolved nations would not be severe and that civil defense would ameliorate fallout in belligerent nations. Teller criticized Sagan's claim that the TTAPS smoke data were, in Teller's paraphrase, "scientifically robust," even though TTAPS had not used the term. He also asserted that smoke particles would rain out of the atmosphere more quickly than TTAPS suggested. "A severe climatic change must be considered dubious rather than robust," he argued, though he admitted that a nuclear winter of some severity could not be entirely ruled out. In conclusion, Teller scolded Sagan: "Highly speculative theories of worldwide destruction—even the end of life on Earth—used as a call for a particular kind of political action serve neither the good reputation of science nor dispassionate political thought."[55]

Sagan counterpunched with a mostly scientific rebuttal in *Nature* more than a year later, though the original draft from late 1984 contained a great deal of anti-Teller vitriol, beginning with an epigraph from Robert Browning clearly intended as a barb at Sagan's rival: "So absolutely good is truth, truth never hurts / The teller." Although Sagan expected and accepted "competent criticism" as "natural and healthy," he bemoaned "a tendency in many expert pronouncements to downplay these consequences [of nuclear war]." He accused Teller of "selective inattention to the data, misquotation of sources, occasional distortion of the facts, and simple misconceptions" in his attempt to explain away nuclear winter by "invoking a 'meteorological miracle.'"[56]

Sagan pointed out explicit technical flaws, but Teller's "marked propensity for mixing science and politics" truly riled him. For forty-five years, Sagan wrote, Teller had accepted that nuclear weapons had no long-term effects. But now that scientists had found the opposite, Teller "is vigorous in minimizing these consequences, and in reminding us that not all the evidence is in. There is a clear double standard of scientific evidence at work." Teller never counseled caution or calm, never wanted to wait until the data were in during hysterias such as the missile gap or the bomber gap. Only for antinuclear science did he counsel patience.[57] But Teller's influence within the halls of government and national security made his intransigence more than just an annoyance for Sagan.

U.S. Government

While scientists explored the possibility of nuclear winter, the U.S. government followed suit. In contrast to one historian's claim that the "policy debate over nuclear winter was largely limited to voices from the scientific community," many government officials embraced nuclear winter as a scientific basis for the criticism of deterrence in general, and the Reagan administration in particular, especially its forecast of "winnable" nuclear wars and promotion of SDI.[58] The executive branch, in contrast, steeled itself against changing course.

Documents declassified during the 1980s indicate that the navy instantly accepted the nuclear winter theory as plausible and kept tabs on the research even in its earliest stages. A memo written in the summer of 1983 discussed the research by a "Cornell group"—evidently TTAPS—that "indicates important implications for military planning." The memo's author described the theory as a "scientifically sound first cut," while a second navy memo suggested that the DOD study nuclear winter, as it "might be a source of embarrassment" if the Pentagon appeared oblivious to it.[59]

A memo to the chief of naval operations written just days after the Halloween conference stated that nuclear winter theories "are probably generally valid and will be widely accepted in the scientific community." It described the science behind nuclear winter as "extensively reviewed" by scientific experts, while the claims were "generally similar" to a study conducted by the undersecretary of defense. The navy did not oppose the theory but expressed great concern that the Soviet Union would exploit nuclear winter for propaganda purposes. The memo even stated that the results of nuclear winter "deserve serious study." Overall, the navy appreciated the scientists' presentation as "a serious, credible, result of a scientific enquiry."[60] A subsequent memo agreed with the scientists' claim that a full-scale nuclear exchange "could result in the extinction of man" and ordered policy studies in light of this finding.[61]

As the navy observed the Halloween conference, Congress reacted as well. On the morning after Sagan's Sunday *Parade* article appeared, congressmen rushed to endorse Sagan's theory. Senator William Proxmire (D-WI) was one of several to have the article inserted into the *Congressional Record*. For Proxmire, the implications of nuclear winter were obvious: enact arms control measures before the arms race takes humans "down the road to suicide." He specifically proposed a "mutual and verifiable" freeze and "an antiproliferation agreement" with "teeth." In the lower house that same day, Mel Levine (D-CA) also put Sagan's article into the *Record*, stressing that nuclear winter showed how the Reagan administration's pet projects of the MX, Pershing II, and cruise missiles were "destabilizing and threaten to weaken deterrence." Levine called Sagan's article "sober reading" that disputed the Pentagon's belief that "nuclear wars are somehow winnable."[62]

On December 8, 1983, Senators Edward Kennedy and Mark Hatfield, cosponsors of a 1982 freeze resolution, brought Sagan to their forum on the worldwide consequences of nuclear war. Sagan mentioned the broad array of scientific institutions in the United States and overseas studying nuclear winter and claimed that three-dimensional models appeared to confirm the TTAPS study. He adamantly implored his congressional hosts to rethink nuclear policies. If U.S. nuclear weapons can accidentally destroy the United States, he asked, is a huge arsenal even a credible deterrent? Sagan made it clear that a minimum deterrent—with a maximum explosive power below the nuclear winter threshold—was feasible and patriotic for both superpowers. He described a nuclear first strike as "an elaborate way of committing national suicide," adding that "the ashes of communism and capitalism will be indistinguishable."[63]

The forum also included Soviet scientists who had been studying nuclear winter. Vladimir Alexandrov discussed how his three-dimensional model showed "significant cooling" and presented other evidence that the postnuclear war environment would be "hostile to human beings." Alexander Pavlov stated that a nuclear war would destroy humanity, while Sergei Kapitza dubbed deterrence "dubious" and mentioned a freeze. Yevgeny Velikhov spoke last and described nuclear weapons as suicidal. A commentary in the *Times* saw the forum as having "made short work" of the Pentagon's arguments for SDI and claims that a nuclear war could remain limited and winnable.[64]

Later in the Senate, Proxmire again brought up nuclear winter as a strong argument for arms control. Proxmire highlighted Sagan's scientific credibility, praising the theory as "based on elaborate and careful calculations by a number of scientists from a number of countries." Recognizing the critics of nuclear winter, Proxmire declared, "I shall take Sagan and the scientific evidence." When Proxmire placed a summary of Sagan's *Foreign Affairs* article into the *Record,* he professed that "a comprehensive nuclear arms freeze, followed by a massive reduction of all nuclear armaments, should remain our prime objective." On May 4 Senator William Cohen (R-ME) wrote to Reagan, alerting the president to nuclear winter and the TTAPS study. He urged him to consider the "very serious policy implications" of the possibility that "even a limited nuclear exchange" could produce "devastating results, affecting . . . perhaps all of the globe." Cohen then asked Reagan to put the power of the executive behind a serious study of nuclear winter's policy ramifications.[65]

Sagan was eager to return to Congress and influence debates over nuclear weapons, pointing out that members of the public wrote to him complaining about the government's lack of knowledge about nuclear winter.[66] In May 1984 members of Congress, especially Representative Tim Wirth (D-CO), were equally eager to bring Sagan back to the Capitol. Thus, Sagan arrived for a whirlwind visit at National Airport on the morning of Tuesday, May 15, where a member of Wirth's staff whisked him to a lunch meeting with the Democratic Caucus Committee on Party Effectiveness. A briefing of legislative assistants followed, where he spoke on the "long-term and environmental dimensions" of nuclear weapons. The first day culminated in a Congressional Clearinghouse on the Future event with cocktails and "a delicious dinner"; the forty-one attendees quickly set the room to "overflowing." Wednesday,

May 16, started early with a meeting with the Democratic Steering and Policy Committee and Democratic whips. After Sagan had discussions with Senators Cohen and Proxmire, the editorial board of the *Washington Post* hosted Sagan at a luncheon. The highlight of the day was a "members only" event featuring an "off-the-record dialogue" between Sagan and Teller from 3:00 p.m. to 5:00 p.m. on the first floor of the Capitol, with eighty-two members of Congress in attendance.[67]

According to Wirth, while Sagan spoke, Teller's assistant Lowell Wood caused a "racket" by jostling a table with glasses of water and bowls of ice stacked on flat metal trays, "making a ton of noise in the process." After Wirth reprimanded Wood four or five times, he finally stopped. "The point is," Wirth reflected, "that this protégé of Teller's didn't want Sagan to be heard."[68] At 8:22 p.m. Sagan finally left Washington, having for the most part charmed Congress.

After Sagan's hectic tour of the Capitol, Wirth immediately took action. Along with Representatives Jim Leach (R-IA), Newt Gingrich (R-GA), Al Gore (D-TN), and Charles Roemer (D-LA), Wirth drafted an amendment to the pending DOD budget reauthorization. The amendment mandated "comprehensive study of the atmospheric, climatic, environmental, and biological consequences of nuclear war and the implications that such consequences have for the nuclear weapons strategy and policy, the arms control policy, and the civil defense policy of the United States." A letter to their peers in the House described Sagan's theory as "a sobering premonition of a dying world," while in an interview about the amendment Wirth stated that nuclear winter "requires a complete rethinking" of U.S. national security and arms control.[69]

On May 31 Wirth and his allies introduced the amendment on the House floor, where it sparked only brief debate. Wirth justified the amendment as necessary for full understanding of the strategic and tactical nuclear weapons programs that Congress was responsible for funding. In particular, he mentioned the "sobering" TTAPS study and described the amendment as "a moral imperative," as nuclear winter could cause "national suicide." In support of the amendment, Gore praised the credibility of nuclear winter studies and added that "we need to know what these experts make of the threat of nuclear winter." But because Congress could easily get scientific input from hearings and other studies, such claims suggest that the amendment amounted to an attempt by members of Congress to assert control over the DOD and force it to adopt its concerns about nuclear weapons. Representative Samuel Stratton (D-NY) had earlier introduced an amendment essentially barring the DOD from conducting nuclear winter studies; after that amendment failed, Wirth's passed easily, 298–98. In between the two votes on nuclear winter, however, the House passed funding for the MX missile by the narrow margin of 199–196.[70]

Deterrence on Trial, Part 1

Sagan's romance with Congress continued at congressional hearings on nuclear winter. At the time, Democrats held a majority of the seats in Congress, and many of them were eager to challenge Reagan on defense policy. No one who appeared in front of Congress denied the possibility of a nuclear winter, while many witnesses and members of Congress alike used the theory to challenge the Reagan administration and the DOD. Certain themes permeated the hearings: believers in nuclear winter emphasized its scientific credibility, its profound implications for nuclear policy, and its challenge to nuclear deterrence. Opponents of nuclear winter incessantly attacked the theory's uncertainties yet paradoxically felt that enough certainty existed to state that the nuclear winter prediction only reinforced the nuclear policies of the Reagan administration.

As vice chairman of the Subcommittee on International Trade, Finance, and Security Economics, Proxmire brought the first hearings on nuclear winter to order on July 11, 1984. He declared the government's lack of reaction to the theory of nuclear winter "a sad commentary" and asked the witnesses to instruct the committee on what questions Congress and the Reagan administration should be asking. Sagan spoke first, showing an assortment of slides, including charts, graphs, and artists' renderings of nuclear winter. He hoped that nuclear winter would convince "those who have not yet seen the light" to admit that a nuclear first strike was madness, an "elaborate and very expensive form of national suicide." In addition, he wanted to alert those nations that had assumed they could safely sit out a nuclear war. Finally, he dismissed civil defense as a political prop. The witnesses who followed hailed Sagan and his research on nuclear winter: Admiral Noel Gayler deemed nuclear winter scenarios "quite reasonable," while former arms control official Paul Warnke stated that Sagan had "convincingly demonstrated" that more nuclear weapons had not made the United States more secure. The members of the subcommittee were impressed with what they saw. Senator James Sasser (D-TN) referred to Sagan as a "very distinguished" expert doing "a great service to all mankind" and used nuclear winter to criticize mutually assured destruction as "a cocked hat." Proxmire brought the first session to a close by describing nuclear winter as "enormous" but also "plausible."[71]

On the following morning, representatives of the DOD, the Arms Control and Disarmament Agency, and the Federal Emergency Management Agency (FEMA) appeared before the subcommittee. Relatively hostile to these witnesses, the subcommittee essentially put deterrence on trial. Proxmire began by announcing that using nuclear weapons "may be shooting ourselves in the head" and that "the strategic options we have adopted to assure deterrence could also assure our self-destruction." Richard Wagner, assistant secretary of defense for atomic energy, surprisingly admitted that despite some uncertainties, "there could indeed be a nuclear winter." But, he added, nuclear winter "does not change the most fundamental aspects of our policy." In questioning, Wagner was asked about the strategy of deterrence by Representative Parren Mitchell (D-MD), who argued that because the use of U.S. nuclear weapons would also destroy the United States, deterrence lacked credibility. Wagner responded that deterrence aimed to show the Soviets that it was not in their best interests to attack. When Mitchell offered that "the deterring factor becomes a destruction factor," Wagner replied, "That is the essence of deterrence."[72]

After Proxmire noted the importance of a DOD representative recognizing the possibility of nuclear winter, he brought Sagan back in to critique the administration witnesses. Sagan proclaimed himself "delighted" that the DOD and ACDA took nuclear winter seriously. But when Proxmire attempted to link nuclear winter to a freeze, David Emery of FEMA objected. To the contrary, he stated, the threats to the global climate "reinforce" the administration's arms control policies, stressing, "I can't envision any study that would invalidate deterrence." When Proxmire suggested that the prospect of nuclear winter made nuclear weapons obsolete, Emery responded that "it would depend on whether or not the Soviets reacted accordingly." Proxmire persisted, stating that "the most eminent scientists in the world who are agreeing and we have the Defense Department representative saying this morning that in his judgment this is probably going to turn out to be verified and correct. It's a fact now." Emery, however, remained adamant that the threat of nuclear winter could be ameliorated by current Reagan administration policy, including SDI.[73]

In the final session, the aptly named Sidney Winter of the Yale Economics Department exclaimed that the TTAPS study "is quite unprecedented in the credibility and explicitness of its apocalyptic speculations" and "must be considered to inaugurate a new era in the discussion of nuclear armaments." Furthermore, nuclear winter gave moral critiques of nuclear weapons new validity, though such views were once "dismissed as naïve and uninformed."

A United Press International wire story from that same day was headlined "Pentagon Aides Agree on a 'Nuclear Winter'" and quoted Wagner's admission that "there could indeed be a 'nuclear winter' or there could be little effect." The story also emphasized that the Pentagon aides "held fast to the policy of deterrence," but the hearing had established Sagan's role as the scientific authority lending credence to Congress's defiance of deterrence.[74]

A second hearing on nuclear winter amplified the opposition to deterrence brewing in Congress. James Scheuer (D-NY), chairman of the House Natural Resources Subcommittee, opened the hearings on September 12, 1984, by stating that a nuclear winter might threaten earth's ability to sustain life. If accurate, he continued, "the implications of this hypothesis impose new realities on our thinking about nuclear deterrence." Introducing Sagan, the well-known evolutionary biologist Stephen Jay Gould, and Teller, Scheuer described the panel members as "some of this country's most eminent scientists." Sagan spoke first, explaining the development of the nuclear winter theory as it had progressed from Mars back to earth. He again made a point of emphasizing the theory's scientific credentials. Despite "differences of opinion," he said, most of the "published work" showed TTAPS as being "somewhere in the neighborhood of what might happen." Referring to the July hearing, Sagan noted Wagner's admission that a nuclear winter could follow a nuclear war as an indication of how "the convergence of opinion" reflected a growing consensus. He then listed the policy implications, including that a first strike would be suicidal, uninvolved nations would be destroyed, and civil defense would not work. Gould, one of the twenty coauthors of Ehrlich's *Science* article, followed Sagan. He emphasized as well the "substantial agreement" with the TTAPS paper by "distinguished scientists." Gould himself was "impressed" by the "convergence of basic results." Nuclear winter, he declared, was not "fanciful conjecture" but a "remarkable convergence" that reflected the "widespread scrutiny" to which the theory had been subjected.[75]

Teller spoke last and went on the offensive against nuclear winter, telling the committee that he had worried about far-graver threats to national security. He deflected attention from his inability to deny the possibility of a nuclear winter and instead said the TTAPS assertions were as bland a statement as 2 + 2 = 4, that no one would disagree with the result given their assumptions, but "if you make the wrong assumptions, you get the wrong results." He disputed the idea of scientific agreement on nuclear winter, claiming that repeated verification of the TTAPS model "shows nothing except that our computing machines are working."[76] While Teller could not refute nuclear winter altogether, he managed to offer more than just token opposition to Sagan's antinuclear campaign.

The hearings had supplied critics of the Reagan administration with ample ammunition. The executive branch appeared to feel the heat and took action to address—and co-opt—nuclear winter. An August 1984 State Department memo to Secretary of State George Shultz stated that "the implications for US policy of the nuclear winter theory . . . could be profound if the administration-sponsored studies agree with Turco *et al.*'s conclusions and/or if, by default, congressional and public attitudes are moulded by those results." In September 1984 the White House Office of Science and Technology Policy announced a multimillion-dollar study of nuclear winter involving the National Oceanic and Atmospheric Administration, the Department of Energy, and the Defense Nuclear Agency. One unnamed scientist, however, told *Nature* that he feared that "the administration may seek to use the scientific uncertainties as an excuse to respond only by commissioning research."[77]

In late September 1984, Sagan appeared on CNN, where he argued—in contrast to some of his defenders in Congress—that nuclear winter need not invalidate deterrence. Though Sagan personally opposed the concept, he suggested that deterrence could remain with just a "tiny" number of nuclear weapons. Because a single U.S. nuclear submarine could hold enough warheads to destroy 160 Soviet cities, Sagan explained, "how many nuclear weapons . . . do you need in order to have a reliable retaliatory capability and invulnerable deterrent? And the answer is, you do not need ten thousand strategic warheads." The U.S. and Soviet arsenals were "absurdly more than is needed for strategic deterrence," he said, recommending arsenal reductions of 90 percent or more. After the interview, he immediately joined an all-night vigil for disarmament at Lafayette Park, across from the White House.[78]

New Study, Renewed Controversy: September 1984–April 1985

Sagan's antinuclear activism took him from Congress to Lafayette Park to sites overseas and back again, even to the nuclear testing site in Nevada where police twice arrested him during protests.[79] He also defended the nuclear winter theory in print. Responding to *Nature*'s dismissive editorials, TTAPS wrote to the journal's editor in September 1984. The scientists argued that "we took extraordinary measures to have our calculations reviewed by a large number of experts" and questioned "whether Maddox has carefully read the work he is criticizing." Sensing that Maddox ultimately disapproved of the public campaign based on nuclear winter, they countered that "open and informed debate on this issue is the only responsible approach, given the gravity of the potential climatic catastrophe we believe we have uncovered." Maddox confirmed their suspicions in his response and revealed the clash between scientific and political conventions when he wrote, "It seems to me improper that the results of calculations should be published even in sober language without a warning to all potential readers of the pitfalls there must be. This is doubly unfortunate when, as on this occasion, a purportedly scientific publication is so fully amplified by popular articles . . . in *Parade*."[80] It was the popularization that burned more than the science as well as the fact that *Nature* had been scooped by a common newspaper insert. After accusations of faulty evidence, political bias, and headline seeking, the fate of the nuclear winter hypothesis appeared to hinge on the judgment of the NAS.

The NAS Report

The NAS released its highly anticipated report on nuclear winter in late 1984, but rather than settle the debate, confusion ensued over what the report actually said. The NAS scientists did appear to endorse Sagan's urgency, stating that because so much was at stake, they found it prudent to make at least general predictions. Despite "enormous uncertainties," the NAS recognized the possibility of "severe" effects. They offered "qualified, preliminary" estimates, "clearly and emphatically of an interim character," that the planet "could be severely affected." Fires, smoke, soot, and dust would block sunlight, but the amount of any temperature drops remained uncertain. Ozone could be substantially reduced, while damage to the climate of the Southern Hemisphere "cannot be ruled out." Because specific quantitative conclusions were impossible, the academy recommended "a major effort" to remove the uncertainties.[81]

With such a vague statement, both sides claimed vindication. A *New York Times* article on the NAS report by William Broad received the headline "'Nuclear Winter' Is Seen as Possible." The article stated the "clear possibility," according to the NAS, that a nuclear war could cause "severe drops in temperature." Broad quoted the chair of the NAS study group as describing the findings as "quite consistent" with the original nuclear winter studies and explained that "reaction to the report was that it enhanced the topic's overall credibility," though to support this statement he quoted one of the original TTAPS authors. This interpretation contrasted greatly with a *Times* editorial published two days later that argued that the NAS report had proven nuclear winter "increasingly uncertain" and its effects "impossible to define."

A dissenting view in a column that appeared opposite the editorial argued that the NAS had "given legitimacy" to nuclear winter, adding that "nuclear winter raises at least the possibility of human extinction following a Soviet-U.S. war."[82]

Nature, however, contended that claims that the NAS endorsed the nuclear winter hypothesis were gross misinterpretations, with the NAS study-group chair telling *Nature* that Sagan had been taking "recent calculations . . . too literally." Maddox himself argued that the significance of the NAS report was "to emphasize more clearly than has been customary the uncertainties . . . of what a nuclear winter would be like." Although Maddox admitted that the NAS report "qualitatively confirmed" the TTAPS prediction, he also stated that the NAS assessment was "hedged around with so many qualifications that a null outcome could well be compatible with the academy committee's analysis." Maddox worried that scientists who believed in the possibility of nuclear winter "give the impression that the issue has been decided before the study is complete," and Maddox suspected that they did so "not for reasons that are political in the partisan sense but apparently in the belief that the threat of nuclear winter will persuade governments towards effective arms control."[83]

In a letter to the *Times,* Sagan denounced the obsession with uncertainties as an excuse for inaction. "Nuclear winter is not amenable to experimental verification—at least not more than once," he wrote, "and few of us wish to perform the experiment." Uncertainty could be resolved only by a nuclear war, Sagan explained, adding, "This is not an unfamiliar circumstance for policy makers who must make decisions in the face of uncertainty." He also stated that the NAS report supported the possibility of nuclear winter, a claim that a member of the NAS study group later disputed, interpreting the report as only identifying "the very large uncertainties plaguing all calculations of this phenomenon."[84]

The NAS report failed to solve the impasse over the theory, but science still suffered from nuclear winter fever, as the phenomenon infected the realms of international science, geopolitics, and even criminal intrigue. In *Nature* scientists from Czechoslovakia defended the TTAPS model, while two Norwegian scientists criticized "the overly detailed examination of minutiae" of nuclear winter as "deflect[ing] attention and concern from . . . the death and suffering of hundreds of millions of human beings, starting milliseconds after the first flash and continuing for years and generations." Teller counterrebutted Sagan's rebuttal of his article as "ambiguous and inaccurate," while a British scientist argued that "there are many areas of uncertainty . . . but the *risk* of a nuclear winter now seems undeniable." Meanwhile, Canadian scientists set controlled forest fires to create data for nuclear winter studies, and *Nature's* editor noted that attempts to understand nuclear winter had inspired numerous environmental studies and spurred new developments in computer modeling and simulations.[85]

On January 28, 1985, the leaders of Argentina, Greece, India, Mexico, Sweden, and Tanzania gathered in New Delhi to issue a "Declaration on the Arms Race." Their statement showed that the nuclear winter campaign had indeed alerted nonnuclear states to their own peril at the hands of the super-powers. They stated, "It is a small group of men and machines in cities far away who can decide our fate. . . . Nuclear war, even on a limited scale, would trigger an arctic nuclear winter which may transform the earth into a dark-ened, frozen planet, posing unprecedented peril to all nations, even those far removed from the nuclear explosions."[86]

Most bizarrely, Vladimir Alexandrov, the Soviet scientist who had been involved with nuclear winter modeling since the 1983 peer-review meet-ing, "disappeared" while in Spain, never seen again after apparently being abducted by unidentified thugs. His associates in the United States feared a KGB plot; their Soviet counterparts saw evidence of an identical plot by the CIA. Apparently, some Soviet scientists took to calling Alexandrov "the first casualty of nuclear winter." His disappearance is still unexplained.[87]

Reagan Reacts

Back in the United States, Sagan had convinced many in Congress that nuclear winter had substantial implications for Cold War policy, especially SDI. At a Committee on Foreign Relations hearing, Senator John Kerry (D-MA) suggested to the Pentagon aide Richard Perle that researching nuclear winter would be a better use of the $3.7 billion being squandered on the pos-sibly "irrelevant" SDI.[88] For its part, the Reagan administration continued its awkward balancing act of questioning the validity of nuclear winter while halfheartedly trying to co-opt it as justification for existing policy. A *New York Times* article on the many government nuclear winter studies included an interview with Reagan's science adviser George Keyworth, who stated that nuclear winter "deserves far better scientific assessment than it's had to date, [and] if the gravest impacts turn out to be true . . . it would limit serious consideration by the Soviets of a first strike." Elsewhere, President Reagan plainly accepted nuclear winter. He mentioned that "as a great many repu-table scientists are telling us . . . such a war could just end up in no victory for anyone because we would wipe out the earth as we know it." After discussing the Tambora eruption that erased summer in 1816 (an event TTAPS referred to frequently), Reagan rhetorically asked his interviewer, "Now if one volcano can do that, what are we talking about with the whole nuclear exchange, the nuclear winter that the scientists have been talking about?" Reagan conceded, "It's possible," though he instantly linked nuclear winter to SDI, stating, "I think if you have a defensive weapon . . . Let's put it in such a way that those missiles aren't going to get to their target."[89]

The DOD delivered its report on nuclear winter as ordered to Congress in March 1985. The report contained a scientific explanation of the temperature drops possible after a nuclear war, though it avoided use of the phrase *nuclear winter*. The report discussed the likelihood of effects spreading to the Southern Hemisphere but overwhelmingly emphasized the uncertainties of TTAPS, detailed over several pages. The document insisted that no method or formula could predict the biological consequences.[90]

In its discussion of policy implications, the DOD wrote that nuclear winter helps "strengthen" existing U.S. policy that a nuclear war can and must be prevented in the present through deterrence and arms control and in the future with SDI—elements of U.S. policy that "remain fundamentally sound." To those who argued that nuclear winter made deterrence obsolete, the DOD responded, "We strongly disagree, and believe we cannot lower our standards for deterrence because of any such hope"; the many uncertainties with nuclear winter demanded no less. *Nature* summarized the DOD report tersely: "Pentagon says yes, it may happen, but 'so what?'"[91] Ensuing hearings proved that Congress did not appreciate the Pentagon's flippancy.

Deterrence on Trial, Part 2

The March 1985 joint hearing on nuclear winter most explicitly challenged the notion that the Pentagon successfully co-opted nuclear winter, as the hearing's purpose was ostensibly to evaluate—but actually to harangue— the DOD's report. Representative Morris Udall (D-AZ) began the hearing by innocently expressing his hope that witnesses would answer questions about nuclear winter, such as "What is it?" But because the basic questions of nuclear winter had been addressed in hearings before, the political goals quickly became clear. Udall doubted that salvation would come from "strategic snake oil" such as SDI. "The belated discovery of nuclear winter," he said, "would help us to realize at long last that the path to peace may be through arms control rather than through a never-ending succession of weapons systems disguised as bargaining chips." Scheuer followed with a description of nuclear winter as the "ghoulish season" and challenged the DOD's analysis of nuclear winter, declaring, "The implications of nuclear winter impose new realities on nuclear arms control strategy and nuclear deterrence." Claudine Schneider (R-RI) piled on, calling the DOD report "delusional thinking" and unscientific. She hoped for experts "courageous enough to follow the data wherever that may lead," while Wirth similarly chimed in that the DOD ignored the many policy implications of nuclear winter.[92]

Somewhat predictably, Sagan appeared as the first witness and instantly castigated the DOD report. He joked that if it had been a seminar paper at Cornell, he would have given it a D, or "maybe a C minus if I was in a friendly mood." While TTAPS had recognized the "serious policy implications" of nuclear winter early on, gleaned from discussions with "senior" nuclear experts "and other masters of dark arts," the DOD had shown no evidence of similar awareness. He criticized the DOD for clinging to current nuclear policy and could not fathom why the report showed "no agonizing reappraisals" of policy in the face of "the destruction of our global civilization." Asked about disagreement among scientists, Sagan responded that "increasing numbers of competent scientists" agreed that nuclear winter "looks serious." Though he admitted there would never be 100 percent consensus, he defended some uncertainty as well within normal bounds. "Scientists tend to cloak their predictions in a shroud of ifs and buts," he explained.[93]

Assistant Secretary of Defense Richard Perle followed Sagan's appearance with an aggressive condemnation of the astronomer. "I didn't hear a word of science this morning. I heard a shallow, demagogic, rambling policy pronouncement," he began, and he gave Sagan an F. Perle fumed that "there hasn't been a shred of evidence" to support any reconsideration of current policy. He admitted that nuclear winter might deserve consideration but not until the many uncertainties had been resolved. In response to a question from Schneider about the biological and social implications of nuclear winter, Perle scoffed, "It's a bottomless pit for research." When Schneider pointed out that Perle had just advocated more research but also disdained such research as useless, Perle responded, "I realize there is disappointment that we did not at the conclusion of this report say we are going to abandon our historic attitude toward the construction of our strategic forces and the nature of our deterrent." Later he explained that current policy was undoubtedly reinforced by nuclear winter, not changed by it, despite the many doubts that surround the theory.[94]

Next, Jeremy Stone of the FAS argued that, in spite of Perle's claims, nuclear winter compelled "a new approach to deterrence." In sharp contrast to Stone,

George Rathjens of MIT stated that despite being a "dove" and a "disarmer," he believed the "public has been misled . . . aided and abetted by the scientific community . . . where there have been careless and hyperbolic statements, even irresponsible ones." He argued that the oceans would help retain warmth and smoke would rain out, preventing a disastrous nuclear winter. Stephen Schneider of the National Center for Atmospheric Research (NCAR) addressed such uncertainties, describing them as "not the same thing as no effect." Rather, there was a high probability of bad consequences and a lower probability of the worst-case scenario, the extinction of humans. Congresswoman Schneider agreed, stating that although nuclear winter might have some "fuzzy parameters" and lack "scientific precision," it was "accepted" by science and even the DOD, which insisted on overstating the uncertainties.[95]

In a letter distributed to their congressional colleagues, Wirth and Representative Jim Leach (R-IA) deemed the DOD report unsatisfactory for its review of a paltry three nuclear winter studies, its narrow focus on SDI, and its scornful attitude toward the idea of nuclear winter in general. In February 1986 Wirth and eleven other members of Congress officially informed the DOD that the report was unacceptable and mandated a second analysis. This directive ordered the DOD to look at the NCAR and Los Alamos studies as well as more rigorous analysis of policy implications, including first-strike suicide, targeting of cities, civil defense, and SDI. The second report, however, also disappointed Wirth, who described it as a "shallow" five pages.[96] With nuclear winter still contested, scientists eagerly awaited the International Council of Scientific Unions report due in late 1985, hoping it would put the controversy to rest.

Confirmation: Summer 1985–Winter 1986

The ICSU's Scientific Committee on Problems of the Environment (SCOPE) began to study the environmental effects of nuclear war in October 1983 with a distinct effort "to arrive at something approaching consensus." In a letter to Wirth, a member of the committee emphasized the unique aspects of SCOPE: the study would emanate from an international group of hundreds of scientists from more than twenty nations and include a full study of climatic and biological effects.[97] When SCOPE finally released its study on the environmental consequences of nuclear war (ENUWAR) in late 1985, nuclear winter received a serious boost in credibility but also a significant shift in emphasis. The SCOPE-ENUWAR study predicted "near- or sub-freezing summer temperatures over much of North America, Europe, and north and central Asia during the first few weeks following a nuclear war." Even temperature drops of just 10°C "would probably have very significant environmental effects." Climatic disturbances could continue for months or years, rainfall would lessen, and sunlight reaching earth's surface could decrease by 10 to 20 percent.[98]

In the *Bulletin of the Atomic Scientists,* Thomas Malone, general secretary of SCOPE in the 1970s, summarized the two volumes of the SCOPE report and emphasized that "the majority of the world's population is at risk of starvation in the aftermath of a nuclear war." As for the extinction of humanity that Ehrlich had insisted "cannot be excluded" as a possibility, the SCOPE report deemed it unlikely. Yet "the indirect effects [of nuclear war] could result in the loss of one to several *billions* of humans." Addressing the uncertainties that had dogged nuclear winter research from the start, Malone explained, "Whatever uncertainties remain . . . do not call into question the credibility of the report's findings." SCOPE had avoided use of the term *nuclear winter* not because it was misleading, Malone explained, but because "even modest temperature changes would devastate global agriculture. It is not necessary to envision a world dripping with ice before such disasters would occur." The study offered "substantial reason to believe" that temperature and precipitation changes and a decrease in sunlight would follow a nuclear war. Such disruptions "would cause large numbers of deaths associated with insufficient food." In conclusion, "The indirect effects on populations of a large-scale nuclear war—particularly the climatic effects caused by smoke—could be more consequential globally than the direct effects, and *the risks of unprecedented consequences are great for noncombatant and combatant countries alike.*" "The scientists have spoken," Malone averred, "and policy-makers now have much to do by way of framing an appropriate response." Malone praised the SCOPE-ENUWAR report in distinctly moral terms, hoping it would provide "scientific foundation" to the "intuitive ethical concern" of scientists.[99]

A memo from Wirth's office praised the "comprehensive" nature of the SCOPE study and noted that the "survival of our species may depend on re-tooling our nuclear defense policy." After the study's broad release, even many of the nuclear winter theory's old antagonists began to change their minds. The *New York Times* asserted that the new study "sharply questioned" previous judgments that a nuclear war could be survived. The new findings on smoke in particular convinced the editors that a nuclear conflict "could be followed by a nuclear winter that would kill hundreds of millions more." The editorial went on to state that "these judgments of nuclear effects carry many possible implications for nuclear strategy." Overall, "deterrence must not be allowed to fail," and nuclear arsenals must be reduced. An article in *Nature* stated, "The likelihood of a nuclear winter . . . is thus given further support," while Schneider of the NCAR said that SCOPE's findings "should enhance the credibility of suggestions of a nuclear winter."[100]

The SCOPE study even forced Maddox to begrudgingly admit that TTAPS had not been too far off the mark. After trudging through SCOPE's "monumental report," Maddox relented that, "for the time being, the nuclear winter must firmly be listed among the consequences of substantial nuclear wars, remembering that time (but, it is hoped, not experience) will show that even present fears are immoderate." He added that "from now on it will probably be wise to follow SCOPE's conclusion that nuclear winter is a probable consequence of nuclear war." But Maddox, determined to find something to criticize, chastised SCOPE for having "steered clear of taking up the implications of its conclusions." He worried about the "obvious danger" that "technical arguments and conclusions will be misinterpreted." Yet just two weeks earlier, Maddox had attacked those who accepted the nuclear winter theory for trumpeting its policy implications. Nuclear winter, he had argued, was not a "unique" argument for arms reductions—"people's fond wish to sleep at night is a sufficient case for that." He had also complained that "the assumption that all nuclear wars must be all-out wars is surely mistaken." To the contrary, Maddox wrote, "There is no obvious way in which the concept of nuclear winter affects strategy and international relations in ways that are unique."[101]

Further discussions in *Nature* revealed that for many critics of the nuclear winter theory, Sagan's primary sin had not been bad science but the poor taste of using science to support political activism. One critic wrote that the fear of nuclear winter grew out of many scientists' beliefs that "responsibility for the influence of their achievements rests partially with them and should not reside solely with politicians," an attitude that "has at times tainted the objectivity that is crucial to the scientific endeavor." In particular, nuclear winter research "has become notorious for its lack of scientific integrity," despite the SCOPE report. Especially unfortunate was "the appearance of the results in popular literature before being exposed to the rigours of peer review," even though the TTAPS article had in fact been accepted by *Science* by the time the *Parade* article appeared.[102] Schneider and Starley Thompson defended their own work on nuclear winter as exemplary precisely because they had refrained from political statements and instead followed "a logical progression of scientific research," while yet another attack on Sagan fretted that because of inaccurate statements, "credibility is lost and messages from the scientific community will eventually be ignored." Still another critic scorned TTAPS for "grasping at some very strange straws" to prove their hypothesis and accused them of ignoring evidence against nuclear winter.[103] To Sagan, of course, separating nuclear winter from politics would have made no sense whatsoever.

As scientists started to come to terms with nuclear winter, members of Congress continued to wrestle with the Reagan administration and the defense establishment. The final nuclear winter hearing took place in October 1985, under the auspices of the Committee on Armed Services, but added little to the debates that had already occurred. Predictably, Sagan appeared as a witness and Perle followed to counter his claims, while other witnesses expressed belief in or doubt of nuclear winter based on their opinion for or against nuclear deterrence.[104]

As Congress and defense officials remained locked in the struggle over nuclear winter, the theory continued to move people worldwide. With Cold War ideology losing its grip on the world as the 1980s continued, ideas that challenged the bipolar paradigm held special appeal. In April 1986 bishops of the United Methodist Church released a statement on Cold War nuclear policy that expressed moral outrage at nuclear winter. Their "foundation document" directly linked their challenge to nuclear winter: "We write in defense of Creation. We do so because the Creation itself is under attack. Air and water, trees and fruits and flowers, birds and fish and cattle, all children and youth, women and men live under the darkening shadows of a threatening nuclear winter." The declaration continued, "*Nuclear deterrence* has too long been reverenced as the idol of national security. . . . The moral case for deterrence, even as an interim ethic, has been undermined by unrelenting arms escalation." The bishops refused to give "the ideology of deterrence . . . the churches' blessing."[105]

Soviet officials and other leaders also endorsed the theory. In a speech at the United Nations, Soviet foreign minister Eduard Shevardnadze mentioned nuclear winter and expressed his desire that, in the future, the word *winter* would "retain in all languages of the world the one and only meaning, its original one, and be identified solely with the season of the year which is beautiful and joyful in its own way." Even Mikhail Gorbachev, general secretary of the Communist Party and leader of the Soviet Union, said in August 1986, "The explosion of even a small part of the existing nuclear arsenal would be a catastrophe, an irreversible catastrophe, and if someone still dares to make a first nuclear strike, he will doom himself to agonizing death, not even from a retaliatory strike, but from the consequences of the explosion of his own war-heads." After France paid New Zealand reparations for sinking Greenpeace's *Rainbow Warrior* vessel, the New Zealand government used the money to fund a study of nuclear winter, while the British Labour Party relied specifically on nuclear winter for its opposition to the nuclear defense of Europe in 1986. At the June 1985 END conference, a workshop on British-French cooperation rec-ommended the dubbing into French of a nuclear winter film.[106]

Nuclear Winter in the Soviet Union

Sagan's nuclear winter campaign had alleged that both superpowers had failed to adequately address the danger of, and even at times the possibility of, nuclear winter. Hoping to influence Soviet scientists and government offi-cials, Sagan brought Vladimir Alexandrov into nuclear winter studies during the early stages of research. In congressional hearings Sagan expressed plea-sure that "publications in Pravda and programs on Soviet television" con-tained "widespread coverage in the Soviet Union of the nuclear winter issue," encouraging continued discussion of nuclear winter in the Soviet Union. Alexandrov himself addressed Congress, stating that "I think we have pretty good coverage of this topic in the Soviet Union." Elsewhere, Sagan explained that "there has been at least some permeation of the understanding of nuclear winter to the Soviet public."[107]

But the nuclear winter theory also appeared in the Soviet Union as part of the brewing dissent movement of the mid-1980s. Sagan probably did not know that nuclear winter formed the basis of a demonstration conducted by the dissidents of the Moscow Trust Group, a human rights and peace organi-zation that served "as a forum for independent discussion about major world problems, and for the exchange of knowledge and suggestions with visiting peace activists from the west." While the Trust Group did not publicly crit-icize the Soviet government for fear that it would be "brutally repressed," members of the group were frequently arrested and imprisoned. END con-tacts reported that Soviet officials arrested the physician Vladimir Brodsky in July 1985 on charges of "hooliganism," which included "transmitting a let-ter to the Soviet Academy of Sciences requesting greater publicity about the nuclear winter." In late November Brodsky was transferred to a Siberian labor camp "so that he will experience the coldest possible conditions during his 3-year term of enslavement." Brodsky went on a hunger strike for two months at prison and subsequently endured forced feedings.[108]

Actions such as Brodsky's nuclear winter demands were part of a broad array of nonviolent demonstrations. During a rally at Gagarin Square on Cosmonaut's Day, April 12, 1985, protesters shouted, "Tell the truth about the Nuclear Winter phenomenon to our people." This demonstration came on the heels of one on March 9, where protesters chanted, "No more prisoners of peace," and on May 16, the Trust Group demonstrated for "solidarity of grass-roots peace activists East and West." Mass arrests followed each demonstration.[109] Soviet activists thus demonstrated their willingness to go to jail for nuclear winter and that information on nuclear winter was on par with other freedom demands. In dissidents' minds, Soviet authorities' refusal to inform the public about the possibility of nuclear winter reinforced their belief that the Soviet Union cared nothing for its people. In contrast to the reception of nuclear winter in the United States, which largely focused on professional mores and scientific validity, Soviet activists and authorities respectively saw the theory as an eminently plausible rejection of established policy and scientific dissent as a threat to the Communist Party's monopoly on information and state power.

A Growing Consensus: Late 1986 to 1989

While Soviet scientists fought for their basic rights, scientists in the West approached nuclear winter as a scientific question, one that was quickly becoming answered. The Los Alamos study initiated by Bethe resulted in four articles that gradually appeared between 1983 and 1986 showing the results of a three-dimensional simulation of nuclear winter.[110] Bethe later explained how the study showed that a combination of factors "makes Nuclear Winter worse, especially if the nuclear weapons are exploded in summer." In recognition of the work, Los Alamos officials nominated the authors for a Distinguished Performance Award in 1986 and praised Bethe's "large role in getting this work started." Bethe himself described the work on nuclear winter as "outstanding. In my opinion it is by far the best that has been done in this active field" and "one of the best scientific efforts that has come out of the Los Alamos laboratory ever."[111]

Other studies took shots at the credibility of the original TTAPS paper while basically confirming its findings, aside from human extinction. In the summer of 1986, Thompson and Schneider of the NCAR published "Nuclear Winter Reappraised" in *Foreign Affairs,* the same venue where Sagan announced the dire policy implications of nuclear winter years earlier. Its authors intended for this article to sound the death knell of the nuclear winter theory. Thompson and Schneider began, as had Sagan, with a scientific discussion of doomsday scenarios. Compared to other outlandish concepts, nuclear winter "has been much more compelling scientifically," they wrote. The NAS and SCOPE studies had "helped to legitimize" nuclear winter as a topic of serious scientific research. But the main importance of nuclear winter, they argued, was its three serious challenges to the credibility of U.S. nuclear policy: the threat of human extinction, the suicidal risk of a first strike, and the existence of a nuclear winter threshold. Their survey of recent studies had convinced Thompson and Schneider that nuclear winter had been reduced "to a vanishingly low level of probability." The original "global freeze scenarios" and "apocalyptic conclusions" predicted by TTAPS were not likely "on scientific grounds," nor did they find evidence of any threshold. Thus, the two aspects of nuclear winter "with the most important implications for policy have been removed." The three-dimensional models showed, according to Thompson and Schneider, that average temperature changes "are considerably smaller" than the TTAPS one-dimensional model, changes that more closely resembled a "nuclear fall" than winter. Specifically, ocean warmth, smoke rainout, and a smoke-enhanced greenhouse effect would prevent severe cooling. They somewhat incongruously added that the remaining problems of nuclear "fall" could "produce unprecedented world-wide human misery," such as "mass starvation" in India. In all, Thompson and Schneider concluded, the global effects could still outweigh the direct effects of nuclear war.[112] Although heralding the defeat of the nuclear winter theory, Thompson and Schneider's article merely gave the effects of nuclear winter a different and less catchy name.

As nuclear winter became established science, its political relevance seemed to disappear as Cold War tensions dwindled, revealing that, to a great extent, the science behind nuclear winter was not the real issue. Rather, Cold War politics, the state of U.S.-Soviet relations, and the likelihood of nuclear war shaped people's interpretations of the theory. In a 1986 *Times* story about "nuclear autumn," Thompson regretted how scientists had gone public with nuclear winter: "People really have in their minds the image of frozen lakes and frozen cornfields and having to dig through frozen ground to bury the dead, and those images are too extreme. It was an excellent attention grabber, but those deep-freeze images are an exaggeration." Turco disputed the notion that a milder scenario overturned the original concern, asking, "Does the world have to freeze to an ice cube before people become concerned about what's going to happen?" Schneider admitted receiving "a lot of unhappy reaction from our former friends" but consoled himself by standing on the high ground of scientific objectivity: "We're trying to substitute credibility for drama."[113]

In a similar vein, at the February 1987 American Association for the Advancement of Science meeting in Chicago, scientists "clashed sharply" over nuclear winter. According to the *Times*, "Some speakers contended that the public image of science had been seriously damaged" by the debate, and "few recent issues had so highlighted the perils of injecting uncertain scientific conclusions into public policy debates," although such claims were impossible to measure concretely. The article heralded "nuclear fall" as the new standard and quoted a distraught George Rathjens on nuclear winter: "I think in the long run it will discredit this community of which we are all a part." *Nature* mentioned Singer's contention that the infrared radiation of smoke and ice clouds would mitigate nuclear winter, arguments that Schneider dismissed as an "infrared herring," while elsewhere Teller held fast to deterrence. A Sagan biographer also accepted nuclear fall as the final word, praising the NCAR as having created the "freest research climate" possible.[114]

But a continuation of the SCOPE-ENUWAR studies showed that nuclear fall was not the final word. Members of SCOPE decided that the concept of nuclear fall, derived from Thompson and Schneider's analyses suggesting that the temperature drop would be one of 15°C (27°F) in summer, failed as a descriptor. The predictions of milder effects were a distraction and had been "refuted by numerous scientific studies, undertaken both in the United States and abroad, which document a much broader, more compelling basis for the conclusion that a global nuclear war would create devastating environmental consequences."[115]

A February 1987 ENUWAR workshop in Bangkok again studied nuclear winter, finding no reason to revise the 1985 conclusions and reaffirming that agricultural systems "are the most vulnerable to the physical and societal disruptions that could follow a large-scale nuclear war." Agriculture in the Northern Hemisphere would be limited or even shut down for the first (and maybe other) growing seasons after nuclear war. "For most countries, and thus for most of the people on earth," the scientists agreed, "the food would run out in a matter of a few months if there were no agricultural production for just one season. . . . *Consequently, the majority of the earth's human populations is vulnerable to starvation following a large-scale nuclear war.*" As had Sagan, SCOPE pointed out that "people living far from the scenes of direct destruction and playing no central role in a nuclear war would be at a risk of losing their lives through the *indirect* effects of nuclear war," such as starvation or death from diseases associated with malnourishment and hunger. These victims "could vastly exceed the number of people who would die from direct effects of such a war." With Reagan and Gorbachev increasingly agreeing on the need to end the arms race, most government figures had lost interest in nuclear winter. But Wirth, by this time a senator, trumpeted the results of the 1987 SCOPE study, stating, "So long as responsible scientists . . . say that nuclear winter cannot be ruled out, the proper course to follow is one of caution, not business as usual." He added, "Nuclear winter is simply too important to our national security to be ignored."[116]

But nuclear winter fears increasingly fell on deaf political ears. When Gorbachev suggested eliminating nuclear weapons at a summit with Reagan at Reykjavik, Iceland, the end of the arms race was in sight, even though Reagan rebuffed Gorbachev's proposal. At the same time, science continued to accept the predictions of the nuclear winter theory. The June 1988 issue of *Environment* hailed the recent SCOPE results and a UN study as a "new scientific consensus." An overview by Frederick Warner of SCOPE hailed the five years of "unprecedented scientific cooperation" of the ENUWAR study and explained that three-dimensional models "confirmed the predictions that the smoke produced by the burning of the majority of cities in the combatant nations could lead temperatures to drop by as much as 15° to 30°C [27° to 54°F] for days to weeks in some regions during the Northern Hemisphere summer." Smoke particles, SCOPE discovered, had actually five times more absorption capacity than assumed in early nuclear winter studies; in essence, "smoke has become darker." The indirect effects of nuclear war could be greater than the direct effects, with "unprecedented consequences" for combatants and noncombatants alike, leaving a "majority of the world's population at risk of starvation." Uncertainties remained, but "confidence in the forecast of nuclear winter is now much broader and stronger than that just following its discovery in 1983." A UN report, completed in April 1988, came to almost identical conclusions.[117]

The nuclear winter controversy was less about scientific data and more about the procedures and rituals for presenting that information publicly. Near the Cold War's end, scientists continued to confirm the nuclear winter thesis. Maddox had finally made peace with nuclear winter, announcing in 1988 that nuclear winter had "come of age" as "an accepted ingredient of academic study." Although Maddox scorned the nuclear winter "bandwagon" for its distasteful "press conferences," he confessed that *Nature* "was probably over-sour in its comments on the affair." Maddox connected nuclear winter to new concerns about global warming and the greenhouse effect but relished a final sting at nuclear winter, hoping that scientists concerned about climate change "will respond more confidently than to the issue of nuclear winter with opinions properly hedged with specific qualifications about the ways in which the models are incorrect."[118] The end of the Cold War made this consensus possible because it removed nuclear winter's political significance. Divorced from contemporary policy debates, nuclear winter could become a normal scientific concept.

The meteorologist Alan Robock summarized new experiments in 1989, stating that the "basic theory of nuclear winter has remained unchanged since it was first described." The cold and the dark would ruin at least one growing season, "resulting in a global famine." A nuclear war between the superpowers would kill more people in India or China than in the United States and Soviet Union combined. Continued research since 1983 had only "strengthened the scientific basis of the theory," he asserted, citing a "consensus" based on studies by the NAS, the Soviet Academy of Sciences, Los Alamos, Livermore, and many others. Noting with regret the decreased interest in Congress, Robock maintained that "the implications of nuclear winter are clear: the use of nuclear weapons would be suicide for all the peoples of the planet." Still other experiments and analyses added to the consensus.[119]

Acceptance of nuclear winter has only increased since the 1980s. Indeed, the concept has shown staying power in science. As war erupted in the Middle East in 1991, scientists—including but by no means limited to Sagan—worried that Iraq might set Kuwaiti oil wells on fire, causing thick black clouds on a par with those predicted by nuclear winter.[120] Nuclear winter earned the ultimate sign of maturation in the early 1990s when one science textbook devoted an entire chapter to the concept. After the Cold War, Sagan transformed nuclear winter into an environmental argument, incorporating the greenhouse effect and global warming. In 2006 and 2007, further analyses by Robock using the most recent computer models indicated that in some scenarios, just "100 Hiroshima-sized" nuclear weapons could trigger a nuclear winter, a number startlingly lower than the original TTAPS estimate.[121]

In 1984 Wirth had been asked how historians would judge Sagan and the idea of nuclear winter. "With admiration and gratitude for pursuing the study of Nuclear Winter and forcing our leaders and the Department of Defense to consider the implications of this phenomenon," he had optimistically predicted. But history has not been nearly so kind. Despite the eventual scientific acceptance of the theory, vindication has not yet arrived for Sagan. One assessment in the late 1980s accused Sagan of "willful misrepresentation" and a "relaxation of professional standards" regarding nuclear winter.[122] In a "postmortem" on nuclear winter, a Sagan biographer suggests that out of kindness, obituaries of the man "downplayed or omitted nuclear winter." But because Sagan's science held up, it seems more likely that his efforts to popularize the nuclear winter theory are to blame for its poor reputation. Several writers have gone so far as to claim that the NAS punished Sagan for his nuclear winter campaign by rejecting his nomination for membership in 1992. Notably, the NAS awarded Sagan not with membership but its Public Welfare Medal in 1994, which specifically praised his popularization achievements.[123] In using science to support changes in public policy, then, Sagan found—as had Pauling—that science can support political points of view, but it cannot easily change them. Although modern life is fraught with technological peril, the structures and mores of the scientific discipline reinforced the boundaries between science and politics established by the AEC in 1954.

Sagan and Turco argued in their book on nuclear winter that the controversy over nuclear winter was not about the science behind it but about the theory's political implications and that the nuclear winter theory had "evolved in an orderly manner."[124] Nuclear winter did not end the Cold War, it is true. But the failure of the nuclear winter campaign to drastically reshape Cold War policy should not lead anyone to ignore or disparage it. Before its scientific plausibility could be fully established, historic events ended the Cold War, making the study of nuclear winter seem less urgent. But at a time when one scientist wanted science to speak to society, other scientists tried to silence him. It was not the theory's specific political arguments but rather that the theory was political at all that harmed it. The zero-sum result of nuclear winter came from the widespread belief that politically active scientists could not be objective scientists.

Aside from nuclear winter, science did not play an especially large role in the antinuclear movement of the 1980s. Activists appeared to prefer moral urgency in denouncing nuclear weapons instead of esoteric debates over complex scientific data. Scientists therefore had to all but step aside as a massive grassroots movement against nuclear weapons swept across the Western world, and this was no coincidence, as morality was the one argument against nuclear weapons that most scientists had refused to make when the national security state redefined the concept of scientific objectivity.

8

"An Emotional Grassroots Offensive"

Scientists, SDI, and the Moral Challenge to Nuclear Weapons, 1980–1991

N UCLEAR WINTER REPRESENTED JUST ONE CURRENT of antinuclear sentiment that arose during the 1980s. The broader antinuclear movement drew activists who criticized nuclear weapons from a wide array of perspectives, including feminism, environmentalism, and religion. These activists consequently had little use for the highly technical arguments for arms control offered by many scientists; the approach to arms control and disarmament that many scientists had adhered to since the 1950s had almost entirely divided them from grassroots antinuclear activists. Meanwhile, government proponents of nuclear weapons painted their scientific opponents as advocates of mutually assured destruction in another attempt to co-opt the antinuclear claims of scientists. Scientists thus had little role in the antinuclear movement of the 1980s, and where they had once provided leadership in the opposition to nuclear weapons, they now could offer their support only as citizens rather than as experts. Since the early Cold War redefinition of science, scientists had been divided along various lines, but none more rigid than the line between those challenging deterrence and those who, however they might feel about nuclear weapons, ultimately upheld its basic premises. By the end of the Cold War, the principle of deterrence remained intact, and science's challenge had been neutralized.

The Antinuclear Movement of the 1980s

At the dawn of the 1980s, legions of people around the world mobilized for disarmament, as grassroots antinuclear activism erupted on many fronts.[1] For some activists, the caustic remarks and flippant quips members of the Reagan administration made about the "evil" Soviet "empire" and "winnable" nuclear wars aroused ire. In other cases, antinuclear efforts evolved out of traditions forged in the civil rights, counterculture, and environmental protest movements of the 1960s and 1970s. Across the Atlantic, European protesters rushed to confront the attempts to station nuclear cruise and Pershing missiles in NATO nations as well as the deployment of Soviet SS-20 missiles in Eastern Europe. Reflecting its many origins, the antinuclear movement of the 1980s encompassed a wide array of activists and causes. In the United States, many movement participants came to focus on Randall Forsberg's "nuclear freeze" proposal that endeavored "to stop the nuclear arms race quite literally, by stopping the development and production of all nuclear-weapon systems" in the United States and Soviet Union.[2] A large coalition of groups under that name led a nationwide campaign for local and federal freeze legislation. The organization Ground Zero engaged in public demonstrations, while many smaller movements, such as Connecticut's Coalition to Stop Trident, embarked on protests against nuclear weapons in distinctly local fashion.

The flood of policy proposals unleashed in the 1980s could have quickly become more ineffective "first steps" in ending the nuclear arms race. One engineer endorsing the freeze wrote that although "the nuclear freeze is crucial, it is only a first step." The One Less Bomb Committee in Concord, Massachusetts, distributed a petition asking the president "to take the *first step* toward disarmament by ordering the disassembling of 1 nuclear bomb."[3] But for a great many activists, the 1980s movement transcended policy demands and looked toward the end of the arms race, not just the beginning of the end. One of the leaders of the European Nuclear Disarmament movement asserted that "END is not an arms control proposal but a political objective," envisioned as "a Europe free of nuclear weapons from Poland to Portugal." The global movement embraced a wide array of activists, a great many of them bound by solidarity in the belief that nuclear weapons were immoral. The editorial of the first issue of *END: Journal of European Nuclear Disarmament* declared, "The peace movement is here to stay. . . . The strength of the movement grows through the spread of ideas. . . . The very diversity of the movement is the source of inspiration and creativity."[4]

Much of the inspiration and creativity of the 1980s antinuclear movement came from feminist movements that opposed nuclear weapons as emblematic of patriarchal oppression. In 1983, inspired by the Greenham Common occupation, female antinuclear activists in the United States established the Women's Encampment for a Future of Peace and Justice in order to blockade the Seneca Army Depot, in Seneca Falls, New York, where nuclear missiles were housed. A vision statement, written by women at the encampment, framed the arms race as just one tool—albeit a particularly dangerous one—of female oppression and celebrated the female gender as a method of resistance in itself. "We are many women with many dreams, who speak now as one, in our common concern for life on this planet. . . . We stand in solidarity with our sisters and brothers and all life on this planet. If one of us is starving, all of us are starving. If one of us is beaten and raped, we are all beaten and raped. If one of us lives in danger of nuclear war—total annihilation, we all live in danger of total annihilation." The women at Seneca Falls declared that they were fighting an enemy that existed long before nuclear weapons and linked themselves to a feminist tradition just as old. "As women we have been traditionally silenced and ignored when we speak out," the statement continued. "Our suffragist foremothers here in New York State worked for women's rights and the abolition of slavery. And just as they struggled against the problems of a dominating, male-controlled power structure, we women today continue that struggle."[5]

The group Feminists Insist on a Safe Tomorrow (FIST) made similar connections between nuclear weapons and the historical oppression of women. An organizing letter from the group stated that "many feminist groups, in addition to our diverse work on rape, battering, reproductive rights, marriage laws, national liberation, fishing rights, land tenure, etc. feel a growing urgency to do work against militarism and imperialism. The arms race endangers the future of all life on earth. . . . Militarism is an expression of a rampant masculine ethic of domination by force which feminists struggle against in many forms." FIST activists planned to assemble a "quilt/banner" composed of squares crafted by women and women's groups worldwide, intended as "a symbolic international presence at U.S. demonstrations against the arms race, militarism, and imperialism." The quilt's first stop was to be the Women's Encampment at Seneca Falls.[6]

As the likely ground zero of a nuclear war, Europe saw the most antinuclear activity, spurred on by the continent's general dissent from Cold War bipolarity in the 1980s but reflecting similar origins in morality, environmentalism, and feminism. In *END Journal,* the West German activist Eva Quistrop wrote that in the mid-1970s, she began to see connections between the nuclear complex and the patriarchal society around her. While "not aggressive in the male sense," she wrote, "we declare war, not on another nation, or race or sex, but against this destructive technology. This is the form patriarchy takes today, and it is a destructive form of power that affects everything." Like her American counterparts, Quistrop saw nuclear protest as one aspect of "feminist issues, ecological issues, Third World issues and the issue of freedom. In particular we had to focus on nuclear technology because it simply is not compatible with a female future." Eventually, Quistrop helped start a movement called German Women for Peace. "Together with the women of the world we will turn our powerlessness into power," her movement declared. "We will no longer continue to accept the struggle for power waged by the superpowers."[7]

The Nobel Peace Prize–winning Swedish activist Alva Myrdal rejected the term *peace movement* as inadequate to describe "the newly rekindled fire of resistance" to nuclear weapons. She preferred the term *resistance movement,* which, she wrote, offered a way of life that refused to be "snared by the allurements of either the one or the other of the superpowers, not by the one in the east nor by the one in the west." Myrdal demanded that both the United States and the Soviet Union remove their intermediate-range nuclear missiles destined for deployment in the European theater.[8] In the fall of 1983, according to one estimate, roughly five million West Europeans participated in antinuclear demonstrations.[9]

Back in the United States, nuclear protest had a distinctly different tone from scientists' efforts in earlier decades. During the late 1960s and 1970s, many Americans (and some scientists themselves) had begun to fear a trend toward technocracy, while left-leaning scientists decried the militarism and class, race, and gender inequalities rampant in U.S. science; consequently, many Americans began to return to religion as a moral arbiter in society.[10] As fears of nuclear war revived in the 1980s, moral messages became crucial to the peace movement, as they resonated with the public in a way that strictly technical arguments for nuclear disarmament could not. In just a single issue of the U.S. antinuclear magazine *Nuclear Times,* ecoreligious claims— "The solution to avoiding nuclear annihilation is to convince everyone on Spaceship Earth that we are all God's children and that it is His desire that we live peacefully together"—mingled with appeals for the movement to reach out to labor unions, endorsements of a freeze from financial experts concerned about fiscal responsibility, and calls to unite the antinuclear and civil rights movements.[11] The antinuclear movement brought together a great variety of activism, of which religion was just one among many. But the religious aspect of activism bears further analysis because religion's moral critique of nuclear weapons in general contrasted greatly with many scientists' technical opposition to nuclear weapons.

Religion in the Antinuclear Movement

In the 1980s religious antinuclear activists added a distinct sense of morality to the antinuclear movement. Jack Joppa, the founder of the National No-Nukes Prison Support Collective, a U.S. organization that assisted activists of any sort imprisoned for antinuclear civil disobedience, explained in 1981 that "many of those imprisoned for longer periods of time are religious activists." This imprisonment resulted, Joppa claimed, from the fact that religious believers felt a greater sense of urgency about the antinuclear cause, and "a consciousness of the urgency is just the beginning of the personal journey that leads one to accept jail time as part of the struggle." Joppa also explained that religious communities buttressed antinuclear resisters with "pre-established networks of support for their members." Church members had people to visit them, watch their children, and feed their pets while in prison, which "enables more religious activists to be currently risking longer sentences."[12]

More mainstream religious activists supported the antinuclear movement as well. An auxiliary bishop of Detroit praised *Nuclear Times*, telling the magazine, "I hope you will continue the fine work you are doing to encourage understanding and involvement in this important issue [of peace]."[13] Not everyone saw the church as a force for peace; a letter from the president of American Atheists asked, "Where, indeed, have the churches been?" The writer blamed churches for supporting the U.S. government "in the spiraling cold war and armaments race . . . in return for innumerable favors," including "positions of prestige, tax exemptions, government largess, and leading places in implementing social policies."[14] But in *Nuclear Times*, at least, coverage emphasized the antinuclear side of many churches and congregations, featuring articles such as "Churches Attack Weapon Business" and "Churches to Kick Off Peace with Justice Week." An article in the June 1983 issue hailed Catholic bishops' endorsement of a nuclear freeze and declaration that the use of nuclear weapons "could not be morally justified." The Catholic bishop of Amarillo, Texas, home of the Pantex nuclear weapons assembly plant, wrote to *Nuclear Times* himself. While he worried that activists accepted only the church's antinuclear stand while rejecting the other aspects of its belief system, he assuaged his doubts with the thought that "the urgency of the nuclear threat is such that we must all work together on it with courage and commitment."[15]

Pope John Paul II directly called on scientists to embrace morality in an address titled "Science, Technology, and Peace," delivered at Hiroshima in late February 1981. The pope described scientists as bearing "the anxiety of the scientific world in the face of an irresponsible use of science, which too often does grievous damage to the balance of nature, or brings with it the ruin and oppression of man by man." The fact that nuclear war threatened the world compelled everyone to confront a "basic moral consideration: from now on, it is only through a conscious choice and through a deliberate policy that humanity can survive." To make the correct moral choices, humanity must put "science . . . at the service of peace." The pope urged scientists to study the ethical problems of modern society more deeply and resist the subjugation of scientific development to military purposes.[16] By embracing an antinuclear ethos, the Catholic Church—though not known for an especially progressive view of women—found itself allied with feminists as well as many other types of activists against the common nuclear menace.

Clergy of all denominations spoke out, unburdened by scientists' restraints of objectivity. One letter to the *Bulletin of the Atomic Scientists* in 1982 criticized world leaders for absolving themselves of responsibility for the nuclear danger. "The most grotesque aspect of the nuclear arms race," the Reverend William Rankin of All Saints Church in Pasadena, California, declared, "is the sense we have that its momentum is invincible and that no one is in charge." The "rising military expenditures, boisterous foreign policy rhetoric, and the piling up of nuclear weapons" amounted to "provocation," which "in the nuclear age is tantamount to criminal insanity." Rankin closed his letter with a call to action: "Never before has the urgency of personal morality been so starkly apparent. Never before have we felt so desperately the need for courage, imagination and vision. Never before have the stakes been higher."[17]

Religious activism in the United States may have been somewhat limited by the evangelical revival of the 1980s, with a good many of these congregations supporting conservative politicians and causes, including a hard line against the atheistic Soviet Union. Across the Atlantic, however, the Church of England endorsed disarmament in 1983 and advocated cancellation of the Trident program, refusal of the Polaris missile, and a halt to the production of cruise missiles. *END: Journal of European Nuclear Disarmament* also reported on churches in East Germany that actively participated in the peace movement.[18] One petition, distributed by Pastor Reiner Eppelmann, declared that nuclear weapons "won't save us, but destroy us." Signers of his petition included craftsmen, white- and blue-collar workers, deacons, a writer, a scientist, a nurse, and a mechanic.[19]

Religion had long been a factor in Britain's largest and most mainstream antinuclear organization, the Campaign for Nuclear Disarmament, which had featured a Christian subgroup since the late 1950s. In the 1980s Christian CND grew larger and bolder, announcing that "the possession of nuclear weapons is totally incompatible with being a follower of Jesus Christ." The organization estimated in 1983 that 23 percent of all CND members considered themselves practicing Christians, a percentage that exceeded that of practicing Christians in Britain as a whole. Christian CND celebrated this embrace of nuclear disarmament by launching a "Nuclear-Free Parishes Campaign" that promoted grassroots efforts, such as "urging Christian congregations to pledge support for nuclear disarmament in their churches" and "actively seeking ways of becoming peacemakers and helping to create a nuclear-free future."[20]

In 1984 Christian CND also challenged the Church of England General Synod to follow up on its antinuclear statement from a year earlier. An open letter from Christian CND argued that the Church of England could not provide "a moral lead if its central body remains silent while the nuclear governments persist with so-called defence policies which . . . involve the conditional intention to inflict genocide on millions of innocent people." Christian CND believed that "God is now calling the Christian community in this country to . . . influence public policy by proclaiming the judgement and peace of the Gospel to a government and people overshadowed by the darkness of death."[21]

A New Voice of Expertise

Antinuclear activists still envisioned a role for scientists, but one based on a fairly generic image of them as experts rather than activists. In her 1983 manifesto, Myrdal described the antinuclear resistance movement as entering a second phase. The first phase had been "the massive emotional protest against nuclear weapons." The second phase, now begun, opposed the state's attempts to stifle the movement by "meeting with realistic counter-arguments all subterfuges, all false arguments and alibis." Scientists stood at the front of this second wave, and she called on them to counter the "superpower and allied propaganda" that opposed the antinuclear movement. "Scientists do not lie . . . [and] their evidence stands invincible," she wrote, evidently unaware of the vast and rancorous disputes between scientists over nuclear weapons. She had faith that scientists and other technical experts could influence public opinion because of their mastery of knowledge. But scientists were just one influential group among many professionals that she identified, including engineers, architects, writers, psychologists, nurses, clergy, physicians, and, most important, "the workers in their great numbers."[22] Scientists still mattered to the antinuclear movement, but no longer as leaders.

Some scientists, physicians, and engineers joined this vibrant mixture of religious, feminist, internationalist, and moral sentiment, creating a new voice of nuclear protest. In particular, the Australian pediatrician and antinuclear activist Helen Caldicott of the Physicians for Social Responsibility (PSR) stood out. She expressed her point of view during a debate over the nuclear freeze against the actor and conservative activist Charlton Heston, the retired navy admiral Gene La Rocque, and—of course—Edward Teller that took place on Valentine's Day 1983 at Clemson University in South Carolina. Caldicott's opening statement discussed the effects of a nuclear war in numerical terms, befitting her identity as a doctor: "750 million of the 1.3 billion people who live in urban areas in this hemisphere would be killed, and 350 million would be seriously injured, to die later." She detailed the effects and casualties at ground zero of a twenty-megaton H-bomb explosion: "a crater three-quarters of a mile wide and 800 feet deep—converting the people, the buildings, and the earth below to radioactive fallout, which would be injected up into the mushroom cloud in the stratosphere to circulate from west to east around the earth, coming down as fallout with low pressure systems." Everyone within a radius of six miles would be killed—or "vaporized," more precisely. She extended her analysis out to twenty miles, where "every person would be killed or lethally injured." At twenty-six miles, "the heat is still so intense that your clothes could instantaneously ignite, and you would become a walking, flaming torch." At thirty-five to forty miles, the cataclysm could start "a firestorm . . . of 1,500 to 3,000 square miles." True to the scientific nature of her field, Caldicott explained that her predictions offered only an educated hypothesis. But she then mixed scientific and religious language: "The only way to find out scientifically is to do the experiment, and I would submit, as a physician, that that is medically contraindicated, that this would create the final epidemic that the human race would ever know. In fact, we are talking about destroying God's creation."[23]

In the question-and-answer session, Caldicott further revealed the moral, religious, and feminist underpinnings of the 1980s antinuclear movement. Though trained in the scientific and medical disciplines, she spoke as not just a doctor but a doctor who cared for children. "I hear what Mr. Heston and Dr. Teller are saying, but I would like to submit, as a woman, a pediatrician, and a mother, that this is prenuclear thinking," she stated. "The thing is," she continued, "I am a woman. You can tell I am a woman. And I do not think it is the right way to settle a conflict. . . . That does not produce conflict resolution in a marriage. If you come on with strengths from both sides, the marriage ends in divorce. Russia and America are married on this planet. If we do not live together, we die together."[24] Here Caldicott rejected the belief that nuclear wars were somehow "winnable" and incorporated the concept of a shared coexistence from the environmental ethos.

A question from the audience directly addressed religion and biblical prophecy, asking the speakers if they agreed that world destruction, as foretold in the book of Revelation, was inevitable. After Heston disputed the idea that God wanted to destroy the world and affirmed Americans' duty to protect the country, Caldicott responded in language that revealed the internationalist and moral ideals of the antinuclear movement. She stated, "About 92 percent of the world's people do not live in Russia or America. I come from Australia, so I am one of them. And these people want to live. . . . As a pediatrician and a mother, I am talking about preserving God's creation for the rest of time. So to talk about patriotism now is anachronistic."[25]

Caldicott's closing statement again emphasized a female perspective on nuclear weapons. Asking the audience to understand nuclear war emotionally, she asked, "How many leaders of the world have witnessed the miracle of the birth of a baby? How many leaders of the world have helped a child to die and supported the parents in their grief?" She closed by outlining a plan for the world's "acute clinical emergency where we are about to die," emphasizing a bilateral nuclear weapons freeze.[26] Caldicott could speak in a way the typical arms control scientist could not. Many of the earlier antinuclear scientists had come from physics, a field dominated by men and, because of its need for massive equipment, one that frequently depended on defense-establishment funding. In addition, physicians had research norms and interests not shared by physicists. Caldicott embraced the moral ethos of the 1980s antinuclear movement and crafted political arguments based on medical expertise and female identity. Such a chorus of expert authority, environmental alarm, and quasi-millennial prophecy helped challenge the arms race and the strategy of deterrence on a level beyond highly technical arms control proposals.

Meanwhile, advocates of nuclear weapons in the 1980s scorned the peace movement. Aghast over the widespread concern about nuclear winter and support for antinuclear proposals in general, a civil defense consultant and geologist wrote to Teller about this moral resistance movement. "Will an emotional grassroots offensive," he asked, "undermine the hope of the Free World's developing and deploying effective, truly defensive weapons?"[27] Moral arguments, more than scientific ones, worried pronuclear supporters of the 1980s.

"Mutually Assured Survival"

Nuclear advocates of the 1980s clearly admired the power of religious and moral arguments, as they used such rhetoric themselves. In 1983 Reagan himself told an Israeli lobbyist, "You know, I turn back to your ancient prophets in the Old Testament and the signs foretelling Armageddon, and I find myself wondering if we're the generation that's going to see that come about. I don't know if you've noted any of those prophecies lately, but believe me, they certainly describe the times we're going through." One year earlier, Secretary of Defense Caspar Weinberger had said, "I have read the Book of Revelation and yes, I believe the world is going to end—by an act of God, I hope—but every day I think that time is running out." James Watt, Reagan's secretary of the interior, had chimed in, "I do not know how many future generations we can count on before the Lord returns." Such apocalyptic talk often indicated hostility to disarmament, as in 1983 when the evangelist Jerry Falwell called the freeze campaign a "suicidal effort." Many Americans began to think that belief in millennial prophecy indicated that these leaders would not attempt to prevent World War III, seeing it as the Almighty's plan.[28]

But when Reagan introduced the Strategic Defense Initiative, his tone changed from impending apocalypse to technological salvation. Accordingly, Reagan administration officials often tried to smear their antinuclear opponents and critics of SDI as immoral advocates of mutually assured destruction. During a 1985 Committee on Armed Services hearing on nuclear winter, the Pentagon aide Richard Perle had argued that Carl Sagan's proposal to reduce nuclear arsenals to a number low enough to avoid nuclear winter but still capable of deterring the Soviets simply—and irresponsibly—endorsed mutually assured destruction.[29] The Pentagon official in charge of the Strategic Defense Initiative Organization (SDIO), James Abrahamson, repeated these accusations in a 1986 debate with Sagan. When Sagan questioned the reliability of SDI, Abrahamson changed the subject, countering that the only alternative to SDI was a policy of mutually assured destruction. In his memoirs Teller framed opponents of SDI, including Hans Bethe and Victor Weisskopf, as believing "the policy of mutually assured destruction [was] a better, more stable policy" (even though SDI and arms reductions were not mutually exclusive).[30]

Teller had spent the 1970s out of the limelight to an extent. He popped up periodically, such as during debates over the energy crisis, when he urged that for the sake of national security, "we should immediately cut gasoline consumption massively." During the Three Mile Island nuclear power plant meltdown, Teller frantically defended nuclear power to various news media as well as in front of Congress.[31] But the conservative revival that swept U.S. politics in the early 1980s poised Teller to once again influence U.S. nuclear policy. Although in 1978 Teller had declared that his preferred candidate for the 1980 presidency was Dixy Lee Ray, the conservative former chair of the Atomic Energy Commission and Democratic governor of Washington, he quickly became a fan of the new president. Reagan's Presidential Transition Office asked Teller to give his opinion on cabinet appointments, though none of his recommendations was selected.[32] He nevertheless wrote a friend in April 1981 that "I am on the whole very much satisfied with what is going on at present."[33]

In a 1980 interview Teller expressed a new interpretation of his approach to nuclear weapons. "I am not an advocate of the arms race," he announced, "I am an advocate of a technological race which is something very different because you produce new, different, surprising things which [are] the real source of power." The technological race was the "real" way to defeat the Soviet Union. By 1981 Teller had largely set aside his other interests in order to focus on his horse of choice in the technological race: nuclear weapons defense systems. Well before Reagan announced SDI, Teller pushed defensive nuclear weapons as the most important breakthrough physicists could achieve in the 1980s. He characterized missile defense as comparable to the urgency and nobility of scientists' efforts during World War II, writing, "Those of us who remember the mid-1930s know that Britain was saved by the development of radar and . . . code breaking." In contrast to Hitler, however, "the men of the Kremlin are cool, practical and conservative. This time, success in developing defense could prevent war." In testimony before the House Committee on Armed Services, Teller continued to hammer home his warnings of appeasement when he deemed nuclear freeze proposals "as effective as Chamberlain's umbrella was in preventing the Second World War."[34]

Along with advocating missile defense, Teller continued to attack those who threatened the weapons he advocated. In a 1982 article in the *Journal of Civil Defense,* he focused his ire on the "new tidal wave of disarmament propaganda." In particular, opposition to nuclear weapons among religious organizations alarmed Teller. "When church people support peace, they do not differ from any other Americans," he wrote. "When church people raise rigid opposition to the preparation of weaponry that decreases the danger of war itself, their action appears more dubious." Worried by the moral and religious challenge to nuclear weapons, he continued, "We should pray that revolutionary students, politicians and archbishops do not make common cause in supporting an oversimplified solution which will lead to disaster."[35]

Embroiled at the time in the bitter debate with Sagan over nuclear winter, Teller reserved some vitriol for activists of all sorts, including Caldicott's PSR. "Who are these physicians who call themselves 'Physicians for Social Responsibility'?" he rhetorically asked an interviewer. "Does that mean all other physicians not belonging to this small group are not responsible?" He answered himself: "The so-called 'Physicians for Social Responsibility' . . . are, in fact, highly irresponsible." Furthermore, a nuclear freeze would make nuclear war a "practical certainty." Shifting to a defense of his allies, Teller stated that "President Reagan is the first U.S. leader who has had the guts to tell his people this sad and terrible fact. That we are second best. We may be 10 years behind, we may be as much as 15 years behind, or we may be only six years behind. But we are decisively behind." Such a "fact" was highly dubious at best, but hyperbole came naturally to Teller by this point. He continued to try to smear his opponents with the same Red Scare tropes he had used since the late 1940s: "Physicians who try to scare people about nuclear war are right in trying to prevent war, but they are wrong in trying to disarm the U.S. as the means of preventing war." With typical exaggeration, Teller claimed that "the anti-war groups in Britain, France, and the U.S. . . . helped bring Hitler to power and helped encourage the Germans to launch an even greater slaughter in World War II. . . . I do not want history to repeat itself."[36]

When not on the attack, Teller's moral language attempted to put a positive spin on nuclear weapons, especially SDI, the plan to arm satellites with nuclear-powered X-ray lasers that would blast enemy missiles. In the summer of 1982, Teller wrote to inform Reagan about this "important new class of defensive nuclear weapons systems." The weapons would be "spectacularly destructive," Teller wrote; "however, it is enemy warheads, rockets and satellites, not lives, which will be destroyed." Calling it "the most important [matter] in strategic military affairs since the advent of the hydrogen bomb,"

Teller requested an additional fifty-five million dollars in research funds for Livermore laboratory. Emphasizing their morality, Teller wrote that with these weapons, "we may end the Mutual Assured Destruction era and commence a period of assured survival on terms favorable to the Western Alliance." As an added bonus, satellite weapons would eliminate a pesky nuisance by serving as "a uniquely effective reply to those advocating the dangerous inferiority implied by a 'nuclear freeze.'" On September 14 Teller visited Reagan to tell him about how nuclear-powered lasers could defend the United States from Soviet missiles, an idea the president described as "exciting" in his diary.[37]

While not religious himself, Teller saw the value of supporting his position on nuclear weapons in moral terms. In a letter to the conservative icon William F. Buckley, Teller again used the language of morality to justify nuclear weapons, writing, "What is really immoral is not nuclear weapons, but rather aggression. Defense is justified." The "proper and morally correct purpose" of nuclear weapons was to serve as "defensive instruments," he explained. "Our difficulty is that this idea is contrary to general assumptions, and it is extremely hard to make people believe it. A nuclear freeze would preclude ongoing development of purely defensive nuclear devices."[38]

On March 23, 1983, with Teller, Bethe, and other influential scientists watching, Reagan announced SDI to the public. "What if free people could live secure in the knowledge that their security did not rest upon the threat of instant U.S. retaliation to deter a Soviet attack, that we could intercept and destroy ballistic missiles before they reached our own soil or that of our allies?" the president asked. "I call upon the scientific community of our country, those who gave us nuclear weapons, to turn their great talents now to the cause of mankind and world peace, to give us the means of rendering these nuclear weapons impotent and obsolete." Teller later wrote that Reagan's "wonderful words moved me deeply." But how could Reagan's statement not have pleased Teller? After all, he had practically provided the president with the speech. In July Teller and other SDI advocates again visited Reagan, urging that SDI should receive the same priority as the Manhattan Project during World War II. After the meeting Reagan wrote in his diary, "I have to agree with them it's the way to go."[39]

In contrast, other elite U.S. scientists advocated a ban on space weapons. Even before Reagan's SDI announcement, a February 1983 petition signed by scientists, drafted by Sagan and the physicist Richard Garwin, had declared, "We believe that the testing or deployment of any weapons in space—in part by threatening vital satellite assets—significantly increases the likelihood of warfare on Earth. . . . Once such weapons systems are established in national arsenals they become very difficult to displace. . . . If space weapons are ever to be banned, this may be close to the last moment in which it can be done." Signatories included such U.S. scientific luminaries as Bethe, Sidney Drell, Lee DuBridge, Frank Long, Carson Mark, Philip Morrison, Wolfgang Panofsky, I. I. Rabi, Glenn Seaborg, Victor Weisskopf, Jerome Wiesner, and Herbert York.[40]

To Congress, Teller described defensive nuclear weapons, including SDI and the X-ray laser, as "a third generation of nuclear weapons," adding that the "big size" and "enormous destructive power" of nuclear weapons no longer mattered. Because the X-ray laser would use a nuclear explosion to power a laser, the explosives no longer needed to be devastatingly large. He branded his opponents as "stuck in the old concept of no defense."[41] During House debate over SDI, a representative from Arizona advocated for the program based on Teller's judgment, inaccurately claiming that Teller had also been the sole advocate of the hydrogen bomb in the late 1940s and early 1950s. "Again in the scientific world he becomes a lone voice," Republican Eldon Rudd declared. "Thank God for Dr. Teller."[42]

Ensconced at the Hoover Institution on the campus of Stanford University, Teller defended SDI and his new conception of deterrence. The derisive nickname "Star Wars" particularly galled him because it evoked images of fantastic and impractical battle stations.[43] He bemoaned the "wide-spread anti-Reagan attitude of the press" for confusing the public over defensive weapons (though he also faulted excessive U.S. secrecy restrictions). Reagan had not proposed "Star Wars," Teller argued; instead, he had proposed a system "to replace the truly horrible idea of mutual assured destruction." Answering criticisms that the system was not 100 percent effective, Teller urged the public not to discount an 80 percent effective defense system and claimed that "two hostile camps primarily armed with shields is less dangerous than if armed with swords." Teller dismissed deterrence based on "devastating retaliation," preferring instead deterrence based on defense. This method he deemed more effective because it relied on uncertainty by creating doubt in the minds of the Soviets. "Our purpose is to deter war by making the success of aggression less likely, thereby we can contribute to deterring aggression," he told Congress.[44]

Far from being a lone voice in the scientific wilderness, Teller had the backing of many other scientists on SDI, including the Science and Engineering Committee for a Secure World, formed in May 1986. The organization counted on "thousands of scientists and engineers across America and elsewhere who agree with us that it is unscientific and unwise to hastily oppose the promising

Strategic Defense Initiative proposal at this early stage of its research and development." To them, a system to protect people from nuclear destruction made "good common and good moral sense." The group argued that SDI would turn U.S. policy "away from the unreliable, outdated MAD doctrine and its death dealing nuclear missiles, to a Mutually Assured Survival policy based on new, life protecting defensive systems," a policy they described as "ethically superior." Former National Academy of Sciences president Frederick Seitz chaired the group; other members included Teller, Eugene Wigner, S. Fred Singer, Hans Mark, Alvin Weinberg, John Wheeler, Harold Agnew, and Dixy Lee Ray.[45]

Teller made no secret of his political persuasion. After Reagan underwent surgery to remove a potentially cancerous polyp in his large intestine, Teller showered him with flattery and sycophancy. "There are few occasions when I dare to use the name of God," the normally irreligious Teller wrote. "Now I thank him for your recovery from your operation." He went on to thank Reagan for his continuing support of SDI and advised the president not to trade it away for some short-term arms control agreements. Instead, establishing SDI "as the protector of the free world . . . would make your role more remarkable than that of Lincoln. He saved the Union. You have set out to save freedom." He concluded by pledging to do his best to turn Reagan's SDI "dream into reality"; he did not need to add that it was his own dream as well.[46]

Antinuclear Scientists in the 1980s

While Teller could get away with making moral arguments because he was pronuclear and anticommunist, many scientists continued to oppose nuclear weapons by favoring technical arguments and remaining ambivalent to grassroots efforts. Because moral arguments against nuclear weapons most effectively mobilized the grassroots, the old guard of antinuclear scientists found themselves followers rather than leaders of the movement because— unlike when they spoke about scientific and technical issues—they had no unique authority over moral concerns. In contrast to earlier eras, the movement in the 1980s valued moral authority over technical expertise, which paralleled the Reagan administration's attempt to reframe the Cold War in the 1980s as a morally justified struggle against atheistic communism rather than an ideological competition contested on a technological level. This definition put Cold War policy beyond the purview of scientists and served to make them less influential as a social force. Some of these scientists felt a sense of paternalism toward the antinuclear movement, since they had given birth to nuclear dissent decades earlier. "The community of physical scientists has been struggling with the problem of avoiding nuclear war since the end of World War II," wrote Bernard Feld, the new editor of the *Bulletin of the Atomic Scientists*.[47] This was, of course, true, but scientists were being overtaken as many other activists representing a wide array of causes catalyzed the antinuclear movement.

Scientists shared no single reaction to the grassroots antinuclear movement; a survey of the *Bulletin* reveals a variety of positions. One writer dismissed grassroots efforts such as the enormous antinuclear rally in Central Park on June 12, 1982, where roughly three-quarters of a million people demonstrated for disarmament. John Isaacs, a member of the Council for a Livable World, discussed the political prospects for freeze legislation in the 1982 November elections. In one of the *Bulletin*'s rare mentions of the Central Park rally, Isaacs gave the rally a nice pat on the head. "Demonstrations such as the huge June 12 New York rally were important in the campaign to stop the nuclear arms race," he wrote, "but a definite political focus is also necessary to have an impact on decision-makers in Congress." Scientists had been mentioned only as an afterthought in a *New York Times* description of the rally's participants, near the bottom of a list including pacifists, anarchists, Buddhist monks, and jugglers.[48]

Still, some scientists could be supportive of grassroots activism. The *Bulletin* began a "Bulletins" section devoted to "public interest organizations and activities," such as the first Ground Zero week of protest in 1982. Douglas Mattern, an electronics engineer and disarmament activist, hailed the antinuclear movement in the *Bulletin* and blasted the Reagan administration for running the arms race at full speed. "The failure [of disarmament measures] cannot be blamed on the lack of public support," Mattern wrote, praising the June 12 demonstrations. Instead, "The U.S. government poses the main problem in the disarmament dilemma." Mattern called on "the American people" to "build enough pressure to force the Administration to abandon its escalation program and accept the bilateral nuclear freeze."[49]

When it came to freeze legislation, the U.S. Congress did not turn to scientists for guidance. Instead, government officials, foreign relations specialists, and arms control experts were more likely to be consulted. A 1983 hearing by the House Foreign Affairs Committee, for example, brought Perle, the Sovietologist Raymond Garthoff, and Randall Forsberg to the hill for their views on freeze proposals. In contrast, scientists were heavily consulted during hearings on nuclear winter and less frequently for their views on SDI.[50]

As for scientists'—specifically physicists'—personal attitudes toward the arms race in the 1980s, at least one survey was conducted. In 1986 Peter D. Hart Research Associates surveyed 549 physicists selected randomly from the American Physical Society's directory. By a margin of 54 percent to 29 percent, the confidential report stated, physicists viewed SDI as "a step in the wrong direction for America's national security policy." But physicists took a different view of other weapons that made up U.S. nuclear defenses, including Trident submarines (63 percent right direction, 11 percent wrong direction), cruise missiles (45 percent right direction, 26 percent wrong direction), and the Stealth Bomber (39 percent right direction, 24 percent wrong direction).[51] Many scientists clearly opposed SDI, but unlike grassroots activists in the United States and Europe, they viewed some nuclear weapons as acceptable. Just as Oppenheimer had argued in 1954 that he had supported the development of the H-bomb once a "technically sweet" design had been conceived, perhaps many scientists in the 1980s felt comfortable opposing only those weapons that they could contest on technical grounds.

Computer scientists also mobilized against SDI on technical grounds. The Computer Professionals for Social Responsibility challenged the program in terms of the inherent complexity and difficulty of the computing requirements such a weapons system would require. One critic wrote, "Even if we could somehow magically build computers which were fast enough and reliable enough, even if we could devise systems which [were] completely reliable, even if we could write software which would be completely error free—the bottom line is that no one knows what to tell the computers to do." At least one British computer scientist demonstrated that such skepticism was not limited to U.S. scientists. Richard Ennals resigned his government research position to protest the British government's decision to participate in "Star Wars" research, and he and several of his fellow Imperial College computer scientists explained their reasons in a letter to Margaret Thatcher. They deemed it "not possible" to build a reliable SDI and argued that the attempt to do so would "divert scarce human and technological resources away from civil applications." Furthermore, they feared that SDI research would spark a nihilistic "Star Wars Race" between East and West.[52]

While not prone to such public demonstrations, Bethe had continued to do what he could for arms control and disarmament since the early 1960s. When the Kennedy administration signed a test ban agreement with the Soviet Union in 1963, Bethe reconsidered his earlier doubts and voiced his belief that the Senate should ratify the treaty. During the ensuing decades, Bethe had continued to pursue arms control measures, always in the technical language of the scientist. The 1980s found Bethe still active in arms control efforts and still viewing disarmament through the lens of U.S. national security.

On September 22, 1982, the *New York Times* published an op-ed piece coauthored by Bethe that refuted the Reagan administration's reasons for rejecting a freeze. An early draft of the editorial argued that "the U.S. should want a freeze" and predicted that such a measure would "reduce the risks of war and the costs of military programs." Bethe also spoke in favor of the measure at the October 13, 1981, meeting of the Tompkins County Nuclear Weapons Freeze Campaign.[53] But at an arms race colloquium at Sandia Laboratories in July 1982, Bethe was asked to comment on the freeze proposal and revealed a complex position. He began by stating that he did not actually advocate a freeze. The freeze was an important but simple "political movement," he said. "It has to be simple to be understood by the public." While the public understood the concept of a freeze, Bethe suspected the public would have difficulty understanding his highly technical discussion of arms control. The freeze existed, in Bethe's mind, "as a means of alerting the public and, thereby, giving a signal to our government that we do not want to continue the arms race." But what made sense to the public did not necessarily make sense in reality. He opposed stopping the production of the cruise missile, for example, "because I consider it the second-most important part of our arsenal. Therefore, I don't endorse the freeze as an actual measure, but I do endorse it as an easily understood public movement. I think it has done its job in this respect."[54] Bethe approved of new nuclear weapons as long as they replaced the larger and more destabilizing ones of previous generations, but such nuance did not easily jibe with the moral opposition to nuclear weapons that drove grassroots antinuclear movements. While antinuclear activists had begun to challenge deterrence and the fundamental principles of U.S. Cold War policy, Bethe's paradigm continued to rely on nuclear weapons.

Bethe had an ambivalent view of social movements. In 1949 he had mistakenly dismissed the National Association for the Advancement of Colored People as "a Communist front organization," and in 1963 he remained skeptical of antinuclear activism. Referring to disarmament and public opinion, Bethe dismissed "going directly to the people" as unwise. "The people," he explained, "are unfortunately swayed by the political climate of the moment. For instance, the German hating campaign of the first World War, the McCarthy Era and much worse, operations in dictatorship countries like Nazi Germany and Russia. In the heat of international conflict I would not trust the people to remain loyal to the disarmament agency in preference to their own country."[55]

In the 1980s Bethe attempted to walk a fine line between supporting the freeze as a "public movement," on the one hand, and opposing the freeze "as an actual measure," on the other. When a November 11, 1981, national anti-nuclear teach-in organized by the Union of Concerned Scientists brought together scientists, academics, and students in grassroots actions modeled after teach-ins during the Vietnam War, Bethe took part. About a month before, Bethe informed a colleague that he would participate in the event and included a list of talking points for himself and other scientists. The list clearly demonstrated the technical nature of Bethe's arms control advocacy, as he defended arms control and disarmament as not detrimental to the military security of the United States. Bethe began his list with the statement that the "premise of the Reagan government that we are inferior to the Soviet Union in nuclear weapons is false. What matters for our security from surprise attacks are submarines and bombers. The penetration of the latter will be assured by cruise missiles, which will become operational in a few months. In these two categories we are superior to the USSR." The next item asserted that "since cruise missiles assure the ability to penetrate into the Soviet Union the B1 is unnecessary." The accuracy of Trident missiles, he added, ensured that "MX is not needed from this point of view."[56] Just as he had in the late 1950s, Bethe chose to argue that arms control would not harm U.S. nuclear superiority rather than vocally embrace the moral appeal of disarmament.

Bethe also endorsed the freeze in a public appeal signed by just under one hundred scientists from four continents on both sides of the Iron Curtain in 1982. The petition aimed at "our colleagues of the world's scientific community," asking them to "accept responsibility and become directly involved in actions to avert nuclear war." The accompanying text endorsed a freeze: "To reverse the present arms race we must first stop racing. This calls for a 'standstill freeze' on current nuclear arsenals as an effective way of initiating the essential process of nuclear disarmament."[57]

Eventually, Bethe's conflicting private and public thoughts on a freeze caused confusion, forcing him to clarify his ambivalent stand. In 1983 he wrote to the news editor of the *Ithaca (NY) Journal* after the paper printed an interview with him that ruffled some feathers. Bethe complained that his statement, "I don't think the freeze, taken literally, is the right thing to do," had been "misinterpreted" by many people. "The emphasis," he explained, "is on 'taken literally.' I am very much in favor of the freeze as a popular movement, because it is a signal to our government that the people of the U.S. want to stop the arms race. But I don't believe it would be helpful just to stop exactly where we are." Such nuance was typical of Bethe; he believed in deployment of the cruise missile on U.S. bombers, though only because it would alleviate the "need" for the B-1 bomber. He opposed deployment of the cruise missiles either on ships or on the ground but endorsed submarine-launched ballistic missiles because they were impervious to enemy attack.[58]

Elsewhere, Bethe considered a pet project of Teller's, the X-ray laser. Although the jury was still out, he wrote to a Pentagon official that "the x-ray laser should not be disqualified simply because it exploits a nuclear explosion as a power source." In the absence of a comprehensive nuclear test ban, he vowed to support research exploring the X-ray laser.[59] Though an avid arms controller, Bethe did not express his personal opposition to nuclear weapons in moral terms. Instead, he coolly calculated each new weapon and analyzed it in regard to other weapons and the political context, accepting or rejecting it after logical, unemotional thought. While this approach suited Bethe's personal temperament, it ensured that he and other scientists like him would be out of step with the antinuclear activists of the 1980s, who often saw nuclear weapons as misogynistic threats to God's creation.

Bethe expressed his own ideology in a January 20, 1983, talk at the Center for the Study of Democratic Institutions on the subject titled "Scientists' Responsibility." He spoke specifically on whether scientists should participate in military research, mentioning radar as a clear-cut case where participation had no down side, while participation in the A-bomb and H-bomb projects had more ambiguity. Nevertheless, Bethe stated, "Non-participation is not an effective way to stop a military development." Instead, "Decisions about these programs must be made by the elected representatives of the people." In a rationalization similar to Teller's, Bethe believed that it was scientists' duty to inform the public and government of the implications of their discoveries. Over time officials "will and should take over." A note to himself tellingly added, "Important that they [scientists] get informed & not argue on emotional grounds"—words that again echoed the AEC's redefinition of science. The section concluded with a touch of pragmatism and a grasp of political realities. "It is important," he said, "that scientists dedicated to restraining armaments be in weapons development, just as dovish senators should be on [the] Armed Services Comm[ittee]."[60]

But even as he endorsed some nuclear weapons, he opposed the most controversial technology of the 1980s, SDI. Like Teller, Bethe attended the White House briefing just prior to Reagan's announcement of SDI in March 1983. Less than a week later, he wrote to the president expressing his concerns, in particular gauging "the chances of success of an effective defense to be incredibly small." Even more troubling to Bethe, such a system would create far more instability than any other Cold War weapon. He felt certain that the Soviets would see SDI as aggressive and would subsequently launch attacks on U.S. satellites. Without "far-reaching conciliatory diplomatic moves toward the Soviet Union, the program of developing these defensive weapons would make this country far less secure than we are today."[61]

In November 1983 Bethe appeared at Harvard's JFK School of Government to debate Teller on SDI. Teller began by framing SDI as a humane alternative to the "repulsive" policy of mutually assured destruction. Because the officials in the Kremlin were cautious, Teller explained, they would overestimate the efficacy of U.S. defenses. Thus, a system that was only 50 percent or 80 percent effective in actuality would, because of the Kremlin's mind-set, be essentially 95 percent effective. At the very least, "we have raised the level of uncertainty and gained time for cooperation." Later he added, "I believe it is a moral and practical necessity to develop defense."[62]

When it was his turn, Bethe carefully rebutted his onetime friend and longtime rival. The Soviets would consider Star Wars, in Bethe's words, an aggressive move and would build more weapons to compensate. The United States would respond in kind, further escalating the arms race. Furthermore, no weapon could attack missiles effectively because although missiles are vulnerable in their launch phase, the time window of that phase lasts only briefly. Once the missiles made it out of the atmosphere, there would be, because of multiple independent reentry vehicles, roughly one hundred thousand objects to target, far too many for the satellites to destroy. The weight of three hundred satellites weighing one hundred tons each made them prohibitively expensive to launch, and, finally, if the superpowers pursued SDI, the public would lose interest in the more valuable goals of arms control and disarmament.[63]

Teller responded (as usual) by saying that he could not counter Bethe's arguments without revealing classified information. Instead, he simply argued that arms control agreements would not work. Bethe nevertheless expressed confidence that nuclear weapons treaties could be policed and that SDI would be prohibitively expensive, costing "hundreds of billions of dollars." Teller grumbled that "I would be very happy to be exceedingly quiet if only Hans Bethe would come and help, and thereby, even beyond contributing his own talents, provide an example to young people that we must search for a ballistic-missile defense."[64]

Bethe continued to do his best to prevent what he saw as futile and expensive SDI research efforts. He wrote to a scientist with the Pentagon's SDIO in 1985 to express his opinion, again questioning the cost-effectiveness of the system and its vulnerability to attack. In a speech later that summer, he touched on the arms race that began after Hiroshima. For forty years, "U.S. policy has tried to rely on superior technology. Whenever there was a chance to make nuclear weapons more devastating, we took it." The United States introduced the hydrogen bomb and the transcontinental bomber to the world and increased the number of nuclear bombs and later missiles and, "worst of all," MIRVs. "In every case," he continued, "the Soviets followed suit, 3 to 5 years later, and we were less secure than before." SDI, the "newest technological escalation . . . will end up the same way, by making us still less secure."[65]

One month later, Teller complained to Bethe about his anti-SDI activities, telling him "your published stance has made our national effort in a vital field much more difficult. This single fact has a greater influence on me than everything else put together." Teller's lament echoed his belief that in the late 1940s and early 1950s, Oppenheimer had single-handedly hampered H-bomb research. Such disagreements wounded Teller in a personal way: "All this is very sad and I suspect that your feelings may be similar." But he had to place his professional responsibilities above his feelings. "Indeed, the hope and effort for a useful defense in the strict and narrow sense of the word is the one remaining motivation for which I continue to work."[66]

In his notes for a response to Teller, Bethe wrote that they each differed fundamentally over how to achieve U.S. security. Teller wanted "a technology race," while Bethe believed "we must talk, negotiate." He wrote that Teller "spends full time on persuading others . . . [while] I spend maybe 1/3 of my time on it, [and] still try to do physics." He defended his anti-SDI beliefs and also spoke about their personal relationship: "I remember fondly the years of our friendship, back in 30's & early 40's. I am sorry that politics has separated us so far. But can't we be personally friendly?"[67]

Frustrated by their private correspondence, Teller took his complaints public. In an "Open Letter to Hans Bethe," Teller repeated his claim that Bethe was bringing down the entire SDI effort almost single-handedly. Because Bethe was "at the core of an increasingly vocal movement of scientists against SDI," Teller had written this open letter "in the hope that you and others may find some way to move from polemic debate and confrontation toward technical criticism, understanding, and cooperation." In response, Bethe wrote simply that "SDI is not science" and that his efforts countered the "false claims" of the SDIO. He also told Teller, "I don't agree at all on your assessment of SDI, technically as well as politically."[68]

Teller even mentioned Bethe by name in testimony before Congress. He explained that many scientists' opposition to SDI "arises from their being uninformed." Although Bethe had, according to Teller, once said that SDI was "a splendid idea," Bethe did not change his public position. "Instead of objecting on scientific and technical grounds, which he thoroughly understands, he now objects on the grounds of politics, on grounds of feasibility of military deployment, on other grounds of difficult issues which are quite outside the range of his professional cognizance or mine." Bethe's dissent, in Teller's mind, led to a sort of antinuclear proliferation: "For every Bethe, there are a hundred others who speak up and who don't even know the basics of what they are talking about."[69]

For many U.S. scientists who objected to SDI, the idea of nuclear-powered satellite lasers bristled not just as a weapon but as a tool the Pentagon used to dominate U.S. science and control its funding. In 1986, a Yale mathematician wrote to Bethe: "The whole SDI enterprise is serving the unavowed purpose (conscious in some, unconscious in others) of funding science, technology, and engineering via the Defense Department, and starving the [National Science Foundation], among other things. My clear opinion is that I object to this sleight of hand and deviousness."[70] To the antinuclear segment of the world public, however, SDI transcended science. The program was just one more nuclear weapon in an already bloated arsenal that consisted of MX, cruise, and Trident missiles. The resistance movement against nuclear weapons had moved beyond the debate over different weapons to call for a halt to nuclear weapons production and the removal of missiles from Europe. In a sense, the antinuclear movement thus challenged scientists to transcend science as well.

Scientists and Moral Arguments

No longer the leaders of antinuclear protest and growing more distant from the public, some of the scientists who had been active in arms control and disarmament debates throughout the Cold War felt compelled to shift to moral and religious critiques of nuclear weapons during the 1980s. While doing so, they tried to balance this moral shift with continued reliance on their credibility as objective, scientific experts. Breaking from decades of keeping science and morality separate, some scientists found themselves in new territory as they allied with religious leaders and grassroots movements.

One such alliance occurred in 1980, when Pope John Paul II convened the Pontifical Academy, an honorary group of papal science advisers—most of them not Catholic—in order to discuss the aftereffects of nuclear war and to come up with ways the pope might help. These scientists took quickly to their charge. At the final meeting, in October 1981, the academy issued a final statement that deplored nuclear weapons as immoral and made a special appeal to scientists: "Science can offer the world no real defense against the consequences of nuclear war," they wrote. Instead, scientists must "stress that the future of humankind depends upon the acceptance by all nations of moral principles transcending all other considerations." Aside from "the powers of intelligence," scientists needed to rely on "the powers of ethics, morality and conviction. . . . This is the greatest moral issue that humanity has ever faced, and there is no time to be lost." In all, fifty-eight scientists from five continents participated and signed the declaration.[71]

John Paul II then asked the leaders of the nuclear powers as well as the United Nations to receive his scientific delegates. On December 14, 1981, Reagan met with the U.S. delegation, consisting of the Manhattan Project veteran Victor Weisskopf, David Baltimore of MIT, Marshal Nirenberg of the National Institutes of Health, and Howard Hiatt, dean of Harvard's School of Public Health. Hiatt began the presentation in terms designed to startle the president by describing a one-megaton bomb detonated directly over the White House, instantly killing six hundred thousand people, including most of the district's doctors, meaning that survivors would have nowhere to go for treatment.[72]

In an attached postscript to his report, Weisskopf recounted that he had received a mild but distinct impression of what it felt like to be a political activist when the Reagan administration had subtly resisted the scientists' visit. "We were received by the President standing up, and he never asked us to sit down," he noted. For fifteen minutes the delegation stood as the presentation proceeded. At one moment in the meeting, Weisskopf made reference to the pope's letter of introduction, "a moving document about nuclear war," as he described it. Reagan, however, "said he did not remember ever having received such a letter. . . . This showed how little attention and how little briefing the President devoted to this reception." At the end of the meeting, Reagan made sure to reference the biblical passage from Revelations on Armageddon.[73] Reagan's reaction to the presentation is somewhat surprising, since it seemed to support the president's oft-stated fear of nuclear war, though he generally dismissed the claims of antinuclear activists on the political Left. Despite Weisskopf's frustrations, other antinuclear scientists also saw religion as a good way to spread their message. In 1984 Sagan had put aside his atheism to join with the pope and other religious leaders to bring attention to the threat of nuclear winter.[74]

While not adopting a religious focus, one of the more active antinuclear organizations to feature a moral argument was the PSR, described by the

Bulletin editor Bernard Feld as "the most hopeful sign that has appeared on the international horizon in more than a decade." An explanation of the organization's fundamental values appeared in the March 1981 *Bulletin,* written by the head of the San Francisco Bay Area PSR, Peter Joseph. He explained the vision of the group as an optimistic affirmation of life rooted in science, but more human than technical. "Physicians are constantly confronted with bad news," he wrote, facing difficult matters of life and death. While "the present situation is grave, the prognosis guarded . . . in medicine there is always hope. . . . Hope is a prerequisite for medical practice. It is an absolute necessity for functioning in the nuclear age."[75]

Finally, some veteran scientist activists endorsed grassroots actions. Former Manhattan Project chemist and presidential science adviser George Kistiakowsky had once questioned the value of scientists' disarmament efforts. But over time he was converted to the cause, eventually cutting ties with the Pentagon in 1968 over the Vietnam War. In 1981 he hailed PSR and the Council for a Livable World because warnings about the effects of nuclear war "must be carried throughout the world." With slight oversimplification (more appropriate to the activist than the scientist), he wrote that "public protest" had resulted in the 1963 test ban treaty, declared that "the youth movement forced the termination of the Vietnam War," and added that grassroots opposition had halted U.S. antiballistic missile deployment. "When a large number of people understand the monstrous consequences of nuclear wars," he concluded, "they will force governments to move toward arms control and disarmament negotiations and the peaceful settlement of disputes."[76] Once the science adviser to President Eisenhower, Kistiakowsky had become a cheerleader for the grassroots antinuclear movement.

This new role for scientists was exquisitely captured by the physicist Barry Casper in an endorsement of grassroots activism in the *Bulletin.* Casper wrote that his journey from student to activist had begun during his graduate school years at Cornell University. His mentors Bethe, Philip Morrison, and Jay Orear—the "vanguard" of antinuclear physicists—were pivotal. "Their commitment [to arms control] was infectious. Concerned from the beginning about the threat of nuclear war, in a matter of months, I came to share their commitment," he wrote. A summer arms control study group had initiated him into "the physics fraternity" as much as learning quantum field theory had. "Ever since then," he confessed, "nuclear war has been my issue too." But by the 1970s, Casper was "saddened to see how many of my friends in the academic arms control community had adapted themselves to the Washington version of reality." What had begun as a "countervailing force" in the 1960s had become "professionalized" in later decades. Casper called for a true social movement dedicated to stopping the arms race, and he made a plea to the community of physicists based on his experiences in the civil rights movement and the anti–Vietnam War movement. "Do whatever you can," he challenged physicists, including research, education, and community outreach. The world needed "experts to lend authoritative support to the notion that the arms race has gone too far and must be stopped." But even more urgent was for "experts to carry the message to ordinary citizens that you don't have to be an expert to know that this is true." Scientists had been told they had to choose between professional "respectability" or "meaningful action," but this was a false dichotomy. "We can choose instead a role of moral leadership," he argued, "joining with the physicians and church leaders and other courageous figures in sounding the alarm and helping to stop the world's mad rush toward nuclear suicide."[77] Scientists, then, had to spread the message that one need not be a scientist to engage in antinuclear protest, essentially to proclaim that they were not unique as advocates of arms control.

The redefinition of the antinuclear movement as a moral challenge to nuclear weapons failed to fully reconfigure scientists' role in the movement, however. During the 1980s, many elite antinuclear U.S. scientists remained wedded to the official avenues of arms control advocacy—diplomacy, expertise, and advising. Near the end of the decade, antinuclear activists witnessed the ratification of the Intermediate-Range Nuclear Forces treaty, an arms control measure that—at last—actually reduced weapons.[78] In the *Bulletin's* first issue of 1988, the editors hailed the INF treaty, setting the clock back three minutes, to six minutes to midnight. And with the requisite optimism, the editors followed this announcement with the obligatory praise: "The INF Treaty, combined with improvements in U.S.-Soviet relations and greater international concern about common security matters, are significant *first steps* in a new direction."[79]

Soon the Cold War ended—not with a thermonuclear bang, but an uprising of protest and reform in the economically stagnating Soviet Union. The U.S. national security state, dedicated to both piling up enough nuclear weapons to destroy the Soviet Union several times over and beating it into economic submission with a costly arms race, ended up outlasting its communist rivals in large part by redefining science along Cold War lines and neutralizing the most powerful scientific challenges to nuclear weapons. For decades, the U.S. government had most often stifled antinuclear dissent and devoted billions of dollars to a bloated nuclear arsenal that all but a scant few professed to despise. Furthermore, scientists contributed to the enduring strategy of deterrence by mostly avoiding powerful moral arguments against nuclear weapons and ostracizing those who stepped out of line. The Cold War consensus and the manufacture of consent sometimes forced and sometimes asked the state's experts to withhold free expression and uphold the continued buildup of nuclear weapons. Only the end of the Cold War brought this conformist mind-set into question.

Conclusion

The Future of Nuclear Weapons

I N 1989 EDWARD TELLER TURNED EIGHTY-ONE years old. At a birthday celebration for the elder physicist, his friends encouraged him to "Go for a hundred!" and "Don't Stop Now!" Others exclaimed in the guest book, "Looking forward to magic Nos. 82–126," and "You have always been an inspiration and an example. 1000 years."[1]

Entering his ninth decade had not dimmed Teller's enthusiasm for both nuclear weapons and technological defenses against them. During the late 1980s, his pet project had been Brilliant Pebbles, a more nimble version of the Strategic Defense Initiative consisting of small satellites weighing just over one hundred pounds each. According to Teller's plans, thousands of the devices would patrol the atmosphere until they sensed an incoming missile. At that point, those satellites within range of the missile would, as Teller explained, "scatter destructive pebbles in the path of the attack missile." In the words of Teller's ally Hans Mark, a former NASA missile scientist and chancellor of the University of Texas system at the time, Brilliant Pebbles served "to keep the strategic defense program alive over the long haul." Mark had written to Teller to explain that strategic defense programs like Brilliant Pebbles could be neither tested nor deployed "without violating the ABM Treaty." Not that Mark was bothered by the prospect of violating the treaty; rather, he was upset that the George H. W. Bush administration lacked the will to revise, violate, "or even seem to violate" the treaty. He told Teller, "They will support 'Brilliant Pebbles' with lots of money to keep us quiet but they will not deploy a system based on the concept."[2]

Along with strategic defense, Mark also reassured Teller that the alignment between the national security state, science, and academic institutions remained tight. "We have done well here in Texas in bringing defense related research work to the University," Mark boasted, and mentioned twenty million dollars a year for "electro-magnetic guns for the Army," thirty million dollars a year for navy "anti-submarine devices," and eight hundred million dollars a year to research "Over the Horizon radars" for the air force.[3]

After the end of the Cold War, Teller pondered the future of the Livermore laboratory, which he had served in many capacities since its founding in the 1950s. Determined to keep the lab thriving, he continued to emphasize defensive weapons systems. He declared it "essential" that Livermore "maintain its work on radically innovative developments in defense" in a 1994 letter to his fellow former Livermore director John Foster. "It is a mistake to assume that elimination of weapons and elimination of new ideas equals stability," he asserted. In Teller's mind, this unstable, post–Cold War world required "new types of weapons and ideas," with Los Alamos and Livermore leading the way.[4]

As Teller looked to the future, his old rival Hans Bethe reflected on his own career in arms control and science. In a speech accepting the Einstein Peace Prize in 1992, Bethe asked rhetorically how the Cold War ended. "Did we bring this about by Arms Control?" he asked. "No!" he answered. The main factors had been the "peaceful revolution" of the Soviet people and the reforms of Mikhail Gorbachev. But, he added, "we, the Arms Control community, also contributed." Bethe specifically mentioned promoting alternatives to the arms race and "getting to know each other" at Pugwash conferences, in addition to "the actual negotiations of treaties." Turning to the future, Bethe set an agenda for arms control. As though responding to Teller's vision of the post–Cold War world, he saw "no longer any good reason to design still more sophisticated nuclear weapons." But Bethe did not endorse getting rid of the nuclear deterrent entirely, explaining, "Of course, we shall still need to keep some nuclear weapons, and a competent group to maintain and supervise them."[5]

Bethe's desire to retain some nuclear weapons was based on the possible proliferation of nuclear weapons to countries like Iraq and the former states of the Soviet Union. Even after the Soviet Union had dissolved and most of the communist world along with it, Bethe could not envision a future without nuclear weapons, though he hoped an arsenal of a mere one hundred nuclear weapons would suffice to deter new countries from joining the nuclear club. Bethe ended by saying that "the nuclear world looks much better today . . . but a lot remains for us to do."[6]

What remained to be done? The most urgent nuclear fear after the end of the Cold War was that Soviet nuclear weapons would vanish from their arsenals amid the chaos of societal collapse in the former Soviet Union. The general consensus was that only Russia possessed the means of adequately securing the weapons against theft and use, and even if the weapons remained safe, hardly anyone wanted what would amount to nuclear proliferation to three new countries (Ukraine, Belarus, and Kazakhstan). Senator Sam Nunn (D-GA) sponsored legislation authorizing aid to implement the transfer to Russia, while Secretary of State James Baker helped convince the new republics to release the weapons. Like arms control agreements since détente, the solution to this nuclear issue hinged more on politics and diplomacy than scientific expertise.[7]

The pendulum of nuclear weapons swung wildly after the Cold War. Proliferation occurred—inevitably, perhaps—with India drastically increasing its production of weapons and Pakistan following suit. North Korea produced nuclear weapons of a sort, and Iran vacillated until agreeing in 2015 to limit its nuclear program. In the direction of arms control, some progress was made, including the Comprehensive Test Ban Treaty (CTBT), long sought by scientists. President Bill Clinton signed the agreement, passed by the United Nations in 1996, but although the United States abides by it, the Senate has not ratified the treaty. The pendulum swung back again under the George W. Bush administration, which withdrew from the ABM treaty in order to pursue a new generation of missile defense and launched a war with Iraq based on false pretenses and claims of weapons of mass destruction, including a nuclear program. Although controversies and causes like these occupied many scientists' time during the Cold War, scientists have been less visible in the post–Cold War iterations of these issues, as other problems seemed more urgent, especially global climate change.

But an idealistic call for the abolition of nuclear weapons came from some unexpected voices. In the January 4, 2007, edition of the *Wall Street Journal*, George Shultz, William Perry, Henry Kissinger, and Sam Nunn published an op-ed enthusiastically endorsing "the goal of a world free of nuclear weapons." While Nunn, no longer a senator, had worked extensively for arms control, the appearance of Shultz and Kissinger in the antinuclear camp was more surprising. As secretary of state during the Reagan administration, Shultz had been part of an administration that simultaneously opposed and co-opted the tremendous antinuclear resistance movement of the 1980s; Kissinger, of course, had been a close correspondent of Teller's and, while serving in the Nixon administration, had actively disdained antinuclear sentiments. But the end of the Cold War had changed the game for these old hands of the national security state. Despite the idealistic nature of their proposal, however, they couched it in realist terms, writing, "Reliance on nuclear weapons for [deterrence] is becoming increasingly hazardous and decreasingly effective" and that a substantial reduction in the size of nuclear forces in all states, including the United States, demanded the highest priority. In making this argument, they echoed the sentiment that antinuclear scientists had made throughout the Cold War: that more nuclear weapons make the United States less secure and that nuclear disarmament would not harm the nation's security. Shultz, Perry, Kissinger, and Nunn closed their editorial by stating that achieving a world without nuclear weapons would be "a bold initiative consistent with America's moral heritage."[8] The end of the Cold War had the potential to upend the nation's reliance on nuclear deterrence for its security.

Further progress appeared imminent in April 2009, when President Barack Obama declared "America's commitment to seek the peace and security of a world without nuclear weapons" to a massive audience in Prague. Obama promised nothing less than "to put an end to Cold War thinking . . . [and] reduce the role of nuclear weapons in our national security strategy." In concrete terms, this would be achieved by a new strategic arms reduction treaty, Senate ratification of the CTBT, a halt to the production of fissile materials, and the strengthening of the Nonproliferation Treaty. Yet underneath new visions lay old ways of thinking, as the president could not renounce deterrence entirely. "Make no mistake," Obama emphasized. "As long as these weapons exist, the United States will maintain a safe, secure and effective arsenal to deter any adversary."[9]

In a democratic society, it is important to recognize the deep interplay between political protesters and foreign relations. Activists who internationalized their protest and transcended borders and the nation-state system have been particularly effective at creating change. In the 1950s and 1960s, civil rights activists put pressure on policymakers for social and political change by contrasting the differences between the expressed values of the United States in waging the Cold War overseas with the Jim Crow treatment of African Americans at home. At the same time, politicians often achieved civil rights measures by justifying them in Cold War terms.[10] Such efforts were not limited to grassroots activists. In the twentieth century and into the present day, international nongovernmental organizations have often bypassed the nation-state system in order to create a "global community" that has influenced geopolitical affairs in a progressive manner.[11] Regarding the Cold War in particular, transnational protesters altered the foreign policies of both the United States and the Soviet Union, as a potent mix of NGOs, diplomats, and social movements forced the superpowers toward arms control, respect for human rights, and coexistence; these peaceful protest movements led the superpowers away from conflict, shook the foundations of the nation-state system, and spurred the tectonic shifts and uprisings that brought an end to the Cold War.[12]

In contrast, by turning back scientists' challenge to nuclear weapons, the national security state managed to stifle a major segment of this turmoil. Effectively resisting this challenge often meant muting protest or adapting only slightly in order to prevent truly dramatic change. Scientists' attempts to oppose nuclear weapons from within the government managed not to overturn Cold War nuclearism but perpetuate it. Those scientists who attempted to work for disarmament outside the government found themselves policed by both red-baiters and their peers who had subconsciously (and sometimes willingly) adopted the state's conception of science. Other scientists, by choosing to ally with the government and accepting the fundamental importance of deterrence, found it possible to influence policy and still come hardly any closer to nuclear disarmament. Objections to nuclear weapons were channeled into mainstream politics that argued not over the morality of deterrence but the best way to implement it. This division hinged on the redefinition of science during the Cold War, when "objective" science advice supported the nuclear deterrent and "emotional" science based on morality was dismissed as patently unscientific.

The government's suppression of its scientists' moral arguments against nuclear weapons had great consequences for science, society, and the nation. Scientists' socially formed inclinations to let political concerns guide their technical advice had to be eradicated, as a distinction between the two, while clear, had never been explicitly enforced. With social and moral concerns unwelcome in policymaking circles, the supposedly objective natural sciences (physics in particular) became aligned with and dependent on the economic, political, and militaristic elements of U.S. society. For example, the Department of Defense became science's greatest single patron in the ten years after World War II, a relationship that changed little during the remainder of the Cold War.[13] As the Cold War state increased its influence over science, scientists also played a role in the militarization of their discipline. Neither powerless victims nor uncontested power brokers, elite natural and physical scientists of all political beliefs reconfigured themselves and their relationship to science, politics, and the national security state. In the aftermath, avenues of dissent disappeared, and science became subordinate to political beliefs in public policy debates.

In modern times, scientists have faced a dilemma about both creating and controlling the forces of technology quickly demolishing old ways of life. The Pugwash conferences long included discussions on the social responsibilities of scientists, which built on earlier concerns about science's impact on society. In his landmark *Age of Extremes,* the historian Eric Hobsbawm notes, "No period in history has been more penetrated by and more dependent on the natural sciences than the twentieth century. Yet no period, since Galileo's recantation, has been less at ease with it."[14] There is no reason to think that clamor from the public and the government for scientific expertise will cease in the near future, as the planet and nation-state system face stiff challenges from biological weapons, nuclear proliferation, toxic wastes from modern technologies, energy consumption and production, and global climate change. In addition, nation-states around the globe—from North Korea to Israel to Russia to the United States—still see nuclear weapons as the ultimate means of protecting their national security. Consequently, states will continue to rely on scientists to develop both life-affirming and life-destroying technologies.

When nuclear weapons initiated a potentially more deadly era of international relations at the beginning of the Cold War, U.S. scientists, as the guardians of nuclear knowledge, played a substantial role in shaping their nation's nuclear policy. The end of the Cold War has diminished the number but not the danger of nuclear weapons, and scientists have largely disappeared from foreign policymaking circles, even as they continue to serve in the laboratories that create military technologies. Referring to recent advances in biological weapons, the sociologist Jeanne Guillemin explains that "the participation of capable experts is as essential to any programmatic degradation of the life sciences as it is to their protection." Another scholar has written that "scientific disciplines reshaped by Cold War politics will continue to align American science along a military axis long after the end of the Cold War."[15]

The role of scientists in public policy in the United States has shifted since the end of the Cold War. The dismantling of the Office of Technology Assessment in 1995 left Congress to confront threats such as global climate change, stem cell research, genetically modified organisms, diseases from AIDS to bird flu, and nuclear terrorism without a ready supply of independent scientific advice.[16] With science less powerful than partisanship, journalists and other observers have decried that as a consequence, policies are shaped by politicians with little or no understanding of the science and technology behind them. To these critics, scientists' lack of active involvement in policymaking can only have a detrimental effect on the life of the nation.

If this skewed dynamic is to change, many observers argue, scientists will have to assert themselves in the realm of politics and society.[17] If they fail to do so, scientists might find themselves with their objective reputations fully intact but completely divorced from the greater society and devoid of public authority.

Yet such claims reach only partial truths because they have been based on a limited understanding of the development of this disconnect. During the Cold War, the public and government instinctively turned to scientists for advice on the burning questions of the day. But scientists' battles over nuclear policy harmed their image as public experts, lessening their authority in matters over which they should have logically held sway. In the realm of climate change, for example, scientists' general consensus about the urgency and cause of the problem has failed to fully negate the very different claims of other interest groups and experts, including corporations and economists.

Serving as a politically active scientist does not guarantee influence. Scientists prefer to speak with nuance and tentative conclusions, two types of rhetoric that presidents and members of Congress particularly dislike hearing from advisers and witnesses.[18] Many scientists attempted to shape nuclear policy in many ways during the Cold War, from quasi-grassroots campaigns to scientific internationalism to cabinet-level access, but just as many obstacles blocked these efforts. Bringing science to bear on political issues was not as easy as it seemed, not as easy as men like Pauling, Sagan, and Bethe hoped. Science remains an incredibly powerful worldview and social force, but even so it cannot easily overturn an entrenched ideology. In the contemporary United States, science has been drowned out—just one competing voice among many others in the political life of the nation. Scientists determine the mores of their own discipline, to be sure, but it bears reminding that the distinction between objective and activist brands of science was created by the national security state during the Cold War as the means to achieve a distinct political end.

Notes

Introduction

1. Linus Pauling to G. W. Beadle, October 25, 1956, LP Peace 6: Other Peace Activism, 6.012: Pauling Peace Research Notes, 12.2: Assorted Pauling Peace Research Notes, 1950s, Ava Helen and Linus Pauling Papers, Oregon State University (hereafter LP Papers).
2. *Testimony of Dr. Linus Pauling*, Hearing before the Internal Security Subcommittee, 86th Cong., 2nd sess., October 11, 1960 (Washington, DC: Government Printing Office, 1960), 366, 414, 416, 419.
3. *Strategic and Foreign Policy Implications of ABM Systems*, Hearings before the Subcommittee on International Organization and Disarmament Affairs, 91st Cong., 1st sess., March 6, 11, 13, 21, 26, and 28 and May 14 and 21, 1969 (Washington, DC: Government Printing Office, 1969), 73–74, 90, 117–18.
4. Ibid., 77–78, 92–94, 105–10, 117, 119.
5. Campbell Craig and Frederik Logevall, *America's Cold War: The Politics of Insecurity* (Cambridge, MA: Harvard University Press, 2009).
6. Daniel Kevles, *The Physicists: The History of a Scientific Community in Modern America* (New York: Alfred A. Knopf, 1978); Stuart Leslie, *The Cold War and American Science: The Military-Industrial-Academic Complex at MIT and Stanford* (New York: Columbia University Press, 1993); Joy Rohde, *Armed with Expertise: The Militarization of American Social Research during the Cold War* (Ithaca, NY: Cornell University Press, 2013).
7. Lawrence Wittner, *Toward Nuclear Abolition: A History of the World Nuclear Disarmament Movement, 1971 to the Present* (Stanford, CA: Stanford University Press, 2003), 485; Jennifer Sims, *Icarus Restrained: An Intellectual History of Nuclear Arms Control, 1945–1960* (Boulder, CO: Westview Press, 1990), 141–63.
8. Peter Kuznick, *Beyond the Laboratory: Scientists as Political Activists in 1930s America* (Chicago: University of Chicago Press, 1987).
9. Gerard DeGroot, *The Bomb: A Life* (Cambridge, MA: Harvard University Press,

2005), 4; U.S. Atomic Energy Commission, *In the Matter of J. Robert Oppenheimer: Transcript of Hearing before Personnel Security Board and Texts of Principal Documents and Letters* (Cambridge, MA: MIT Press, 1970), 1016–18.

10. Fred Kaplan, *The Wizards of Armageddon* (Stanford, CA: Stanford University Press, 1991); Sarah Bridger, *Scientists at War: The Ethics of Cold War Weapons Research* (Cambridge, MA: Harvard University Press, 2015); Jessica Wang, *American Science in an Age of Anxiety: Scientists, Anticommunism, and the Cold War* (Chapel Hill: University of North Carolina Press, 1999).

11. Martin Sherwin, *A World Destroyed: Hiroshima and Its Legacies*, 3rd ed. (Stanford, CA: Stanford University Press, 2003); Alice Smith, *A Peril and a Hope: The Scientists' Movement in America, 1945–47* (Chicago: University of Chicago Press, 1965); Jeffrey Knopf, *Domestic Society and International Cooperation: The Impact of Protest on U.S. Arms Control Policy* (Cambridge: Cambridge University Press, 1998); Matthew Evangelista, *Unarmed Forces: The Transnational Movement to End the Cold War* (Ithaca, NY: Cornell University Press, 1999); Kelly Moore, *Disrupting Science: Social Movements, American Scientists, and the Politics of the Military, 1945–1975* (Princeton, NJ: Princeton University Press, 2008); Rebecca Slayton, *Arguments That Count: Physics, Computing, and Missile Defense, 1949–2012* (Cambridge, MA: MIT Press, 2013); Gabrielle Hecht, *The Radiance of France: Nuclear Power and National Identity after World War II* (Cambridge, MA: MIT Press, 2009).

12. Benjamin Greene, *Eisenhower, Science Advice, and the Nuclear Test-Ban Debate, 1945–1963* (Stanford, CA: Stanford University Press, 2007); David Kaiser, "The Postwar Suburbanization of American Physics," *American Quarterly* 56, no. 4 (2004): 851–88.

13. David Cassidy, *J. Robert Oppenheimer and the American Century* (New York: Pi Press, 2005), 323, 335.

14. Zuoyue Wang, *In Sputnik's Shadow: The President's Science Advisory Committee and Cold War America* (New Brunswick, NJ: Rutgers University Press, 2008).

15. Joseph Rotblat, *Pugwash—the First Ten Years: History of the Conferences of Science and World Affairs* (New York: Humanities Press, 1968), 77.

16. Lawrence Wittner, *Resisting the Bomb: A History of the World Nuclear Disarmament Movement, 1954–1970* (Stanford, CA: Stanford University Press, 1997), 292–96.

17. Ralph Lapp, "Toward Nuclear Education," *Bulletin of the Atomic Scientists* 29, no. 6 (1973): 6.

1. From "Highly Unreliable" to "Patriotic and Prompt"

1. Harry Truman, *Memoirs by Harry S. Truman*, vol. 1, *Year of Decisions* (New York: Doubleday, 1955), 421; quoted in John Dower, *Embracing Defeat: Japan in the Wake of World War II* (New York: W. W. Norton / New Press, 1999), 36; Paul Boyer, *By the Bomb's Early Light: American Thought and Culture at the Dawn of the Atomic Age*, 2nd ed. (Chapel Hill: University of North Carolina Press, 1994), 5.

2. Martin Sherwin, *A World Destroyed: Hiroshima and Its Legacies*, 3rd ed. (Stanford, CA: Stanford University Press, 2003), 9. On "the Bomb" as an eponymous entity,

see Gerard DeGroot, *The Bomb: A Life* (Cambridge, MA: Harvard University Press, 2005), 2.

3. Spencer Weart and Gertrud Szilard, eds., *Leo Szilard: His Version of the Facts; Selected Recollections and Correspondence* (Cambridge, MA: MIT Press, 1978) 55; C. F. von Weizsacker, *The Politics of Peril: Economics, Society, and the Prevention of War* (New York: Seabury Press, 1978), 199; quoted in Richard Rhodes, *The Making of the Atomic Bomb* (New York: Simon and Schuster, 1986), 532; quoted in Charles Thorpe, *Oppenheimer: The Tragic Intellect* (Chicago: University of Chicago Press, 2006), 180.

4. Alice Smith and Charles Weiner, eds., *Robert Oppenheimer: Letters and Recollections* (Cambridge, MA: Harvard University Press, 1980), 316–17; Edward Teller, *Memoirs: A Twentieth-Century Journey in Science and Politics* (Cambridge, MA: Perseus Books, 2001), 222; "Press Release by the White House, August 6, 1945," Subject File, Eben A. Ayers Papers, Harry S. Truman Library, http://www.trumanlibrary.org/whistlestop/study_collections/bomb/large/documents/pdfs/59.pdf#zoom=100. On Wilson's meeting, see Thorpe, *Oppenheimer: The Tragic Intellect*, 154–55; and Kai Bird and Martin Sherwin, *American Prometheus: The Triumph and Tragedy of J. Robert Oppenheimer* (New York: Alfred A. Knopf, 2005), 287–89.

5. Sherwin, *World Destroyed,* 5; Greenglass quoted in Sam Roberts, *The Brother* (New York: Random House, 2001), 136; Stalin's reaction in Simon Montefiore, *Stalin: Court of the Red Tsar* (New York: Alfred A. Knopf, 2004), 599; Mao quoted in David Holloway, *Stalin and the Bomb: The Soviet Union and Atomic Energy, 1939–1956* (New Haven, CT: Yale University Press, 1994), 282.

6. Smith and Weiner, *Robert Oppenheimer,* 319.

7. Alice Smith, *A Peril and a Hope: The Scientists' Movement in America, 1945–47* (Cambridge, MA: MIT Press, 1971); Boyer, *Bomb's Early Light*, 59–75; William Lanouette, *Genius in the Shadows: A Biography of Leo Szilard, the Man behind the Bomb* (New York: Charles Scribner's Sons, 1992); Sherwin, *World Destroyed*, 58–60; Lawrence Wittner, *One World or None: A History of the World Nuclear Disarmament through 1953* (Stanford, CA: Stanford University Press, 1993). On the creation of the AEC, see Richard Hewlett and Oscar Anderson, *A History of the United States Atomic Energy Commission*, vol. 1, *The New World, 1939–1946* (University Park: Pennsylvania State University Press, 1962).

8. Wittner, *One World or None,* 162–63, 250–53, 269–71, 314–28; Boyer, *Bomb's Early Light*, 53–58; Bird and Sherwin, *American Prometheus*, 342–45.

9. David Kaiser, "The Atomic Secret in Red Hands? American Suspicions of Theoretical Physicists during the Early Cold War," in *Reappraising Oppenheimer: Centennial Studies and Reflections,* edited by Cathryn Carson and David Hollinger, Berkeley Papers in the History of Science, vol. 21 (Berkeley, CA: Office for History of Science and Technology, 2005), 186; Stanley Livingston to Libby, November 26, 1954, folder: Libby, AEC Commissioner, box 5 (SL), Hans Bethe Papers, Cornell University, Ithaca, NY (hereafter HB Papers); Jessica Wang, *American Science in an Age of Anxiety: Scientists, Anticommunism, and the Cold War* (Chapel Hill: University of North Carolina Press, 1999); Stephanie Young,

"'Something Resembling Justice': John Francis Neylan and the AEC Personnel Security Hearings at Berkeley, 1948–49," in *Reappraising Oppenheimer*, edited by Carson and Hollinger.

10. Gregg Herken, "Was Robert Oppenheimer a 'Closet Communist'? The Debate and the Evidence," in *Reappraising Oppenheimer,* edited by Carson and Hollinger; Bird and Sherwin, "Robert Oppenheimer and the Communist Party"; Barton Bernstein, "The Puzzles of Interpreting J. Robert Oppenheimer, His Politics, and the Issues of His Possible Communist Party Membership," in *Reappraising Oppenheimer,* edited by Carson and Hollinger.

11. David Hecht, *Storytelling and Science: Rewriting Oppenheimer in the Nuclear Age* (Amherst: University of Massachusetts Press, 2015).

12. U.S. Atomic Energy Commission, *In the Matter of J. Robert Oppenheimer: Transcript of Hearing before Personnel Security Board and Texts of Principal Documents and Letters* (Cambridge, MA: MIT Press, 1970), 137; Smith and Weiner, *Robert Oppenheimer*, 311; Robert Williams and Philip Cantelon, eds., *The American Atom: A Documentary History of Nuclear Policies from the Discovery of Fission to the Present* (Philadelphia: University of Pennsylvania Press, 1984), 122, 125–26.

13. The studies include Richard Polenberg, ed., *In the Matter of J. Robert Oppenheimer: The Security Clearance Hearing* (Ithaca, NY: Cornell University Press, 2002); Bird and Sherwin, *American Prometheus*; David Cassidy, *J. Robert Oppenheimer and the American Century* (New York: Pi Press, 2005); Thorpe, *Oppenheimer: The Tragic Intellect*; Jeremy Bernstein, *Oppenheimer: Portrait of an Enigma* (Chicago: Ivan R. Dee, 2004); Priscilla McMillan, *The Ruin of J. Robert Oppenheimer and the Birth of the Modern Arms Race* (New York: Viking, 2005); Jeremy Bernstein, "In the Matter of J. Robert Oppenheimer," *Historical Studies in the Physical Sciences* 12, no. 2 (1982): 195–252; Philip Stern, *The Oppenheimer Case: Security on Trial* (New York: Harper & Row, 1969).

14. Bird and Sherwin, *American Prometheus,* 401; Polenberg, *Security Clearance Hearing,* 361; U.S. Atomic Energy Commission, *In the Matter of J. Robert Oppenheimer*, 710, 1019; McMillan, *Ruin of Oppenheimer*; FBI teletype, June 12, 1952, folder: "Re: Oppenheimer Hearing," box 446: Topic File, Papers of Edward Teller, Hoover Institution, Stanford University, Stanford, CA (hereafter ET Papers). In *Memoirs*, Teller denies that he told the agent that he wanted Oppenheimer removed from the GAC (372).

15. Polenberg, *Security Clearance Hearing,* 178; Thorpe, *Oppenheimer: The Tragic Intellect*, 200.

16. Polenberg, *Security Clearance Hearing,* 359–60; Cassidy, *Oppenheimer and the American Century*, 323; U.S. Atomic Energy Commission, *In the Matter of J. Robert Oppenheimer*, 1016–18.

17. Ibid.

18. FBI teletype, 1, June 12, 1952, folder: "Re: Oppenheimer Hearing," box 446: Topic File, ET Papers; Williams and Cantelon, *American Atom*, 126–27.

19. S. S. Schweber, *In the Shadow of the Bomb: Bethe, Oppenheimer, and the Moral Responsibility of the Scientist* (Princeton, NJ: Princeton University Press, 2000);

Bethe to Norris Bradbury, folder: Bethe, Hans A., box 273: Correspondence, Personal, ET Papers (also in Bethe to Bradbury, February 14, 1950, folder: Correspondence on H-bomb with Bradbury, box 21 [SL], HB Papers); Bethe to Robert Bacher, April 4, 1950, folder 10.5: Bacher, R. F., box 8, HB Papers.

20. Teller to Bethe, November 29, 1950, folder: Bethe-Teller Correspondence, 1950–57, 1982–85, box 21 (SL), HB Papers.

21. Bethe to Teller, December 8, 1950, folder: Bethe, Hans A., box 273: Correspondence, Personal, ET Papers.

22. U.S. Atomic Energy Commission, *In the Matter of J. Robert Oppenheimer*, 7–8, 660.

23. "Scientists Affirm Faith in Oppenheimer," *Bulletin of the Atomic Scientists* 10, no. 5 (1954): 189.

24. Bethe to Samuel Silverman, March 18, 1954, folder 12.4: Oppenheimer Case (2), box 12, HB Papers.

25. Courant to Bethe, May 12, 1954, folder 10: R. Courant, box 2, ET Papers (also in folder 12.4: Oppenheimer Case [2], box 12, HB Papers); Bethe to Courant, May 18, 1954, folder 10.13: (Correspondence) C (3), box 10, HB Papers.

26. Platt to Libby, November 24, 1954, folder: Libby, AEC Commissioner, box 5 (SL), HB Papers.

27. Livingston to Libby, November 26, 1954, folder: Libby, AEC Commissioner, box 5 (SL), HB Papers.

28. Breit to Libby, December 8, 1954, folder: Libby, AEC Commissioner, box 5 (SL), HB Papers; Richard Hewlett and Jack Holl, *Atoms for Peace and War: Eisenhower and the Atomic Energy Commission, 1958–1961* (Berkeley: University of California Press, 1989), 111–12.

29. Bethe to Teller, November 30, 1954, folder 12.36: (Correspondence) T (2), box 12, HB Papers (emphasis in the original); Teller, *Memoirs,* 367–68; Peter Goodchild, *Edward Teller: The Real Dr. Strangelove* (Cambridge, MA: Harvard University Press, 2004), 212–13; Hans Bethe, "Comments on the History of the H-bomb," *Los Alamos Science* 3, no. 3 (1982): 42–53.

30. Teller to George Stewart, September 23, 1954, folder: Re: Oppenheimer, J. R., box 446: Topic Files, ET Papers.

31. Walkowicz to Wiesner, June 5, 1962, 3–4, folder: PSAC 1971, Members and Consultants, box 5/5, George B. Kistiakowsky Papers, Harvard University, Cambridge, MA.

32. U.S. Atomic Energy Commission, *In the Matter of J. Robert Oppenheimer*, 1065.

33. "Scientists Affirm Faith in Oppenheimer," 188; "Transcript of Meeting with the President, May 19, 1959," 2, U.S. PSAC, Records 1957–61, box 1, Meeting Notes: May 1959, Dwight D. Eisenhower Library, Abilene, KS; quotation is from Edwin Land.

34. "Science in National Security," 2–7, transcript of presidential address delivered November 7, 1957, folder 1.2: General Security Policy, box 187, Jerome B. Wiesner Papers, MIT, Cambridge (hereafter JBW Papers).

35. "Memorandum of Conference with the President, May 19, 1959," May 20, 1959, folder 3.5: Test Ban Policy Proposals, 1 of 4, box 189, JBW Papers.

36. U.S. State Department, *Foreign Relations of the United States, 1958–1960* (Washington, DC: Government Printing Office, 1996), 3:184.

37. Bethe to Paul Doty, December 3, 1957, folder 23.13: 1956–65, F including FAS, box 23, HB Papers.

38. Bethe to Rockefeller, November 4, 1959, folder 4.23: Test Ban: Correspondence, Talks (Outlines), Other People's Articles, box 4, HB Papers.

39. Bethe, "Cornell University Lecture, January 5, 1962," 16, folder: Strategy and Disarmament/Bulletin, box 15 (SL), unprocessed collection, HB Papers.

40. Teller to Nancy Weil, November 4, 1983, folder 6: October–December 1983, box 433: Chronological Correspondence, 1981–1991, ET Papers.

2. Linus Pauling's "Science of Morality"

1. Spencer Weart, *Nuclear Fear: A History of Images* (Cambridge, MA: Harvard University Press, 1988), 203, 212, 214; Robert Divine, *Blowing on the Wind: The Nuclear Test Ban Debate, 1954–1960* (New York: Oxford University Press, 1978), 321; Harold Jacobson and Eric Stein, *Diplomats, Scientists, and Politicians: The United States and the Nuclear Test Ban Negotiations* (Ann Arbor: University of Michigan Press, 1966), 479–80; Lawrence Wittner, *Resisting the Bomb: A History of the World Nuclear Disarmament Movement, 1954–1970* (Stanford, CA: Stanford University Press, 1997), 37–39.

2. Thomas Hager, *Force of Nature: The Life of Linus Pauling* (New York: Simon and Schuster, 1995), 113, 151, 258–59.

3. Ibid., 246–47; Andrew Brown, *J. D. Bernal: The Sage of Science* (New York: Oxford University Press, 2005).

4. Hager, *Force of Nature*, 296–98.

5. Barbara Marinacci and Ramesh Krishnamurthy, eds., *Linus Pauling on Peace: A Scientist Speaks Out on Humanism and World Survival* (Los Altos, CA: Rising Star Press, 1998), 89–90; Clifford Mead and Thomas Hager, eds., *Linus Pauling: Scientist and Peacemaker* (Corvallis: Oregon State University Press, 2001), 6; Hager, *Force of Nature*, 174, 247.

6. Barbara Marinacci, ed., *Linus Pauling in His Own Words: Selections from His Writings, Speeches, and Interviews* (New York: Touchstone Press, 1995), 147.

7. Ibid., 150.

8. Brenda Maddox, *Rosalind Franklin: The Dark Lady of DNA* (New York: Perennial, 2002), 254; Gautam Desiraju, "The All-Chemist," *Nature* 408, no. 6811 (2000): 407.

9. Hager, *Force of Nature*, 547; Marinacci, *Pauling in His Own Words*, 11.

10. Quoted in Michael Bess, *Realism, Utopia, and the Mushroom Cloud: Four Activist Intellectuals and Their Strategies for Peace, 1945–1989* (Chicago: University of Chicago Press, 1993), 50.

11. Divine, *Blowing on the Wind*, 323; Weart, *Nuclear Fear*, 212.

12. Linus Pauling, *No More War! 25th Anniversary Edition* (New York: Dodd, Mead, 1983), 215–17 (emphasis in the original).

13. Hager, *Force of Nature*, 528, 531–32; Marinacci and Krishnamurthy, *Pauling on Peace*, 127.

14. Marinacci and Krishnamurthy, *Pauling on Peace,* 164–65; undated notes, "Threat of Destruction—Terrible Danger," LP Peace, 6.0: Other Peace Activism, 6.012: Pauling Peace Research Notes, 12.1: Assorted Pauling Peace Research Notes, 1930s–1940s, Ava Helen and Linus Pauling Papers, Oregon State University, Corvallis (hereafter LP Papers). (This document must be from the 1960s, not the 1930s or 1940s, as it mentions the H-bomb and MIRVs [multiple independent reentry vehicles].) "An Exclusive: Nobel Prize Winner Linus Pauling Answers Edward Teller's Recent *Life* Magazine Article on 'The Compelling Need for Nuclear Tests,'" *I. F. Stone's Weekly,* February 24, 1958, LP Peace 6.0: Other Peace Activism, 6.001: The Fallout Suits, 1958–62, 1.3: Publication: "An Exclusive . . . Nuclear Tests," LP Papers.

15. Linus Pauling, "Genetic and Somatic Effects of Carbon-14," *Science* 128, no. 3333 (1958): 1183.

16. Pauling to Robert Gilmore, undated, LP Peace 4: Peace Groups, 4.003: SANE, 1958–1966, 3.1: Correspondence: SANE, Local Chapters, 1958, LP Papers.

17. Marinacci, *Pauling in His Own Words,* 12, 150; Marinacci and Krishnamurthy, *Pauling on Peace,* 114.

18. Pauling to Richard Wyse, May 15, 1958, folder: Pauling-Teller Debate, box 437: Topic Files, Papers of Edward Teller, Hoover Institution, Stanford University, Stanford, CA (hereafter ET Papers).

19. "Scientists Affirm Faith in Oppenheimer," *Bulletin of the Atomic Scientists* 10, no. 5 (1954): 188–89.

20. Marinacci and Krishnamurthy, *Pauling on Peace,* 113.

21. W. F. Libby, "Radioactive Fallout and Radioactive Strontium," *Science,* n.s., 123, no. 3199 (1956): 657–60. Fusion weapons used a fission bomb to trigger thermonuclear fusion, although much of the energy released actually came from the fission of U238 by high-energy neutrons released during fusion. Such information would have been strictly classified during the 1950s and reflects the barriers between Pauling and official knowledge. With access to classified knowledge, Pauling may have even found that his estimates were conservative. Thanks to Bruce Hunt for explaining this point.

22. Pauling, "Genetic and Somatic Effects," 1186.

23. Marinacci and Krishnamurthy, *Pauling on Peace,* 114.

24. Ibid., 113; *The Nature of Radioactive Fallout and Its Effects on Man,* Hearings before the Special Subcommittee on Radiation, 85th Cong., 1st sess., May 27–29 and June 3–7, 1957 (Washington, DC: Government Printing Office, 1957), 19, 691, 1989, 1991; *Fallout from Nuclear Weapons Tests,* Hearings before the Special Subcommittee on Radiation, 86th Cong., 1st sess., May 5–8, 1959 (Washington, DC: Government Printing Office, 1959), 60, 2347–62, 2455–60, 2462–65. See, for example, "Test Ban," March 3, 1961, LP Peace 6: Other Peace Activism, 6.012: Pauling Peace Research Notes, 12.3: Assorted Pauling Peace Research Notes, 1960s, LP Papers.

25. While protesting nuclear weapons in the 1950s, Pauling also participated in the race to uncover the structure of DNA, a race he eventually lost to the Cavendish Laboratory. The State Department had refused his passport request after he had accepted an invitation to address the Royal Society of London about protein structures, but learning the most recent British advances in DNA research was

also on his agenda. Looking back on his travails, Pauling claimed that had he traveled to Britain, he would have seen Rosalind Franklin's X-ray photos of DNA and, in his words, "Well, who knows?" Franklin's photos eventually led James Watson and Francis Crick to recognize DNA's double-helical structure, possibly the greatest scientific discovery of the twentieth century. Marinacci and Krishnamurthy, *Pauling on Peace*, 63, 67; Hager, *Force of Nature*, 339, 343, 356, 400.

26. Wittner, *Resisting the Bomb*, 138–40.

27. Harry Kalven Jr., "Congressional Testing of Linus Pauling, Part I: The Legal Framework," *Bulletin of the Atomic Scientists* 16, no. 10 (1960): 383–90; Kalven, "Congressional Testing of Linus Pauling, Part II: Sourwine in an Old Bottle," *Bulletin of the Atomic Scientists* 17, no. 1 (1961): 12–19.

28. Pauling to Fred Okrand, April 28, 1960, and Ava Helen Pauling to Dorothy Crowfoot Hodgkin, September 23, 1960, Correspondence, All Documents and Media, Linus Pauling and the International Peace Movement, http://scarc.library. oregonstate.edu/coll/pauling/peace/index.html.

29. Internal Security Subcommittee, *The Pugwash Conferences: A Staff Analysis*, 87th Cong., 1st sess. (Washington, DC: Government Printing Office, 1961), 1.

30. Ibid., 54–55.

31. See Joseph Rotblat, *Scientists in the Quest for Peace: A History of the Pugwash Conferences* (Cambridge, MA: MIT Press, 1972), 105.

32. U.S. State Department, *Foreign Relations of the United States, 1958–1960* (Washington, DC: Government Printing Office, 1996), 3:694.

33. See LP Peace 6: Other Peace Activism, 6.001: The Fallout Suits, 1958–62, 1.9: Correspondence re: the Fallout Suits, 1958–62, LP Papers.

34. Einstein to Pauling, May 21, 1952 (2.32), LP Safe Contents, Drawer 2, folder 2.002, LP Papers.

35. Pauling, "Science in the Modern World," 1, August 12, 1951, LP Peace 4: Peace Groups, 4.001: First Unitarian Church, (Reverend Stephen H. Fritchman) Correspondence, 1948–1980, folder 1.1: Correspondence: Rev. Stephen H. Fritchman, 1948–1980, LP Papers.

36. Pauling, *No More War!*, 180–81, 187; Pauling to Dag Hammarskjöld, January 13, 1958, LP Peace 5: Nuclear Bomb Test and Proliferation Petition, 5.002: *An Appeal by Scientists to the Governments and People of the World*, 1957–58, 2.4: Correspondence: Dag Hammarskjöld, United Nations, 1957–58, LP Papers.

37. Helen Allison, "Outspoken Scientist," *Bulletin of the Atomic Scientists* 16, no. 10 (1960): 382, 390.

38. Marinacci and Krishnamurthy, *Pauling on Peace*, 114 (elided text in the original).

39. Pauling to Eisenhower, June 4, 1957, LP Peace 5: Nuclear Bomb Test and Proliferation Petitions, Section 5.002: *An Appeal by Scientists to the Governments and People of the World*, 1957–1958, 2.3: Correspondence: Dwight D. Eisenhower, June 4, 1957, LP Papers; Pauling to James Arnold, December 10, 1957, (1.100) LP Safe Contents, Drawer 2, folder 2.001, LP Papers.

40. In *Resisting the Bomb*, Wittner writes that most biologists approved of the petition, while physicists were "more standoffish" (38).

41. Burton to Pauling, May 27, 1957, LP Peace 5: Nuclear Bomb Test and Proliferation

Petitions, 5.002: *An Appeal by Scientists to the Governments and People of the World*, 1957–68, 2.1: Correspondence, Notes re: Circulation and Signing of *An Appeal by Scientists to the Governments and People of the World*, 1957–69, LP Papers; Inglis to Pauling, May 17, 1957, (1.6); Brode to Pauling, May 23, 1957, (1.9); Bloch to Pauling, May 20, 1957, (1.7), LP Safe Contents, Drawer 2, folder 2.001, LP Papers.

42. Bridgman to Pauling, May 17, 1957, (1.92); Rehberg to Pauling, October 12, 1957, (1.96), LP Safe Contents, Drawer 2, folder 2.001, LP Papers.

43. Goudsmit to Pauling, June 18, 1957, (1.58) LP Safe Contents, Drawer 2, folder 2.001, LP Papers.

44. Unknown to Pauling, December 2, 1957, (1.140); Purcell to Pauling, May 17, 1957, (1.84), LP Safe Contents, Drawer 2, folder 2.001, LP Papers.

45. Franck to Pauling, May 20, 1957, (1.108); Franck to Pauling, December 12, 1957, (1.107), LP Safe Contents, Drawer 2, folder 2.001, LP Papers.

46. Doty to Pauling, May 24, 1957, LP Peace 5: Nuclear Bomb Test and Proliferation Petitions, 5.002: *An Appeal by Scientists to the Governments and People of the World*, 1957–58, 2.1: Correspondence, Notes re: Circulation and Signing of *An Appeal by Scientists to the Governments and People of the World*, 1957–59, LP Papers; Blackett to Pauling, November 11, 1957, (1.124) LP Safe Contents, Drawer 2, folder 2.001, LP Papers.

47. Bethe to Pauling, May 17, 1957, (1.80) LP Safe Contents, Drawer 2, folder 2.001, LP Papers.

48. Szilard "often abstained from [Pugwash] conference statements, although substantially helping in their preparation" (Rotblat, *Scientists in the Quest for Peace*, 5). Szilard to Pauling, May 27, 1957, (1.50); Wald to Pauling, December 6, 1957, (1.74) LP Safe Contents, Drawer 2, folder 2.001, LP Papers.

49. Panofsky to Pauling, December 3, 1957, (1.28) LP Safe Contents, Drawer 2, folder 2.001, LP Papers.

50. Edsall to Pauling, May 20, 1957, (1.137) LP Safe Contents, Drawer 2, folder 2.001, LP Papers.

51. Goldberg to Pauling, May 29, 1957, (1.120), and Puck to Pauling, October 1, 1957, (1.12) LP Safe Contents, Drawer 2, folder 2.001, LP Papers; Beadle, "Statement on the Pauling Petition," LP Peace 5: Nuclear Bomb Test and Proliferation Petition, Section 5.001: *An Appeal by Scientists to the Governments and People of the World*, 1957–1958, 1.3: Typescript, Correspondence: "Statement on the Pauling Petition," by G. W. Beadle, 1957, LP Papers; Beadle to Pauling, May 20, 1957, (1.105) LP Safe Contents, Drawer 2, folder 2.001, LP Papers.

52. Conant to Pauling, November 19, 1957, (1.3); Bush to Pauling, November 21, 1957, (1.76); Allison to Pauling, November 20, 1957, (1.110); Seitz to Pauling, November 21, 1957, (1.44); Wheeler to Pauling, December 11, 1957, (1.41); and Griggs to Pauling, November 25, 1957, (1.61), LP Safe Contents, Drawer 2, folder 2.001, LP Papers.

53. Pitzer to Pauling, May 27, 1957, (1.32) LP Safe Contents, Drawer 2, folder 2.001, LP Papers.

54. Pauling to Dag Hammarskjöld, February 16, 1961, LP Peace 5: Nuclear Bomb

Test and Proliferation Petitions, 5.011: *An Appeal to Stop the Spread of Nuclear Weapons, 1961,* 11.10: Correspondence: Dag Hammarskjöld, LP Papers.

55. Alice Smith, *A Peril and a Hope: The Scientists' Movement in America, 1945–47* (Chicago: University of Chicago Press, 1965), 22–23, 41–48.

56. Rabinowitch to Pauling, May 18, 1957, LP Peace 5: Nuclear Bomb Test and Proliferation Petitions, 5.002: *An Appeal by Scientists to the Governments and People of the World, 1957–58,* 2.1: Correspondence, Notes re: Circulation and Signing of *An Appeal by Scientists to the Governments and People of the World, 1957–59,* LP Papers.

57. Bentley Glass, "Scientists in Politics," *Bulletin of the Atomic Scientists* 18, no. 5 (1962): 2–7; Linus Pauling, "Scientists in Politics," *Bulletin of the Atomic Scientists* 18, no. 10 (1962): 32.

58. See, for example, Pauling to Harry Kalven Jr., August 19, 1962, folder 5.43: Correspondence Related to Linus Pauling, box 5, Hans Bethe Papers, Cornell University, Ithaca, NY.

59. Pauling to Bethe, September 26, 1963, (2.4) LP Safe Contents, Drawer 2, folder 2.002, LP Papers; Pauling to Bethe, May 18, 1966, folder: Bulletin of Atomic Scientists Board of Sponsors Correspondence, box 443: Topic Files, ET Papers.

60. Pauling to Rotblat, May 10, 1962, LP Peace 1: Pugwash Conferences, 1.005: Materials re: Tenth through Thirteenth Pugwash Conferences; Pugwash Symposia; International Student Pugwash, 5.1 (tenth conference), LP Papers. See Rotblat, *Scientists in the Quest for Peace,* 2, 137–40.

61. Pauling to Russell, May 10, 1962, LP Peace 1: Pugwash Conferences, 1.005: Materials re: Tenth through Thirteenth Pugwash Conferences; Pugwash Symposia; International Student Pugwash, 5.1 (tenth conference), LP Papers; Russell to Pauling, June 30, 1962, (2.28) LP Safe Contents, Drawer 2, folder 2.002, LP Papers.

62. Pauling to Robert Scheer, February 23, 1967, LP Peace 1: Pugwash Conferences, 1.001: Materials re: First through Eighth Pugwash Conferences, 1.1 (first conference), LP Papers. On the collaboration between the CIA and the Ford Foundation, see John Krige, *American Hegemony and the Postwar Reconstruction of Science in Europe* (Cambridge, MA: MIT Press, 2006), 155–89.

63. Pauling to Norman Cousins, August 11, 1960, LP Peace 4: Peace Groups, 4.003: SANE, 1958–1966, 1982, 3.9: National Chapter, Correspondence and Miscellaneous, 1960, LP Papers; Pauling to Clarence Pickett, May 29, 1961, LP Peace 4: Peace Groups, 4.003: SANE, 1958–1966, 1982, 3.10: National Chapter: Correspondence, 1961–1964, LP Papers. On SANE, see Milton Katz, *Ban the Bomb: A History of SANE, the Committee for a Sane Nuclear Policy, 1957–85* (New York: Greenwood Press, 1986); and Pauling to Nolan Kerschner, November 8, 1960, LP Peace 4: Peace Groups, 4.003: SANE, 1958–1966, 1982, 3.3: Correspondence: SANE, Local Chapters, 1960, LP Papers.

64. Mass letter, Peggy Duff, June 7, 1962, 2–3, 1/62; "Minutes of the A.G.M. of the Scientist's Group of C.N.D.," May 28, 1962, 4–6, 1/62, Scientist Group, 1962, Section 1: CND Central Constitution, Minutes of Committees, Subject Files, 1958–1971, Campaign for Nuclear Disarmament Papers, London School of Economics and Political Science (hereafter CND Papers).

65. "Minutes of a Committee Meeting of the Scientist's Group Following the A.G.M. on Monday, May 28, 1962," 1/62; "C.N.D. Scientists' Group," minutes, January 2, 1964, 10, 1/62: Scientist Group, 1962, Section 1: CND Central Constitution, Minutes of Committees, Subject Files, 1958–1971, CND Papers; Jill Harrington to Peggy Duff, January 11, 1960; Duff to Harrington, January 15, 1960; Duff to Anna Steele, CND, January 27, 1960; Steele, London CND, to Duff, February 2, 1960; Duff to Steele, February 12, 1960; 5/11: Policy (2); Structure, Strategy, and Relations with Other Organisations: Correspondence and Circulars, CND policy, resignation of Bertrand Russell from CND, Section 5: London Region Minutes, Correspondence, CND Papers.

66. "Minutes of the A.G.M. of the Scientist's Group of C.N.D.," May 28, 1962, 4–6, 1/62; "Minutes of a Meeting of the Scientists Group of CND," December 14, 1962, 9, 1/62: Scientist Group, 1962, Section 1: CND Central Constitution, Minutes of Committees, Subject Files, 1958–1971, CND Papers.

67. "To the Rt. Hon. Harold Macmillan, M.P., F.R.S.," 12, 1/62: Scientist Group, 1962, Section 1: CND Central Constitution, Minutes of Committees, Subject Files, 1958–1971, CND Papers (emphasis added).

3. Edward Teller's Flexible Response

1. See Fred Kaplan, *The Wizards of Armageddon* (New York: Simon and Schuster, 1983); William Broad, *Teller's War: The Top-Secret Story behind the Star Wars Deception* (New York: Simon and Schuster, 1992); Peter Goodchild, *Edward Teller: The Real Dr. Strangelove* (Cambridge, MA: Harvard University Press, 2004); Edward Teller, *Memoirs: A Twentieth-Century Journey in Science and Politics* (Cambridge, MA: Perseus Books, 2001); Gregg Herken, *Brotherhood of the Bomb: The Tangled Lives and Loyalties of Robert Oppenheimer, Ernest Lawrence, and Edward Teller* (New York: Henry Holt, 2002); and István Hargittai, *Judging Edward Teller: A Closer Look at One of the Most Influential Scientists of the Twentieth Century* (New York: Prometheus Books, 2010). See also Patrick McGrath, *Scientists, Business, and the State, 1890–1960* (Chapel Hill: University of North Carolina Press, 2002), chaps. 5–6.

2. Herman Kahn, *On Thermonuclear War* (Princeton, NJ: Princeton University Press, 1961), 145–49; Sharon Ghamari-Tabrizi, *The Worlds of Herman Kahn: The Intuitive Science of Thermonuclear War* (Cambridge, MA: Harvard University Press, 2005), 41, 212.

3. Ghamari-Tabrizi, *Worlds of Herman Kahn,* 36–37; D. G. Brennan to Teller, August 14, 1964, folder: Hudson Institute, box 443: Topic File, Papers of Edward Teller, Hoover Institution, Stanford University, Stanford, CA (hereafter ET Papers) (emphasis in the original). It is unclear why Brennan suggested U238 instead of U235; a possible explanation is that while U235 is vastly more conducive to nuclear fission, U238 is a much more common isotope of uranium. A huge quantity of U238 might presumably make up for its lack of quality as an explosive. Teller to Brennan, August 25, 1964, folder: Hudson Institute, box 443: Topic File, ET Papers.

4. Quoted in Goodchild, *Edward Teller,* 287.

5. Herbert York, *The Advisors: Oppenheimer, Teller, and the Superbomb* (Stanford, CA: Stanford University Press, 1989), 146.

6. Teller, *Memoirs*, 13–14, 16.

7. Ibid., 95.

8. Richard Rhodes, *The Making of the Atomic Bomb* (New York: Simon and Schuster, 1986), 545–46; Kai Bird and Martin Sherwin, *American Prometheus: The Triumph and Tragedy of J. Robert Oppenheimer* (New York: Alfred A. Knopf, 2005), 282–83; Goodchild, *Edward Teller*, 79–91; Herken, *Brotherhood of the Bomb*, 85–86.

9. Teller, *Memoirs*, 177.

10. Ibid., 177–78.

11. Ibid., 219.

12. Ibid., 183.

13. Teller, *Memoirs*, 279, 307, 404; Edward Teller, "To Sagittarius," *Bulletin of the Atomic Scientists* 7, no. 1 (1951): 22.

14. Teller, *Memoirs*, 397, 401.

15. Luis Alvarez to Teller, undated, folder 1: General, box 2, ET Papers.

16. Telegram, October 1954, folder 5: Oppenheimer, J. Robert, Miscellaneous, box 30, ET Papers.

17. U.S. State Department, *Foreign Relations of the United States, 1955–1957,* vol. 20 (Washington, DC: Government Printing Office, 1990), 639 (hereafter *FRUS, 1955–1957*).

18. Memo, "Plans for the Peaceful Use of Thermonuclear Explosives (Plowshare) in Alaska and Elsewhere"; Teller to Jackson, September 22, 1958, folder 1: Reading File, June–October 1958, box 420: Chronological Correspondence, 1956–58, ET Papers.

19. Ibid.

20. Ibid.

21. Teller to John Morse Jr., July 14, 1958, folder 1: Reading File, June–October 1958, box 420: Chronological Correspondence, 1956–58, ET Papers; Teller to Ernest Patty, June 9, 1959, folder 3: Reading File, June–September 1959, box 423: Chronological Correspondence, 1959–1961, ET Papers; Dan O'Neill, *The Firecracker Boys* (New York: St. Martin's, 1995).

22. PSAC January 23–24, 1967, meeting agenda, box 5, folder: PSAC, 1967—All Correspondence, HUG (FP) 94.14, George B. Kistiakowsky Papers, Harvard University, Cambridge, MA; "Presenting the Real Life Dr. Strangelove," *Gamut*, May 24, 1977, folder 4, box 1, ET Papers; Teller to Hans Mark, September 10, 1958, folder 1: Reading File, June–October 1958, box 420: Chronological Correspondence, 1956–58, ET Papers; Teller to Warren Johnson, February 24, 1958, folder: GAC: Opinions on GAC issues, box 439: Topic Files, ET Papers.

23. Teller, *Memoirs*, 205.

24. Ibid., 207–8. Szilard had expressly asked Teller not to seek Oppenheimer's permission to circulate the petition.

25. Ibid., 209; Teller to Thomas Paradine, January 13, 1960, folder 5: Reading File: January–April 1960, box 423: Chronological Correspondence, 1959–1961, ET Papers.

26. Quoted in Charles Thorpe, *Oppenheimer: The Tragic Intellect* (Chicago: University of Chicago Press, 2006), 165–66.

27. Teller to Robert Gilpin, November 24, 1961, folder 6: Reading File, October–December 1961, box 422: Chronological Correspondence, 1959–61, ET Papers.

28. Quoted in Teller, *Memoirs,* 436; Teller to Szilard, December 15, 1957, and Teller to Szilard, September 15, 1957, folder 2: Reading File, May–December 1957, box 421: Chronological Correspondence, 1956–58, ET Papers.

29. Teller to Ferenc Nagy, May 13, 1960, folder 1: Reading File, May–June 1960, box 422: Chronological Correspondence, 1959–61; Teller to Nagy, January 12, 1962, folder 5: Reading File, January–March 1962, box 426: Chronological Correspondence, 1962–66, ET Papers.

30. Lawrence Wittner, *Resisting the Bomb: A History of the World Nuclear Disarmament Movement, 1954–1970* (Stanford, CA: Stanford University Press, 1997).

31. Robert Divine, *Blowing on the Wind: The Nuclear Test Ban Debate, 1954–1960* (New York: Oxford University Press, 1978); Benjamin Greene, *Eisenhower, Science Advice, and the Nuclear Test-Ban Debate, 1945–1963* (Stanford, CA: Stanford University Press, 2007), 7, 59, 90, 142; Teller to Al Latter, May 29, 1957, folder 2: Reading File, May–December 1957, box 421: Chronological Correspondence, 1956–58, ET Papers.

32. Teller to Weaver, February 24, 1958, folder 2: Reading File: January–May 1958, box 420: Chronological Correspondence, 1956–58, ET Papers.

33. Teller to Norman Caine, June 2, 1958, folder 1: Reading File, June–October 1958, box 420: Chronological Correspondence, 1956–58, ET Papers.

34. Greene tabs Willard Libby as the source of this comparison (*Eisenhower,* 65). Teller to A. H. Schwichtenberg, undated, folder 1: Reading File, June–October 1958, box 420: Chronological Correspondence, 1956–58, ET Papers.

35. Teller to Frank Berry, October 23, 1961, folder 6: October–December 1961, box 422: Chronological Correspondence, 1959–61, ET Papers.

36. Teller to Kissinger, May 7, 1960, folder 1: Reading File, May–June 1960, box 422: Chronological Correspondence, 1959–61, ET Papers. C14 and Sr90 are incorporated into human tissue and decay immediately, making them vastly more damaging than elements that decay outside the body, where damaging effects can be blocked by the skin. *Nuclear Test Ban Treaty,* Hearings before the Senate Committee on Foreign Relations, 88th Cong., 1st sess., August 12–15, 19–23, and 26–27, 1963 (Washington, DC: Government Printing Office, 1963), 455.

37. Teller to Strauss, March 20, 1958, folder 2: Reading File, January–May 1958, box 420: Chronological Correspondence, 1956–58; Teller to Stuart Foster, October 29, 1959, folder 4: Reading File, October–December 1959, box 423: Chronological Correspondence, 1959–1961, ET Papers.

38. Teller to Kissinger, May 7, 1960, folder 1: Reading File, May–June 1960, box 422: Chronological Correspondence, 1959–61, ET Papers.

39. Teller to Symington, May 23, 1958, folder 2: Reading File, January–May 1958, box 420: Chronological Correspondence, 1956–58, ET Papers.

40. *FRUS, 1955–1957,* 640–41 (elided text in the original).

41. Genevieve Greteman to Donald Robinson, June 27, 1957, folder 2: Reading File, 1957, box 421: Chronological Correspondence, 1956–58, ET Papers.

42. Teller to Jackson, May 15, 1956, folder 3: Reading File, 1956, box 420: Chronological Correspondence, 1956–58, ET Papers.

43. Teller to David Griggs, undated, folder 5: Reading File, January–April 1966, box 423: Chronological Correspondence, 1959–1961, ET Papers.

44. Teller to Floyd Odlum, August 9, 1958, folder 1: Reading File, June–October 1958, box 420: Chronological Correspondence, 1956–58; Teller to Anderson, March 25, 1960, folder 5: Reading File, January–April 1960, box 423: Chronological Correspondence, 1959–1961, ET Papers.

45. Teller to Bradbury, August 28, 1958, folder 1: Reading File, June–October 1958, box 420: Chronological Correspondence, 1956–58, ET Papers.

46. Teller to McCone, March 8, 1960, folder 5: Reading File, January–April 1960, box 423: Chronological Correspondence, 1959–1961; Teller to McCone, November 25, 1960, folder 4: Reading File, October–December 1959, box 423: Chronological Correspondence, 1959–1961, ET Papers; Hugh Gusterson, *Nuclear Rites: A Nuclear Weapons Laboratory at the End of the Cold War* (Berkeley: University of California Press, 1998), 131–64.

47. See, for example, Teller to Norman Caine, June 2, 1958, folder 1: Reading File, June–October 1958, box 420: Chronological Correspondence, 1956–58, ET Papers.

48. Teller to Pauling, February 1, 1960, folder 5: Reading File, January–April 1960, box 423: Chronological Correspondence, 1959–1961, ET Papers.

49. Teller to Mrs. William McKeeman, June 30, 1960, folder 1: Reading File, May–June 1960, box 422: Chronological Correspondence, 1959–61; Teller to Jimmy Allen, September 13, 1958, folder 1: Reading File, June–October 1958, box 420: Chronological Correspondence, 1956–58, ET Papers.

50. Teller to Arthur Adamson, undated, folder 1: Reading File, April–June 1963, box 425: Chronological Correspondence, 1962–66, ET Papers; Alden Emery to Pauling, LP Safe Contents, Drawer 2, folder 2.013, Item 13.46, Ava Helen and Linus Pauling Papers, Oregon State University, Corvallis; Emery to Pauling, LP Science: (American Chemical Society: Correspondence, 1950–1964), box 14.006, folder 6.5, Pauling Papers.

51. Teller to David Martin, May 31, 1960, folder 1: Reading File, May–June 1960, box 422: Chronological Correspondence, 1959–61, ET Papers; "Ex-Senator Dodd Is Dead at 64," *New York Times,* May 25, 1971; Thomas Dodd, "The Summit and the Test Ban Fallacy," *Congressional Record—Senate,* May 12, 1960, 10137; Teller to T. F. Walkowicz, May 27, 1960, and Teller to Floyd Odlum, June 29, 1960, folder 1: Reading File, May–June 1960, box 422: Chronological Correspondence, 1959–61, ET Papers.

52. Teller to James Straubel, June 29, 1960, folder 1: Reading File, May–June 1960, box 422: Chronological Correspondence, 1959–61, ET Papers.

53. Teller to Robert Messier, October 12, 1960, folder 1: Reading File, October–December 1960, box 423: Chronological Correspondence, 1959–1961; Teller to Nagy, May 13, 1960; Teller to Truman, May 11, 1960, folder 1: Reading File, May–June 1960, box 422: Chronological Correspondence, 1959–61; Teller to Kahn, February 28, 1964, folder 1: Reading File, January–March 1964, box 424: Chronological Correspondence, 1962–66, ET Papers.

54. Teller to Francis Walter, April 7, 1961, folder 4: Reading File, April–June 1961, box 422: Chronological Correspondence, 1959–61, ET Papers.

55. U.S. State Department, *Foreign Relations of the United States, 1958–1960*, vol. 3 (Washington, DC: Government Printing Office, 1996), 696 (hereafter *FRUS, 1958–1960*); Teller to Charter Heslep, August 2, 1962, folder: AEC/Public Info Office Heslep re: Bethe Meeting in 1962, box 444: Topic Files; Teller to Walter Selove, June 14, 1958, folder 1: Reading File, June–October 1958, box 420: Chronological Correspondence, 1956–58, ET Papers; Bethe to Teller, September 9, 1941, folder 8.53 (untitled), box 8, Hans Bethe Papers, Cornell University, Ithaca, NY; Teller to Strauss, April 25, 1958, folder 2: Reading File: January–May 1958, box 420: Chronological Correspondence, 1956–58, ET Papers.

56. Teller to Kissinger, August 8, 1962, folder 3: Reading File, July–September 1962, box 426: Chronological Correspondence, 1962–66, ET Papers.

57. Ibid.

58. Teller to Arthur Adamson, undated, folder 1: Reading File, April–June 1963, box 425: Chronological Correspondence, 1962–66; interview with Hahn, July 31, 1963, folder: Test Ban: 1963 Press Coverage, box 448: Topic Files; Teller to Walter Selove, June 14, 1958, folder 1: Reading File, June–October 1958, box 420: Chronological Correspondence, 1956–58, ET Papers.

59. Teller to Bethe, October 3, 1960, folder 1: Reading File, October–December 1960, box 423: Chronological Correspondence, 1959–1961 (emphasis added); Teller to Rabinowitch, January 20, 1958, folder 1: Reading File, June–October 1958, box 420: Chronological Correspondence, 1956–58; Teller to Jay Orear, March 8, 1958, folder 2: Reading File: January–May 1958, box 420: Chronological Correspondence, 1956–58, ET Papers.

60. Bentley Glass, "Scientists in Politics," *Bulletin of the Atomic Scientists* 18, no. 5 (1962): 2–7; Teller to Rabinowitch, April 18, 1957, folder 2: Reading File, 1957, box 421: Chronological Correspondence, 1956–58, ET Papers.

61. Teller to Rabinowitch, December 14, 1959, folder 4: Reading File, October–December 1959; Teller to Wigner, January 19, 1960, folder 5: Reading File, January–April 1960, box 423: Chronological Correspondence, 1959–1961; Teller to Rabinowitch, July 13, 1960, folder 2: Reading File, July–September 1960, box 422: Chronological Correspondence, 1959–61, ET Papers.

62. Teller to Laurence Kuter, folder 1: Reading File, October–December 1960, box 423: Chronological Correspondence, 1959–1961; Teller to Burke, September 26, 1957, folder 2: Reading File, May–December 1957; Teller to James Doolittle, November 5, 1958, folder 1: Reading File, November–December 1958, box 421: Chronological Correspondence, 1956–58, ET Papers.

63. Teller to Bethe, January 8, 1958, folder 2: Reading File: January–May 1958; Teller to Jackson, September 22, 1958, folder 1: Reading File, June–October 1958, box 420: Chronological Correspondence, 1956–58, ET Papers; *The Nature of Radioactive Fallout and Its Effects on Man,* Hearings before the Subcommittee on Radiation, 85th Cong., 1st sess., May 27–29 and June 3–7, 1957 (Washington, DC: Government Printing Office, 1957), 983.

64. Teller to Jackson, August 8, 1962, folder 3: Reading File, July–September 1962,

box 426: Chronological Correspondence, 1962–66, ET Papers. Naturally, making nominations and suggestions was perfectly reasonable and normal for scientists. For a full list of PSAC members, see Zuoyue Wang, *In Sputnik's Shadow: The President's Science Advisory Committee and Cold War America* (New Brunswick, NJ: Rutgers University Press, 2008), 325–28.

65. Teller to T. G. Lanphier Jr., February 16, 1960, folder 5: Reading File, January–April 1960; Teller to Lanphier Jr., May 7, 1959, folder 2: Reading File, January–May 1959, box 423: Chronological Correspondence, 1959–1961; Teller to Symington, February 5, 1958; Teller to Symington, March 10 and April 25, 1958, folder 2: Reading File, January–May 1958, box 420: Chronological Correspondence, 1956–58, ET Papers.

66. Teller to William F. Buckley Jr., May 9, 1958, folder 2: Reading File: January–May 1958; Teller to Nelson Rockefeller, July 5, 1958, folder 1: Reading File, June–October 1958, box 420: Chronological Correspondence, 1956–58; Teller to Kissinger, January 11, 1960, folder 5: Reading File, January–April 1960, box 423: Chronological Correspondence, 1959–61, ET Papers.

67. Teller to Kissinger, September 18, 1957, folder 2: Reading File, May–December 1957, box 421: Chronological Correspondence, 1956–58, ET Papers.

68. *FRUS, 1958–1960,* 537.

69. Teller to Johnson, October 18, 1958, folder 1: Reading File, June–October 1958, box 420: Chronological Correspondence, 1956–58, ET Papers.

70. Teller to Johnson, June 14, 1958, folder 1: Reading File, June–October 1958; Teller to Strauss, March 20, 1958, folder 2: Reading File, January–May 1958, box 420: Chronological Correspondence, 1956–58, ET Papers; Herken, *Brotherhood of the Bomb,* 330; Teller to Albert Latter, August 28, 1957, folder 2: Reading File, May–December 1957, box 421: Chronological Correspondence, 1956–58, ET Papers.

71. Teller to Kissinger, May 2, 1962, folder 4: Reading File, April–June 1962, box 426: Chronological Correspondence, 1962–66, ET Papers.

72. Teller to Kissinger, September 6 and August 26, 1963, folder 2: Reading File, July–September 1963, box 425: Chronological Correspondence, 1962–66, ET Papers.

73. Teller to Rockefeller, August 13, 1964, and Teller to Kissinger, August 17, 1964, folder 5: Reading File, July–September 1964, box 425: Chronological Correspondence, 1962–66, ET Papers.

74. Teller, *Memoirs,* 465; Goodchild, *Edward Teller,* 306; David Cassidy, *J. Robert Oppenheimer and the American Century* (New York: Pi Press, 2005), 349. Bird and Sherwin, *American Prometheus,* sound more skeptical (681n).

75. Teller to Wigner, January 19, 1960, folder 5: Reading File, January–April 1960, box 423: Chronological Correspondence, 1959–1961; Teller to Manson Benedict, February 18, 1963, folder 3, Reading File, January–March 1963, box 425: Chronological Correspondence, 1962–66, ET Papers; William Lanouette, *Genius in the Shadows: A Biography of Leo Szilard, the Man behind the Bomb* (New York: Charles Scribner's Sons, 1992), 353–55; Bird and Sherwin, *American Prometheus,* 574–76; Glenn Seaborg, *Adventures in the Atomic Age: From Watts to Washington* (New York: Farrar, Straus, and Giroux, 2001), 224–26.

76. Teller to Wheeler, January 21, 1964, and Teller to Raymond Mar, February

20, 1964, folder 1: Reading File, January–March 1964, box 424: Chronological Correspondence, 1962–66, ET Papers; Teller, *Memoirs*, 485–91; Teller to McCone, March 8, 1960, folder 5: Reading File, January–April 1960, box 423: Chronological Correspondence, 1959–1961, ET Papers.

77. Teller, *Memoirs*, 307; Teller to Brown, April 3, 1956, folder 3: Reading File 1956, box 420: Chronological Correspondence, 1956–58, ET Papers. Teller's son, Paul, did not become a quarterback but did become a philosopher of science.

78. July 15, 1958, memo from Barney Oldfield and attached preamble and summary remarks, folder: USAF re: Pauling Teller Debate, box 457: Topic file/Alphabetical file, ET Papers.

4. "Crucified on a Cross of Atoms"

1. John Gaddis, *We Now Know: Rethinking Cold War History* (New York: Oxford University Press, 1997); Marc Trachtenberg, *A Constructed Peace: The Making of the European Settlement, 1945-1963* (Princeton, NJ: Princeton University Press, 1999).

2. In *Kennedy, Khrushchev, and the Test Ban* (Berkeley: University of California Press, 1981), Glenn Seaborg makes clear his and other scientists' deep regret that the test ban was not comprehensive (xiv, 242, 293–99).

3. Eugene Rabinowitch, *The Dawn of a New Age: Reflections on Science and Human Affairs* (Chicago: University of Chicago Press, 1963), 99.

4. M. Losada to Rabinowitch, March 11, 1964, Series IV, Addenda II, box 6, folder 13: General Correspondence, Eugene Rabinowitch Papers, Regenstein Library, University of Chicago (hereafter ER Papers).

5. Joseph Rotblat, *Scientists in the Quest for Peace: A History of the Pugwash Conferences* (Cambridge, MA: MIT Press, 1972), 141; Rabinowitch, *Dawn of a New Age*, 5.

6. Rotblat, *Quest for Peace*, 143.

7. Rabinowitch, "About Pugwash," *Bulletin of the Atomic Scientists* 21, no. 4 (1965): 9; Feld to Rabinowitch, February 4, 1970, Series IV, Addenda II, box 7, folder 1: General Correspondence, ER Papers.

8. Joseph Rotblat, *Pugwash—the First Ten Years: History of the Conferences of Science and World Affairs* (New York: Humanities Press, 1968), 17; Rotblat, *Quest for Peace*.

9. "Private Meeting in London to Discuss the Nuclear Test Ban Deadlock," March 16–17, 1963, part 1, 1, box 35: Correspondence, 1961–1965, folder: Nuclear Test Ban, HUG (FP) 94.8, George B. Kistiakowsky Papers, Harvard University, Cambridge, MA (hereafter GBK Papers).

10. Rotblat, *Pugwash*, 19, 23.

11. Ibid., 78.

12. Benjamin Greene, *Eisenhower, Science Advice, and the Nuclear Test-Ban Debate, 1945–1963* (Stanford, CA: Stanford University Press, 2007), 24.

13. U.S. State Department, *Foreign Relations of the United States, 1955–1957*, vol. 20 (Washington, DC: Government Printing Office, 1990), 273 (hereafter *FRUS, 1955–1957*).

14. Ibid., 419–21.

15. Walter Rosenblith, ed., *Jerry Wiesner, Scientist, Statesman, Humanist: Memories and Memoirs* (Cambridge, MA: MIT Press, 2003), 257; Bethe to Rabinowitch, February 12, 1958, box 8, folder 16, ER Papers.

16. James Killian, *Sputnik, Scientists, and Eisenhower: A Memoir of the First Special Assistant to the President for Science and Technology* (Cambridge, MA: Harvard University Press, 1977), 150; U.S. State Department, *Foreign Relations of the United States, 1958–1960*, vol. 3 (Washington, DC: Government Printing Office, 1996), 544 (hereafter *FRUS, 1958–1960*).

17. Greene, *Eisenhower*, 134–64; Harold Jacobson and Eric Stein, *Diplomats, Scientists, and Politicians: The United States and the Nuclear Test Ban Negotiations* (Ann Arbor: University of Michigan Press, 1966), 119.

18. Hans Bethe Oral History, November 3, 1977, 22, Dwight D. Eisenhower Library, Abilene, KS (hereafter DDEL); Killian to Eisenhower, April 3, 1958, White House Office of the Special Assistant for Science and Technology (James R. Killian and George B. Kistiakowsky): Records, 1957–1961, Alphabetical File, Disarmament— Nuclear [March–April 1958] (1) box 1, DDEL; *FRUS, 1958–1960*, 585–86, 603.

19. Rosenblith, *Jerry Wiesner*, 263; George Kistiakowsky, *A Scientist at the White House: The Private Diary of President Eisenhower's Special Assistant for Science and Technology* (Cambridge, MA: Harvard University Press, 1976), 292, 322; Weisskopf to Killian, September 27, 1958, White House Office of the Special Assistant for Science and Technology (James R. Killian and George B. Kistiakowsky): Records, 1957–1961, Alphabetical File, Nuclear Test Policy [May 1958–October 1960] (1) box 8, DDEL.

20. Jacobson and Stein, *Diplomats, Scientists, and Politicians*, 52–56, 62–71, 76, 81.

21. Ibid., 135–47, 155, 217, 220, 222.

22. George Kistiakowsky Oral History, November 3, 1977, 16, DDEL.

23. Kistiakowsky, *Scientist at the White House*, 228.

24. Subcommittee on Disarmament, *Controlling the Further Development of Nuclear Weapons: A Collection of Excerpts and a Bibliography*, 85th Cong., 2nd sess. (Washington, DC: Government Printing Office, 1958), 29, 39–40; "Meeting on Arms Limitations," 2, March 1960, U.S. President's Science Advisory Committee: Records, 1957–1961, box 2, DDEL.

25. Teller to Latter, March 20, 1964, folder 1: Reading File, January–March 1964, box 424: Chronological Correspondence, 1962–66, Papers of Edward Teller, Hoover Institution, Stanford University, Stanford, CA (hereafter ET Papers). Teller was barely exaggerating: as of 2015 the recipient of a Lawrence Award received twenty thousand dollars and "a gold medal bearing the likeness of E. O. Lawrence," according to the Department of Energy (http://science.energy.gov/lawrence/).

26. "Private Meeting," part 2, 14, folder: Nuclear Test Ban, box 35: Correspondence, 1961–1965, HUG (FP) 94.8, GBK Papers. See also Kistiakowsky to Thomas Morgan, August 25, 1961, folder: ACDA (Arms Control and Disarmament Agency), 1961–64, box 31: Correspondence, 1961–1965, HUG (FP) 94.8, GBK Papers.

27. Killian, *Sputnik, Scientists, and Eisenhower*, 168.

28. Kistiakowsky, *Scientist at the White House*, xlvii, 49, 73, 198.

29. *FRUS, 1955–1957,* 638–40 (elided text in the original).

30. Eisenhower to Strauss, July 2, 1957, and Strauss to Eisenhower, July 3, 1957, Ann Whitman File, Administrative Series, box 5, Atomic Energy Commission, 1957 (2), DDEL. See also Bethe Oral History, 8.

31. *FRUS, 1955–1957,* 754–55; Bethe Oral History, 8.

32. *FRUS, 1958–1960,* 604.

33. *FRUS, 1955–1957,* 477.

34. *FRUS, 1958–1960,* 533–37.

35. Ibid., 692–94, 796.

36. Zuoyue Wang, *In* Sputnik's *Shadow: The President's Science Advisory Committee and Cold War America* (New Brunswick, NJ: Rutgers University Press, 2008), 4.

37. *FRUS, 1955–1957,* 478–79, 662–65, 754–55.

38. Rosenblith, *Jerry Wiesner,* 441.

39. Ibid., 409; Feld to Rabinowitch, March 17, 1960, box 30: Committee on Pugwash Conferences on Science and World Affairs (P-COSWA), folder 304: 1959–1965, Bernard T. Feld Papers, Massachusetts Institute of Technology, Cambridge (hereafter BTF Papers).

40. Feld, unpublished autobiography, "VIII: Nuclear Politics in the U.S.A.," Doc. 11, March 8, 1988, box 65: Writings, folder unnumbered: Autobiographical, BTF Papers; Bethe Oral History, 18.

41. Jacobson and Stein, *Diplomats, Scientists, and Politicians,* 231–61.

42. "Farewell Radio and Television Address to the American People, January 17, 1961," in *Public Papers of the Presidents of the United States: Dwight D. Eisenhower, 1960–61* (Washington, DC: Government Printing Office, 1961), 1035–40; Killian, Sputnik, *Scientists, and Eisenhower,* 224.

43. Kistiakowsky, Memo to Members, PSAC, January 19, 1961, box 5: PSAC, All Correspondence, 1968–1969, folder: PSAC, 1968, HUG (FP) 94.14, GBK Papers; Herbert York, *Arms and the Physicist* (Woodbury, NY: American Institute of Physics, 1995), 147. Eisenhower also mentioned Wernher von Braun, the U.S. missile engineer.

44. Ruth Adams to Feld, November 8, 1961, box 5: Arms Control, folder 42: 1960–61, BTF Papers; Feld, unpublished autobiography, "VIII: Nuclear Politics in the U.S.A."

45. Carl Kaysen, interview, MIT, March 16, 2005.

46. Rosenblith, *Jerry Wiesner,* xiii–xiv, 40, 509.

47. Theodore Sorensen, *Kennedy* (New York: Harper and Row, 1965), 621–22; Rosenblith, *Jerry Wiesner,* 58; Kaysen interview.

48. U.S. State Department, *Foreign Relations of the United States, 1961–1963,* vol. 7 (Washington, DC: Government Printing Office, 1995), 268, 271 (hereafter *FRUS, 1961–1963*).

49. Ibid., 576–77, 585, 623–24.

50. Kistiakowsky, *Scientist at the White House,* 292.

51. Ibid., 423–24; "Private Meeting," part 1, 14, folder: Nuclear Test Ban, box 35: Correspondence, 1961–1965, HUG (FP) 94.8, GBK Papers.

52. Seaborg, *Kennedy, Khrushchev, and the Test Ban,* 172–76.

53. Ibid., 227, 242.

54. Ibid., 241; Kaysen interview.

55. Seaborg, *Kennedy, Khrushchev, and the Test Ban,* 235, 241.

56. *FRUS, 1961–1963,* 821.

57. Teller to Kissinger, September 6, 1963, folder 2: Reading File, July–September 1963, box 425: Chronological Correspondence, 1962–1966; Teller to Symington and Teller to Stennis, August 8, 1962, folder 3: Reading File, July–September 1962, box 426: Chronological Correspondence, 1962–66; Teller to Jackson, August 29, 1963, folder 2: Reading File, July–September 1963, box 425: Chronological Correspondence, 1962–1966, ET Papers.

58. *Military Aspects and Implications of Nuclear Test Ban Proposals and Related Matters,* Hearings before the Preparedness Investigating Subcommittee, 88th Cong., 1st sess., May 7, 15, and 28; June 5 and 25–27; August 1–2, 9, 12, 14, 16, 19–20, 22–23, and 27, 1963 (Washington, DC: Government Printing Office, 1964), 594 (hereafter Preparedness Hearings).

59. Ibid., 356, 471, 944–45.

60. *Nuclear Test Ban Treaty,* Hearings before the Committee on Foreign Relations, 88th Cong., 1st sess., August 12–15, 19–23, and 26–27, 1963 (Washington, DC: Government Printing Office, 1963), 227 (hereafter CFR Hearings).

61. Preparedness Hearings, 543, 546, 549.

62. CFR Hearings, 506.

63. Ibid., 137 (McNamara), 557 (Brown), 584–85 (Bradbury), 763 (York), 267 (Seaborg); Kistiakowsky, *Scientist at the White House,* 859.

64. CFR Hearings, 859.

65. Preparedness Hearings, 206.

66. CFR Hearings, 81, 165, 541; Kaysen interview.

67. Kistiakowsky to Eisenhower, August 18, 1963, folder: General Eisenhower, box 32: Correspondence, 1961–1965, HUG (FP) 94.8, GBK Papers.

68. CFR Hearings, 767.

69. Kistiakowsky to Eisenhower, August 18, 1963.

70. CFR Hearings, 996, 1007.

71. Preparedness Hearings, 536, 750, 772.

72. CFR Hearings, 639, 836.

73. Preparedness Hearings, 590, 594.

74. Solly Zuckerman to the prime minister, June 24, 1963, PREM 11/4159, UK National Archives, London; Seaborg, *Kennedy, Khrushchev, and the Test Ban,* 269–71; Kaysen interview.

75. CFR Hearings, 405. Of 638 U.S. tests between 1945 and 1980, 345 (54 percent) took place after the LTBT. In the Soviet Union, of the 298 tests between 1949 and 1980, 168 (56 percent) occurred after the LTBT (Seaborg, *Kennedy, Khrushchev, and the Test Ban,* 288). Feld, unpublished autobiography, "VIII: Nuclear Politics in the U.S.A."

76. Peter Goodchild, *Edward Teller: The Real Dr. Strangelove* (Cambridge, MA: Harvard University Press, 2004), 305–7.

77. Preparedness Hearings, 772. For voting results, see "Roll Call Vote in Senate on the

Test Ban Treaty," *New York Times,* September 25, 1963. Jackson and Hickenlooper also voted for the treaty, while Stennis voted against it. Symington endorsed the Preparedness Subcommittee's report that recommended rejection of the treaty but voiced his intent to vote for ratification in the Senate nonetheless. Seaborg, *Kennedy, Khrushchev, and the Test Ban,* 278.

78. "War and Peace," *New York Times,* August 23, 1963; Harold Macmillan to Secretary General, Pugwash, Dubrovnik, Yugoslavia, 1963, FO 371 IA D1092/ 30, UK National Archives.

79. Paul Boyer, "From Activism to Apathy: The American People and Nuclear Weapons, 1963–1980," *Journal of American History* 70, no. 4 (1984): 821–44; Feld, unpublished autobiography, "VIII: Nuclear Politics in the U.S.A."; Rabinowitch, "Editorial: The Test Ban," *Bulletin of the Atomic Scientists* 19, no. 7 (1963): 2; Long to Feld, October 2, 1963, box 33: Eleventh Pugwash Conference, Dubrovnik, folder 329: Correspondence, 1963, BTF Papers.

80. Kistiakowsky Oral History, 21; Bethe Oral History, 23–24.

81. Kistiakowsky to David Tunick, September 4, 1964; Kistiakowsky to M. Kasha, November 19, 1964, folder: Scientists and Engineers for LBJ, 1 of 2, box 36: Correspondence, 1961-1965, HUG (FP) 94.8, GBK Papers.

82. Jacobson and Stein, *Diplomats, Scientists, and Politicians,* 481; Goodchild, *Edward Teller,* 268.

5. To "Sail Before the Wind of Time"

1. Eugene Rabinowitch, "Editorial: The Test Ban," *Bulletin of the Atomic Scientists* 19, no. 7 (1963): 2; Rabinowitch, "Editorial: First Step—to Where?," *Bulletin of the Atomic Scientists* 19, no. 8 (1963): 2–3.

2. Eugene Rabinowitch, "Nuclear Bomb Tests: A Skeptical View," in *The Atomic Age: Scientists in National and World Affairs,* edited by Rabinowitch (New York: Basic Books, 1963), 341.

3. Marc Trachtenberg, *A Constructed Peace: The Making of the European Settlement, 1945-1963* (Princeton, NJ: Princeton University Press, 1999); John Gaddis, *We Now Know: Rethinking Cold War History* (New York: Oxford University Press, 1997). The phrase "eyeball to eyeball" refers to Dean Rusk's comment about U.S.-Soviet relations during the Cuban Missile Crisis.

4. Paul Boyer, "From Activism to Apathy: The American People and Nuclear Weapons, 1963–1980," *Journal of American History* 70, no. 4 (1984): 821, 837.

5. Lawrence Wittner, *Toward Nuclear Abolition: A History of the World Nuclear Disarmament Movement, 1971 to the Present* (Stanford, CA: Stanford University Press, 2003), 14.

6. George Kistiakowsky, *A Scientist at the White House: The Private Diary of President Eisenhower's Special Assistant for Science and Technology* (Cambridge, MA: Harvard University Press, 1976), 423-24; Joseph Rotblat, "Movements of Scientists," in *Scientists, the Arms Race, and Disarmament,* edited by Rotblat (London: Taylor & Francis, 1982), 139; Rotblat, *Pugwash—the First Ten Years: History of the Conferences of Science and World Affairs* (New York: Humanities

Press, 1968), 42; Rotblat, *Scientists in the Quest for Peace: A History of the Pugwash Conferences* (Cambridge, MA: MIT Press, 1972), 33.

7. Rotblat, *Pugwash,* 44; David Binder, "Scientists Begin East-West Talks," *New York Times*, September 21, 1963.

8. W. E. Kerr, "Impressions from Dubrovnik," *Pugwash Newsletter* 2, no. 3 (1964): 43, Series IV, Addenda II, box 1, folder 2: 13th Pugwash Conference on Science and World Affairs; "Preamble to Continuing Committee Press Release," 1963, Series I, box 6, folder 9: Press Releases, Internal Memoranda, Miscellaneous Notes; J. D. Cockcroft, "The Nuclear Test Ban," Paper XI.9, box 6, folder 11: Conference Papers, Aubert-Cockcroft, Eugene Rabinowitch Papers, Regenstein Library, University of Chicago (hereafter ER Papers).

9. "Scientists Discuss Germany's Division," *New York Times,* September 23, 1963; "World Scientists Hail U.S. and Soviet Peace Plans," *New York Times,* September 24, 1963; "Study of Quakes," *New York Times,* September 26, 1963.

10. Rabinowitch, "Pugwash," from *Retort,* undated (mid-1965), Series IV, Addenda II, box 6, folder 7: Disarmament, Proposed Publication On; Rabinowitch to Bernard Feld, October 7, 1963, Series I, box 8, folder 20: Feld-Goldsmith, ER Papers.

11. David Riesman, "Report from Moscow," *Committees of Correspondence Newsletter* (April 1961), Series I, box 10, folder 11: Committees of Correspondence, National Headquarters, ER Papers; Eugene Rabinowitch, *The Dawn of a New Age: Reflections on Science and Human Affairs* (Chicago: University of Chicago Press, 1963), 98; Rabinowitch to Feld, October 7, 1963, Series I, box 8, folder 20: Feld-Goldsmith, ER Papers.

12. "Recommendations from the Continuing Committee to the Committee on Future Activities and Organization," 1962, Series I, box 6, folder 1: Cambridge Pugwash Conference, August 1962; Rabinowitch, Memo to Possible U.S. Pugwash Delegates, April 27, 1964, Series IV, Addenda II, box 1, folder 2: 13th Pugwash Conference on Science and World Affairs, ER Papers.

13. Rotblat, *Quest for Peace,* 26; Wilton Dillon, Memo to Harrison Brown and Murray Todd, Office Files of Bill Moyers: Pugwash, box 74 (1390), Lyndon Baines Johnson Library (hereafter LBJL).

14. Rotblat, *Quest for Peace,* viii; "Scientists at Parley Discuss Atom Issue," *New York Times,* September 15, 1964; "Scientists' Parley Asks Antiwar Pact," *New York Times,* September 21, 1964; "Atom Ban Called Possibility Soon," *New York Times,* September 12, 1966; "New Step Is Urged to Ban Atom Tests," *New York Times,* September 18, 1966.

15. Rabinowitch to Seldes, October 29, 1958, Series III, Addenda I, box 12, folder 30: Post Third Pugwash Conference Correspondence, ER Papers; Rabinowitch, *Dawn of a New Age,* 209, 47, 94; (Draft) Memorandum on Future Development of the COSWA [Pugwash] Conferences, Series I, box 6, folder 20: U.S. Pugwash Continuing Committee, ER Papers.

16. Matthew Meselson, "Impressions from Dubrovnik," *Pugwash Newsletter* 2, no. 3 (1964): 43, Addenda II, box 1, folder 2: 13th Pugwash Conference on Science and World Affairs, ER Papers.

17. Rabinowitch to Harrison Brown, June 10, 1964, Series IV, Addenda II, box 6, folder 13: General Correspondence, ER Papers; Eugene Rabinowitch, "About

Pugwash," *Bulletin of the Atomic Scientists* 21, no. 4 (1965): 9; Rabinowitch, *Atomic Age*, 500; Rabinowitch, *Dawn of a New Age*, 229. On Rabinowitch, see Patrick David Slaney, "Eugene Rabinowitch, the *Bulletin of the Atomic Scientists*, and the Nature of Scientific Internationalism in the Early Cold War," *Historical Studies in the Natural Sciences* 42, no. 2 (2012): 114–42.

18. "Minutes of Pugwash Continuing Committee," September 7–8 and 16–17, 1966, Series IV, Addenda II, box 1, folder 6: 16th Pugwash Conference, ER Papers; Rotblat, *Quest for Peace*, 66, 246–55.

19. Wilton Dillon to Harrison Brown and Murray Todd, Office Files of Bill Moyers: Pugwash, box 74 (1390), LBJL; Rotblat, *Quest for Peace*, 67. See Y. Peter and B. Winid to Rabinowitch, May 31, 1966, Series IV, Addenda II, box 1, folder 4: 15th Pugwash Conference; and Paul Freund to Harrison Brown, October 28, 1966, Series IV, Addenda II, box 1, folder 6: 16th Pugwash Conference, ER Papers.

20. "Peace Moves at Pugwash," *New York Times*, October 11, 1964; Telegram from Jerome Wiesner and Paul Doty to McGeorge Bundy, Department of State, Czechoslovakia Cables, vol. 1, November 1963–August 1967, 23, National Security File, Country File, Europe and USSR, Czechoslovakia, box 179, LBJL; for Kennedy's messages to Pugwash, see *Pugwash Newsletter* 2, no. 3 (January 1964), Series IV, Addenda II, box 1, folder 2: 13th Pugwash Conference on Science and World Affairs, ER Papers; Rotblat, *Quest for Peace*, 59; telegram from McGeorge Bundy, Department of State, to Jerome Wiesner and Paul Doty, Czechoslovakia Cables, vol. 1, November 1963–August 1967, 24, National Security File, Country File, Europe and USSR, Czechoslovakia, box 179, LBJL.

21. J. Kretzman to McGeorge Bundy, undated [September 1964], 82, 82a, Czechoslovakia Memos, vol. 1, November 1963–August 1967, National Security File, Country File, Europe and USSR, Czechoslovakia, box 179, LBJL; *Congressional Record* (1963), appx. A7185.

22. "Ex-Senator Dodd Is Dead at 64," *New York Times*, May 25, 1971; Lawrence Wittner, *Resisting the Bomb: A History of the World Nuclear Disarmament Movement, 1954–1970* (Stanford, CA: Stanford University Press, 1997), 363–64; press release from Senate Internal Security Subcommittee, May 28, 1961, Series II, box 8, folder 10: The President and Foreign Policy—Publication, ER Papers; "Senate Staff Study Hits Science Talks Promoted by Eaton," *New York Times*, May 28, 1961; *Congressional Record*, vol. 107, pt. 11, 15059; Internal Security Subcommittee, *The Pugwash Conferences: A Staff Analysis*, 87th Cong., 1st sess. (Washington, DC: Government Printing Office, 1961).

23. S. M. Levitas to Rabinowitch, May 7, 1958, Series II, box 9, folder 2: Magat–Phil; Rabinowitch to Walt Whitman, February 23, 1960, Series I, box 6, folder 19: U.S. Pugwash Continuing Committee, ER Papers; Rabinowitch, *Atomic Age*, 570.

24. "Ex-Senator Dodd Is Dead."

25. Kai Bird, *The Color of Truth: McGeorge Bundy and William Bundy, Brothers in Arms* (New York: Touchstone, 1998), 309; Lyndon Johnson phone conversation with Abe Fortas, May 19, 1965, in *Reaching for Glory: Lyndon Johnson's Secret White House Tapes, 1965–65*, edited by Michael Beschloss (New York: Simon and Schuster, 2001), 332; *Congressional Record*, vol. 112, pt. 15, 1966, 19441.

26. Kistiakowsky to Morris Marden, December 6, 1965, box 33: General Correspondence, ca. 1928–1982, folder: Don Hornig, HUG (FP) 94.8, George B. Kistiakowsky Papers, Harvard University (hereafter GBK Papers).

27. Donald Hornig, Memo to the President, April 8, 1965, April–June 1965, box 2, Chronological File; Hornig to McGeorge Bundy, December 23, 1965, October–December 1965, box 3, Chronological File; Hornig to Bernard Feld, March 15, 1966, January–March, 1966, box 3, Chronological File, Papers of Donald F. Horning, LBJL (hereafter DFH Papers).

28. Hornig to Frank Long, September 27, 1965, July–September 1965, box 2, Chronological File; Hornig to George Kistiakowsky, September 27, 1965, July–September 1965, box 2, Chronological File, DFH Papers.

29. Hornig to Herbert York, January 10, 1966, January–March 1966, box 3, Chronological File, DFH Papers; Rabinowitch to Todd Murray, November 29, 1970, Series IV, Addenda II, box 7, folder 10: General Correspondence, ER Papers; Frank Long to Kenneth Pitzer, October 19, 1966, October–December 1966, box 4, Chronological File, DFH Papers.

30. Hornig to Joshua Lederberg, November 19, 1965, October–December 1965, box 3, Chronological File; "The Role of Science and Technology in Aid to Developing Countries," June 7, 1966, April–June 1966, box 4, Chronological File, DFH Papers.

31. Hornig, Memo to Walt Rostow, September 9, 1966, July–September 1966, box 4, Chronological File, DFH Papers; Rotblat, Memo to Continuing Committee, "Nice Pugwash Conference Agenda (Tentative)," February 19, 1968, Series IV, Addenda II, box 1, folder 10: 18th Pugwash Conference, ER Papers; Memorandum for Members and Consultants-at-Large, President's Science Advisory Committee, October 6, 1967, box 5, folder: PSAC Reports, 1967, HUG (FP) 94.14, GBK Papers.

32. Hornig, Memo for Jack Valenti, May 26, 1964, April–May 1964, box 1, Chronological File; October 8, 1965, October–December 1965, box 3, Chronological File; Hornig to Solly Zuckerman, July 24, 1967, July–September 1967, Chronological File, box 5, DFH Papers.

33. Hornig, Memo for Marvin Watson, February 19, 1968, January–March 1968, box 6, Chronological File, DFH Papers.

34. "Report of Working Group 5"; Wilton Dillon to Hayes Redman, April 15, 1966; Dillon, Memo to Harrison Brown and Murray Todd, April 15, 1966, Office Files of Bill Moyers: Pugwash, box 74 (1390), LBJL.

35. Rotblat, *Pugwash,* 51–52; "U.N. Urged to Lead a Year for Science," *New York Times,* April 17, 1965; Eugene Rabinowitch, "Pugwash XVI," *Bulletin of the Atomic Scientists* 23, no. 1 (1967): 43; "Pugwash in Africa," *New York Times,* January 28, 1966; Richard Burling to Rabinowitch, August 24, 1966, Series IV, Addenda II, box 1, folder 9: 17th Pugwash Conference, ER Papers.

36. Rotblat, *Pugwash,* 56; Bernard Feld memo, September 29, 1966, Series IV, Addenda II, box 1, folder 9: 17th Pugwash Conference, ER Papers; Rotblat, *Quest for Peace,* 68–69, 262; Rotblat, *Pugwash,* 56; Rabinowitch, Agenda for Sopot Pugwash Meeting, September 1966, Series IV, Addenda II, box 1, folder 7: 16th Pugwash Conference, ER Papers; "Vietnam War Condemned by Pugwash Conference," *New York Times,* January 5, 1966; Rotblat, *Pugwash,* 206.

37. Eugene Rabinowitch, "Pugwash," *Retort,* undated [mid-1965], Series IV, Addenda II, box 6, folder 7: Disarmament, Proposed Publication On, ER Papers.

38. Harrison Brown to Rabinowitch, June 10, 1966; Frederick Seitz to Rabinowitch, June 13, 1966; Rabinowitch to Harrison Brown, June 23, 1966, Series IV, Addenda II, box 1, folder 5: 16th Pugwash Conference, ER Papers.

39. Rabinowitch, "Pugwash XVI," 43.

40. David Inglis to John Voss, October 12, 1967, Series IV, Addenda II, box 6, folder 14: General Correspondence, ER Papers; Rotblat, *Quest for Peace,* 72; "'Secret' Mission Described" and "French Engineer Silent," *New York Times,* April 5, 1968; "Frenchman Took U.S. Plan to Hanoi," *New York Times,* April 9, 1968; Robin Clarke, "Science and Technology Comment," *Science Journal,* undated [probably 1968], Series IV, Addenda II, box 7, folder 1: General Correspondence; "Minutes for the Pugwash Continuing Committee Meeting," December 10–11, 1967, Series IV, Addenda II, box 7, folder 5: General Correspondence, ER Papers; George Herring, *America's Longest War: The United States and Vietnam, 1950–1975,* 3rd ed. (New York: McGraw-Hill, 1996), 196.

41. Cyrus Eaton letter, 1969, Series IV, Addenda II, box 2, folder 4: 19th Pugwash Conference; Paul Doty, "On the Current Impasse," 1968, Series IV, Addenda II, box 2, folder 1: 18th Pugwash Conference, ER Papers; Rotblat, *Quest for Peace,* 320–21.

42. Edward Teller, *Memoirs: A Twentieth-Century Journey in Science and Politics* (Cambridge, MA: Perseus Books, 2001), 492, 501, 504.

43. *Bulletin of the Atomic Scientists* 21, no. 6 (1965); "World Court or U.N. Decision to End Vietnam War Urged," *New York Times,* January 2, 1966; Eugene Rabinowitch, "New Year's Thoughts, 1968," *Bulletin of the Atomic Scientists* 24, no. 1 (1968): 2–4.

44. PSAC, December 14–15, 1964, meeting agenda, box 3, folder: PSAC, 1964—All Correspondence; PSAC, June 7–8, 1965, meeting agenda, box 3, folder: PSAC, 1965—All Correspondence; PSAC, February 14–15, 1966, meeting agenda, box 4, folder: PSAC, 1966—All Correspondence; PSAC, May 16–17, May 20–21, and June 17–18, 1966, meeting agendas, box 4, folder: PSAC, 1966–1969, HUG (FP) 94.14, GBK Papers.

45. Max Frankel, "Intellectuals to Johnson: War's the Rub," *New York Times,* May 22, 1967; Hornig, Memo to the President, May 29, 1967, April–June 1967, and Donald Greenspan to Hornig, June 8, 1967, April–June 1967, box 5, Chronological File, DFH Papers. See also August 7, 1967, July–September 1967, box 5, Chronological File, DFH Papers.

46. Hornig, Memo to Secretary Katzenbach, August 16, 1967; Hornig to W. W. Rostow, August 26, 1967; Hornig, Memo to Members of the PSAC Ad Hoc Vietnam Group, August 25, 1967, July–September 1967, box 5, Chronological File, DFH Papers; Rotblat, *Quest for Peace,* 293–94.

47. "Excerpt from Dr. Drell to Dr. Hornig, December 30, 1967," PSAC 1971: Members and Consultants, box 5/5, HUG (FP) 94.14, GBK Papers.

48. Hornig to J. James Moore, January 19, 1968; Hornig to Robert Komer, January 31, 1968; Hornig, Memo for the President, March 7, 1968; Hornig to John Foster, March 15, 1968, January–March 1968, box 6, Chronological File; Hornig, Memo

to the President, April 10, 1968, April–June 1968, box 6, Chronological File, DFH Papers. Apparently, "Snoopy" suffered from "reliability problems" (Hornig to John Foster, May 20, 1968, April–June 1968, box 6, Chronological File, DFH Papers).

49. Hornig, Memo for Marvin Watson, April 18, 1968, April–June 1968, box 6, Chronological File, DFH Papers; Evert Clark, "Top Scientist Cuts All Links to War," *New York Times,* March 1, 1968; Hornig to LBJ, December 8, 1967, October–December 1967, box 5, Chronological File; Hornig, Memo for Marvin Watson, February 19, 1968, January–March 1968, box 6, Chronological File, DFH Papers.

50. Herbert York and Allen Greb, "Scientists as Advisers to Governments," in *Scientists, the Arms Race, and Disarmament,* edited by Rotblat, 94.

51. David Inglis to John Voss, October 12, 1967, Series IV, Addenda II, box 6, folder 14: General Correspondence; Feld to Rotblat, July 2, 1968, Series IV, Addenda II, box 6, folder 6: Disarmament Studies, ER Papers.

52. Wittner, *Resisting the Bomb,* 155–56; Glenn Seaborg, *Stemming the Tide: Arms Control in the Johnson Years* (Lexington, MA: Lexington Books, 1987), 201.

53. Seaborg, *Stemming the Tide,* 136–43.

54. Ibid., 356–69; Wittner, *Toward Nuclear Abolition,* 432–34; Ronald Powaski, *March to Armageddon: The United States and the Nuclear Arms Race, 1939 to the Present* (New York: Oxford University Press, 1987), 122–23.

55. Seaborg, *Stemming the Tide,* 77, 377; *Nonproliferation Treaty,* Hearings before the Committee on Foreign Relations, 90th Cong., 2nd sess., pt. 1: July 10–12 and 17, 1968 (Washington, DC: Government Printing Office, 1968), iii; *Nonproliferation Treaty,* Hearings before the Committee on Foreign Relations, 91st Cong., 1st sess., pt. 2: July 10–12 and 17, 1969 (Washington, DC: Government Printing Office, 1969), iii.

56. Seaborg, *Stemming the Tide,* 267–304.

57. Herbert York, *Arms and the Physicist* (Woodbury, NY: American Institute of Physics, 1995), 20.

58. Seaborg, *Stemming the Tide,* 252–59.

59. Glenn Seaborg, *A Chemist in the White House: From the Manhattan Project to the End of the Cold War* (Washington, DC: American Chemical Society, 1998), 143, 190.

60. Seaborg, *Stemming the Tide,* 137; Seaborg, *Chemist in the White House,* 157–60.

61. Glenn Seaborg, *Adventures in the Atomic Age: From Watts to Washington* (New York: Farrar, Straus, and Giroux, 2001), 142; Seaborg, *Stemming the Tide,* 236.

62. Rotblat, "Movements of Scientists," 139–40; Rotblat, *Quest for Peace,* 272; Matthew Evangelista, *Unarmed Forces: The Transnational Movement to End the Cold War* (Ithaca, NY: Cornell University Press, 1999), 143.

63. Eugene Rabinowitch, "NPT: Movement toward a Viable World," *Bulletin of the Atomic Scientists* 25, no. 4 (1969): 48.

64. "Humphrey Appoints Panel to Advise Him on Science," *New York Times,* August 17, 1968; Eugene Rabinowitch, "Humphrey's Assets," *New York Times,* October 2, 1968; Bernard Feld, "Life-and-Death Issue," *New York Times,* November 2, 1968; Detlev Bronk and George Kistiakowsky, "Humphrey Backed," *New York Times,* November 3, 1968; Peter Bing to Hans Bethe, October 15, 1968; Lewis Strauss to Bethe, October 11, 1968; folder 17.5: Scientists for Humphrey, 1968, box 17, Hans Bethe Papers, Cornell University, Ithaca, NY.

65. Bethe to Drell, October 17, 1968, folder 7.42: [Correspondence] D, box 7, Bethe Papers.

66. R. W. Apple Jr., "DuBridge to Aid Nixon on Science," *New York Times,* December 4, 1968; Robert Reinhold, "Scholars Praise 2 Nixon Choices," *New York Times,* December 4, 1968; Lee DuBridge to Rabinowitch, January 31, 1958, box 8, folder 19: DuBridge–Einstein, ER Papers.

67. Glenn Seaborg, *The Atomic Energy Commission under Nixon* (New York: St. Martin's Press, 1993), 5–6; York and Greb, "Scientists as Advisers to Governments," 94; Richard Lyons, "DuBridge Resigns as Nixon's Science Adviser; Computer Expert Named," *New York Times,* August 20, 1970; "Physics Journal Decries Role of Scientist in Capital," *New York Times,* January 5, 1972; Richard Lyons, "Science Adviser to Nixon Leaving for Industry Job," *New York Times,* January 3, 1973; "Downgrading Science," *New York Times,* February 7, 1973.

68. "Against the Misuse of Science: An Appeal by M.I.T. Scientists," *Bulletin of the Atomic Scientists* 25, no. 3 (1969): 8; Kelly Moore, *Disrupting Science: Social Movements, American Scientists, and the Politics of the Military, 1945–1975* (Princeton, NJ: Princeton University Press, 2008), 158–89.

69. Joseph Rotblat, "'Black Box' Discussion," *New York Times,* January 25, 1963; Henry Kissinger, "Reference to 'Black Box,'" *New York Times,* March 13, 1963.

70. Walter Sullivan, "Pugwash Experts Offer Arms Plan," *New York Times,* October 30, 1969; Eugene Rabinowitch, "Speech for Lake Geneva Conference," 1970, Series IV, Addenda II, box 3, folder 10: 20th Pugwash Conference, ER Papers.

71. *Chicago Tribune,* September 20, 1970, Series IV, Addenda II, box 3, folder 11: 20th Pugwash Conference, Press Clippings; Rabinowitch to Rotblat, November 17, 1970, Series IV, Addenda II, box 7, folder 10: General Correspondence, ER Papers.

72. Rabinowitch to Todd Murray, November 29, 1970, and Rabinowitch to Carl Djerassi, January 22, 1971, Series IV, Addenda II, box 7, folder 10: General Correspondence; Feld, Memo to Rabinowitch, December 8, 1971, Series IV, Addenda II, box 7, folder 8: General Correspondence, ER Papers.

73. "The Nuclear Weapons Test Ban," *Bulletin of the Atomic Scientists* 12, no. 7 (1956): 268.

74. "Test Ban Dialogue," *Bulletin of the Atomic Scientists* 12, no. 9 (1956): 324.

75. Eugene Rabinowitch, "Nuclear Bomb Tests," *Bulletin of the Atomic Scientists* 14, no. 8 (1958): 282–83; Rabinowitch, "Editorial: First Step—to Where?," 2–3.

76. Indu Shekhar Mishra, "The NPT Is Not Enough for India," *Bulletin of the Atomic Scientists* 24, no. 6 (1968): 4; Eugene Rabinowitch, "NPT: Movement toward a Viable World," *Bulletin of the Atomic Scientists* 25, no. 3 (1969): 48.

77. Bernard Feld, "Looking to SALT-II," *Bulletin of the Atomic Scientists* 28, no. 6 (1972): 2; Eugene Rabinowitch, "The Moscow Summit," *Bulletin of the Atomic Scientists* 28, no. 6 (1972): 50.

78. Joseph Rotblat, "Report on Pugwash Activities during the Period 1967–72," *Pugwash Newsletter* 10, no. 3 (1973): 72–81; "Background Paper by the Polish Group," *Pugwash Newsletter* 7, no. 1 (1974): 7, Great Britain, Collective Box, Swarthmore College Peace Collection (hereafter SCPC).

79. Lawrence Wittner explains this occurrence as public policy "catching up" with

the antinuclear movement, whereas Geir Lundestad, on the other hand, argues that the United States initiated arms control agreements during the 1970s as a way of slowing U.S. decline in world leadership. Wittner, *Resisting the Bomb,* 415; Lundestad, *The United States and Western Europe since 1945: From "Empire" by Invitation to Transatlantic Drift* (Oxford: Oxford University Press, 2003), 193.

80. "The Uncontrolled Atom: A Crisis of Complacency," *Pugwash Newsletter* 12, no. 1 (1974): 30–32, Great Britain, Collective Box, SCPC.

6. The Dilemmas of Herbert York

1. Jim Bear to Herbert York, December 28, 1973, box 8, folder 1: Chronological File, 9/6/73–2/1/74; York to Harold Brown, May 11, 1976, MSS 107, box 11, folder 5, Herbert F. York Papers, Mandeville Special Collections Library, University of California, San Diego (hereafter HFY Papers).

2. York to Joseph Kraft, February 11, 1974, box 8, folder 2: Chronological File, 2/4/74–3/28/74, HFY Papers; Herbert York, *Making Weapons, Talking Peace: A Physicist's Odyssey from Hiroshima to Geneva* (New York: Basic Books, 1987), 254–55.

3. Herbert York, *Race to Oblivion: A Participant's View of the Arms Race* (New York: Simon and Schuster, 1970), 12, 24, 237; York to Herman Kahn, June 1, 1981, box 17, folder 4, HFY Papers.

4. Kelly Moore, *Disrupting Science: Social Movements, American Scientists, and the Politics of the Military, 1945–1975* (Princeton, NJ: Princeton University Press, 2008).

5. York, *Making Weapons,* 155, 158–59.

6. York to Charles Schwartz, June 11, 1974, box 8, folder 2, HFY Papers. York uses the phrase "hawkish to super-hawkish" in his book *The Advisors: Oppenheimer, Teller, and the Superbomb* (Stanford, CA: Stanford University Press, 1989), so the phrase could be his, or he could be borrowing Schwartz's phrase.

7. Schwartz to York, March 11 and 20, 1982, box 18, folder 4, HFY Papers.

8. York, *Making Weapons,* 27, 77, 119, 124, 184, 264, 333.

9. Herbert York, *Arms and the Physicist* (Woodbury, NY: American Institute of Physics, 1995), x–xi.

10. York, *Making Weapons,* 6–25; York, *Arms and the Physicist,* xi.

11. York, *Making Weapons,* 31–40.

12. Ibid., 53; "Transcript of Interview—Five Men in the Establishment—Herbert York, 1987," by Karyn Gladstone, box 66, folder 15, HFY Papers, 17; York, *Making Weapons,* 43–60.

13. István Hargittai, *Judging Edward Teller: A Closer Look at One of the Most Influential Scientists of the Twentieth Century* (New York: Prometheus Books, 2010), 243–44.

14. York, *Making Weapons,* 63–66.

15. Ibid., 67–69.

16. Ibid., 70.

17. J. S. Foster to York, October 6, 1976, box 12, folder 4: Chronological File, October 1976, HFY Papers; York, *Making Weapons,* 75.

18. York, *Making Weapons,* 76–77.

19. Ibid., 83.

20. "Five Men in the Establishment," 14, 17–19, 22, 27; York, *Arms and the Physicist,* xii.

21. Ibid.

22. Edward Teller, *Memoirs: A Twentieth-Century Journey in Science and Politics* (Cambridge, MA: Perseus Books, 2001), 434; "Five Men in the Establishment," 22–23.

23. "Five Men in the Establishment," 22–23.

24. York, *Making Weapons,* 100–107.

25. Ibid., 109–10, 117.

26. Ibid., 118–19.

27. Ibid., 120–23, 136–37, 142.

28. Ibid., 168–69, 174–76, 179, 182.

29. Ibid., 183–86.

30. Richard Nixon, *RN: The Memoirs of Richard Nixon* (New York: Warner Books, 1978), 1:269–70.

31. York, *Making Weapons,* 189–90, 192, 201, 205.

32. Ibid., 198, 200.

33. "Interview with Karyn Gladstone," box 66, folder 15, HFY Papers, 44.

34. York, *Making Weapons,* 209, 211–14.

35. "Interview with Karyn Gladstone," 34, 41; York, *Making Weapons,* 226–29.

36. York, *Making Weapons,* 214–17.

37. "Transcript of Interview of HFY by Dr. Maurice Matloff, 1985," November 15, box 66, folder 13, HFY Papers, 46.

38. "Five Men in the Establishment," 38–39.

39. York to Norris Bradbury, April 30, 1974, box 8, folder 4: Chron. File, 10/4/73–7/22/74, HFY Papers.

40. York to John Holum, July 10, 1973, box 8, folder 3, HFY Papers.

41. York to Robert Woito, undated, box 11, folder 6: Chron. File, June 1976, HFY Papers.

42. York, *Making Weapons,* 176–77.

43. Ronald Powaski, *March to Armageddon: The United States and the Nuclear Arms Race, 1939 to the Present* (New York: Oxford University Press, 1989), 116–21.

44. Teller to McGeorge Bundy, May 10, 1965, folder 3, Reading File, April–June 1965, box 424: Chronological Correspondence, 1962–66, Papers of Edward Teller, Hoover Institution, Stanford University, Stanford, CA (hereafter ET Papers).

45. Edward Teller, "Needed Now: Transatlantic ABM Defense—and Union," *Freedom & Union* 22, no. 11 (1967): 4, folder 5.3: Speeches and Writings, "Needed Now," box 5; Teller, "Draft Statement on ABMs," undated, folder: Anti-Ballistic Missiles, Statements, box 443: Topic Files, ET Papers.

46. York, *Making Weapons,* 237.

47. Glenn Seaborg, *Stemming the Tide: Arms Control in the Johnson Years* (Lexington, MA: Lexington Books, 1987), 431; York, *Race to Oblivion,* 195.

48. York, *Making Weapons,* 240; Powaski, *March to Armageddon,* 132–33; York, *Race to Oblivion,* 195–209.

49. Thomas Halsted, "Lobbying against the ABM, 1967–1970," *Bulletin of the Atomic Scientists* 27, no. 4 (1971): 26.

50. York, *Making Weapons*, 238–39; "Statement by Herbert F. York," March 11, 1969, box 44, folder 5, HFY Papers.

51. York, *Race to Oblivion*, 219.

52. York, *Making Weapons*, 240–41.

53. "Draft of a Statement by One Group of Scientists with Prof. York," undated, box 45, folder 9: Antiballistic Missile (ABM), Testimony, 1969, 1984–87, Testimony and Statements, 2 of 2, HFY Papers.

54. Teller to Sharon Weldon, undated, and Teller to Harold Wynne, April 25, 1969, folder: ABM's, box 444: Topic Files, ET Papers; Bethe to Sharon Weldon, March 17, 1969, folder 8.8: [Correspondence] W (2), box 8, HB Papers.

55. "Statement by Professor Hans A. Bethe at the Hearings before the Committee on Foreign Relations of the United States Senate, March 6, 1969, Subcommittee on International Organization and Disarmament Affairs," box 44, folder 5: Antiballistic Missile (ABM), Controversy, 1969–70—Statements, HFY Papers.

56. York, *Making Weapons*, 242 (emphasis in the original).

57. Bethe to York, October 9, 1978, folder 22.18: Test Ban, box 22, HB Papers. On the MX, see Ronald Powaski, *Return to Armageddon: The United States and the Nuclear Arms Race, 1981–1999* (New York: Oxford University Press, 2000), 35–37.

58. Rabinowitch to York, April 2, 1969, box 44, folder 7: Antiballistic Missile (ABM), Correspondence, 1969, 2 of 3, HFY Papers.

59. Powaski, *March to Armageddon*, 132–33; York, *Making Weapons*, 242.

60. "Interview with Karyn Gladstone," 33, 37; York, *Making Weapons*, 258–59.

61. York to Harold Brown, May 11, 1976, box 11, folder 5, HFY Papers; York, *Making Weapons*, 261, 265, 271, 280.

62. York, *Making Weapons*, 282–84; Jimmy Carter, *Keeping Faith: Memoirs of a President* (Fayetteville: University of Arkansas Press, 1995), 222–23; "Interview with Karyn Gladstone," 44.

63. York to Philip Abelson, undated, box 6, folder 1: Miscellaneous Correspondence, 1963–64, HFY Papers. See also York to Marvin Goldberger, August 23, 1963, and York to Harold Brown, August 23, 1963, box 33, folder 4: Arms Control and Disarmament Agency, York's Testimony on Test-Ban Treaty, 1963, HFY Papers.

64. York to Jozef Goldblat, May 21, 1973, box 7, folder 2: Chron. File, 4/3/73–5/7/73, HFY Papers.

65. York to Garwin, October 18, 1978, box 15, folder 4, HFY Papers; York, *Making Weapons*, 285–87.

66. Bethe to Spurgeon Keeny, October 30, 1978; Jeremy Stone to York, November 1, 1978, box 15, folder 4: Chron. File, October–November 1978; York to Michael May, undated, box 16, folder 6: Chron. File, January–February 1981; York to Harold Brown, September 12, 1978, box 86, folder 11, HFY Papers; York, *Making Weapons*, 289; York to Ralph Goldman, February 19, 1979, box 85, folder 22: Part 1: Geneva Memorabilia, 1979–1980, HFY Papers.

67. York, *Making Weapons*, 294–95.

68. Ibid., 301–3; Steven Seymour, Memorandum of Conversation, February 5, 1979, box 64, folder 11, HFY Papers.

69. York, *Making Weapons*, 303–4; York, "Moscow Visit," report to the NSC, July 1979, box 63, folder 8, HFY Papers.

70. York, *Making Weapons*, 305–9.

71. York to Jorma Miettinen, May 19, 1980, box 16, folder 3: Chron. File, January–June 1980, HFY Papers.

72. York, *Making Weapons*, 317–22.

73. Ibid., 314–16.

74. York to Frank Maestrone, December 31, 1980, box 16, folder 5: Chron. File, October–December 1980; York to Ernst Haas, February 25, 1981, box 16, folder 6: Chron. File, January–February 1981; York to Gerard Piel, May 19, 1981, box 17, folder 3, Chron. File, May 1981, HFY Papers; "Interview with Karyn Gladstone," 51.

75. York to Weisskopf, January 22, 1982, box 18, folder 3, HFY Papers; Katie Walter, "Herbert York (1921-2009): A Life of Firsts, an Ambassador for Peace," *Science and Technology Review* (September 2009): 4–9.

76. "Interview with Karyn Gladstone," 49; York, *Arms and the Physicist*, 6.

77. "Interview with Karyn Gladstone," 38.

78. Bethe to York, October 9, 1978, box 15, folder 4, HFY Papers.

79. York, *Making Weapons*, 258–59.

80. "Interview with Karyn Gladstone," 40.

7. "An Elaborate Way of Committing National Suicide"

1. "Washington Forum on the World-Wide Consequences of Nuclear War," *Disarmament: A Periodic Review by the United Nations* 7, no. 3 (1984): 39; Philip Shabecoff, "U.S.-Soviet Panel Sees No Hope in an Atomic War," *New York Times*, December 9, 1983.

2. Carl Sagan, *The Varieties of Scientific Experience: A Personal View of the Search for God* (New York: Penguin, 2006), 195; Keay Davidson, *Carl Sagan: A Life* (New York: John Wiley and Sons, 1999), 281; William Poundstone, *Carl Sagan: A Life in the Cosmos* (New York: Henry Holt, 1999), 205.

3. Indeed, they postulated that such an event had already occurred when the Tambora volcano eruption in 1815 kept temperatures so low that 1816 came to be known as the "year without a summer." Carl Sagan and Richard Turco, *A Path Where No Man Thought: Nuclear Winter and the End of the Arms Race* (New York: Random House, 1990), 95–101.

4. Paul Ehrlich et al., *The Cold and the Dark: The World after Nuclear War* (New York: W. W. Norton, 1984), 3–4, 88; Sagan and Turco, *Path Where No Man Thought*, 39; *The Consequences of Nuclear War*, Hearings before the International Trade, Finance, and Security Economics Subcommittee, 98th Cong., 2nd sess., July 11–12, 1984 (Washington, DC: Government Printing Office, 1986), 4–11.

5. In his epic history of the antinuclear movement, *Toward Nuclear Abolition: A History of the World Nuclear Disarmament Movement, 1971 to the Present* (Stanford, CA: Stanford University Press, 2003), Lawrence Wittner barely mentions the theory and its charismatic proselytizer. Lawrence Badash, "Nuclear Winter: Scientists in the Political Arena," *Physics in Perspective* 3, no. 1 (2001): 76–105. Badash, *A*

Nuclear Winter's Tale: Science and Politics in the 1980s (Cambridge, MA: MIT Press, 2009), looks at the nuclear winter controversy from an almost exclusively scientific perspective.

6. Davidson, *Carl Sagan: A Life*, 76–77, 194, 234, 288.

7. Sagan, *Varieties of Scientific Experience*, 31; Davidson, *Carl Sagan: A Life*, xii, 1, 237, 260, 336; Poundstone, *Carl Sagan*, 291, 388; Yervant Terzian and Elizabeth Bilson, *Carl Sagan's Universe* (Cambridge: Cambridge University Press), 147, 155, 160.

8. Tom Head, ed., *Conversations with Carl Sagan* (Jackson: University Press of Mississippi, 2006), 37.

9. Davidson, *Carl Sagan: A Life*, 120, 130, 135, 151, 226–32, 268–71; Poundstone, *Carl Sagan*, 155.

10. Davidson, *Carl Sagan: A Life*, 126–30, 185. *L* stood for "the average lifespan of a technologically advanced civilization," for which there was only one example, human civilization on earth. The estimated value of *L* rose and fell as the world drifted toward and away from thermonuclear conflict in the late 1950s and early 1960s. Thus, the equation hinged on a single variable that was, at best, difficult to estimate.

11. Christopher Chyba, "An Exobiologist's Life Search," *Nature* 401, no. 6756 (1999): 857; Terzian and Bilson, *Carl Sagan's Universe*, 3; Poundstone, *Carl Sagan*, 288; Head, *Conversations with Carl Sagan*, 57, 138. Ken Burns's *Civil War* later surpassed *Cosmos* in number of U.S. viewers, though *Cosmos* presumably remains unsurpassed worldwide.

12. Poundstone, *Carl Sagan*, 292; Head, *Conversations with Carl Sagan*, 117; Carter quoted in Douglas Brinkley, *The Unfinished Presidency: Jimmy Carter's Journey beyond the White House* (New York: Penguin, 1998), 32–33.

13. Paul Boyer, *Fallout: A Historian Reflects on America's Half-Century Encounter with Nuclear Weapons* (Columbus: Ohio State University Press, 1998), 150–55; Jonathan Schell, *The Fate of the Earth* (New York: Alfred A. Knopf, 1982); *Consequences of Nuclear War on the Global Environment*, Hearing before the Investigations and Oversight Subcommittee, 97th Cong., 2nd sess., September 15, 1982 (Washington, DC: Government Printing Office, 1983), 1–2, 177.

14. Luis Alvarez et al., "Extraterrestrial Cause for the Cretaceous-Tertiary Extinction," *Science*, n.s., 208, no. 4448 (1980): 1095–1108; "The Atmosphere after a Nuclear War: Twilight at Noon," *Ambio* (1982): 114–25.

15. The one-dimensional model treated debris as capable of moving up or down (or both) in the atmosphere, but not in any other direction. TTAPS, "Nuclear Winter: Global Consequences of Multiple Nuclear Explosions," *Science*, n.s., 222, no. 4630 (1983): 1283–92.

16. Ehrlich et al., *Cold and the Dark*, xv–xvi, 31; Anne Ehrlich, "About the Conference," in "Nuclear Winter: A Forecast of the Climatic and Biological Effects of Nuclear War," *Bulletin of the Atomic Scientists* 40, no. 4 (1984): 12S–13S.

17. A. Ehrlich, "About the Conference," 12S–13S; Ehrlich et al., *Cold and the Dark*, xvi (emphasis in the original).

18. Sagan to Bethe, March 2, 1983, folder 22.28: Nuclear Winter, continued, box 22, Hans Bethe Papers, Cornell University, Ithaca, NY (hereafter HB Papers); list of Scientific Advisory Board in Ehrlich et al., *Cold and the Dark*, 218–21; Bethe,

memo to TTAPS, August 1, 1983, folder: 22.8: Nuclear Winter, continued, box 22, HB Papers.

19. Undated handwritten notes by Bethe, folder 22.25: Sagan, box 22; handwritten notes by Bethe: "11–11 Panel, 1983," folder 22.27: Nuclear Winter, continued, box 22, HB Papers (emphasis in the original).

20. Sagan to Teller, April 25 and June 24, 1983, and February 23, 1984, folder: Sagan, Carl Dr., box 283: Correspondence, Personal, Papers of Edward Teller, Hoover Institution, Stanford University, Stanford, CA (hereafter ET Papers) (also in folder 22.27: Nuclear Winter, continued, box 22, HB Papers).

21. Teller to Sagan, August 16, 1983, folder: Sagan, Carl, Dr., box 283: Correspondence, Personal, ET Papers.

22. Kennan to Sagan, November 1, 1983, folder 22.27: Nuclear Winter, continued, box 22, HB Papers.

23. Sagan and Turco, *Path Where No Man Thought,* xx–xxii. See also acknowledgments in Ehrlich et al., *Cold and the Dark,* 29; "The Chilling Aftermath of a Nuclear War," reprinted in *Congressional Record,* Senate, February 23, 1984, 3083.

24. Ehrlich et al., *Cold and the Dark,* xviii.

25. A. Ehrlich, "About the Conference," 12S–13S; Ehrlich et al., *Cold and the Dark,* xv.

26. Carl Sagan, "The Nuclear Winter," *Parade,* October 30, 1983.

27. Ibid.

28. Ibid. This prediction assumed that the weapons would be used on cities that would then burn. The same amount of nuclear weapons used on relatively empty areas would not have the same effect.

29. Ibid.

30. Ehrlich et al., *Cold and the Dark,* xviii, 35.

31. Ibid., xxi, xxiv–xxv, xxxiii, 9, 24, 26.

32. Ibid., 31.

33. Ibid., 43–59, 128, 155.

34. Richard Turco et al., "Nuclear Winter: Global Consequences of Multiple Nuclear Explosions," and Paul Ehrlich et al., "Long-Term Biological Consequences of Nuclear War," *Science,* n.s., 222, no. 4630 (1983): 1283–90, 1293–99.

35. Extensions of Remarks, George Miller, "Carl Sagan's New Year's Resolution," *Congressional Record,* January 24, 1984, 326–27.

36. This need not be true, of course, and one might consider it somewhat disloyal to the scientific method to require varying standards of evidence, no matter the prediction.

37. Carl Sagan, "Nuclear War and Climatic Catastrophe: Some Policy Implications," *Foreign Affairs* 62, no. 2 (1983–84): 257–59, 275. It is unclear why Sagan chose to include unborn generations in his calculations, though it is worth noting that Pauling also did so in his 1950s estimates of the human cost of nuclear fallout.

38. Ibid., 276, 292 (emphasis in the original).

39. "The Winter after the Bomb," *New York Times,* November 6, 1983; "Nuclear Winter and Its Smoke," *New York Times,* August 19, 1984.

40. Robert Lieber and Dan Horowitz, "Live, Die: Moot Point," *New York Times,* November 20, 1983; William Broad, "Review 7," *New York Times,* August 12, 1984.

41. Davidson, *Carl Sagan: A Life*, 57, 80, 349, 377–78.

42. Glenn Collins, "Students Voice Fear and Hopelessness in Talks the Day after 'The Day After,'" *New York Times*, November 22, 1983.

43. Peter Kerr, "Physicians Urge End to Arms Race," *New York Times*, January 10, 1984.

44. "Open Letter to the General Synod of the Church of England," November 15, 1984, doc. 73, 6/1 Christian CND (33/127), CND Additions (I), Campaign for Nuclear Disarmament Papers, London School of Economics and Political Science. Sagan himself would have pointed out that the possibility of nuclear winter did not mean that the threat of nuclear weapons had "grown worse," but rather meant that the threat of nuclear winter had been recognized only in the 1980s; the superpowers had possessed enough nuclear weapons to initiate a nuclear winter since at least the 1960s.

45. "Introduction," *ENDpapers Eight, Spokesman 46* (Summer 1984): 1.

46. In his personal papers at Cornell University, Bethe left a handwritten note for future researchers to find on the folder titled "Nuclear Winter" that boasts, "Note: This work was initiated at Los Alamos by H. A. Bethe in summer 1983," folder 22.26: Nuclear Winter, box 22, HB Papers.

47. Robert Malone to Bethe, September 13, 1983, folder 22.26: Nuclear Winter, box 22, HB Papers. See also Memo, Malone to C. P. Robinson, November 30, 1984: Annual Progress Report, Nuclear War Climate Studies, folder 22.26: Nuclear Winter, box 22, HB Papers.

48. S. Fred Singer, "Nuclear Winter and Nuclear Freeze," *Disarmament: A Periodic Review by the United Nations 7*, no. 3 (1984): 63–71; Singer, "The Big Chill? Challenging a Nuclear Scenario," *Wall Street Journal*, February 3, 1984.

49. "The Chilling Aftermath of a Nuclear War," reprinted in *Congressional Record, Senate*, February 23, 1984, 3083; *The Climatic, Biological, and Strategic Effects of Nuclear War*, Hearing before the Natural Resources, Agriculture Research and Environment Subcommittee, 98th Cong., 2nd sess., September 12, 1984 (Washington, DC: Government Printing Office, 1985), 7.

50. Editors' introduction, "Nuclear Winter: A Forecast of the Climatic and Biological Effects of Nuclear War," *Bulletin of the Atomic Scientists 40*, no. 4 (1984): 2S; Joseph Smith, review of *Cold and the Dark*, by Ehrlich et al., *Bulletin of the Atomic Scientists 41*, no. 1 (1985): 49–51.

51. John Maddox, "From Santorini to Armageddon," *Nature 307*, no. 5947 (1984): 107; Maddox, "Nuclear Winter Not Yet Established," *Nature 308*, no. 5954 (1984): 11.

52. Tom Reuter, "Telling All," *Nature 311*, no. 5988 (1984): 700; A. D. Brown, "Teller's Cold Comfort," *Nature 312*, no. 5995 (1984): 587; Valmore LaMarche Jr. and Katherine Hirschboeck, "Nuclear War Models," *Nature 309*, no. 5965 (1984): 203; William Bown and Jan Peczkis, "Nuclear War: Counting the Cost," *Nature 310*, no. 5977 (1984), 455; Alan Robock, "Snow and Ice Feedbacks Prolong Effects of Nuclear Winter," *Nature 310*, no. 5979 (1984): 667, 670; Jonathan Katz, "Atmospheric Humidity in the Nuclear Winter," *Nature 311*, no. 5985 (1984): 417; Starley Thompson, Stephen Schneider, and Curt Covey, "Is the 'Nuclear Winter' Real?," *Nature 310*, no. 5979 (1984): 625.

53. Teller to Sagan, Art Broyles Version, undated, folder: Sagan, Carl, Dr., box 283: Correspondence, Personal, ET Papers.

54. Sagan to Teller, February 23, 1984, folder: Sagan, Carl, Dr., box 283: Correspondence, Personal, ET Papers (also in folder 22.27: Nuclear Winter, continued, box 22, HB Papers); Teller to Sagan, Teller Version, undated, folder: Sagan, Carl, Dr., box 283: Correspondence, Personal, ET Papers.

55. Edward Teller, "Widespread After-effects of Nuclear War," *Nature* 310, no. 5979 (1984): 621–22, 623–24.

56. Carl Sagan, "Confidential Draft: On Minimizing the Consequences of Nuclear War," 1–2, 6–9, late 1984, folder 22.25: Sagan, box 22, HB Papers; Sagan, "On Minimizing the Consequences of Nuclear War," *Nature* 317, no. 6037 (1985): 485–88.

57. Sagan, "Confidential Draft," 19–22.

58. Badash, "Nuclear Winter," 79.

59. R. F. Bacon, "Memorandum for the Chairman, Military Liaison Committee," July 26, 1983, and "Memorandum for the Chief of Naval Operations," October 7, 1983, reprinted in *Climatic, Biological, and Strategic Effects of Nuclear War*, 229–30.

60. J. A. Lyons, "Memorandum for the Chief of Naval Operations," including "Technical Summary" and "Conference Synopsis," November 7, 1983, reprinted in *Climatic, Biological, and Strategic Effects of Nuclear War*, 214–21.

61. L. F. Brooks, "New In-house Study," November 7, 1983, and J. A. Lyons, "Memorandum for the Chief of Naval Operations," November 19, 1983, reprinted in *Climatic, Biological, and Strategic Effects of Nuclear War*, 222–25.

62. "Carl Sagan on the Consequences of Nuclear War," *Congressional Record*, Senate, October 31, 1983, 30031–32; "Dangers of Nuclear War," *Congressional Record*, Extensions of Remarks, October 31, 1983, 30175. Representative Ted Weiss (D-NY) also put the *Parade* article into the *Record*. Extensions of Remarks, "The Chilling Effects of Nuclear War," November 18, 1983, 34872.

63. "A Partial Transcript of the DC Forum on the World-Wide Consequences of Nuclear War, Sponsored by Senators Kennedy and Hatfield, December 8, 1983," *Disarmament: A Periodic Review by the United Nations* 7, no. 3 (1984): 34–35, 37–38; Philip Shabecoff, "U.S.-Soviet Panel Sees No Hope in an Atomic War," *New York Times*, December 9, 1983.

64. "Partial Transcript," 40–42, 47, 54–57, 62; Tom Wicker, "A Grim Agreement," *New York Times*, December 12, 1983.

65. "The Real Argument for Comprehensive Arms Control," *Congressional Record*, Senate, February 23, 1984, 3082; "Why Survival Depends on Reducing Strategic Nuclear Weapons by 97 Percent," *Congressional Record*, Senate, April 25, 1984, 9805–6; William Cohen to Ronald Reagan, May 4, 1984, folder 3: Nuclear Winter, box 196, Timothy E. Wirth Papers, University of Colorado, Boulder (hereafter TEW Papers).

66. Thomas Peterson to Sagan, February 16, 1984, folder 3: Nuclear Winter, box 196, TEW Papers.

67. "United States Congress Congressional Clearinghouse on the Future Invitation"; Wirth and Gillis Long, invitation, May 4, 1984; Wirth and Gingrich invitation;

invitation to Democratic Steering and Policy Committee, May 9, 1983; "Congressional Staff Briefing"; "Master Schedule for Dr. Sagan"; "Sagan—Teller Meeting Attendees," May 16, 1984; Memo to TEW from CC, undated; "Carl Sagan Dinner," May 15, 1984, folder 3: Nuclear Winter, box 196, TEW Papers.

68. Telephone interview with Tim Wirth, January 24, 2008.

69. "Amendment to H.R. 5167," Leach, Gingrich, Wirth, Gore, and Roemer letter, May 21, 1984, folder 3: Nuclear Winter, box 196, TEW Papers; Caspar Weinberger, "The Potential Effects of Nuclear War on the Climate," March 1985, reprinted in *Nuclear Winter and Its Implications,* Hearings before the Committee on Armed Services, 99th Cong., 1st sess., October 2–3, 1985 (Washington, DC: Government Printing Office, 1986), 73; "Nuclear Winter Interview Question Responses," 3, December 5, 1984, folder 7: Nuclear Winter—Correspondence, box 195, TEW Papers.

70. *Congressional Record,* House, May 31, 1984, 5089–5100.

71. *Consequences of Nuclear War,* 1–2, 56, 65, 75–76, 80, 86.

72. Ibid., 99–102, 112–13, 116–19.

73. Ibid., 130–31, 135–39.

74. Ibid., 147; "Pentagon Aides Agree on a 'Nuclear Winter,'" *New York Times,* July 13, 1984.

75. *Climatic, Biological, and Strategic Effects of Nuclear War,* 1–9.

76. Ibid., 18–22.

77. Shultz quoted in Tim Beardsley, "Mechanics of SCOPE Report," *Nature* 317, no. 6034 (1985): 192; Tim Beardsley, "US Plans for Studies Proliferate," *Nature* 311, no. 5984 (1984): 287.

78. "Carl Sagan on Nuclear Winter," transcript of interview with CNN, September 25, 1984, 1, 7, 22, folder 3: Nuclear Winter, box 196, TEW Papers.

79. Davidson, *Carl Sagan: A Life,* 376; Poundstone, *Carl Sagan,* 339.

80. TTAPS and John Maddox, "Nuclear Winter to Be Taken Seriously," *Nature* 311, no. 5984 (1984): 307.

81. "Report of the United States National Academy of Sciences: Summary and Conclusions," *Disarmament: A Periodic Review by the United Nations* 8, no. 1 (1985): 110–20.

82. William Broad, "'Nuclear Winter' Is Seen as Possible," *New York Times,* December 12, 1984; "Nuclear Winter, Star Wars," *New York Times,* December 14, 1984; Tom Wicker, "Tambora's Lesson," *New York Times,* December 14, 1984.

83. Stephen Budiansky, "US National Academy Urges Greater Caution," *Nature* 312, no. 5996 (1984): 683; John Maddox, "Nuclear Winter and Carbon Dioxide," *Nature* 312, no. 5995 (1984): 593; Maddox, "Where Now with Nuclear Winter?," *Nature* 312, no. 5996 (1984): 696.

84. Carl Sagan, "A Nuclear Theory That Can't Be Tested," *New York Times,* December 29, 1984; Jonathan Katz, "Nuclear Winter Effects Not Settled," *New York Times,* January 5, 1985.

85. Per Oftedal et al., "Aftermath of Nuclear War," *Nature* 313, no. 6005 (1985): 732; Edward Teller, "Climatic Change with Nuclear War," *Nature* 318, no. 6042 (1985): 99; P. M. Kelly, "In the Aftermath," *Nature* 315, no. 6015 (1985): 161 (emphasis in the original); Tim Beardsley, "Canadian Forest Burn as Model," *Nature* 316, no. 6028

(1985): 479; John Maddox, "New Ways with Aggregation," *Nature* 314, no. 6013 (1985): 667; Beardsley, "Looking to the Future," *Nature* 315, no. 6021 (1985): 620.

86. Edmund Jan Ozmanczyk, "New Delhi Declaration on the Nuclear Arms Race, 1985," in *Encyclopedia of the United Nations and International Agreements*, edited by Anthony Mango (New York: Routledge, 2003), 1548–50. See also Sagan and Turco, *Path Where No Man Thought*, 179.

87. Vera Rich, "Nuclear Winter Expert Vanishes without Trace," *Nature* 316, no. 6023 (1985): 3; Rich, "Aleksandrov Still Not Found," *Nature* 316, no. 6028 (1985): 479; Tim Beardsley, "Soviet Missing Person," *Nature* 317, no. 6034 (1985): 191; Sagan and Turco, *Path Where No Man Thought*, 135–42; Badash, *Nuclear Winter's Tale*, 227.

88. Notes, February 25, 1985, folder 7: Nuclear Winter—Correspondence, box 175, TEW Papers.

89. William Broad, "U.S. Weighs Risk That Atom War Could Bring Fatal Nuclear Winter," *New York Times*, August 5, 1984; "Middle East Review," *New York Times*, February 12, 1985.

90. Caspar Weinberger, "The Potential Effects of Nuclear War on the Climate," March 1985, reprinted in *Nuclear Winter and Its Implications*, 75–77, 83.

91. Ibid., 83–85. See also Wayne Biddle, "Pentagon Agrees Nuclear Warfare Could Block Sun, Freezing Earth," *New York Times*, March 2, 1985; Stephen Budiansky, "Pentagon Says Yes, It May Happen, but 'So What?,'" *Nature* 314, no. 6007 (1985): 121.

92. *Nuclear Winter*, Hearing before the Natural Resources, Agriculture Research, and Environment Subcommittee and the Subcommittee on Energy and the Environment, 99th Cong., 1st sess., March 14, 1985 (Washington, DC: Government Printing Office, 1985), 1–2, 6, 10–12.

93. Ibid., 19–36.

94. Ibid., 37–67.

95. Ibid., 69–79, 81–82, 125, 153–54.

96. Letter from Jim Leach and Timothy Wirth, March 6, 1985, and "Statement—SCOPE Press Conference," May 28, 1987, folder 7: Nuclear Winter—Correspondence, box 195, TEW Papers; Wirth et al. to Weinberger, February 3, 1986, folder 7: Nuclear Winter—Correspondence, box 195, TEW Papers. The other signers were Proxmire, Gary Hart, Newt Gingrich, Schneider, Udall, Gore, Leach, Roemer, Scheuer, Levine, and McKinney.

97. Gilbert White to Wirth, March 6, 1985, and "Report on the Progress of the SCOPE ENUWAR Project since October 1983," folder 7: Nuclear Winter—Correspondence, box 195, TEW Papers; *SCOPE 28: Environmental Consequences of Nuclear War*, 2nd ed. (Chichester: John Wiley & Sons, 1989); "ICSU Project Hunts for Data," *Nature* 309, no. 5969 (1984): 577.

98. Mark Harwell and Christine Harwell, "Updating the 'Nuclear Winter' Debate," *Bulletin of the Atomic Scientists* 43, no. 8 (1987): 42–44.

99. Thomas Malone, "International Scientists on Nuclear Winter," *Bulletin of the Atomic Scientists* 41, no. 11 (1985): 52–55 (emphasis in the original); "Declaration on Prevention of Nuclear War," *Bulletin of the Atomic Scientists* 38, no. 10 (1982): 4–5; *SCOPE 28*, 2:490.

100. Memorandum/Talking Points, September 11, 1985, folder 7: Nuclear Winter—Correspondence, box 175, TEW Papers; "Rethinking Nuclear War," *New York Times,* September 29, 1985; Peter Gambles, "Cautious Support from SCOPE," *Nature* 315, no. 6020 (1985): 534; Tim Beardsley, "International Committee Echoes Gloomy Forecasts," *Nature* 317, no. 6034 (1985): 191.

101. John Maddox, "What to Make of Nuclear Winter," *Nature* 317, no. 6034 (1985): 189–90; Maddox, "Nuclear Winter Can Cross Equator," *Nature* 317, no. 6032 (1985): 11.

102. K. A. Emanuel, "Towards a Scientific Exercise," *Nature* 319, no. 6051 (1986): 259.

103. Stephen Schneider and Starley Thompson, "The Mesoscale Effects of Nuclear Winter," *Nature* 320, no. 6062 (1986): 491–92; Tim Beardsley, "Has Winter Become Fall?," *Nature* 320, no. 6058 (1986): 103; Joseph Knox and Charles Shapiro, "The Real Hazards of Nuclear Fallout," *Nature* 321, no. 6065 (1986): 21–22; S. B. Idso, "Nuclear Winter and the Greenhouse Effect," *Nature* 321, no. 6066 (1986): 122.

104. *Nuclear Winter and Its Implications,* 2, 5–9, 15–18, 93–110, 124–37, 140–43, 147, 150–51; Maxine Clarke, "US Arms Control Policy Doubts," *Nature* 317, no. 6037 (1985): 466.

105. "Excerpts from Pastoral Plan," *New York Times,* April 27, 1986 (emphasis in the original).

106. "Excerpts from U.N. Speeches by Shultz and Shevardnadze," *New York Times,* September 25, 1985; Sagan and Turco, *Path Where No Man Thought,* 183 (quote), 181; *END French Group Newsletter* 3, no. 2 (1985), European Nuclear Disarmament Papers, London School of Economics and Political Science (hereafter END Papers).

107. Ehrlich et al., *Cold and the Dark,* xviii; *Climatic, Biological, and Strategic Effects of Nuclear War,* 45, 52; *Nuclear Winter,* 34.

108. Roderic Pitty, "A Brief Report on the Situation of the MOSCOW TRUST GROUP," November 23, 1985, S1–85–11–23–1; letter from Peter Murphy, September 12, 1985, S1B-85-9-12-1, END Papers.

109. "Visit to Yuri and Olga Medvedkov, 7.11.85," November 7, 1985, S1–85–11–7-1; "Yori to Oleg Popov," August 4, 1985, S1A-85-8-4-1, END Papers.

110. Robert Malone et al., "Influence of Solar Heating and Precipitation Scavenging on the Simulated Lifetime of Post-nuclear War Smoke," *Science* 230, no. 4723 (1985): 317–19; Eric Pitcher et al., "January and July Simulations with a Spectral General Circulation Model," *Journal of the Atmospheric Sciences* 40, no. 3 (1983): 580–604; V. Ramanathan et al., "The Response of a Spectral General Circulation Model to Refinements in Radiative Processes," *Journal of the Atmospheric Sciences* 40, no. 3 (1983): 605–30; Robert Malone et al., "Nuclear Winter: Three-Dimensional Simulations Including Interactive Transport, Scavenging, and Solar Heating of Smoke," *Journal of Geophysical Research* 91, no. D1 (1986): 1039–53.

111. Eric Jones to C. F. Keller, March 13, 1986; Jones to Bethe, March 13, 1986; Bethe to Charles Keller, March 18, 1986, folder 22.26: Nuclear Winter, box 22, HB Papers.

112. Starley Thompson and Stephen Schneider, "Nuclear Winter Reappraised," *Foreign Affairs* 64, no. 5 (1986): 981–83, 989, 993–94, 998, 1005.

113. James Gleick, "Less Drastic Theory Emerges on Freezing after a Nuclear War," *New York Times*, June 22, 1986.

114. James Gleick, "Science and Politics: 'Nuclear Winter' Clash," *New York Times*, February 17, 1987; John Maddox and Joseph Palca, "Chiefs Dominate Indians at an Annual Science Smorgasbord," *Nature* 324, no. 6107 (1987): 750; Edward Teller, "In the Worst Event," *Nature* 328, no. 6125 (1987): 23; Poundstone, *Carl Sagan*, 332–37.

115. Harwell and Harwell, "Updating the 'Nuclear Winter' Debate," 42–44.

116. Ibid. (emphasis in the original); "Statement—SCOPE Press Conference," May 28, 1987, folder 7: Nuclear Winter—Correspondence, box 195, TEW Papers.

117. Introduction, *Environment* 30, no. 5 (1988): 1; Frederick Warner, "Consensus and Uncertainties: The Environmental Effects of Nuclear War," *Environment* 30, no. 5 (1988): 2–7; Richard Turco and G. S. Golitsyn, "A Status Report: Global Effects of Nuclear War," *Environment* 30, no. 5 (1988): 14; Department for Disarmament Affairs, Report of the Secretary-General, *Study on the Climatic and Other Global Effects of Nuclear War*, Disarmament Study Series 18 (New York: United Nations, 1989).

118. John Maddox, "What Happened to Nuclear Winter?," *Nature* 333, no. 6170 (1988): 203.

119. Alan Robock, "New Models Confirm Nuclear Winter," *Bulletin of the Atomic Scientists* 45, no. 7 (1989): 32–35; Jenny Nelson, "Fractality of Sooty Smoke: Implications for the Severity of Nuclear Winter," *Nature* 339, no. 6226 (1989): 611.

120. "The Technology of Wednesday's War," *Nature* 349, no. 6305 (1991): 91; Peter Aldhous, "Oil-Well Climate Catastrophe," *Nature* 349, no. 6305 (1991): 96; K. A. Browning et al., "Environmental Effects from Burning Oil Wells in Kuwait," *Nature* 351, no. 6325 (1991): 363.

121. John Birks, "The End of Innocence," *Nature* 349, no. 6309 (1991): 472; Carl Sagan, *Billions and Billions: Thoughts on Life and Death at the Brink of the Millennium* (New York: Random House, 1997), 99–107; Rex Dalton, "What Happens When Two Nations Battle with Nukes?," *Nature* (online) (December 12, 2006); Harvey Leifert, "Extreme Events: Climate Catastrophe," *Nature Reports: Climate Change* 4 (September 2007): 50. In 2010 members of International Physicians for the Prevention of Nuclear War and Physicians for Social Responsibility mentioned nuclear winter and the "billions of people" who would starve in an editorial arguing for ratification of the recent Strategic Arms Reduction Talks treaty. Ira Helfand et al., "A New START for the World," *Tampa Tribune*, April 8, 2010.

122. "Nuclear Winter Interview Question Responses," December 5, 1984, folder 7: Nuclear Winter—Correspondence, box 195, TEW Papers; J. L. Heilbron, "Honesty's the Best Policy," *Nature* 340, no. 6325 (1989): 608.

123. Chris Mooney, "Hard Science," *New Republic* 238, no. 4834 (2008): 11–12; Poundstone, *Carl Sagan*, 346–47, 356–58; Davidson, *Carl Sagan: A Life*, 389–92, 397. At the same time, it is equally plausible that Sagan's purely scientific work, though prolific, did not measure up to the high standards of the academy or that his interest in extraterrestrial life harmed his standing in the eyes of conservative members of the NAS.

124. Sagan and Turco, *Path Where No Man Thought*, 33–34.

8. "An Emotional Grassroots Offensive"

1. Paul Boyer, *Fallout: A Historian Reflects on America's Half-Century Encounter with Nuclear Weapons* (Columbus: Ohio State University Press, 1998), 167–93; Boyer, "From Activism to Apathy: The American People and Nuclear Weapons, 1963–1980," *Journal of American History* 70, no. 4 (1984): 821–44; Lawrence Wittner, *Toward Nuclear Abolition: A History of the World Nuclear Disarmament Movement, 1971 to the Present* (Stanford, CA: Stanford University Press, 2004).

2. Randall Forsberg, "A Bilateral Nuclear-Weapons Freeze," *Scientific American* 247, no. 5 (1982): 52.

3. Douglas Mattern, "Requiem for a Not So Special Session," *Bulletin of the Atomic Scientists* 38, no. 9 (1982): 59; advertisement, "One Less Bomb," *Bulletin of the Atomic Scientists* 37, no. 4 (1981): 7 (emphasis in the original).

4. Mary Kaldor, "END Can Be a Beginning," *Bulletin of the Atomic Scientists* 37, no. 10 (1981): 45; "Editorial," *END: Journal of European Nuclear Disarmament*, no. 1 (1982–83): 2.

5. "Vision Statement," folder: Mailings, flyers, press release, etc., CDGA: Women's Encampment for a Future of Peace and Justice, Swarthmore College Peace Collection (hereafter SCPC).

6. "Dear Women," CDGA: Feminists Insist on a Safe Tomorrow, SCPC.

7. Eva Quistrop, "Women Reclaim the Future," *END: Journal of European Nuclear Disarmament*, no. 1 (1982–83): 28–29.

8. Alva Myrdal, "The New Resistance Movement," *ENDpapers Six, Spokesman* 44 (Winter 1983–84): 3–4.

9. Myrna Greenfield, "Peace Camp Inspirations," *END: Journal of European Nuclear Disarmament*, no. 6 (1983): 6–7; Wittner, *Toward Nuclear Abolition*, 133–39, 168.

10. Maurice Isserman and Michael Kazin, *America Divided: The Civil War of the 1960s* (New York: Oxford University Press, 2000); Bruce Schulman, *The Seventies: The Great Shift in American Culture, Society, and Politics* (New York: Free Press, 2001); Kelly Moore, *Disrupting Science: Social Movements, American Scientists, and the Politics of the Military, 1945–75* (Princeton, NJ: Princeton University Press, 2008), 130–33.

11. Richard Grossman, "Unions Concerned"; Anthony Benedetto, "Genie No Dream"; "Dollars & Sense"; and "Growing Bold in Washington," *Nuclear Times* 1, no. 3 (1983): 3, 5, 8.

12. Jack Joppa to *Sojourners*, January 2, 1981, Nuclear Resister, DG261, box 1: Correspondence, 1981, SCPC.

13. Thomas Gumbleton, "Peace and War," *Nuclear Times* 1, no. 6 (1983): 2.

14. Madalyn Murray O'Hair, "Church Key," *Nuclear Times* 1, no. 6 (1983): 2.

15. Corinna Gardner, "Churches Attack Weapon Business," *Nuclear Times* 1, no. 6 (1983): 9; Walter Lew, "Churches to Kick Off Peace with Justice Week," *Nuclear Times* 1, no. 7 (1983): 12; Patty Edmonds, "The Greater Work Still Ahead," *Nuclear Times* 1, no. 8 (1983): 16; L. T. Matthiesen, "Meddling Prophets?," *Nuclear Times* 1, no. 7 (1983): 2.

16. Pope John Paul II, "Science and Conscience," *Bulletin of the Atomic Scientists* 37, no. 4 (1981): 7–8.

17. William Rankin, "Where Are Our Leaders?," *Bulletin of the Atomic Scientists* 38, no. 6 (1982): 70.

18. Barbara Eggleston, "Controversy over Church Report," *END: Journal of European Nuclear Disarmament,* no. 1 (1982–83): 2; Wolfgang Muller, "Delicate Compromise between State and Grassroots: The Difficult Task of the East German Churches," *END: Journal of European Nuclear Disarmament,* no. 1 (1982–83): 12–13.

19. "What Will Bring about Peace?," CC Docs 1982, April 1982 Meeting, European Nuclear Disarmament Papers, London School of Economics and Political Science.

20. "Christian CND School for Action," doc. 2, folder 6/1 Christian CND (33/127), CND Additions (I), Campaign for Nuclear Disarmament Papers, London School of Economics and Political Science (hereafter CND Papers); "Press Statement," April 27, 1983, doc. 10, folder 6/1 Christian CND (33/127), CND Additions (I), CND Papers; press release: "Christian CND on 'Church and the Bomb' 'Nuclear-Free Parishes Campaign' Launched," doc. 2a, folder 6/1 Christian CND (33/127), CND Additions (I), CND Papers.

21. "Open Letter to the General Synod of the Church of England," November 15, 1984, doc. 73, folder 6/1 Christian CND (33/127), CND Additions (I), CND Papers.

22. Myrdal, "The New Resistance Movement," 4–5.

23. "The Nuclear Arms Freeze," Proceedings of a Roundtable Discussion, 5–7, February 14, 1983, folder 29.6: Nuclear Arms Freeze, box 29, Papers of Edward Teller, Hoover Institution, Stanford University, Stanford, CA (hereafter ET Papers). Caldicott recognized that contemporary nuclear strategy recommended using "many small bombs on one city [rather] than one big bomb," but because she believed that "the Russians have big crude weapons," she focused on the effects of one twenty-megaton H-bomb. She also said that the effects of such a bomb were "simpler and easier to describe." She might also have added more startling. Much of Caldicott's data came from Jonathan Schell's *Fate of the Earth* (New York: Alfred A. Knopf, 1982).

24. Ibid., 13.

25. Ibid., 15–16.

26. Ibid., 18.

27. Cresson Kearny to Teller, February 11, 1985, folder 1: Cresson H. Kearny, box 3, ET Papers.

28. Boyer, *Fallout,* 150–55.

29. *Nuclear Winter and Its Implications,* Hearings before the Committee on Armed Services, 99th Cong., 1st sess., October 2–3, 1985 (Washington, DC: Government Printing Office, 1986), 147.

30. "Transcript of Debate between Dr. Carl Sagan and Lt. Gen. James Abrahamson, July 31, 1986," 3, 19, folder 20.46: Sagan-Abrahamson Debate, box 20, Hans Bethe Papers, Cornell University, Ithaca, NY (hereafter HB Papers); Edward Teller, *Memoirs: A Twentieth-Century Journey in Science and Politics* (Cambridge, MA: Perseus Books, 2001), 532.

31. Edward Teller, "Conflict in the Middle East: Time for an American Energy

Contingency Plan," *Congressional Record,* House, 2365–66; Peter Goodchild, *Edward Teller: The Real Dr. Strangelove* (Cambridge, MA: Harvard University Press, 2004), 326–27.

32. Teller to Richard Allen, undated, folder: Reagan, Ronald, box 282: Correspondence: Personal, ET Papers.

33. Teller to H. Peter Metzger, December 29, 1978, box 3, folder 7: H. Peter Metzger; Teller to Gina Hayward, April 17, 1981, box 1, folder 4, ET Papers.

34. World Research, Inc., "The Energy Crisis: No Contingency Plan; An Exclusive Interview with Dr. Edward Teller," 1980, folder 1: "The Energy Crisis," box 7, ET Papers; Edward Teller, "Role of Physicists in the 1980's," reprinted in *Congressional Record,* Extensions of Remarks, March 2, 1981, 3341–42; *Defense Department Authorization and Oversight,* Hearings before the Committee on Armed Services, 98th Cong., 1st sess., March 1–2, 9, 15, 17, and 23–24; and April 12, 18–20, 22, and 25–28, 1983 (Washington, DC: Government Printing Office, 1984), 1367.

35. Edward Teller, "Deep Freeze for Nuclear Arms," reprinted in *Congressional Record,* Extensions of Remarks, June 7, 1982, 12859.

36. "Father of H-Bomb Warns of U.S. Weakness," reprinted in *Congressional Record,* House, August 5, 1982, 19663–64.

37. Teller to Reagan, July 23, 1982, folder: Reagan, Ronald, box 282 Correspondence—Personal, ET Papers; Douglas Brinkley, ed., *The Reagan Diaries* (New York: HarperCollins, 2007), 100.

38. Teller to William F. Buckley, May 19, 1982, folder: Buckley, William F., box 274: Correspondence: Personal, ET Papers.

39. Teller, *Memoirs,* 531–32; Brinkley, *The Reagan Diaries,* 165.

40. AAAS, *Science 83* 4, no. 5 (1983): 17 (also in "Ban Space Weapons," *Bulletin of the Atomic Scientists* 39, no. 9 [1983]: 2–3).

41. *Defense Department Authorization and Oversight,* 1355–56.

42. "Strategic Defense Initiative Is Truly a Reagan Initiative," *Congressional Record,* House, October 23, 1985, 28681.

43. Teller to James Fletcher, July 28, 1983, folder 5, July–September 1983, box 433: Chronological Correspondence, 1981–1991, ET Papers.

44. Teller to Peter Renz, July 30, 1984, folder 3.11: Peter Renz, Correspondence, box 3, ET Papers. Even a mere 20 percent of Soviet missiles would have been more than enough to annihilate the United States. "Testimony of Dr. Teller on SDI," *Congressional Record,* Senate, May 15, 1986, 10766–68.

45. "Statement on SDI by the Science and Engineering Committee for a Secure World," reprinted in "Testimony of Dr. Martin J. Hoffert on SDI," *Congressional Record,* Senate, May 15, 1986, 10768–70.

46. Teller to Reagan, August 6, 1985, folder: Reagan, President Ronald, box 282: Correspondence: Personal, ET Papers.

47. Bernard Feld, "Campaign for a Livable World," *Bulletin of the Atomic Scientists* 37, no. 6 (1981): 1.

48. John Isaacs, "The Freeze," *Bulletin of the Atomic Scientists* 38, no. 8 (1982): 9–10; Paul Montgomery, "Throngs Fill Manhattan to Protest Nuclear Weapons," *New York Times,* June 13, 1982.

49. "Ground Zero Week, 1982," *Bulletin of the Atomic Scientists* 38, no. 4 (1982): 57; Mattern, "Requiem for a Not So Special Session," 58–59.

50. *Calling for a Mutual and Verifiable Freeze on and Reductions in Nuclear Weapons,* Hearings before the Committee on Foreign Affairs, 98th Cong., 1st sess., February 17 and March 2 and 8, 1983 (Washington, DC: Government Printing Office, 1983).

51. Peter D. Hart Research Associates, "A Survey of Physicists' Attitudes toward the Strategic Defense Initiative," March 1986, folder 20.51: Reaction to Star Wars Announcement, box 20, HB Papers.

52. Quoted in Rebecca Slayton, "Speaking as Scientists: Computer Professionals in the Star Wars Debate," *History and Technology* 19, no. 4 (2003): 357; Richard Ennals, "Why I Quit over SDI," *END: Journal of European Nuclear Disarmament,* no. 20 (1986): 10–11.

53. Hans Bethe and Frank Long, "The Value of a Freeze," *New York Times,* September 22, 1982; Bethe and Long, "The Case for a Nuclear Freeze between the U.S. and the U.S.S.R.: A Response to Richard Perle," undated, folder 17.16: Arms Control, box 17; Ruth Yarrow to Bethe, October 18, 1981; Bethe to Henry Kendall, October 12, 1981, folder 33.26: November 11, 1981, National Teach-in on Nuclear War, box 33, HB Papers.

54. "The Arms Race: A Sandia Colloquium by Hans A. Bethe, July 28, 1982," 15–16, folder 17.12: Arms Control Sandia Colloq. '82, box 17, HB Papers.

55. Bethe to E. T. Dunham, June 26, 1962, folder 5.41: Correspondence Related to Disarmament, box 5, HB Papers.

56. Bethe to Henry Kendall, October 12, 1981, folder 33.26: November 11, 1981, National Teach-in on Nuclear War, box 33, HB Papers.

57. "We Now Appeal," *Bulletin of the Atomic Scientists* 38, no. 9 (1982): 3–4.

58. Bethe to the Editor, *Ithaca Journal,* April 4, 1983, folder: Bulletin, Long, box 1 (unprocessed collection), HB Papers.

59. Bethe to Gerold Yonas, April 12, 1985, folder: Government Officials, box 276: Correspondence: Personal, ET Papers.

60. Handwritten notes for talk at Center for Study of Democratic Institutions, January 20, 1983, folder: Responsibility of Scientists/Hutchins Center, box 11 (SL), HB Papers.

61. Bethe to Reagan, March 29, 1983, folder 20.32: SDI: Keyworth, Maj. Worden, box 20, HB Papers.

62. "Transcript of Teller-Bethe Debate," November 1983, folder 20.45: Teller-Bethe Debate, box 20, HB Papers, published in *Technology Review* 87, no. 3 (1984): 38.

63. Ibid.

64. Ibid.

65. Bethe to Gerold Yonas, April 12, 1985, folder: Government Officials, box 276: Correspondence: Personal, ET Papers; Bethe, "July 16, 1985," folder 17.57: Commemoration of Trinity, July 16, 1985, box 17, HB Papers.

66. Teller to Bethe, May 23, 1985, folder 33.54: 1985–86, Livermore–Teller, box 33, HB Papers.

67. Bethe, "Letter to Edward," undated draft, folder 33.54: 1985–86, Livermore–Teller, box 33, HB Papers.

68. "National Defense and the Scientists: An Open Letter to Hans Bethe from

Edward Teller," undated, 1, 17, folder 33.54: 1985–86, Livermore–Teller, box 33, HB Papers; "Teller Open Letter," handwritten notes, undated, folder 33.54: 1985–86, Livermore–Teller, box 33, HB Papers; Bethe to Teller, January 24, 1987, folder 33.54: 1985–86 Livermore–Teller, box 33, HB Papers.

69. *Defense Department Authorization and Oversight,* 1360.

70. Serge Lang to Bethe, October 15, 1986, folder 20.18: Letters and Articles against SDI, box 20, HB Papers.

71. "Declaration on Prevention of Nuclear War," *Bulletin of the Atomic Scientists* 38, no. 10 (1982): 4–5. See also "Declaration on Prevention of Nuclear War," September 24, 1982, folder: Weisskopf, Vatican Declaration, box 1 (unprocessed collection), HB Papers.

72. "Report on the Mission of the Pontifical Academy to President Reagan and the UN," Victor Weisskopf, undated, 1–5, folder: Weisskopf, Vatican Declaration, box 1 (unprocessed collection), HB Papers.

73. "Addendum to the Report on the Visit to President Reagan," Victor Weisskopf, undated, folder: Weisskopf, Vatican Declaration, box 1 (unprocessed collection), HB Papers.

74. Keay Davidson, *Carl Sagan: A Life* (New York: John Wiley and Sons, 1999), 57, 80, 349, 377–78.

75. Feld, "Campaign for a Livable World," 1; Peter Joseph, "Doctors Speak Up," *Bulletin of the Atomic Scientists* 37, no. 3 (1981): 17.

76. George Kistiakowsky, "Carrying the Message," *Bulletin of the Atomic Scientists* 37, no. 3 (1981): 10.

77. Barry Casper, "An Appeal to Physicists," *Bulletin of the Atomic Scientists* 40, no. 8 (1984): 9–13.

78. Ronald Powaski, *Return to Armageddon: The United States and the Nuclear Arms Race, 1981–1999* (New York: Oxford University Press, 2000), 69.

79. "Six Minutes to Midnight," *Bulletin of the Atomic Scientists* 44, no. 1 (1988): 3 (emphasis added).

Conclusion

1. Guest book, folder 2, box 1, Papers of Edward Teller, Hoover Institution, Stanford University (hereafter ET Papers).

2. Hans Mark to Teller, June 5, 1989, folder: Mark, Hans, Correspondence, 1980s, box 279: Correspondence, Personal, ET Papers.

3. Edward Teller, *Memoirs: A Twentieth-Century Journey in Science and Politics* (Cambridge, MA: Perseus Books, 2001), 535–36; Mark to Teller, June 5, 1989, folder: Mark, Hans, Correspondence, 1980s, box 279: Correspondence, Personal, ET Papers.

4. Teller to John Foster, July 1, 1994, folder: Foster, John S., Jr., box 275: Correspondence: Personal, ET Papers.

5. Bethe, "Chicago 3–12–92" (notes for talk), folder 35.23: 1992 Einstein Peace Prize— Chicago Talk, box 35, Hans Bethe Papers, Cornell University, Ithaca, NY.

6. Ibid.

7. Richard Rhodes, *The Twilight of the Bombs: Recent Challenges, New Dangers, and the Prospects for a World without Nuclear Weapons* (New York: Vintage, 2011), 97–117.

8. George Shultz et al., "A World Free of Nuclear Weapons," *Wall Street Journal*, January 4, 2007.

9. "Remarks by President Obama," April 5, 2009, online by Gerhard Peters and John Wooley, *The American Presidency Project,* http://www.presidency.ucsb.edu/ws/?pid=85963.

10. Thomas Borstelmann, *The Cold War and the Color Line: American Race Relations in the Global Arena* (Cambridge, MA: Harvard University Press, 2001); Mary Dudziak, *Cold War Civil Rights: Race and the Image of American Democracy* (Princeton, NJ: Princeton University Press, 2000); Penny von Eschen, *Race against Empire: Black Americans and Anticolonialism, 1937–1957* (Ithaca, NY: Cornell University Press, 1997).

11. Akira Iriye, *Global Community: The Role of International Organizations in the Making of the Contemporary World* (Berkeley: University of California Press, 2002).

12. Matthew Evangelista, *Unarmed Forces: The Transnational Movement to End the Cold War* (Ithaca, NY: Cornell University Press, 1999); Sarah Snyder, *Human Rights Activism and the End of the Cold War: A Transnational History of the Helsinki Network* (Cambridge: Cambridge University Press, 2011); Lawrence Wittner, *Toward Nuclear Abolition: A History of the World Nuclear Disarmament Movement, 1971 to the Present* (Stanford, CA: Stanford University Press, 2003).

13. Stuart Leslie, *The Cold War and American Science: The Military-Industrial-Academic Complex at MIT and Stanford* (New York: Columbia University Press, 1993), 9. See also Daniel Kevles, *The Physicists: The History of a Scientific Community in Modern America* (New York: Alfred A. Knopf, 1977).

14. Eric Hobsbawm, *The Age of Extremes: A History of the World, 1914–1991* (New York: Vintage, 1994), 522.

15. Jeanne Guillemin, "Seduced by the State," *Bulletin of the Atomic Scientists* 63, no. 5 (2007): 14–16; Leslie, *Cold War and American Science*, 11.

16. Chris Mooney, *The Republican War on Science* (New York: Basic Books, 2005).

17. Henry Petroski, *Beyond Engineering* (New York: St. Martin's Press, 1986); Chris Mooney, "Requiem for an Office," *Bulletin of the Atomic Scientists* 61, no. 5 (2005): 40–49; Mooney, "Hard Science," *New Republic* 238, no. 4834 (2008): 11–12.

18. Zuoyue Wang and Naomi Oreskes, "History of Science and American Science Policy," *Isis* 99 (2008): 365–73.

Index

Abrahamson, James, 223–24
Ackerman, Thomas, 176. *See also* TTAPS, TTAPS paper
Adams, Ruth, 106
Advanced Research Projects Agency, 152, 156
Agnew, Harold, 228
Agnew, Spiro, 161
Alexandrov, Vladimir, 192, 200, 207
Allison, Helen, 50
Allison, Samuel, 56
Alvarez, Luis, 69, 175, 179
Alvarez, Walter, 175
American Academy of Arts and Sciences, 122, 177
American Association for the Advancement of Science, 210
American Association of Scientific Workers, 46
American Atheists, 218
American Chemical Society, 80–81, 83
American Civil Liberties Union, 38, 46
American Physical Society, 230
Anderson, Clinton, 79, 125
Andropov, Yuri, 186
antiballistic missiles, 8, 11, 85, 152; activism against, 238; Antiballistic Missile Treaty, 161, 241, 243; hearings

on, 2–3, 155–63; Nixon administration and, 137–38; nuclear winter and, 184; President's Science Advisory Committee and, 126; Safeguard, 157–59, 161; scientists' opposition to, 2–3, 144, 155–63, 169; Sentinel, 157–58, 160; and test ban debate, 110–11
Antiballistic Missile Treaty (1972). *See* antiballistic missiles
antinuclear movement of the 1980s, 215–18, 222, 238. *See also* Central Park Rally for Peace
appeasement, 56, 68, 75, 79–84, 88, 189, 224–25
Argonne National Laboratory, 51
arms control: and 1968 election, 138; end of the Cold War and, 242; negotiations and proposals, 73, 79, 142; and nuclear winter, 172; President's Science Advisory Committee and, 127, 133, 151; and scientists, 5; Strategic Defense Initiative and, 234. *See also* nuclear disarmament
arms control agreements, 11, 94, 101, 113, 117, 162–65, 168–70
Arms Control and Disarmament Agency, 114, 152, 164–65, 195

PAUL RUBINSON was born in Baltimore and graduated with a BA from Vanderbilt University. He served as a predoctoral fellow at Yale University International Security Studies and received his PhD in history from the University of Texas at Austin in 2008. His research interests focus on the relationship between scientists and the Cold War, including opposition to the arms race and defense of human rights. In addition to *Redefining Science,* he is author of the forthcoming *Rethinking the Antinuclear Movement.* His articles have appeared in *Diplomatic History* and *Cold War History* as well as edited collections on the Cold War, science, and human rights. Rubinson is currently assistant professor of history at Bridgewater State University.